"Lorcin's study of the formulation and manipulation of imperial identities is a masterpiece of the genre and makes a significant contribution to Algerian history, to nineteenth-century French intellectual history, and to the broader history of imperialism. Because of its content and because it is such a good read, it should certainly be considered seriously by everyone teaching Middle Eastern/North African history, courses involving Europe's last wave of imperialism, and broader world-history courses."

—John Ruedy, *Journal of Middle East Studies*

"Lorcin's excellent intellectual history investigates in great depth the French colonial 'Kabyle Myth' and the nineteenth-century development of racial stereotypes. . . . Lorcin's highly recommended book also serves anthropological, ethnological, and sociological studies of imperialism."

—*Choice*

"Essential reading for any student of Maghreb history and important in its conclusions. . . . Lorcin's sources are rich and varied, scrupulously referenced. . . . Enjoyable to read as well as being most enlightening."

—Anthony Clayton, *Journal of Imperial and Commonwealth History*

"Lorcin's persuasive and well-written account of the historical development of [postcolonial] attitudes adds much to our understanding."

—William A. Hoisington Jr., *Journal of Interdisciplinary History*

"Lorcin's exemplary study of the 'Kabyle myth' . . . provides striking evidence of the centrality of racial classification to modern colonialism."

—Daniel J. Sherman, *French Historical Studies*

"A very admirable intellectual and social history of nineteenth-century colonial Algeria. . . . Lorcin incorporates an impressive knowledge from a variety of fields—history, sociology, anthropology, philology, ethnology, and literature. Her cross-disciplinary approach will attract a variety of specialists."

—Phillip C. Naylor, *Journal of North African Studies*

"Sets new standards for research in both colonial and intellectual history. . . . *Imperial Identities* would already be important if it merely showed how the Kabyle Myth came into existence, but that is not where Lorcin stops her inquiry, and this is why her work is certain to leave a lasting mark on the field."

—James Le Sueur, *Journal of Modern History*

IMPERIAL
IDENTITIES

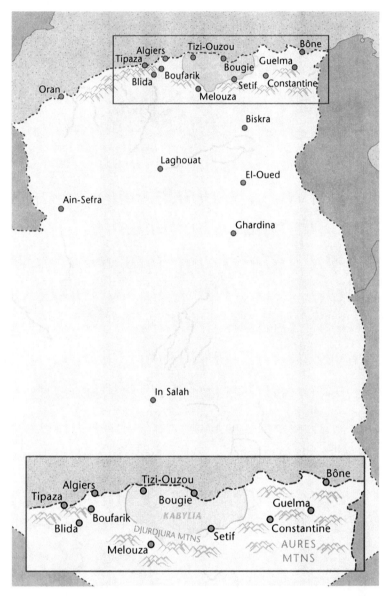

Colonial Algeria. Map created by the University of Minnesota Cartography Lab.

IMPERIAL IDENTITIES

Stereotyping, Prejudice, and Race in Colonial Algeria

NEW EDITION

PATRICIA M. E. LORCIN

Foreword by Hugh Roberts
With a new introduction by the author

UNIVERSITY OF NEBRASKA PRESS
LINCOLN AND LONDON

Foreword

HUGH ROBERTS

The Kabyle myth, the object of Patricia Lorcin's magisterial study, had become a serious obstacle to the analysis of political life in independent Algeria by the time I started to take an interest in the country in the early 1970s. The discrediting of French writings about the Kabyles as "myth" rendered the investigation of Kabyle participation in national politics—and especially of local politics in the Kabylia region—exceptionally delicate and difficult, beset with all kinds of pitfalls. This was not because the regime was engaged in repression or even active discrimination against Algeria's Berber populations in the economic and political spheres, as is sometimes suggested. On the contrary, it was not only careful to include Berbers in high office in almost exact proportion to their percentages of the total population but was also extremely sensitive to the state of opinion in the Berber regions—Kabylia and the Aurès especially—and was actively engaged in a strategy of integrating the populations of these regions into the Algerian national community. The first two *wilayāt* (governorates) to benefit from special development programs in the late 1960s were Tizi Ouzou (Greater Kabylia) and Batna (Aurès); Berber heroes were commemorated in the names of public places, streets, squares, and high schools,[1] and Berber musicians were able to record and sell their songs quite freely.[2] But this era was the high tide of the Algerian national idea; the regime, as the heir to the nationalist movement that had developed from the 1920s onward, was also the heir of this movement's definition of the nation as "Arabo-Muslim," a definition that omitted any reference to the Berber element. Many, probably most, Algerians at that time had internalized the national idea thus defined, and to evoke or inquire about local, regional, or linguistically specific identities was frowned upon as an insensitive intrusion on a septic issue and provoked unease even in interlocutors who were themselves Berbers. To exhibit a special interest in the Kabyles was to lay oneself open to the suspicion—no doubt well founded in some cases—of having no respect for the Algerian national identity and, in particular, of regressing to a research agenda of the colonial era, with all that this might imply.

When it came to investigating postcolonial social and political development in Kabylia (the choice I eventually made for my doctoral thesis), the Kabyle myth loomed up immediately as a source of several difficulties. Like all myths, the Kabyle myth contained a kernel of truth; it would not have had the great potency it did otherwise. The most serious of the nineteenth-century French ethnologists—notably Hanoteau and Letourneux and Masqueray—had all remarked upon the significance of institutions in the political organization of Kabyle society and had emphasized above all the role of the *jema 'a* (in Berber, *thajma 'th*), the village council or assembly, in Kabyle self-government.[3] These observations had a firm basis in reality. But the way they had subsequently been incorporated into the most fanciful elaborations of a far-reaching dichotomy between the Kabyles (or the Berbers in general) and the "Arabs" had almost entirely discredited them by the 1960s. The most influential writings on Berber political organization by that time were those of the British anthropologist Ernest Gellner and the French sociologist Pierre Bourdieu.[4] Gellner's development of Edward Evans-Pritchard's segmentarity theory in the context of the Central High Atlas of Morocco had played down the significance of the *jema 'a* and explicitly denied that Berber society possessed any political institutions at all, emphasizing the role of kinship and religion instead. Bourdieu also emphasized kinship and its ideological corollary, the code of honor, and while evacuating the question of religion tended, like Gellner, to play down the *jema 'a* in what came across as a conscious effort to distance his view from that of his nineteenth-century predecessors. In the course of fieldwork in the Jurjura mountains of Kabylia in 1975 and 1976, however, I found that the *jema 'a* and its associated institutions still existed in the villages I visited and appeared to play a crucial role despite the fact that they had no official existence in the eyes of the Algerian government. I accordingly formed the view that, on this point at least, the observations of the nineteenth-century ethnologists had been sound. How, then, to do justice to the reality of Kabyle life without lapsing into the misconceptions of the nineteenth-century myth-mongers?

The first point to grasp, as Lorcin shows with exemplary thoroughness, is how the makers of the Kabyle myth constructed a stereotype of "the Kabyle" by linking, indeed identifying, several distinct dichotomies with each other. In the Kabyle myth, "the Kabyle" is constructed not only in opposition to "the Arab" but also by identifying this opposition with the oppositions "mountain/plain" and "sedentary/nomad." At the same time, "the Kabyle" is identified with "the Berber" and vice versa. What is remarkable is the blindness that was presupposed by this stereotyping. The Kabyles were certainly a sedentary people of the mountains. But important elements of the Chaouia (or Shawiyya) Berbers of the Aurès region in southeastern Algeria are—or at least used to be— seminomadic pastoralists (especially the Berber-speaking Nememcha to the east of the Aurès mountains proper), and much of the Chaouia population inhabit the high plains to the north of the Aurès rather than the mountains themselves. This is enough to refute the simple-minded identification of the mountain/ plain and sedentary/nomad dichotomies with the Berber/Arab dichotomy. This identification worked only if for "Berber" one read "Kabyle," but even in this

case—ignoring the confusion (or sleight-of-hand) it involved—the identification broke down at the other end, for the identification of "the Arab" with the
"plain" and "nomadism" equally had no warrant in reality.

The geography of Algeria north of the Sahara is dominated by two mountain chains: the Tell Atlas, which reaches its highest point in the peak known as
Tamgout n'Lalla Khedija in the Jurjura range of Greater Kabylia but extends
from the Moroccan border to the Tunisian one, and the Saharan Atlas, which
equally extends right across the country and reaches its highest point in the
Jebel Chelia in the Aurès massif. To the west of the Aurès and its extension in the
Belezma mountains, the populations of the Saharan Atlas are Arabic-speakers, a
significant proportion of whom have long been sedentary. As for the Tell Atlas, it
is only in Greater and Lesser Kabylia, the Mount Chenoua district to the west
of Algiers, and the hills to the south of Tlemcen that Berber-speakers are found
in any numbers. The populations of all the other districts of the Tell Atlas—
the Ouarsenis, Dahra, and Trara mountains in the west; the Blida Atlas in the
center; and the Collo, Edough, Ferjiwa, Hodna, and Mejerda mountains in the
east—are both hillsmen and Arabic-speakers. The apparently willful if not reso-
lutely determined refusal to see the Arabic-speaking hillsmen of Algeria had an
important corollary that was also rooted in a very striking, if secondary, premise.

Whether or not one endorses the positive evaluation that the nineteenth-
century French ethnologists made of Kabyle political organization as exhibiting
"republican" and "democratic" qualities, there is no doubt that the descriptions they provided of this organization—notably regarding the role of the
village *jema'a* and the importance of customary law—were factually accurate
as far as they went. One of the ways in which the Kabyle myth went astray was
in suggesting that it was only the Berbers who possessed such arrangements.
In fact, however, the *jema'a* has been a long-established institution among
the Arabic-speaking hillsmen of Algeria, as certain twentieth-century studies
have made clear.[5] Moreover, it is not only among the mountain and sedentary
populations—whether Berberophone or Arabophone—that the *jema'a* is (or
used to be) encountered. Some and quite possibly most of the "nomadic" and
pastoralist populations—which the Kabyle myth treated as invariably composed
of "Arabs" and in every respect unlike the favored Kabyles—also had the *jema'a*,
as Alain Romey's fine study of one pastoralist tribe of southern Algeria records.[6]
Indeed, just as the role of rudimentary parties (*sfūf*, singular: *saff*, usually written *çof* by the French) was indispensable to the primacy of the *jema'a* in Kabyle
political organization, so too Arab populations that possessed the *jema'a* also
had *sfūf*, as Romey documents.[7]

This element of continuity, of a shared tradition of political organization,
that transcended the linguistic Berber/Arab distinction extended to the sphere
of law. As Lorcin shows in detail, a fundamental element of the Kabyle myth was
the thesis that the Kabyles were only superficially, and not "really," Muslims.
The most important premise of this notion was the observation that they had

their own local law, embodied in what was known as a *qānūn* (plural: *qawānīn*) legislated by their assemblies and so man-made, derived from local customs (*'urf*) rather than from the Qur'ān and the Sharī'a. But the supposition that this radically distinguished the Kabyles from the other populations of the Algerian countryside and the Arabs in particular was entirely mistaken. As Karim Rahem has shown for the predominantly Arabophone hillsmen of the hinterland of Skikda (ex-Philippeville) in the Nord-Constantinois, some of these other populations also governed themselves by reference to custom and customary (*'urfi*) law.[8] And as Mahfoud Bennoune testifies, the Arabic-speaking Beni Kaïd tribe of the El-Milia district not only had customary law but also, like the Berbers of Kabylia, embodied it in a *qānūn*.[9]

The secondary premise of the failure of French colonialism to take into consideration the true character of the Arabic-speaking populations of Algeria was the quite remarkable lack of curiosity about them and the all but systematic failure to investigate them. The superabundance of nineteenth-century literature on Kabylia stands in spectacular contrast to the paucity of comparable studies of Algeria's numerous other regions and their inhabitants. While the category of "the Kabyles" referred with some precision to the particular inhabitants of a clearly defined region, that of "the Arabs" appears as an entirely residual category in which numerous different populations—the hillsmen of the Ouarsenis and the Collo, the sedentary oasis-dwellers of the Saharan *qsūr*, the transhumant pastoralists of the northern Sahara and the High Plateaux, and, indeed, the urban populations of Muslim Algeria's cities and towns—were lumped together pell-mell without any effort of discernment or the kind of serious inquiry required for this.

Lorcin's meticulous tracing of the development of the Kabyle myth identifies the principal reasons for this. The fateful decision in 1840 to abandon the modest objective of *l'occupation restreinte* and to embark instead on the conquest of the interior—a choice that had its equally fateful sequel in 1848 in the decision to incorporate Algeria into the French state—made the security of the French position an intense and abiding preoccupation of the colonizing authorities. This in turn induced them not only to encourage large-scale French and other European settlement in order to consolidate the conquest by arms but also to look for elements of the indigenous population who might be susceptible to co-optation. The policy of assimilation thus broached needed "natives" to assimilate, and the Kabyles were quickly identified as the likeliest candidates for this role. In part this was because, having largely failed to rally to the Emir Abdelkader's cause, they were perceived as having resisted the French incursion quite independently of "the Arabs" and then to have definitely submitted and to be making the best of their new situation, an attitude the French military naturally appreciated. In part it was because their way of life—with its settled agriculture, arboriculture and stock raising, craft manufacture and trade, industriousness, frugal habits, stone houses, compact and picturesque villages, and, finally, an impressive form of self-government—seemed to recall that of the hillsmen of the Massif Central and Savoy. In this way did wishful thinking supplement insecurity and anxiety to produce an enduring collective hallucination.

That the Kabyles were the most suitable human material available for assimilation quickly became *une évidence*, that is, a dogma, but the intellectual process involved in establishing this postulate involved the multifaceted contrast with "the Arabs," which in turn rendered pointless any serious interest in the latter. Thus the fanciful conception of "the Kabyle" became, at least for a time, virtually proof against experience. For had the colonial ethnologists seriously investigated Algeria's other hillsmen (to look no further), they might have come to realize that the Kabyles were not so very different from many of their Arabic-speaking fellow Muslims, and the hopeful conclusions so rapidly jumped to from initial impressions of them might have been undermined far sooner—and perhaps less painfully—than they were.

In what, then, if anything, lay the specificity of the Kabyles, the substantive difference between them and the other indigenous populations of Algeria? The true answer is that it lay in four closely linked facts: the fact that Kabyle society was, with the exception of the cities of the Mzab, the most developed variant of what Jean Morizot has called "la société villageoise" in Algeria,[10] in that their villages were appreciably larger than those found among the other observable variants (the Aurès, the Wad Righ, the *qsūr* of the Sud Oranais and the Saharan oases, etc.); the corresponding fact that theirs was the most elaborate variant of the political tradition of the *jema'a* to be found in Algeria north of the Sahara; and that these aspects of their society were due primarily to two other features that distinguished it—the exceptional density of population of the region and its proximity to Ottoman Algiers. The extraordinary population density—which remained, of course, to be explained—placed exceptional stress on their sociopolitical organization and prompted over time its development and elaboration. The proximity to Algiers and the Kabyles' correspondingly intense relations with the Ottoman authorities supplemented population pressures in impelling these developments in Kabyle organization.

The logics of the remarkable development that had occurred in Kabylia by the time the French got there could only be grasped by historical investigation. Instead, the French engaged in ahistorical stereotyping and intense and far-reaching speculation about race, with—as Lorcin shows—the findings of the observers in the field being taken up and pressed into the service of unscientific theorizing in the metropolis. In this way did French commentators convince themselves that the Kabyles were "democrats" and "republicans," not "really" Muslims, and even "anticlerical" (and accordingly susceptible to assimilation) *because they were Berbers*, that it was *la génie berbère*, the genius of their "race," that explained the impressive and distinctive character of their social and political arrangements.

The development of the race theory of Kabyle organization was thus a surrogate for the historical explanation that alone could really explain it and do justice to it. Intent on consolidating the conquest, permanently anxious about security, and correspondingly inclined to engage in wishful thinking and grasp at straws, the French were wholly disinclined to undertake the historical investigation that was required. In particular, their prejudice against the Ottoman regime they had destroyed and superseded ruled out recognizing that developments in the mountainous hinterland of Algiers owed much to this regime's protracted and complex influence.

Patricia Lorcin's meticulously researched and beautifully written account of the Kabyle myth, of the history of its emergence, the intellectual and political context that produced it, and of its subsequent influence and eventual eclipse, is an object lesson in the methods of rigorous historical investigation and reasoning that a fully grounded understanding of Algeria's complex history unquestionably requires. The republication of her book is an occasion to celebrate; may all those concerned with the history and historiography of Algeria salute it and meditate on the example it sets.

NOTES

1. This recognition even included Abane Ramdane, the FLN leader killed by his peers in 1957; streets in central Algiers and Constantine were already named after him by 1972 if not earlier, as were the main streets in Tizi Ouzou and Bouïra.

2. When I arrived in Bouïra to take up a teaching post at the Lycée there in September 1973, I could hear the music of the Kabyle singer Idir playing in cafés all over town; his song "A Vava Inouva" was a huge hit, and it appeared that the government was tacitly facilitating this expression of Berber culture.

3. Adolphe Hanoteau and Aristide Letourneux, *La Kabylie et les coutumes kabyles*, 3 vols. (Paris: Châllamel, 1872–3; 2nd ed., 1893); Émile Masqueray, *Formation des Cités chez les populations sédentaires de l'Algérie* (Paris: Ernest Leroux, 1886). Republished with an introduction by Fanny Colonna, Centre de Recherches et d'Études sur les Sociétés Méditerranéennes, series "Archives Maghrébines" (Aix-en-Provence: Édisud, 1983).

4. Ernest Gellner, *Saints of the Atlas* (London: Weidenfeld & Nicolson, 1969); Pierre Bourdieu, *Sociologie de l'Algérie* (Paris: Presses Universitaires de France, 1958); *The Algerians* (Boston: Beacon Press, 1962).

5. See especially Mahfoud Bennoune, *El Akbia: Un siècle d'histoire algérienne (1857–1975)* (Algiers: Office des Publications Universitaires, 1986; 2nd ed. 2009), 123 et seq. The village El Akbia is located in the mountains in the vicinity of El Milia to the northwest of Constantine in northeastern Algeria.

6. Alain Romey, *Les Sa'id Atbâ de N'Goussa: Histoire et état actuel de leur nomadisme* (Paris: L'Harmattan, 1983), 73 et seq., 83.

7. Romey, *Les Sa'id Atbâ de N'Goussa*.

8. Karim Rahem, *Le Sillage de la Tribu: Imaginaires politiques et histoire en Algérie (1843–1993)* (Paris: Riveneuve éditions, 2008), 234.

9. Bennoune, *El Akbia*, 27.

10. Jean Morizot, *L'Algérie kabylisée* (Paris: J. Peyronnet, 1962); and *Les Kabyles, Propos d'un Témoin* (Paris: Centre des Hautes Études sur l'Afrique et l'Asie Modernes, 1985).

Introduction to the Nebraska Edition

In the two decades following the 1995 publication of *Imperial Identities*, French colonial history has moved from being a little-explored subdivision of French historiography to one of its leading concerns. Shaped by the imperial and cultural "turns" and stimulated by postcolonial studies and the broadening of Francophonie, the ensuing interdisplinarity has created a broader historical canvas on which scholars of colonial history can work. Although Algeria was not the only "jewel" in France's imperial crown, the legacy of French rule in Algeria has been the most profound of all its territories. In Indochina, also a former French territory of significance, the fallout from the French presence has been overshadowed by the subsequent involvement of the United States and the anguish of the Vietnam War. Indochina's historiography has not been dominated by the trauma of the territory's decolonization from France to the extent that Algeria's has.[1]

Trauma as colonial legacy has stimulated scholarship, even if the focus of that scholarship has not been the traumatic event itself. The French overseas territory of Algeria was *sui generis* in that it was considered to be a departmental extension of the mainland rather than a colony. Losing it resembled the trauma of an amputation, even when that amputation was seen as salutary. Like the phantom limb of an amputation, however, the specter of the past still haunts the present. It is not surprising, therefore, that colonial Algeria was the focus of much of the early scholarly attention of the French "imperial turn," and scholars interested in imperialism have continued to produce a steady stream of scholarly articles and monographs. The bitter and lengthy decolonization (1954–62) of Algeria, which not only occasioned a stubborn official refusal to accept it as a war of independence but also led to its virtual occlusion in the public sphere, contributed to stimulating scholarly interest in the colony.[2] The war had been, after all, a dramatic twentieth-century expression of the Franco-French wars, following closely behind the Vichy period and echoing that time for some scholars.[3] When, in the 1990s, an independent Algeria descended into a bloody civil war, questions about the colonial legacy of violence resurfaced. Even though the events that triggered the conflict had little if anything to do with colonialism and much to do with internal politics, the perception persisted—at least among some present-day critiques of colonialism—that the patterns of violence established during the colonial period were being replicated.[4]

The scholarly issues related to colonial Algeria were not, of course, restricted to events occurring in Algeria. In France immigration politics was closely linked to France's former colonial territories, in particular those of the Maghreb. The Algerian War of Independence had washed up nearly two million dispossessed individuals on France's shore: *pieds-noirs*, *harkis*, and political or intellectual exiles, self-imposed or otherwise—ever-present reminders of the bitterness of a war from which the country wanted to move on.[5] In the public sphere erasure appeared to be the immediate response. By the 1990s, however, a generation of French and Algerian researchers who had not experienced the war had come of age, and they could look at the war with more dispassionate eyes. Coincidently the opening of access to documents at the Service Historique de la Defénse (SHAT) allowed for the examination of new material on the war.

Thus, in much the same way as it took thirty years for scholarship on Vichy to move in a new direction, it took as long for the nature of France's relationship to Algeria to be reexamined in a more penetrating light. Borrowing the concept of a syndrome from Henri Russo's *Vichy Syndrome*, the French "memory loss" in the aftermath of independence was dubbed the Algerian Syndrome. But it wasn't just a question of mimicking a catchy moniker; the experiences of civilians under the German occupation and the experiences of Algerians during the War of Independence had disturbingly unhealthy parallels. Torture, summary executions, and the brutalizing of the civilian population in Algeria flew in the face of French republican ideals of liberty, equality, and fraternity. It took a generation for the dust to settle on atrocities and outrages committed before they could be aired afresh; events in Algeria during the nineties focused attention on the area anew and raised questions not only about the connection between the two wars but also about the colonial project as a whole. Was it a coincidence that when the civil war in Algeria finally subsided, an official acknowledgment that Algeria's struggle for independence had in fact been a war was finally forthcoming and that the atrocities committed at the time were being aired anew? Raphaëlle Branche's admirable treatment of torture during the Algerian War, along with the publication in the same year of the defense of torture by Algerian War veteran Paul Aussaresses (1918–2013), created a commotion in France on both sides of the divide, leading to threats against Branche and a trial for Aussaresses.[6] The scandal of Abu Ghraib (2003–4) during the second Iraq war and the Bush administration's instigation of the practice of "rendition," all but echoing Aussaresses's conviction that torture was a legitimate way of extracting information, ensured that the issue of torture was kept in the public eye. Analyses of the connections between the two practices of torture followed, although the outcry against torture in the United States remained relatively muted.[7]

The scholarly preoccupation with the twentieth century and in particular the Algerian War of Independence meant that scholars interested in colonial

Algeria, specifically those from the Anglophone academy, have only lately turned their attention to the nineteenth century.[8] Recent attention has also focused on the two World Wars and the interwar period in France, especially with regard to issues of gender and race, issues that were hardly touched upon prior to 1995, at least in relation to France and its colonies.[9] The myth that racism was not endemic to French colonies—or to the metropole, for that matter—but was a personal or short-lived aberration has been discredited.

But how have the main themes that run through *Imperial Identities*—stereotyping and race, military Saint-Simonianism, and the Kabyle Myth—been picked up and expanded upon since the book's initial publication in 1995? Historians whose interests focus on France and its empire have shown the most interest in the former two themes, whereas it is historians of the Maghreb that have taken up the theme of the Kabyle-Arab divide. The Kabyle Myth has been examined in passing by scholars whose interests have focused on colonial policies or activities relating to the treatment of the local populations, whether in Algeria, France, or the way the myth informed policies in colonial Morocco.[10]

Most recent scholarship on stereotyping and race in France during the modern colonial period has concentrated on the situation in the metropole, focusing mainly on the twentieth century.[11] Although nearly all former French colonies are sites of emigration, the immigrant majority in France from former colonies comes from North Africa and is predominantly (but not exclusively) Muslim.[12] The uneasiness with and fear of Islam, emotional responses that were prevalent in nineteenth-century colonial Algeria, have resurfaced in the postindependence metropole as anti-Islamic immigrant politics, either in the form of right-wing invective against Islam's perceived menace or as the introduction-actual or projected-of sumptuary laws such as those against the *hijab* and the *burqa*.[13] The symbolic potency of the "veil" predated independence, as evidenced by the public ceremony during the War of Independence when the wives of leading French military officers incited Algerian women to remove their veils as a sign of their emancipation.[14] Current scholarship has focused less on Saint-Simonianism and the military in Algeria, although the influence of Saint-Simonianism continues to be of scholarly interest.[15] Military activity in the nineteenth century has received some attention either in the context of the conquest or as an examination of the violence the military perpetrated in their attempts to subdue the local populations.[16]

FROM THE "KABYLE MYTH" TO THE "KABYLE QUESTION"

The third and most significant theme—the Kabyle Myth or, in its postindependence iteration, the Arab-Kabyle divide—is a recurrent theme in the scholarship on Algerian ethnic politics.[17] The Arab-Kabyle (Berber) binary—the basis for the Kabyle Myth—is, according to James McDougall, "routinely deployed as an explanatory principle of the sociological reality of Maghrebi societies and persistently invoked in the discourses of Maghrebi politics . . . [furthermore the] devise has been fundamental to categorization and representations both among North Africans themselves and by outside observers. In Algeria, in particular, it has provided the idiom for some of the most bitterly fought social conflicts of the past half-century."[18] What then are these conflicts and how, if at all, are they related to the past? Although the "Berber Spring" of the 1980s is most commonly known as the first postindependence clash between Arabs and Kabyles, antagonisms and conflicts existed much earlier. The assassination of the Kabyle leader Abane Ramdane during the War of Independence was due to, among other things, his promotion of the concept of an Algerian Algeria (*Algérie algérienne*) rather than an Arab and Muslim Algeria (*Algérie arabe et musulmane*).[19] His ideas flew in the face of the desire by the FLN (National Liberation Front) to dissociate Algeria from the secularizing culture of the colonial period by emphasizing the importance of Islam.

Following independence, Kabyle elites started to form a tangible identity framed in linguistic and historical terms. They argued that Maghrebi countries had emerged out of "a vast Berber land," thus emphasizing their historical legitimacy.[20] A sense of unity was further created by adopting the designation *Imazighen* as one of self-referral, with *Tamazight* as the unifying term for the Berber language. The sense of unity reinforced by these terms extended beyond the borders of Algeria to the Kabyle/Berber diaspora. According to Jane Goodman, whose anthropological study focuses on Kabyle/Berber cultural modernity, their postindependence identity has been created by both discursive and performative means. Poetry, literature, songs, and social rituals linking Kabyles and other Berbers across time and space, in what Goodman calls "cultural motion," have created a perception that Berber identity is "singular and unique"—a perception that reinforces the position of the Algerian state, which views Berber activities as neocolonialist defiance whose motivation comes from abroad, in particular from France.[21] Is the Kabyle Myth the foundation for these developments, or are they merely postindependence identity politics? To be sure, ideas from the past permeate the present, but in the postcolonial situation they are more often than not used for political ends, as they obviously were in this case by the Algerian state. The Kabyle Myth is an ideological structure of the colonial past, not the postindependence present. Why then this animus?

The "Kabyle Question," which has resurfaced at regular intervals since independence, is due essentially to the absence of adequate institutions to express grievances and channel representation of interests.[22] These grievances started when the government of the newly independent Algerian state sought to Arabize the population by introducing a challenging program, geared at teaching modern Arabic throughout the educational system. The aim was to replace French, which was still used in some key institutions, and in the process eradicate significant traces of the colonial past.[23] Conceivably, without the drive to Arabize, the Kabyles would not have defensively sought to sharpen the definition of their own identity. Whether or not there is a causal link between the two, the shoring up of regional identity politically or culturally—or both— was an evident phenomenon in many areas of the globe in the last quarter of the twentieth century, and the Berbers were no exception. Regionalism, with its demands for cultural (and in some instances political) autonomy, rejects the unifying principles of nationalism. For newly independent countries set on creating a unified state from the social and political disarray engendered by colonialism, any attempt to counteract such a unity by championing a sepa- rate regional identity is, at best, viewed as suspect or, at worst, stamped out. In Algeria, where severe internecine violence had characterized the 1954–62 war and where postindependence purges took countless lives, the necessity to unify the newly established country was especially important. The state would not countenance any impediment to this goal. The ideological impasse between the Algerian state and the Kabyle Berbers gave rise to the 1980 Berber Spring (*Tafsut Imazighen*), which was triggered when the renowned Kabyle author Mouloud Mammeri (1917–89) was stopped from giving a lecture on Kabyle poetry at the university in Tizi Ouzou, in Kabylia. The cancellation of the event provoked violent demonstrations and crystallized the demands for Berber cultural autonomy.[24] Interviews of Kabyles, in the context of Good- man's anthropological monograph, demonstrate that the Berber Spring was an individual turning point and, subsequently, a foundational moment for both academic and popular literature.[25] In the aftermath of the Berber Spring, the Berberist movement founded the Mouvement Culturel Berbère (MCB). It was essentially a Kabyle initiative garnering little support from the other Berber groups in Algeria—initially at least.[26]

In 1989 formal political pluralism was introduced in Algeria, opening the door to the possibility of democratic elections and a multiparty state. In the first round of the ensuing elections, held in 1991, the Islamic Salvation Front (FIS) appeared to be on its way to victory, prompting the ruling party, the FLN, to cancel the second round of elections. New elections were held in 1992, put- ting the military in power and triggering a decade of civil war in which whole villages, districts, and targeted groups were massacred. Although Kabyles were among those targeted, there is no evidence to suggest that they were singled out for particular retribution from either the FIS, which was against secularizing tendencies in the country, or government forces, which were allegedly involved in some of the massacres. Indeed, as a result of the steps taken toward politi- cal pluralism, concessions were made to accommodate some Kabyle cultural demands, although there is still resentment at the fact that the government has so far refused to endow "official" status to *Tamazight* so as to place it on a par with Arabic as a language of public administration.[27]

Conflict between the government and the Kabyles was not at an end, how- ever. In April 2001, at a commemoration of the Berber Spring, a young Kabyle student, Guermah Massinissa, was killed while in custody in the district of Tizi

Ouzou. Two days later several high school students were arrested for allegedly insulting the forces of order, who had claimed that Guermah was a thief. The resulting riots, now known as the "Black Spring," lasted on and off from the end of April to July and claimed over a hundred lives with many more injured, some of them permanently.[28] According to Roberts, the 2001 rioters were reacting to what they characterized as *la hogra*, the contempt of the regime, which was deaf to their demands and blind to their needs. As *Africa News*, reporting on the events, stated: "The people are not only frustrated from the high unemployment rate, the shortage of housing, the deteriorating social conditions, which affect Algerians throughout the country, but also the issue of identity and recognition of the Tamazight language."[29]

According to the *Guardian* (London), "officials . . . attacked the latest protests as a Berber nationalist revolt influenced by outsiders, knowing that many Algerian Arabs suspect[ed] that France [was] behind the Berber national demands."[30] If Algerian leaders overlook or ignore Kabyle demands it is because they are inclined to view events in Kabylia as part of a larger Algerian problem rather than a regional one, which they prefer to see as fomented from the outside. Kabyles, on the other hand, argue that Kabylia is in the vanguard of progressive change and that they are politically in advance of their fellow Algerians.[31] The French press, which closely follows developments in Algeria, echoed these sentiments at the time. Jean-Marcel Bouguereau, writing in *La République des Pyrenees*, stated that the Kabyles were harbingers, in so far as Kabylia was always in the vanguard of Algerian uprisings; Jean Lavallois, in *La Presse de la Manche*, declared that the Kabyles were only expressing more forcefully than demonstrators elsewhere the extent of the national crisis.[32]

Clashes between the Kabyles and government forces continue, albeit not on the scale of the 2001 events; if the "Kabyle Question" is seen by officials to be part of a larger Algerian problem, the debate concerning the position of Kabylia within the Algerian state continues among Kabyle activists. In 2013 the *Amazigh* singer Idir called for the autonomy of Kabylia, prompting Khaled Drareni, anchor person of the Dzaïr Web TV program *Controverse*, to invite the journalist Abdelkrim Ghezali and the writers Abdeslam Abdenour and Mouloud Lounmaouci to respond to Idir's declaration and to discuss the different possibilities of regional autonomy.[33] The discussion was a reflection of the situation as it stands. All three participants agreed that some sort of autonomy was desirable, but there was not much agreement on what form it should take or whether the demands and claims of regionalism for Kabylia were the same as for the other regions of Algeria. Nor did they feel that the government would respond positively to the demands of regionalism. In short, whether at the discursive level or at the political level, the "Kabyle Question" in Algeria remains unresolved.

But what about the Kabyle diaspora and how it has developed in France? Kabyle emigration from Algeria to France started long before independence, when villagers from Kabylia, pauperized as a result of colonial land appropriation, left the region seeking work. They gravitated to the colonial urban centers of Algeria and from there moved on to France. Until the 1940s the majority of the emigrants from Algeria were Kabyle due to the appalling economic conditions in Kabylia—conditions that Albert Camus depicted in his 1938 article "Misère en Kabylie" in the *Alger Républicain*.[34] During that time the emigration comprised young men and bachelors and was temporary. Their aim was to return once conditions in Kabylia improved. After World War II migrants from other Berber regions joined the diaspora.[35] Echoes of the Kabyle Myth accompanied their arrival. According to Amelia Lyons, officials in the Algerian Reform and Planning Office established a program to recruit Algerian peasants to work as farmhands. The program, which was devised in the interwar period, was revived after World War II in order to help France build its shattered economy and repopulate depopulated areas. The intention was to give preference to Kabyle or other Berber families, as family units were more stable than single men and because Kabyles were "more sedentary, more easily adaptable to Western civilization, and only superficially Islamic compared to the Arab majority."[36] The program was never fully implemented because of French resistance at the local level, but it does suggest the impact stereotypes and preconceptions can have on official policy.

A significant characteristic to these diasporic developments was the spatial concentration of Kabyles (and eventually other Berber groups) who gravitated to the same areas and settled according to village or kinship group.[37] This assisted solidarity for activism when it occurred. Diaspora communities seek to consolidate their cultural identities, and the Berber diaspora, whether from Kabylia or from other Berber regions, is no exception.[38] In 1967 the first Berber organization, the Académie Berbère d'échanges et de recherches culturelles, was formed in Paris. In 1972 Berber Studies was established at the University of Paris VIII, Vincennes. This organization served to promote *Amazigh* identity; although they initially reached out to Kabyle communities in Algeria, as time progressed they turned their attention almost exclusively to the diaspora.[39] Today the *Amazigh* network extends beyond France with cultural associations in the United States, Canada, and the Canary Islands, and of course branches exist in the Maghreb countries.[40]

But where does that leave us with the legacy of the Kabyle Myth in Algeria? In 1980, in the wake of the Berber Spring, the Algerian historian Mohammed Harbi stated: "Kabylia's specificity is due to the convergence of several factors: the late and limited character of Arabization and thus the permanence of Berber Culture, the Kabyle policy of French colonialism, which contributed to forming an important elite, [Kabylia's] role as a font of internal and external immigration and its social cohesion."[41] For Harbi, therefore, the impact of the past (whether in the form of the Kabyle Myth or Kabyle immigrant exposure to French culture, politics, and values) is a significant enough factor in the political developments between Kabyles and the government in the postindependence period to warrant consideration.

The privileging of a chosen ethnic group as a useful adjunct to colonization was not restricted to Algeria. European colonialists of the nineteenth century relied on selected groups, whether they formed part of a particular ethnicity or social class. It is the nature of any occupation to do so. But it does not necessarily follow that *divide and rule* is an actual colonial policy: it has less to do with determinism and more to do with expediency. The experiences of occupation have a haphazard quality in that they are responses to developments on the ground, which are seldom those anticipated. Such was the case in Algeria, where the ideologies of assimilation and association were never consistently adhered to and where revolts and rebellions at regular intervals provoked responses that temporarily or permanently disrupted existing or projected policies regarding the local population. The Kabyle Myth was the conjunction of an ideological projection of nineteenth-century racial thought and colonial ethnographic misinterpretations. It never became official colonial policy.[42] The colonial conditions reducing the Kabyles to the itinerant status of impoverished job-seekers, not the misguided elevation of them to superior status in the Kabyle Myth, were the basis of the situation that has troubled the political present in Algeria. The permanent diasporic communities, created as a result of the waves of migration from Kabylia and other Berber regions, not only solidified a diasporic identity but also resulted in an ideological, political, or social relationship to the host country, as any permanent diaspora always does. Such an accommodation leads to various degrees of incompatibly with the inhabitants of the emigration site. Although the processes of identity formation and the political concerns of the diasporic community are framed within the host country, they can tangentially influence the country of origin, causing political, social, or cultural tensions. The past and the present become intertwined in ways that differ from nondiasporic or national communities. Furthermore, when the diaspora comprises individuals from former colonial countries, the relationship and political dynamics between the host country and emigration site are not the same as other forms of diaspora. The postcolonial context—the past fraught as it is with its historical memories of discrimination, marginalization, and violence—becomes a political tool that can be used to intimidate or persecute those who, for whatever reason, unnerve or unsettle the establishment. In discussing the phenomenon of postcoloniality, David Scott reminds us that very little systematic consideration, if any, has been given to *what* present it is that the past is being reimagined for, or, more precisely, "an adequate interrogation of the present (postcolonial or otherwise) depends upon identifying the difference between the questions that animated former presents and those that animate our own."[43] The apparent difficulty in identifying these differences continues to haunt both the politics and historiography of postcolonial Algeria.

Introduction

NOTES

1. The literature on the period 1954–62 is vast. The following are but a few examples: James D. Le Sueur, *Uncivil War: Intellectuals and Identity Politics during the Decolonization of Algeria* (Philadelphia: University of Pennsylvania Press, 2001); Irwin M. Wall, *France, the United States, and the Algerian War* (Berkley: University of California Press, 2001); Matthew James Connelly, *A Diplomatic Revolution: Algeria's Fight for Independence and the Origins of the Post-Cold War Era* (New York: Oxford University Press, 2002); Benjamin Stora and Mohammed Harbi, *La Guerre d'Algérie: 1954–2004, la Fin de L'amnésie* (Paris: R. Laffont, 2004).

2. Among the first to tackle the question of memory in this context was Benjamin Stora, *La Gangrène et L'oubli: La Mémoire de la Guerre d'Algérie* (Paris: La Découverte, 1991). Films originally banned in France include Gillo Pontecorvo, *La Bataille D'alger (the Battle of Algiers)* (Algiers: Casbah Film; Rome: Igor Film, 1966), DVD, 117 min.

3. Martin Evans, *The Memory of Resistance: French Opposition to the Algerian War, 1954–1962,* Berg French Studies (New York: Oxford University Press, 1997); Martin Evans and Kenneth Lunn, *War and Memory in the Twentieth Century* (Oxford: Berg, 1997). Many of the French activists who aided the FLN also made the connection. See Martin Evans, *Mémoires de la Guerre d'Algérie* (Paris: L'Harmattan, 2007). For the debates about memory, see Raphaëlle Branche, *La Guerre d'Algérie: Une Histoire Apaisée?* L'histoire en débats 11351. Paris: Seuil, 2005; Benjamin Stora, *La Guerre des Mémoires: La France Face à Son Passé Colonial* (Paris: Éditions de l'Aube, 2007); Benjamin Stora, "The Algerian War in French Memory: Vengeful Memory's Violence," in *Memory and Violence in the Middle East and North Africa*, ed. Ussama Samir Makdisi and Paul A. Silverstein (Bloomington: Indiana University Press, 2006).

4. For the internal politics, see Hugh Roberts, *The Battlefield: Algeria, 1988–2002; Studies in a Broken Polity* (London and New York: Verso, 2002); Hugh Roberts, *Algerian Socialism and the Kabyle Question*, Monographs in Development Studies (Norwich: School of Development Studies, University of East Anglia, 1981). For a discussion on the links between past and present violence in Algeria, see Abdelmajid Hannoum, *Violent Modernity: France in Algeria* (Cambridge MA: Harvard University Press, 2010).

5. On the treatment of the *harkis*, see Vincent Crapanzano, *The Harkis: The Wound That Never Heals* (Chicago: University of Chicago Press, 2011); Geraldine Enjelvin, "The Harki Identity: A Product of Marginalisation and Resistance to Symbolic Violence," *National Identities* 8 (2006); Abd-El-Aziz Méliani, *Le Drame des Harkis*, reissue (Paris: Perrin, 2001). On the treatment of the *pieds-noirs*, see Todd Shepard, *The Invention of Decolonization: The Algerian War and the Remaking of France* (Ithaca NY: Cornell University Press, 2006). On the silences of war, see the articles on Algeria in Efrat Ben-Ze'ev, Ruth Ginio, and J. M. Winter, eds., *Shadows of War: A Social History of Silence in the Twentieth Century* (Cambridge: Cambridge University Press, 2010). See also the introduction to Patricia M. E. Lorcin, ed., *Algeria and France, 1800–2000: Identity, Memory, Nostalgia* (Syracuse NY: Syracuse University Press, 2006).

6. Torture became an issue during the war following the publication in 1958 of Henri Alleg's experience at the hands of French paratroopers: Henri Alleg, *La Question* (Paris: Éditions de Minuit, 1958). The photographer Dominique Darbois's graphic photographs were visual proof that torture had taken place: Dominique Darbois and Philippe Vigneau, *Les Algériens en Guerre* (Milano: Feltrinelli, 1961). The best recent works are Raphälle Branche, *La Torture et L'armée Pendant la Guerre d'Algérie: 1954–1962* (Paris: Gallimard, 2001); Raphaëlle Branche, "Des Viols Pendant la Guerre d'Algérie," *Vingtième Siècle: Revue d'historie* 75 (2002–3): 123–32; Raphaëlle Branche, "FLN et OAS: Deux Terrorismes en Guerre d'Algérie," *European Review of History / Revue europénne d'Histoire* 14, no. 3 (2007): 325–42;

Introduction

Paul Aussaresses, *Services Spéciaux: Algérie, 1955–1957* (Paris: Perrin, 2001). In 2002, following the trial, Aussaresses was stripped of his rank and fined. Under the amnesties following the end of the Algerian War of Independence he could not be charged with war crimes

7. For the link between French and American practices of torture, see Marie-Monique Robin, *Escadrons de la Mort, L'école Française* (Paris: Découverte, 2004); Marnia Lazreg, *Torture and the Twilight of Empire: From Algiers to Baghdad*, Human Rights and Crimes against Humanity (Princeton: Princeton University Press, 2008). Robin, who is a journalist, focuses on the international expansion of the terror tactics used in the Algerian War thanks to instruction by French officers of select U.S. and South American military personnel. In spite of its title, Lazreg's discussion of Iraq is cursory and her analysis of events in Algeria not nearly as thorough as Branche's work on torture and the army.

8. Recent literature includes Lorcin, *Algeria and France*; Diana K. Davis, *Resurrecting the Granary of Rome: Environmental History and French Colonial Expansion in North Africa* (Athens: Ohio University Press, 2007); Benjamin Claude Brower, *A Desert Named Peace: The Violence of France's Empire in the Algerian Sahara, 1844–1902* (New York: Columbia University Press, 2009); George R Trumbull IV, *An Empire of Facts: Colonial Power, Cultural Knowledge, and Islam in Algeria, 1870–1914* (Cambridge: Cambridge University Press, 2009); Rebecca Rogers, "Telling Stories About the Colonies: British and French Women in Algeria in the Nineteenth Century," *Gender and History* 21, no. 1 (2009); Jennifer E. Sessions, *By Sword and Plow: France and the Conquest of Algeria* (Ithaca NY: Cornell University Press, 2011); Rebecca Rogers, *A Frenchwoman's Imperial Story: Madame Luce in Nineteenth-Century Algeria* (Stanford CA: Stanford University Press, 2013); William Gallois, *A History of Violence in the Early Algerian Colony* (New York: Palgrave, 2013).

9. For Algeria during Vichy, see Jacques Cantier, *L'algérie Sous le Régime de Vichy* (Paris: Jacob, 2002). For women, gender, and race, see Julia Clancy-Smith, "Islam, Gender, and Identities in the Making of French Algeria, 1830–1962," in *Domesticating the Empire: Race, Gender, and Family Life in French and Dutch Colonialism*, ed. Julia Clancy-Smith and Frances Gouda (Charlottesville: University Press of Virginia, 1998); Herrick Chapman and Laura Levine Frader, *Race in France: Interdisciplinary Perspectives on the Politics of Difference* (New York: Berghahn Books, 2004).

10. An exception that focuses on the myth in Algeria is Paul A. Silverstein, "The Kabyle Myth: Colonization and the Production of Ethnicity," in *From the Margins: Historical Anthropology and Its Futures*, ed. B. K. Axel, 122–55 (Durham NC: Duke University Press, 2002). For the impact of the myth in Morocco, see Adam Guerin, "Racial Myth, Colonial Reform and the Invention of Customary Law in Morocco, 1912–1930," *Journal of North African Studies* 16, no. 3 (2011): 361–80. For echoes of the Kabyle Myth in France, see Amelia H. Lyons, *The Civilizing Mission in the Metropole: Algerian Families and the French Welfare State during Decolonization* (Stanford CA: Stanford University Press, 2013), 33.

11. Some exceptions: Owen White, *Children of the French Empire: Miscegenation and Colonial Society in French West Africa, 1895–1960* (New York: Oxford University Press, 1999); Jonathan K. Gosnell, *The Politics of Frenchness in Colonial Algeria, 1930–1954* (Rochester NY: University of Rochester Press, 2002); Martin S. Staum, *Labeling People: French Scholars on Society, Race and Empire, 1815–1848* (Montreal: McGill-Queen's University Press, 2003); Dana S. Hale, *Races on Display: French Representation of Colonized Peoples, 1886–1940* (Bloomington: Indiana University Press, 2008).

12. According to the OEDC, 11.5 percent (7.2 million) of the population in France (as of 2010) is foreign-born. http://www.oecd.org/migration/integrationindicators/keyindicators bycountry/name,219043,en.htm (accessed March 8, 2014). Miguel Mora, the correspondent for *El Pais* in Paris, reporting in May 2013, puts the immigrant population at 26.6

Introduction

percent, of which 30 percent come from the Maghreb, 14 percent from Asia, and 11 percent from sub-Saharan Africa. The remaining 45 percent therefore come from the EU and elsewhere. http://www.fdesouche.com/377212-france-30-de-maghrebins-14-dasiatiques-et-11-dafricains-subsahariens (accessed March 8, 2014).

13. Trica Danielle Keaton, *Muslim Girls and the Other France: Race, Identity Politics, and Social Exclusion* (Bloomington: Indiana University Press, 2006); Joan Wallach Scott, *The Politics of the Veil* (Princeton: Princeton University Press, 2007).

14. Neil MacMaster, *Burning the Veil: Military Propaganda and the Emancipation of Women during the Algeria War 1954–1962* (Manchester: Manchester University Press, 2009); Patricia M. E. Lorcin, *Historicizing Colonial Nostalgia: European Women's Narratives of Colonial Algeria and Kenya 1900–Present* (New York: Palgrave, 2012), 151.

15. Abdallah Zouache, "Eléments D'économie Coloniale Saint-Simonienne: Le Cas de l'Algérie," *Economies et sociétés* 43 (2009); Michel Levallois and Sarga Moussa, *L'orientalisme des Saint-Simoniens* (Paris: Maisonneuve & Larose, 2006); Osama Abi-Mershed, *Apostles of Modernity: Saint-Simonians and the Civilizing Mission in Algeria* (Stanford CA: Stanford University Press, 2010).

16. Pierre Péan, *Main Basse Sur Alger: Enquête Sur Un Pillage, Juillet 1830* (Paris: Plon, 2004); Sessions, *By Sword and Plow*; Brower, *A Desert Named Peace*; Gallois, *A History of Violence in the Early Algerian Colony*.

17. Kabyle cultural, political, and religious differences from the Arabs were used to buttress what developed into the colonial Kabyle Myth, namely that these differences made them potentially easier to assimilate to French culture than the Arabs and therefore superior as colonized subjects.

18. James McDougall, "Myth and Counter-Myth: 'The Berber' as National Signifier in Algerian Historiographies," *Radical History Review* 86 (2003).

19. Jane E. Goodman, *Berber Culture on the World Stage: From Village to Video* (Bloomington: Indiana University Press, 2006), 10; Karina Slimani-Direche, *Histoire de L'émigration Kabyle en France au XXe Siècle: Réalités Culturelles et Politiques et Réappropriations Identitaires* (Paris: Harmattan, 1997), 89. For details of the background and politics surrounding the assassination, see Roberts, *The Battlefield*, 47–49. See also Amar Ouerdane, *La Question Berbère Dans le Mouvement National Algérien: 1926–1980* (Sillery, Québec: Septentrion, 1990); Amar Ouerdane, *Les Berbères et L'arabo-Islamisme en Algérie* (Montréal: KMSA, 2003); Judith Scheele, *Village Matters: Knowledge, Politics and Community in Kabylia, Algeria*, African Anthropology (Rochester NY: James Currey, 2009); Mohammed Harbi, "Nationalisme Algérien et Identité Berbère," *Peuples méditerrnéns/Mediterranean Peoples* 11 (1980): 31–37.

20. Goodman, *Berber Culture on the World Stage*, 11.

21. Goodman, *Berber Culture on the World Stage*, 15.

22. Hugh Roberts, "Algeria: Unrest and Impasse in Kabylia" (N.p.: International Crisis Group, 2003), i.

23. On educational policies, see James D. Le Sueur, "France's Arabic Educational Reforms in Algeria during the Colonial Era: Language Instruction in Colonial and Anti-Colonial Minds before and after Algerian Independence," in *The French Colonial Mind, Volume 1: Mental Maps of Empire and Colonial Encounters*, ed. Martin Thomas (Lincoln: University of Nebraska Press, 2012), 194–218.

24. For details of the Berber Spring, see Goodman, *Berber Culture on the World Stage*, chapter 1; Slimani-Direche, *Histoire de L'émigration Kabyle en France au XXe Siècle*, 117–21; Roberts, *The Battlefield*, 140–44; Hugh Roberts, "Co-Opting Identity: The Manipulation of Berberism, the Frustration of Democratisation and the Generation of Violence in Algeria," in *Working Paper no. 7* (London: Destin, LSE; Crisis States Programme; Development Re-

xxi

search Centre, 2001). For the progression of Kabyle and Berber activism from the Berber Spring to 2003, see Roberts, "Algeria: Unrest and Impasse in Kabylia."

25. Goodman, *Berber Culture on the World Stage*, 31. Algerian scholars are inclined to see 1980 as a continuation of earlier Arab-Berber clashes. See, for example, Ouerdane, *La Question Berbère Dans le Mouvement National Algérien*, 47; Harbi, "Nationalisme Algérien et Identité Berbère," 31–37. It is interesting to note that what is often considered to be the watershed moment for the determination to obtain independence also occurred in Kabylia, in Sétif in 1945.

26. Roberts, "Algeria: Unrest and Impasse in Kabylia," 3.

27. For a list of the measures adopted, see Roberts, "Algeria: Unrest and Impasse in Kabylia," 7–8.

28. Roberts, "Algeria: Unrest and Impasse in Kabylia."

29. "Algeria: Bouteflika Promises," in *Africa News* (N.p.: All Africa, 2001). Accessed through LexisNexis@Academic on March 22, 2014.

30. Karen Thomas, "Berber Protests Shake Algeria's Military Elite: President Stalls as Riots Spread Throughout Country," *Guardian*, June 20, 2001, 12.

31. Roberts, "Algeria: Unrest and Impasse in Kabylia," 12.

32. Quoted in "Kabylie: La Revue de Press," *Le Nouvel Observateur*, May 2, 2001.

33. "Kabylie pour ou contre l'autonomie? Kabylie: Particularismes locaux et revendications," Khaled Drareni on *Controverse*, Dzaïr Web TV, aired on December 13, 2013. Accessed on YouTube on March 22, 2014.

34. Reproduced in Albert Camus, *Actuelles, III: Chroniques Algériennes, 1939–1958* (Paris: Gallimard, 1967). See also the introduction to the fine English translation: *Algerian Chronicles* (Cambridge MA: Harvard University Press, 2013).

35. Slimani-Direche, *Histoire de L'émigration Kabyle en France au XXe Siècle*, 14–15. See also Benjamin Stora, *Les Immigrés Algériens en France: Une Histoire Politique, 1912–1962* (Paris: Hachette littératures, 2009); Benjamin Stora and Linda Amiri, *Algériens en France: 1954–1962, la Guerre, L'exil, la Vie* (Paris: Éd. Autrement; Cité nationale de l'histoire de l'immigration, 2012); Lyons, *The Civilizing Mission in the Metropole*; Paul A. Silverstein, *Algeria in France: Transpolitics, Race, and Nation* (Bloomington: Indiana University Press, 2004).

36. Lyons, *The Civilizing Mission in the Metropole*, 33.

37. Slimani-Direche, *Histoire de L'émigration Kabyle en France au XXe Siècle*, 33; Lyons, *The Civilizing Mission in the Metropole*.

38. There are four different groups of Berbers in Algeria; the Kabyles are the predominant group. See page 4 of the introduction to the first edition of this volume.

39. For a chronological table of these organizations, see Slimani-Direche, *Histoire de L'émigration Kabyle en France au XXe Siècle*, 102; Goodman, *Berber Culture on the World Stage*, 37–39.

40. For a list of the various sites, see http://www.tamazgha.org/links.html (accessed March 23, 2014).

41. Harbi, "Nationalisme Algérien et Identité Berbère," 31. My translation from the French.

42. Although it did in Morocco. See Guerin, "Racial Myth"; David M. Hart, "The Berber Dahir of 1930 in Colonial Morocco: Then and Now (1930–1996)," *Journal of North African Studies* 2, no. 2 (2007).

43. David Scott, *Conscripts of Modernity: The Tragedy of Colonial Enlightenment* (Durham NC: Duke University Press, 2004), 2–3.

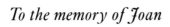
To the memory of Joan

Contents

Acknowledgements

ACKNOWLEDGEMENTS TO THE SECOND EDITION

I would like to thank James Le Sueur and the board of the French Empire series for suggesting the re-edition of *Imperial Identities*. My thanks also go to Alicia Christensen and the editorial board of the University of Nebraska Press for their help in getting the manuscript together to re-edition.

ACKNOWLEDGEMENTS TO THE FIRST EDITION

The contents of this book first saw the light of day as a doctoral dissertation at Columbia University in New York. Although I am indebted to many people and institutions for assistance during my research and its transformation into publishable form, my greatest debt is to my sponsor, Robert O. Paxton. His support and wise guidance were invaluable. My thanks too to Lisa Anderson, and Richard Bulliet of the Middle East Institute, Karen Barkey of the Sociology Department and Elaine Combs-Schilling of the Anthropology Department for their comments and advice. The lively discussions on imperialism which I had with the late Graham Irwin stimulated my interest in the intellectual history of colonial society and set my sights in the direction of this book. Hugh Roberts put me right on a number of important points concerning twentieth-century Algeria, for which I am most grateful.

The book was written while I was living in Brussels and much of the research was undertaken at the Bibliothèque Royale Albert ler, where I was allocated a place in the upper reading room. The members of the library staff with whom I was in contact were always friendly and courteous, but I should like particularly to mention Bernard Gossye and Josef Hermann, the two librarians in the upper reading room, for their patience in locating some of the more obscure volumes and articles necessary for my research and to Ms. Foucart of the inter-library loan department for obtaining innumerable works from other libraries for me to consult. In the same vein I would like to mention M. J.F. Maurel of the overseas section of the French national archives in Aix-en-Provence and the librarians of the Bibliothèque Nationale in Paris and the British Library in London. Finally, I should like to thank Anna Enayat and her colleagues at I.B. Tauris for their advice and help in preparing the manuscript for publication.

Acknowledgements

My greatest personal debt is to the members of my family, Claude, Oliver and Melissa, who never complained when I disappeared or closeted myself away for months on end and who bore my absentmindedness and withdrawal from my domestic surroundings with good humour and much more understanding than I am probably prepared to credit them with.

Introduction

This book arose out of an interest in the mechanics of marginalization and the formation of social hierarchies. What leads society to marginalize an individual or a group of individuals, and how do social elites emerge to impose their will or exercise control over areas beyond the realms of politics and economics? Although a study of this nature could have been undertaken in a variety of fields, my interests lay with racial ideology and imperialism. When I first embarked on my research, as far as nineteenth-century European colonial empires were concerned, racism was usually analysed as an *ex post facto* justification of imperialism. There is undoubtedly truth in this but it seemed to me that a study of attitudes towards ethnic groups in a given colony, over a period of time, would provide a more nuanced portrait of the colonial situation than had hitherto been the case.

The choice of Algeria was made for several reasons. To begin with, it was the first formal colony in France's nineteenth-century or second colonial empire, serving as the exemplar and experimental arena for later colonial acquisitions. What had happened or was happening in Algeria, therefore, was relevant in the whole empire. Second, during the seventy years considered in this work, Algeria was controlled for equally long periods of time by two functionally different types of Frenchmen: military officers and civilian administrators. This offered an insight into the question of the degree to which categories, inherently unstable in themselves and subject to regular redefinition, were formed in relation to a society as a whole, in this case France, or in relation to the interests and anxieties of a particular sector of that society. Third, the colonial setting offered the possibility of analysing category formation and the organizing principles of a given society or, to use Benedict Anderson's perspicacious expression, an 'imagined community', as of its inception and on over a period of time. This type of situation suggested that the mechanics of category formation would be easier to unravel. Finally, category formation in Algeria had already found historiographical expression as the 'Kabyle Myth', or

I

Berber Vulgate as it is sometimes called. This myth is a disconcerting presence in works across the disciplinary board on colonial Algeria for the intellectual space it takes up seems out of proportion to the historical analysis it had hitherto been accorded, namely as essentially a device of the colonial politics of divide and rule. References, allusions and asides to the Arab–Berber dichotomy are ubiquitous and suggested more than a purely political basis for its existence.

The Kabyle Myth: a definition

The population indigenous to Algeria at the time of French conquest numbered about 3 million. Spread over a large area, its small size was emphasized by extreme fragmentation.[1] Its principal components were Arabs and Berbers, but it also included Turks; Kouloughlis (the offspring of Turks and North African women); Andalusians (descendants of the Moors exiled from Spain); blacks (mainly soldiers, emancipated slaves and slaves); Jews; and 'Infidels' (non-Muslim slaves and renegades, many of whom held high office under Turkish occupation).[2] During the colonial period the French were inclined to overlook this diversity and, Jews apart, to view the population as a dichotomy of Arabs and Berbers. To this ethnic dichotomy, the French added a socio-geographic one, namely that Arabs were nomadic plain-dwellers and Berbers sedentary mountain-dwellers, a division that was inaccurate in its exclusiveness as there were not only sedentary Arabs but mountain-dwelling ones as well; there were also nomadic and plain-dwelling Berbers. Misleading blanket qualifications of this sort distorted reality and created a binary imagery which was mythical. French attitudes to the Arabs and Berbers, furthermore, were quite different for, generally speaking, they viewed the former negatively and the latter positively. It is their positive approach to the Berbers (in particular the Kabyles) that has stimulated scholarly interest in French attitudes towards the indigenous population of Algeria and the legacy of these attitudes in the French protectorates of the Maghreb. It is the Manichean dimension of the dichotomy that has come to be known as the 'Kabyle Myth'.

The Kabyle Myth was that the Kabyles were superior to the Arabs; it was not that they were different, which they were. The French used sociological differences and religious disparities between the two groups to create an image of the Kabyle which was good and one of the Arab which was bad and, from this, to extrapolate that the former was more suited to assimilation than the latter. The myth was an assimilationist one in so far as it provided an ideological basis for absorbing the Kabyles into French colonial society to the detriment of the Arabs. It was also a racial myth, for the intellectual concepts of this ideology were essentially ones of race. But it was a myth that never became policy in Algeria, for no pro-Kabyle colonial legislation was ever passed. None the less its impact is undeniable.

It is important to stress that the French did not consciously set out to create a good image of the Kabyle and a bad one of the Arab; rather this imagery was formed due to the circumstances of conquest and occupation coupled with the intellectual, social and political background of the Frenchmen (and in a very few cases, women) who observed, analysed and recorded data on the peoples residing in Algeria during their colonization. The following chapters trace how and why the images of the good Kabyle and the bad Arab emerged and, having done so, how and when they were buttressed by racial ideas prevailing in Europe at the time. It is my contention that it was this conjunction that transformed the Kabyle–Arab imagery into the Kabyle Myth.

The book is organized accordingly. To stress the importance of both a chronological and a thematic approach in this particular instance of the historical development of ideas the four parts of the book follow one line or the other. Part I is chronological, tracing the emergence and evolution of ethnic imagery under the military administration of Algeria. It is a discussion of the sociological, political and administrative factors instrumental in the formation of the blanket categories which gave rise to an analysis of Kabyle *versus* Arab instead of Kabyle *and* Arab. When reading this section it should be born in mind that the yardstick of the colonial observer was French society. How an ethnic group measured up to this yardstick determined what was considered 'good' or 'bad'. With this in mind it is also important to note that much of the ethnological information on the Arabs and Kabyles was exact; it was the value judgements, so often attached to the facts, that created the distortions. For example, as will be seen in this section, one of the most important elements in the triangular comparison was religion. The genuine religious differences between Arab and Kabyle were given an interpretation leading to the conclusion that the Kabyle, in contrast to the Arab, was indifferent to religion (thus could be a good subject for conversion) and his society was intrinsically secular, hence closer to the French. One of the salient facets of the myth was the negative view of Islam, which became inextricably linked to the Arabs. Extrapolations of this sort were made in other domains, as will be seen below. Constant reiteration of what was fact and what was extrapolation would have made for an unwieldy text and done little justice to the reader's intelligence. I have tried, wherever possible, to imply this difference.

Part II of the book is thematic, dealing with the interaction between the social sciences and military personnel in Algeria and with the emergence of ideas on race in France and Algeria. The intellectual trends and development that served as the ideological confirmation of what had become an Arab–Kabyle dichotomy are discussed. This section sees the beginnings of a discussion on the Kabyle Myth *per se*. Racial theory was an attempt to prove moral judgements scientifically, hence a great deal of intellectual nonsense was produced to back up the notion that some groups of humanity were intrinsically better than others. The last chapter of this section sets out to demonstrate how the Kabyle Myth fits into this type of thought. Part III deals with the chronology of the early decades of civilian rule but is also thematic in its consideration of the seminal concepts in the evolution of racial thought in the colony, the nature of the racial dialogue and the language specific to it. It is therefore primarily about the Myth. Part IV, the legacy, is thematic.

Kabylia and the Kabyles

The Berbers of Algeria comprise the Chaouia of the Aurès mountains in southeastern Algeria, the Kabyles (the largest group) of what is now known as Kabylia, the Mozabites of the Mzab in the northern Saharan region and the Tuareg of the central Sahara. Individual exceptions apart, all but the Mozabites are, like the Arabs, Sunni Muslims of the Maleki rite. They are distinguished from the Arabs by their culture and language, of which there are several dialects, but there are none the less Arabic-speaking Berbers and Berber areas, among the Chaouia for example, where Arabic culture has been absorbed into their own. Today a Kabyle is a resident of what is now geographically known as Kabylia, but the term has not always been so precise.

As early as 1857 in polemics about the Kabyles, attention was drawn to the fact that the word Kabylia was coined by the French to designate the region inhabited by Kabyles; initially it was used by neither Arabs nor Berbers.[3] Kabyle, on the other hand, was not a French invention. It is a mutation of the Arabic *kbail* or *qba'il*, a word with two possible etymologies. One definition has it that *kbail* is the plural of *kebila*, meaning tribe among sedentary populations; the second that it derives from the Arabic verb *qbel*, to accept; the Kabyles being those who had accepted the Word of Islam, namely the population indigenous to the area at the time of Arabic conquest.[4] When the French first encountered the term Kabyle, it was used by the local population for hillsmen and mountain-dwellers, residing beyond the limits of lowland and urban influence.[5] Initially the French

4

seemed to have used the term in this sense too and thus during the first decade of French occupation we encounter 'Kabyles' in accounts of campaigns in a variety of mountainous regions: the range around Blida, south of Algiers; the Dahra and Ouarsenis ranges on either side of the Chelif river from Mostaganem in the West to Cherchell in the East; the Trara range near the Moroccan border, and of course in the mountains of what is today known as Greater and Lesser Kabylia.[6] It is probably for this reason too that in early texts on the Kabyles the use of the terms Kabyle and Arab is somewhat confused.

The evolving French concept of Kabylia gradually focused the definition of Kabyle. As the French occupation of Algeria spread, so the definition of Kabylia became more precise. *Kabylie indépendante*, a vague term signifying mountainous regions as yet unconquered by the French, became *La Kabilie proprement dite*, and eventually *La Grande Kabylie* or just *Kabylie*.[7] In a map drawn up in 1847 by the army cartographers of the Arab Affairs Bureau the area of *La Grande Kabylie* was a trapezoid running roughly from the mouth of the Isser river on the Mediterranean between Dellys and Algiers, south to Aumale, east to Sétif and north to Bougie. It is this area which was considered to be Kabylia during the nineteenth century and approximated to what is today known as Greater and Lesser Kabylia. The mountain ranges included in this area are the Djurjura (in Greater Kabylia today) and the Biban and Guergour mountains (in Lesser Kabylia today).

It was, however, the Djurjura which was considered to be the heart of Kabylia and was sometimes used as a metaphor for the region as a whole. Similarly 'Kabyle', strictly speaking an inhabitant of Greater or Lesser Kabylia, was also used, in non-ethnological works, as a metaphor for any Berber-speaker who had 'escaped' the imprint of Arabic culture and the full impact of Islam. It is important to bear in mind that polemical and literary works, travelogues, some histories and other popular works seldom situated Kabylia, nor was any mention made of the other groups of Berbers by way of distinguishing the Kabyles. In fact Kabyle was, on occasion, even used interchangeably with Berber. This allowed for misconceptions among readers without a precise knowledge of Algeria and led to a looser use of the term Kabyle than would be the case today. Even scholars could be misleading on this score. Ernest Renan, reviewing in the September 1873 issue of the *Revue des Deux Mondes* Hanoteau and Letourneux's ethnological work on Kabylia and the Kabyles, still considered to be among the finest of its genre, simply entitled his article 'La Société Berbère'. Similarly Emile Masqueray, although an author of a major ethnological treatise on the different Berber populations of Algeria, could still publish an article whose title qualified Kabylia as *le pays berbère* (my emphasis); not *Kabylie, pays berbère*.[8] In each case the title misleadingly implied that Kabylia, if not the only Berber society (or land), was at least the prototypical one.

To understand why, during the nineteenth century, there was this blurring of concepts between Kabyle and Berber rather than a distinctive notion of the Kabyle as a sub-group of a much larger Berber population, one should remember that knowledge of other Berber groups was very limited. Morocco, whose Berber population was the highest of France's three Maghreb territories, did not become a French protectorate until 1912. Tunisia became a protectorate in 1881, but its Berber population was small. The Kabyles were the largest group of Berbers available for scrutiny. Furthermore, the inaccessibility of the mountainous area now known as Kabylia meant that outside influences had penetrated much more slowly, and in some areas not at all. It is therefore understandable that, during the nineteenth century, the French came to see Kabylia as the best representation of Berber society and the Kabyle as the Berber *par excellence*. This may also help to explain why the Kabyles were the focus of so much attention, scholarly or otherwise. (Collective ethnologies apart, the index of Charles Tailliart's comprehensive bibliography of works on Algeria, published in French to 1924, records nine entries on the Aurès, but none on the Chaouia; eleven on the M'zab; 15 on the Tuareg and three columns on the Kabyles and Kabylia.[9])

The historical context

Algeria was a French colony from 1830 to 1962.[10] From 1830 to 1900, the period covering the principal events described in this book, the colony had two differing colonial regimes: first military, then civilian. The 1830 expedition, allegedly a punitive foray against the Dey of Algiers, extended into 27 years of conquest and pacification followed by 13 years of administrative presence. During the first decade the French were indecisive as to their ultimate aims in the area. As debates intensified in France between advocates of restricted coastal colonization and those of deeper settler penetration, the military spread eastwards along the coast from Sidi Ferruch to present-day Skikda, where the town of Philippeville was established, but local resistance to French encroachment remained strong. Then in 1841 Bugeaud was posted to Algeria as military commander and governor of the colony. The subsequent six years put an end to existing uncertainties. His innovative, but brutal, military tactics gave the French the upper hand militarily, and his theory of colonization, *Par Ense et Aratro* (by sword and plough), encouraged the notion of military occupation and administration. By the time Bugeaud left Algeria in 1847, the Arab leader Abd-el-Kader had been vanquished, military colonization was under way and the idea that Algeria would be French was established. In November 1848 the colony was officially declared a part of France and divided into three departments, but Kabylia had yet to be subdued. This was undertaken by Randon in the 1850s and only in 1857, when Kabylia finally fell, was the French conquest considered complete. Military domination of Algeria continued but, as the civilian settler population increased in size and power, tension escalated between the two occupying elements. The demise of the military regime coincided with the collapse of the Second Empire when the civilians, benefiting from the fact that the French army was discredited in France, took over the administration in Algeria. The Commune in France was echoed in Algiers where, for a brief period, the image of a breakaway republic reared its head. With the collapse in France of the Commune, secessionist ideas in the colony subsided. It was immediately followed by the Great Kabyle Insurrection of 1871. Seen by the settlers as 'a stab in the back' by the ungrateful indigenous population, it brought home the fact that Algeria was not nearly as French as had hitherto been imagined and that without the aid of the metropolis the settlers would be hard pressed to maintain their ascendency.[11] In the ensuing 30 years the patterns of settler domination were formed and, although the colonial boom only really got under way in the twentieth century, it was during the last three decades of the nineteenth century that the interests, ideologies and hierarchies particular to colonial society in Algeria were established.

Nineteenth-century French colonial theory encompassed two doctrines, namely Assimilation and Association.[12] In the former, the traditional colonial doctrine of France, the theory was that the political, economic, and judicial institutions and structures of the colony were to be assimilated into that of the mother country and that the colonized peoples would eventually become Frenchmen. An initial process of civilizing the indigenous populations culturally (*la mission civilisatrice*) would be followed up by naturalization. In practice assimilation was never fully achieved. By the end of the nineteenth century total assimilation was considered to be a pipe-dream and the doctrine, deemed inadequate and unscientific, was replaced by that of association, whereby the colonizing power associated with the colonized, respecting their diverse institutions and progressing in tandem rather than as one.

In Algeria there was never a clear transition from one doctrine to the other, nor was one doctrine ever applied to the exclusion of the other. From the outset theories of colonization proliferated; there was much debate but no hard and fast theory emerged. Assimilation, although the ultimate goal of many of the theories elaborated by officers during the military regime, was, at least as far as the indigenous population was concerned, so distant a prospect as to make it meaningless. It was also a period of trial and error, when, as will be seen below, policies were adopted and then abandoned, either for reasons of security or because it was expedient. As for imposing French culture, this proved a formidable task. The strength of Islamic culture made a recalcitrant pupil of the indigenous population and by the end of the century the French had realized that their culture could never be imposed to the exclusion of all others. With regard to naturalization, the first attempt at establishing guidelines was made by the Senatus Consulte of 1865. Foreign immigrants, Jews and Muslims were included and conditions for their naturalization were laid down. The latter benefited from the protection of France in all circumstances, but should they want to take French citizenship they had to place themselves under the jurisdiction of French law, that is to say renounce their personal statute (statutory rights) under Islamic law, an act equivalent to apostasy. For the Muslim population the 1865 Senatus Consulte remained a dead letter.[13] The 1870 Crémieux Laws naturalized the Jews of Algeria *en masse* but excluded the Muslims. The question of the personal statute was to remain the stumbling-block to naturalization of the Muslims. In the twentieth century the situation did not much improve, and naturalization remained piecemeal as, for example, in 1919 when citizenship was granted to those who had served in the War. Naturalization was again debated at the time of the 1930 Blum-Violette bill, but it was centred around the évolués. Violette, who canvased fervently in 1930 for naturalization without renunciation of the personal statute, was unsuccessful and his bill was shelved.

With the advent of the civilian regime in 1870, the drive to assimilate the institutions of the colony to France accelerated. Financially, politically, educationally and judicially the ties between metropolis and colony were strengthened. From 1871 to 1881 a series of reforms were passed aligning Algeria administratively to France.[14] Fiscal assimilation followed step. The French system of taxation, like many other assimilatory measures, proved detrimental to the Muslims who found themselves with a dual tax burden: Koranic and colonial.[15] In 1872 a department of the Crédit Agricole was opened at the Bank of Algeria to provide credit for agricultural projects. It was this that financed the wine industry, the basis of the colony's economic 'miracle'. Freycinet's 1877 programme of public works in France was

8

extended to Algeria in 1878. In addition to the more obvious results of improved transportation networks, etc., the colony was henceforth stamped with the imprint of French architecture. On the political front, in 1881 colonial representation in the National Assembly, hitherto three deputies and three senators, was increased by three deputies. The indigenous population had no representatives. In education, however, they did slightly better. In 1883 Jules Ferry's education laws were extended to Algeria. Three years earlier had seen the creation of the University of Algiers. The ensuing decade saw the establishment of an institutionalized education system for the indigenous population which was compulsory, free and secular. Judicially too the colony was assimilated to France, but assimilating the Muslim legal system proved too problematic.[16] By the end of the century, whatever side of the fence one was on, assimilation of the indigenous population was being acknowledged as a failure. On one side were those who had no desire to assimilate them, claiming that they were incapable of being assimilated; on the other were those sensitive to indigenous problems who realized that assimilation to date, far from bestowing the benefits of civilization, had been a disaster, causing the indigenous population to lose out in nearly every domain.[17] Association became the more attractive proposition. None the less, in Algeria there had been too much vacillation, too many changes and reversals in indigenous policy to allow association, however viable a theory elsewhere, to become the panacea of the. 'indigenous problem'.

In France the period from 1830 to 1900 opened with the advent of the July Monarchy (1830–1848) and closed when the Third Republic was ceasing to wobble on its feet. In between the country experimented briefly with a Second Republic (1848–52) and, less briefly, a Second Empire (1852–1870). It was also a period marked by the violence of revolution: 1830, 1848 and 1870. To the political factions born of the 1789–99 revolution were added those of successive nineteenth-century regimes. Whatever their achievements or failures, these experiments created a climate of political and ideological diversity and innovation, a factor of importance to the intellectual history of Algeria. Inevitably dissidents and undesirables were thrown up during these various upheavals, and Algeria served to siphon off such elements. Political 'hotheads' were posted to Algeria during the July Monarchy. The revolution of 1848 and the abolition of the National Workshops, the 1851 *coup d'état*, the Commune in 1870, and the occupation of Alsace-Lorraine by the Germans, all occasioned waves of voluntary or forced emigration to Algeria, increasing the civilian population. This contributed to the demographic base that made civilian rule a viable alternative to the military administration and created a settler community, many of whose members were politically at odds with the metropolis. They resented many of the colonial policies originating in France, which they felt were being foisted upon them, and if they did not actually block them they often ignored them. This was especially true as far as the indigenous population was concerned.

Of the diversity and innovation in nineteenth-century France, two developments were fundamental to events in this study. The first had to do with religious ideas; the second with scientific. From the 1789–99 revolution, when the Church was divested of its territorial wealth, to 1905 when Church and state were finally separated, the tide between clerical and anti-clerical elements in France ebbed and flowed as France was gradually transformed into a secular state. It was the period when, to paraphrase Owen Chadwick, the French mind was secularized. The tug-of-war between the secular and the religious was also a feature of nineteenth-century Algeria. Concomitant with the wane of religious power over the state was the rise to pre-eminence of science and scientific ideas. The process, started during the Enlightenment, when advances in scientific knowledge led philosophers to eschew religious argument and review human society in the light of reason, was greatly accelerated. During the nineteenth century scientific discoveries multiplied, as did scientific institutions. As science ousted religion as the explicatory basis for much human behaviour and development, science and technology became a yardstick of progress. Although the European era of Scientism, as it has been dubbed, is usually said to start around 1850, in France science had been given a boost during the 1789–99 revolution. Scientific endeavour had been encouraged, for different reasons, by both the Revolution and the First Empire and, as will be seen below, became linked to the military and hence to colonial experimentation.

The legacy of the 1789–99 revolution to philosophical ideas was a conviction that by creating the right circumstances and banishing entrenched prejudices and superstition, society could be re-fashioned to benefit all its members. The First Empire contributed the notion of a well-established hierarchy in which a meritocratic elite would serve as the beacon. The utopian philosophers who elaborated their visions of such societies dominated the first half of the century.[18] Their ideas were underscored by a belief in progress, however gradual, to an ideal social goal. As the century progressed and the utopian goals seemed no nearer, philosophical optimism was tempered. The positivists, headed by Auguste Comte (1798–1857), still believed that society could be made better by good men, but social pessimism was beginning to be aired by mid-century thinkers such as de Gobineau

(1816–82). Frenchmen paid scant attention to his theories when they were first published in 1853, but the tragic events of the Commune and the loss of Alsace Lorraine cast a pall of gloom conducive to the emergence of more pessimistic lines of thought. The polemics surrounding the Dreyfus Affair encouraged debates on social degeneration and decadence and by the end of the century pessimism was the dominant current. The progression from progress to pessimism in philosophical thought, which is discussed in more detail in the relevant chapters below, was an important element in the development of the Kabyle Myth.

Historiography

The terms Berber Vulgate and Kabyle Myth, used to define the body of thought extolling the Kabyles and denigrating the Arabs, were coined by Charles-Robert Ageron, the first historian to examine French attitudes to the Kabyles of Algeria. In a series of articles spanning 16 years Ageron looked at the origins, chronological development and influence of the Myth.[19] His analysis and periodization evolved during this time, but his approach was political and his conclusions are a reflection of this. He explains it as a historically determined political reflex, Machiavelli's *divide ut imperes*, common to other French colonies. As a colonial polemic, it was most prominent in the early decades of the civilian regime before becoming a key element in colonial ideology. The drive to 'Kabylize' Algeria was the civilian response to Napoleon III's vision of a *Royaume Arabe*.[20] This analysis fails to clarify a number of questions.

To begin with, the role of military men in creating the imagery fundamental to the Myth. Secondly, an analysis of divide and rule as employed in other French colonies suggests that such a policy was axiomatic to French colonial practice. This could not have been the case in Algeria, where policy towards the indigenous population vacillated considerably throughout the century and was subject to the sort of debate that would have made it difficult to produce such a clear line of action. That individual administrators voiced such inclinations is certain; that it formed part of a calculated design is not. Thirdly, under military occupation, which lasted until 1871, the primordial concern was security; the concept of divide and rule, however piecemeal, runs counter to this. Randon's *Organisation kabyle*,[21] was implemented after the conquest of Kabylia in 1858 for reasons of security. If Randon's policy had been based on divide and rule, the civilian regime as exponents of such a policy would not have swept it away. Finally, why, if it was essentially a political phenomenon, were the social sciences (ethnology, anthropology) and even the humanities (history, linguistics) tainted by the notions of the good Berber and the bad Arab?

Two other scholars have undertaken research directly related to the Kabyle Myth. The ethnological aspect of the Myth has been broached twice by Camille Lacoste-Dujardin.[22] The analysis in her article on the geo-political imagery of the Kabyle Myth does not proceed beyond the descriptive, that is to say she sets out what the imagery consists of rather than how and why it developed. Nor does she address the utility of this imagery in developing the organizing principles of colonial society, or consider its evolution in terms of the changing cultural, social and political values of the colony. Colonna has looked at the question of whether or not the French undertook an active educational policy with regard to the Kabyles.[23] Her research led her to conclude that French educational policy in Kabylia was not nearly as aggressive as the number of French-educated Kabyles in the twentieth century appeared to imply. The reality was more closely connected with economic dislocation in Kabylia, and the Kabyle realization that acquiring a French education was the means of escaping their economic plight, than with educational policies imposed by the French. Once again this suggested that the foundation of the Arab–Berber polarity might be more extensive than the political. The presence of a literature on the legacy of the Kabyle Myth and the continuing interest surrounding French attitudes to Arabs and Berbers and its significance, if any, to the post-independence Maghreb only served to endorse the need to re-examine the sources for a broader historical analysis than the political or geo-political.[24]

The political approach to the Kabyle Myth concentrates its conclusions on whether or not there were assimilatory policies in favour of the Kabyles, thus overlooking the relevance of one of the most important aspects of the Myth, the image of Islam in the colony. The Western imagery of Islam and the Orient has been the subject of some excellent studies, which have elaborated on its evolution and significance to imperialism in general, its relevance to France's sub-Saharan empire at the end of the nineteenth century, the development and uses of the image of the Orient and its significance to intellectual research.[25] Said has argued that the Western image of the Orient was closely connected to its political and intellectual domination by the Occident and that Orientalism was a response to *Western* culture rather than to its putative object. In the terms of the historiography of imperialism, Said's research was based mainly on texts assembled at the centre. This suggests that an examination of the image of Islam in a colonial setting might throw some light on a number of interrelated topics, namely the extent to which the image of Islam at the periphery informed intellectual production at the centre and the degree to which it was a response to the events of conquest and occupation or to French culture and values. In his work on the Sudan, Kanya-Forstner had opined that the legacy of the military in Algeria was a 'patho-logical fear of Islam'.[26] Such a statement appeared somewhat para-doxical in the face of the tolerance implied by the sobriquet, *Royaume Arabe*, attached to the decade of military administration which fol-lowed conquest and pacification, and to the pro-indigenous sentiments attributed to it. This suggested that there were double standards in the colony during the period worth investigating from a historical point of view.

Finally, on a non-historiographical note, mention needs to be made of the use of the terms *kabylophile* and *arabophile*, and the word *Algérien*. The terms *kabylophile*, or Kabyle-lover and *arabophile*, or Arab-lover, were popularized during the 1860s and are discussed in their proper context below. Nevertheless it is important to stress that while the *kabylophiles* championed the Kabyles over the Arabs the reverse was not the case: *arabophiles* did not elevate the Arabs over the Kabyles. *Arabophile* was a looser term, implying someone who was pro-indigenous, rather than exclusively pro-Arab, and, more im-portant, sympathetic to Islam. A *kabylophile* could, therefore, also be an *arabophile*. The word Algerian, in its modern sense, did not come into being until the twentieth century. *Algérien*, as used by the French at the time of conquest, meant a resident of Algiers; by the end of the nineteenth century it was used to describe the European settlers who had been born in Algeria. For the purposes of this book, therefore, 'Algerian' will not be used to describe the Arabs and the Berbers unless explicitly specified. The adjective 'indigenous' is employed to describe the totality of the population native to Algeria. This is purely for practical purposes and bears none of the prejudicial connotations associated with the French word *indigène*.

PART I

Algeria 1830–1870

I

The conquest: Kabyles and Arabs in warfare

The pretext for the French invasion of Algeria in 1830 was a diplomatic incident which occurred in April 1827 when the Dey of Algiers hit the French Consul-General with a fly-swatter. The expedition, allegedly punitive in nature and initially restricted in scope, escalated into protracted warfare first against the Arabs, whose tribes were scattered thinly throughout the plains, and then against the Berbers, grouped densely together in the Atlas mountains. The Arabs of the Tell, the fertile coastal zone of Algeria, proved more resilient than the French had anticipated but the point of no return was reached on 22 November 1832 when, on the Eghris Plain, the charismatic Abd-el-Kader was chosen by a collection of tribal leaders to head a *djihad* (holy war) against the French. Although Abd-el-Kader was a *marabout,* whose father had been a dignitary in the Qadiriya brotherhood, he assumed the mantle of leader and undertook to rid Algeria of the French, and later create an independent theocratic state, unsullied by any contact with European Christianity.[1] His emergence as leader hardened resistance to the French, forcing them into a spiral of troop reinforcement and increasing encroachment into the hinterland. From an initial force of 18,000 men, the military presence in Algeria rose to 42,000 in 1837 and 108,000 in 1846.[2] Abd-el-Kader surrendered in 1847 but by this time the French were too involved in the area to withdraw and an all-out assault was launched against the Berber stronghold of Kabylia, the only area as yet unsubjugated and one whose population density per square kilometre was estimated, in contemporary records, to be nearly five times that of the national average[3].

In 1857 the Djurdjura, mountainous heartland of Kabylia, finally fell to the French in the conclusive campaign of the Algerian conquest. It had been the first large-scale incursion into the hitherto unfamiliar territory of the Kabyles and was seminal in the clarification of categories and the formation of stereotypes. Mountain warfare was different from that of the plain and had a bearing on how the military evaluated the opposition they encountered in each. Warfare was the circumstance in which the initial contact between the French and the indigenous population was consummated and, because the French in question were military men who, having conquered, remained to form the administration, the images of the indigenous population formulated during warfare persisted and were absorbed into the received wisdom about the Kabyles and the Arabs. The period of conquest thus started the process of image-making underpinning the Kabyle Myth.

From the landing at Sidi Feruch on 14 June 1830 to the final subjugation of Kabylia in 1857, the conquest of Algeria was arduous and setbacks frequent. Of the initial campaign against Algiers a young officer wrote that 'the ease with which France succeeded would later be exaggerated to enhance its glory'.[4] No such claim was made for Kabylia; the very fact it was conquered at all was in itself a credit. It was a natural barrier which even France's most illustrious precursors, the Romans, had not attempted to breach, a recurrent theme in works on Algeria and Kabylia.[5] The annexation of Kabylia, therefore, was a measure of French military prowess and the crowning achievement of the conquest.

Attitudes to conquest and colonization: the imprint of the past

The reaction in France to the announcement in the *Discours du Trône* on 2 March 1830 of an expedition to Algeria was mixed, and mirrored the divided opinion on the colonization of Algeria which characterized French opinion until the first successful campaigns against Kabylia in the 1840s. There was little opposition to the expedition from parliament but a strong reaction in the press.[6] While in France the debate centred around whether or not to conquer and colonize, in Algeria the problem was not *whether* but *how* to do so. Any strong sentiments of opposition felt among the military manifested themselves either through individual acts of insubordination or through desertion, for which the punishments were severe. Lesser feelings of doubt were shelved or tempered in the business of warfare. For the remainder, attitudes were coloured by prevailing perceptions on colonization and conquest.

The proclamation addressed to the troops on 10 May 1830, prior to their departure for Algiers, exhorted them to remember that the Arab, long oppressed by the Turks, would greet the French as liberators and seek an alliance with them.[7] These sentiments, however, were belied by two dominant intellectual associations with regards to the expedition, namely the antecedents of the Crusades and the Roman colonization of North Africa. Both proffered an aspiration to total subjugation of North Africa; both were to mark the relationship between the French and the Kabyles. Of the two, the former had more to do with French perceptions of Islam and the more immediate imagery surrounding the expedition, the latter with the long-term French image of France as colonizer.

The Crusades and the image of Islam as a belligerent religion

Among the soldiers who embarked for Algiers in 1830, only a small minority of veterans from the Egyptian campaigns could anticipate what the immediate future might hold. To familiarize the troops with the region, the Ministry of War prepared and distributed a number of pamphlets and directives. These included information on the Regency, plans of Algiers, lists of essential Arab and Turkish vocabulary, and a number of directives relating to encampments and bivouacing, troop behaviour under siege, and precautions with regards to health.[8] (The health pamphlet had been drawn up by two veterans of Bonaparte's Egyptian campaign, Desgnettes and Larrey, a fact that added considerable weight in the eyes of the troops.) This theoretical preparation did not detract from the general expectation that they would be confronted with 200,000 Arabs with a daunting cavalry, as well as the Turks, who would defend the walls of Algiers as their compatriots had 'those of Saint Jean d'Acre'.[9] According to a contemporary source, the justification for the campaign was seen by the French troops in various terms. Some were imbued with the same religious exaltation that had spawned the Crusades; others felt a hatred towards the Barbary states kindled by the dire economic straits of the past few years. It was generally held that a settlement on the coast of Africa would provide precious benefits. The loss of Egypt, of African concessions, had caused deep regret. The time to redress these losses and grievances was at hand; hence the impressive machine now deployed in the ports of Provence.[10] Whether inspired by the vision of a crusade, the effect of the loss of Egypt or the promise of a pirate-free Mediterranean, the connotations were of a campaign to achieve a Christian victory over a belligerent Islam.

Once conquest was under way these indefinite designs took on a more concrete form, becoming an imperative. Edouard Lapène, commanding officer at Bougie and first on the spot military observer-

cum-ethnologist of the Kabyles, was expressing a widespread sentiment when he noted that a rapid conquest was necessary to re-
introduce civilization where anarchy and barbaric customs had reigned
since the collapse of the Roman Empire.[11] By 1842 Honoré Fisquet, a
popular historian from Montpellier, was claiming that the initial
ambitions of the troops had been fulfilled. The Mediterranean had
been liberated, Saint Augustine's relics returned to ancient Hippo
and the cross re-erected in Africa, eclipsing the crescent.[12] Commanding officers on the spot were less sanguine. It would never be
possible to lower one's guard against Islam. The Arabs were a belligerent people and, as Bugeaud reminded his subordinates in a speech
after taking Abd-el-Kader's *smala* (mititary encampment), the army
would never put down its sword, and would always brandish it before
the Arabs.[13] The necessity to remain on the alert was constant. In
1848 when, as a result of the February Days, French prestige was
seen to have suffered, the need for vigilance was reiterated by Général
de Rumigny, who declared that it would never be possible for the
French to withdraw from Algeria because a massacre of the Christians
would ensue.[14] (This prediction was revived during the 1956–62
period, contributing to the collection of fears that triggered the mass
exodus of European Algerians once independence had been granted.)

A wariness of Islam was an ever-present feature of the colonial
mentality in Algeria. Once conquest was over the belief that its warlike
and violent propensities served as a barrier to civjlization and progress
handicapped serious attempts at a rapprochement between French
and Arab and militated against the sincerity of the policy of assimilation. If religious fervour made of the Arabs recalcitrant subjects for
the reforms of the *mission civilisatrice*, a lack of such fervour signalled
the possibility of a more flexible response. Thus, when it came to
introducing notions of civilization and progress, a potentially more
malleable element of indigenous society was to be found in Kabylia
for, it was believed, all Kabyles deviated from Islamic practices and
did not share the fanaticism of the Arab tribes.[15] Lapène, who contributed articles to the *Mémoires de l'Académie Royale de Metz* on
Algeria and became an acknowledged authority on the Kabyles after
the publication of *Vingt-Six Mois à Bougie*, stated that it was the
marabouts, the pivots of Kabyle religious life, who were responsible
for any zealous excesses on the part of the Kabyles. At the time of the
Arab conquest in the seventh century, he wrote, priests and *marabouts*,
with the interests of the conqueror at heart, were placed among the
Berbers. These men, less religious than political, insinuated that they
were acting by the will of God for the well-being of humanity. The
Kabyles, he concluded, had no real dogma. They indulged in cult

worship of the *marabouts* while they were alive and revered them as saints when they were dead. It was the *marabouts* who preached holy war against the infidels and were therefore France's most implacable enemies.[16] Rationalizing Kabyle adherence to the creed of Islam in this way endorsed the belief that Islam could be circumvented in Kabylia. The tendency to recoil from Islam blinded the French to the contradiction that the Kabyles, so intractable in conquest, could be the easiest to seduce philanthropically. Islam thus remained the religion whose fanaticism and violence had altered little over the ages. Islam, the belligerent religion: the notion was as alive in the nineteenth century as it had been between the eleventh and the thirteenth.

Roman North Africa and the influence of the classics

While the legacy of the Crusades conjured up images of the barbarity and violence of North Africa's Islamicized population, that of Rome evoked a romanticized vision of *civilization*, of which France was the obvious heir. France looked to the Roman occupation of North Africa for inspiration in its colonial mission, and to the classics as a source of information on its inhabitants; even, on occasion, for guidance in its approach to warfare. Not only was the French *mission civilisatrice* perceived as a modern adaptation of the *Pax Romana* but parallels were constantly drawn between the two. Indeed, the analogy was deemed great enough to imagine that time had 'stood still', producing similar personalities and incidents. The Roman example also served as a justification for French military colonization. Military colonization, or the regime of the garrisons, had long protected civilian colonies in Africa, for Roman domination had been maintained with the help of the army.[17] For the benefit of those doubtful of France's ability to conquer and colonize the area, it was constantly reiterated that Rome had taken 240 years to subdue Numidia and Caesarean Mauritania (the territory of the ex-Regency of Algiers) to the state of a dependent and tributary province.[18]

The main sources for textual comparisons between France and Rome in Kabylia were Sallust's *Jugurthine War* and Tacitus's *The Germania*, although Strabo, Polybius, Ptolemy (Claudius Ptolemæus), Livy (Titus Livius) and Leo Africanus were among the many other classical geographers and historians whose work served as substantiation for the analogies drawn. Lapène's use of Sallust and Tacitus in his 'Notice historique, morale, politique et militaire sur les Kabaïles' (in *Vingt-Six Mois à Bougie*) was almost verbatim. The range of classical sources could be considerable, as in the geographer-historian

Dureau de la Malle's *L'Algérie* (subtitled 'History of the wars of the Romans, Byzantines and Vandals together with examinations of the methods used of old for the conquest and submission of that portion of North Africa today called Algeria'). Of these diverse sources, it was Sallust that had a direct bearing with regard to the Kabyles. As a historical document the *Jugurthine War* was hardly a model of precision, but it contained 'invaluable information' on the inhabitants of ancient Numidia, an area which approximated to Algeria and western Tunisia. The war between Jugurtha, son of Massinissa, and Rome provided insights into warfare with the Berbers, who were considered to be the descendants of Jugurtha's compatriots. Lapène's quoted passages from both Sallust and Tacitus in *Vingt-Six Mois à Bougie* were accompanied by a close textual analysis in which he applied Tacitus's observations to the Kabyles, whose customs, he believed, were strikingly similar to those of the Germanic tribes. He was convinced that his readers would be edified on discovering the link between the Numids, the Vandals from Germany and present-day Kabyle and Berber tribes.[19] Lapène elaborated on these parallels and pointed to the legacy of Roman rule and Vandal conquest in North Africa by suggesting that Kabyle clothing was reminiscent of Roman garments and that the cross tattoo with which Kabyle women adorned themselves was a throwback to the time when the local Aryan Christian inhabitants tattooed themselves with a cross to escape Vandal taxation.[20]

The relevance of the *The Germania* was as a prototype ethnographical study of a people, the Germans. Tacitus presented the objects of his study as being freedom-loving, having a strong sense of honour and a respect for the sanctity of home life, and practising a primal form of equality. He imbued their bellicose natures with virtue and regarded them as overgrown children with a need for Roman tutelage to reach maturity. They were in fact a type of 'noble savage'. The noble characteristics that marked the Germans out from other peoples were frequently to be attached to the Kabyles, and the four characteristics mentioned above were among those which were considered most important in differentiating Kabyles from the Arabs. The comparison of the Kabyles to the Germanic tribes was the initial step in the direction that would lead some synthesizers to claim Aryan origins for the Kabyles.[21]

Dureau de la Malle was one of many who drew attention to the fact that the classics characterized the Libyans as an essentially industrious, agriculturalist people, living in fixed abodes, like the present-day Berbers and Kabyles, who appeared to be their direct descendants.[22] These sources, furthermore, pointed in the direction of a fruitful relationship between the Kabyles and the French. If the Romans and the Carthaginians had established highly successful commercial links and exchanges with the Berbers, it seemed logical, to Dureau de la Malle and his contemporaries, that the French should do the same with the Kabyles.[23] For the French military, in the first decade and a half of conquest, Kabylia was largely uncharted territory. The only access to information concerning its inhabitants was textual, and the most familiar of these texts were the classics. Once on the spot many of the preconceptions acquired through these ancient sources lingered on. Actual contact with Kabyles served to amplify this acquired knowledge rather than to alter it radically.

Early definitions and first contacts

Early definitions of the Kabyles were vague and often inaccurate. Few had had close contact with them and, like the Arabs, they were deemed to be cruel and bellicose, although often described as 'more intelligent'.[24] There was a definite tendency, in the early years, to interchange the designations *Arab* and *Berber*. One of the first on-the-spot accounts of the expedition endorses the fact that in Algiers any mountain-dweller was indiscriminately labelled a Kabyle.[25] Certainly Lapène did so, particularly in his descriptions of the Bougie campaign and in spite of his definition of Berbers as the rural dwellers of the ex-Regency.[26] Lapène, furthermore, separated Berbers into two classes. While all Berbers were descendants of the ancient inhabitants of the area, the *Berbères Bédouins* were the nomadic tribes of the plains and the *Kabaïles* were the sedentary mountain-dwellers of the Atlas.[27] Lapène did not see the Kabyles, or indeed the Berbers, as a separate race but suggested that there had been intermarriage between the original inhabitants of the area and successive conquering peoples. His tendency to use Arab and Berber interchangeably, therefore, suggests that he conceptualized their differences not in terms of ethnicity, but rather in terms of geography or social organization. In his *Notice historique, morale, politique et militaire sur les Kabaïles*, there were no comparisons to the Arabs; he was more interested in probing their 'mysterious origins' and elusive nature.

Alexis de Tocqueville, writing slightly earlier than Lapène, and without the advantage of first-hand experience, declared that if Rousseau had known about the Kabyles he would have found his role models in the Atlas mountains.[28] To the notion of a noble savage Tocqueville added the idea that the Kabyles might be receptive to French civilization, due to their lack of commitment to religion, their pragmatic nature and a curiosity that attached them more to this

23

world than to the next. Thus the French would do better to beguile them with luxury goods rather than canons of wisdom. Tocqueville did draw distinctions between Arabs and Kabyles and while his differences were nuanced, never taking the form of definite categories, he was adamant that contrary to the 'complete equality' that reigned among the Kabyles, in the Arab tribes there were enormous inequalities.[29]

In his 'Second Letter on Algeria', Tocqueville went on to elaborate on the way in which the French could draw the Kabyles into their cultural sphere. If Kabylia was impenetrable territory for the French, the Kabyle soul was not. This was in contrast to the Arab, whose soul was even more mobile than his home. With the Kabyles, he suggested, the French should be even-handed in the civil and commercial domains, and with the Arabs in the religious and political ones.[30] Four years later, having visited Algeria, Tocqueville was to speculate as to why the Kabyles, who had attained the 'first degree of civilization', had not progressed further. It was, he concluded, the result of their mountainous habitat, their proximity to the Arabs, their religion (such as it was) and, above all, their fragmentation into small tribes whose organization maintained their civilization in a preliminary state.[31] As an intellectual and a deputy, Tocqueville took an active interest in French activities in Algeria and consequently in the peoples that populated the area. His statements on the Kabyles were tentative but none the less mirrored some of the sentiments that were being propagated at the time.

The earliest French contacts with the Kabyles were commercial. Prior to French occupation Algeria produced few items in sufficient quantities for exportation. Olive oil and wax from Kabylia were the exceptions and small amounts were exported to the Levant and Europe. Figs, oranges, olives, leather and artisan goods were produced in large enough quantities to be sent out of Kabylia to the urban centres of Algiers and Constantine. The main exchange centre for Kabyle goods was Bougie, and the market each Thursday was attended by approximately two thousand Kabyles.[32] Bougie was also a place of Islamic pilgrimage attracting large numbers of worshippers, most of them Kabyles, during the period of Ramadan and on religious festivals.[33]

French interest in Bougie (Bejaïa today) was aroused soon after Algiers was taken. A coastal town at the base of the Djurdjura mountains, it had been an important port and trading centre in the past but had declined during the Spanish occupation of 1509–1555, never really recovering its former importance. Under the Duc de Rovigo, commander-in-chief of the Army in Algeria from December 1831 to June 1833, a project was put forward to install a French

consul in Bougie, a certain M. Joly, to establish trade with the Kabyles
and open the port to French ships. According to Pellissier de Reynaud,
an officer closely involved in indigenous affairs throughout his twelve
years in Algeria and considered to be the most reliable and important
annalist of the period, this plan was well conceived and could have
been adopted with certain reservations. The French, he believed, could
quite honourably deal on an equal footing with the Kabyles for they
were a free and independent people.[34] After initial enthusiasm on the
part of de Rovigo, the project was abandoned and French troops were
sent in to conquer the town. Eight years later, in his notes taken
during his voyage in Algeria, Tocqueville lamented the French inability to cement commercial ties with the Kabyles. Lieutenant-
Colonel Picouleau, commanding officer of Djidjelli, a port in the
province of Constantine, had told Tocqueville that he believed the
town had a great commercial future. If the French acted with circumspection, Djidjelli, like Bougie, could become the centre of extensive
commerce with the Kabyles. Although the two towns lay next to a
region which contained 'a singular population', Tocqueville doubted
whether the French had the wisdom to develop the area as Picouleau
hoped they would.[35] In the meantime, however, contacts of a less
felicitous sort were being made, namely under conditions of warfare.

The first conflict between French and Kabyles occurred at Médéa
in 1831. Ben Zamoun, chief of the Flissa tribe, inflicted heavy losses
on French troops partaking in the expedition, causing outrage by his
inhuman methods. This sense of outrage was renewed during the
Bougie campaign when, on 29 September 1833, several French soldiers
were decapitated by their captors. The reprisals that followed set the
tone for what seemed to be the beginning of a vicious war between
the French and the Kabyles. Bougie fell to the French shortly afterwards and a military administration was duly set up. Five years of
skirmishes followed, and one incident, the assassination of Salomon
de Musis, left a lasting impact.[36] De Musis, summoned to a meeting
by the Kabyles, was surrounded and killed along with several members
of his entourage as a reprisal for the death of a *marabout* at the hands
of the French. This act of treachery was greeted with consternation
by the French and, according to Pellisier de Reynaud, with seeming
horror by most Kabyles, who made themselves scarce as a result.[37]
Whether or not culpability for this and similar incidents was attributed
to the Kabyles in general, their 'treachery' was rationalized as part of
their indomitable spirit. As Lapène was to put it, extortion, murder
and assassination were their habitual pastime but, being independent
and insubordinate by nature, these were the forceful expressions of
the fact that they had never been and never would be subjugated.[38]

For all their shortcomings, and however repugnant these were deemed to be, the Kabyles were considered redoubtable enemies. Careful surveillance of their movements was necessary. To this end, on 5 June 1837, a decree came into force placing them under the jurisdiction of an *amin* of Kabyle origin, residing in Algiers. Henceforth Kabyles were forbidden to work or live on French-occupied territory until they had been entered in the *amin's* register.[39] Six months later Field-Marshal de Castellane suggested to the commander of the Constantine area, General Negrier, that a census of Kabyles be taken. He argued that if the results indicated that the Kabyles made up half of the 22,000-strong population they should be expelled as they kept arms hidden, which made them doubly dangerous.[40] By the early 1840s, keeping tabs on the Kabyles was no longer sufficient and the notion was emerging that only when Kabylia had been subjugated would the French really be masters of Algeria.

Bugeaud, reluctant at first to undertake the conquest of Kabylia, initiated the move towards final submission in 1843 by attacking those outlying areas that had been organized by ·Abd-el-Kader.[41] The campaigns of the 1840s did not achieve the overall aim of total subjugation, but the territory had been penetrated and contact with the Kabyles was increasing.[42] However, Kabylia was a hostile terrain as the troops under General Changarnier, who led the 1843 expedition, were to discover and as Pierre de Castellane observed in his *Souvenirs*, which were serialized in the *Revue des Deux Mondes* and later translated into English.[43] In addition, disease claimed even more victims than warfare, demoralizing the troops even further.

By 1844 the Arabs of the Tell had been subdued and Kabylia became the centre of French attention. The prospect remained a daunting one, for memories were still alive of the energetic way the army had been repulsed by the Kabyles when French soldiers had attempted to penetrate by means of Bougie, Djedjelli or Setif. Not only was the terrain inhospitable but it was also the most heavily populated area of Algeria. A considerable force was therefore needed to engage these fierce, ubiquitous warriors.[44] In France, the conquest of Kabylia met with considerable opposition, but the arguments in favour were appealing.[45] It was pointed out that when conquest was achieved there would be appreciable strategic, monetary and commercial gains. All of Algeri from Tunisia to Morocco would at last be in French hands. Taxing the dense population of the area would bring added revenue and, finally, from the *colon* point of view, the conquest of Kabylia would considerably increase France's agricultural and commercial riches and provide numerous elements for the future prosperity of the colony.[46]

In Algeria opinion was divided between those who thought it best to neutralize the territory and establish commercial relations and those who felt that only after the submission of Kabylia would France be able to lay true claim to Algeria.[47] But the idea that Kabylia would one day be French was taking hold. The three aghalics grouped around Dellys in central Kabylia, which France now held and whose population numbered 130,000, were seen as the 'mast-head of the future French Kabylia'.[48] The campaigns of the early 1840s, furthermore, had served to dispel any prior misconceptions concerning the Kabyles. The final penetration into the unknown territory, which for so long had been a place of 'mystery and terror', confirmed notions that had started to emerge during earlier operations in the area. It had revealed a sedentary population which was 'calm and industrious with a well-developed sense of the arts and crafts, a somewhat limited intelligence but a stout heart, and energetic, confident character'.[49] To these revelations, the *colon* Maffre added his opinion that, by his nature, the Kabyle was susceptible to civilization and sincerely attached to civilized man.[50] If the Kabyles were a daunting enemy, they were also an honourable one, and the conquest of Kabylia, however hard it proved to be, held the promise of lasting and fruitful ties with its population.

The Conquest of Kabylia

By 1850 the French had acquired some experience of warfare with the Kabyles. Bugeaud, who had been opposed to the penetration of Kabylia initially, came around to the idea soon enough, but the expeditions to Kabylia during his leadership (1841–47) never achieved total subjugation. Between the governorships of Bugeaud and Randon the question of Kabylia was given closer consideration and it was finally decided that conquest was essential. Achieving these ends was now only a matter of time. In a report on the subject, General d'Hautpoul tried to counteract the myth of the invincibility of the area by pointing out that the sedentary nature of the Kabyles militated against their holding out for ever. Anchored to the soil by villages as well built as those in France, by perfectly cultivated properties, by factories and production centres of arms and munitions, the Kabyles could not, like the Arabs, withdraw by fleeing the advancing columns of the French. Once subdued, they would be forced to submit.[51] To this d'Hautpoul added that the economic independence of Kabylia meant that they would never peaceably come under the French yoke. Conquest was therefore vital, not only for the honour of France but also to eliminate the example of an independent entity within a conquered land; an example that could only have a detrimental effect on French control of the Arabs.[52] Concomitant with the belief in the necessity of total subjugation was the idea that the Kabyles could be an important part of the French mission in Algeria. General de Rumigny suggested that their contribution could be both military and economic for, he believed, they would make a perfect infantry which could safeguard the frontiers of Algeria. They were faithful, sober and industrious with responsible habits and remarkable courage. To these desirable traits were added their obvious aptitudes for creating villages, cultivating land and, unlike the forest-destroying Arabs, tending trees and practising the art of grafting.[53]

With the impending conquest, the mystique of Kabylia was about to be assailed, but the process would only serve to reinforce the Arab–Berber divide. Warfare with the Kabyles provided the first real opportunity to formalize definite categories. On Christmas Day 1851 General Randon arrived in Algeria as governor-general. Under his command the final assault on Kabylia was initiated; it was successfully completed in 1857. As predicted, it was not an easy task but, by using Bugeaud's method of mobile strike columns sallying forth from established garrisons, Randon succeeded in wearing down the resistance of the Kabyles.[54]

Warfare and the emergence of categories

In the early campaigns against the Kabyles, French soldiers, ignorant of the terrain and of their opponents, were overwhelmed psychologically, and often literally, by the ferocity of the counter-attack. Unlike the French, the Arabs and Kabyles entered battle with strident war-cries. The silence of the French temporarily unnerved the Kabyles, who then responded (no doubt to counteract this lapse) with 'a sort of wild inebriation'.[55] In turn the blood-curdling shrieks of the Kabyle men and the ululating of their women, who urged them on in the midst of the mêlée, made the obligatory hand-to-hand combat a searing experience for the French soldier. The Kabyle warrior was perceived to be ferocious, a *chien enragé*, but he was also elusive, for he was master of his heights and able to use the terrain to his advantage.[56] In his *Souvenirs*, Pierre de Castellane captures the atmosphere of these encounters admirably.[57] In fact the French army was engaged, for the first time in Africa, in a guerrilla warfare. As guerrillas, the Kabyles forced the French to retrench and rethink their approach to conquest, adding to their mythological stature in the process.[58]

It was now obvious to most observers that the war in Africa, and especially in Kabylia, was imposing an onerous burden on French troops during combat.[59] But other observations had also emerged that made fighting with the Kabyles a singular experience, and a marked contrast to that with the Arabs. In the first place the French were struck by the involvement of the Kabyle women (Lapène is particularly graphic on this point[60]). Second, it was noted that individual action was more important than group manoeuvres.[61] These two observations served to underline the perceived egalitarian tendencies and individuality of the Kabyles. It was clear that in mountain warfare the French, as aggressors, were at a disadvantage.[62] The Kabyles, in their mountain 'nests', provided a very different opposition from that of the Arabs on their plains.[63]

Bugeaud had pointed out the need for a definite strategy to deal with the Kabyles, stating that it was only in the mountains that a real strategy could be useful in Africa. The Kabyles, he stressed, did not flee over great distances like the Arabs and seldom fought head-on, preferring to attack the sides and rear flanks of the French troop columns. Due more to the nature of the terrain than the methods of the defenders, strength was needed to breach the mountain strongholds.[64] The Kabyles were, furthermore, wily and unpredictable, attacking in totally unexpected circumstances. It was necessary, therefore, to be constantly on the alert, never to let one's guard down and constantly to be on the move, as would be the case in the presence of a powerful enemy. Bugeaud advocated attacking the economic interest of the Kabyles, as the most efficacious method of flushing them out of their mountain retreats.[65] The Kabyles responded by burning bales of hay at the entrances of their villages to stop the French advance. In the autumn of 1844 this ruse succeeded. The French were amazed and saddened at the sight of these fires but their admiration was aroused at the 'energetic despair' of the Kabyles, who would rather burn than surrender. The discovery of a deception on the part of the Kabyles in no way diminished them in French eyes; rather it served to confirm 'the daring and skillfulness of the Kabyles in skirmishing'.[66]

By 1851 the question of Kabylia was receiving sustained attention; the differences between Kabyles and Arabs in warfare had ceased to be the prerogative of the military and were being aired in intellectual circles, as was evidenced by the appearance of a two-part article in the *Revue des Deux Mondes*. The journal, which was founded in 1829 as a highbrow cultural review, addressed the upper middle class and the intelligentsia, perpetuating their views and acting, for most of the nineteenth century, as the forum for debating leading intellectual controversies. In the article mountain warfare was discussed using the examples of the campaigns of Navarre (1833–35), which occurred during the Carlist wars, and those of Kabylia (1841–47). The contrast between mountain and plain in warfare was introduced by stating that the destiny of empires could be played out on the renowned plains, but that it was always in the mountains that the genius of resistance of every country was to be found.[67] In the first half of the article, Ducuing presented the varying aspects of mountain warfare by declaring that the two wars of Navarre and Kabylia could be seen as two great complementary military experiences, adding that the similarities between the character, morals, and practices of the Navarrais and the Kabyles were so strikingly obvious that it was hardly necessary to mention them.[68]

In the second part, using as his sources Bugeaud's publications in the *Moniteur Algérien* and the works of Generals Daumas and Yusuf, Ducuing focused on the Kabyles and contrasted them with the Arabs. Theirs was an eminently warlike population, as skilled in firing as the Arabs were on horseback, and these African mountain men were stronger in combat and more united that the men of the plains. The Kabyles, furthermore, were more astute in the tactics of war. Skilled in stratagems and ambushes, they knew how to retreat when necessary and to chose the best vantage points for defence. They were able to disperse in an instant over the rocky slopes, remaining inaccessible to the cavalry.[69]

These qualities as warriors gave rise to an imagery of the Arab as erratic and unreliable and the Kabyle as solid and able to hold his ground. The Arabs 'evaporated like smoke'. When confronted by the French they resorted to innumerable ruses and an uncontrollable fanaticism. As for prisoners, there was no need even to mention them; it was an exterminatory war on both sides. So slippery were the Arabs that two French soldiers were needed to guard each Arab prisoner. Furthermore, when an Arab extended his firearm as a sign of surrender it was merely to assassinate his opponent at closer range. The Kabyle may have been as jealous of his independence as the Arab, but whereas the Arab equated independence with a right to pillage and wander, for the Kabyle it was tied to the right to own a home and enjoy the mountains that formed his habitat. The Arab safeguarded his independence by fleeing, whereas the Kabyle maintained his through resistance. The Arab, having been beaten, escaped in order to rebel again; the Kabyle, having put up a good resistance, resigned himself to defeat.[70] Ducuing's 'La Guerre de Montagne' was a synthesis of the military observations regarding warfare with Kabyles that emerged during the decade of campaigns prior to the culminating assault on Kabylia in 1853 to 1857. Its appearance in the *Revue des Deux Mondes* disseminated military views of the Kabyles and Arabs, based on warfare, among a more general public. The tentative and somewhat vague differences between Kabyle and Arab elaborated in the early years of conquest had now acquired a more substantial framework.

The first-hand experience gained during the 1840s dispelled the aura of the unknown that had hitherto surrounded the Kabyles, making them and their country more accessible. On 24 May 1857 three divisions, under Generals Mac-Mahon, Renault and Yusuf, launched the final assault on Kabylia. According to Colonel Ribourt, the 21,816 bayonets which these divisions represented were the largest mass of infantry that had ever been deployed in Algeria; 30,000 Kabyle muskets opposed the French.[71] The first step in the campaign was an attack on the heights of the Beni Yahia. Reflecting on the French victory, Ribourt declared that the satisfaction at having finally penetrated the heart of Kabylia was tempered by the certainty of future difficulties at the hands of its courageous defenders.[72] By the end of the year the whole of Kabylia was in French hands.

For 17 years the French had grappled with the Kabyles. During the warfare that characterized this period, the image of the Kabyle came sharply into focus. He was, by his tenacity and his wiliness, an admirable and respected opponent. His sedentary nature and the industry by which he lived in his compact, densely populated villages, in marked contrast to the 'errant, pillaging Arab', likened him, in many respects, to the European peasant and more specifically to the Auvergnats or Savoyards.[73] His need to defend his turf and his economic interests, rather than folding up his tent and cantering off into the dust in adversity, had forced on him a courage and steadfastness that the Arab did not need to possess. His women, who accompanied him into the heat of the battle, shared his travails in a way unknown to the Arabs, thus elevating them in his eyes and in the domestic hierarchy. Mountain warfare honed the qualities of individuality, for it was the quick decision, the audacious initiative that won the day. This notion of the Kabyle warrior as an individual, taking his own life-and-death decisions rather than following the herd, confirmed the Kabyle collective will to independence on an individual basis and suggested a further connotation of egalitarianism. The mountains had made them men of stature. Unlike the Arabs 'they had completely escaped the irremediable laxity into which the heady nature of the Maghreb had so often thrown the people of the Sahel and the towns'.[74]

The mountain as a positive category came into its own, in the colonial period, during the campaigns of Kabylia. Later, when the colony was established, the positive nature of the mountain was enhanced by its health-sustaining properties. In Algeria, as in many other sub-tropical and tropical colonies, mountains became the refuge from whence to escape the heat and health hazards of the lowlands. Kabylia became Algeria's 'little Switzerland' as Ifrane and Azrou (in the Middle Atlas) were to become for Morocco. This positiveness accrued to the Kabyles, as mountain people. With time it was considered axiomatic and the individual and collective positive traits of the Kabyles were contrasted to the negative ones of the Arabs. Mountain warfare and the image of the mountain were the first concrete steps in this process.

Islam and the variants of belligerency:
Arab vs. Berber

As far as the French were concerned, the conquest of Algeria was divided into two periods: the submission of Abd-el-Kader and the Arabs of the Tell and the penetration and conquest of Kabylia. As we have seen, the nature of warfare had its own particular impact on the image of Kabyle and Arab, but a second consideration was also influential in the formulation of attitudes concerning these two peoples, namely the role of Islam.

The war against Abd-el-Kader lasted for 15 years and, once Bugeaud arrived on the scene, assumed the character of a contest between two charismatic and strong leaders. From the outset, however, Abd-el-Kader had waged a war of resistance against the French in the name of Islam. The early notions of the French concerning the belligerency of Islam were seemingly substantiated in the person of Abd-el-Kader and his holy war. For Bugeaud the Islamic religion was a considerable obstacle and he warned his compatriots that history had shown that Arabs were quick to revolt and that their antipathy towards the French and Christianity would last for centuries, making it necessary to remain strong in their midst.[75] In a speech given at a banquet in Algiers, a year before his departure and Abd-el-Kader's final submission, Bugeaud reminded his audience that the bellicose, fanatical Arabs would not easily submit to the French yoke.[76] For Bugeaud, the Arabs would always be elusive, difficult to control and a potential danger. Their nomadic social organization and their religion necessitated the use of force to keep them in order and served as a justification for the scorched-earth policy used against them. Arab belligerency was seen essentially in terms of religion.

Kabyle belligerency, on the other hand, was considered to be primarily defensive and unconnected to Islam. Although Abd-el-Kader had originally managed to elicit the help of the Kabyles, they had refused to join him in the latter stages of his *djihad*, a fact that was made much of later. According to Tocqueville, all the scientific commissions of the mid-1840s had strongly advised against the conquest of Kabylia, and this sentiment was shared by the French government.[77] The general feeling was that the area, left alone, would remain peaceful. As Enfantin, a member of the 1840–41 Scientific Commission, explained: 'the Kabyles only screamed when they were being flayed.'[78]

When the decision to make an all-out assault on Kabylia was finally taken, it was not because the Kabyles had waged war on the French, but rather that the presence of a free Kabylia would invigorate the Arab tendency to revolt. Economic considerations may also have added their weight, but the fear of a religious backlash was absent. If the adjective *fanatic* was attached to the Kabyles at all, it was not done so for religious reasons but rather in the more laudable context of uncompromising resistance in the face of attack against their homeland. The Kabyles, being 'sedentary' and 'industrious', were defending a patrimony the French could easily identify with; the Arabs, being 'nomadic' and 'fanatically religious', were defending an ideal the French abhorred.

Conclusion

The period of conquest initiated the trend towards defining Kabyle and Arab in terms of 'good' and 'bad'. The penetration of Kabylia had provided the French with their first prolonged opportunity to evaluate the Kabyles at close quarters. Hitherto the accounts of Kabyle and Arab had been based on hearsay and textual sources only; close contact with the Kabyles confirmed many of the facts acquired by these means. The Kabyles *were* mountain-dwellers. Their lifestyle *was* sedentary. Economically, they *were* commercially minded. Politically, they *did* have a minimally hierarchical society. Kabyle women *did* have more say in the division of labour. Their religious practices *were* other than conventional. These characteristics, however, were the result of demographic, economic and social necessity. Most certainly, they were not due to an innate tendency to a higher civilization than the Arabs nor, above all, to a difference in race. Their social, political and economic organization was not better than that of the Arabs, it was just different.

For the French, the Kabyles were, first and foremost, mountain-dwellers. It was this over-arching environmental category that was most effected by the exigencies of warfare. Paradoxically, the difficulties encountered in the conquest of Kabylia enhanced rather than detracted from the aura that surrounded the mountain and the Kabyles as mountain people. Once the environmental categories of mountain and plain had been coloured by positive and negative connotations; once they had acquired a quasi-moral dimension of good and bad, the door had been opened for these Manichaean value judgements to be extended to more specific disparities of those who dwelled within these environmental confines. In the meantime, however, a second umbrella category, one of societal organization, was being subjected to a similar process. Reconnaissance and security were to imprint the categories of sedentary and nomad as warfare had imprinted those of mountain and plain.

2

Security and reconnaissance
part 1: the elaboration
and confirmation of categories

During the period of conquest, security and reconnaissance were major military preoccupations. It was the need to secure the country durably that had pushed the French into Kabylia. It was the need for security that stimulated the drive for reconnaissance and the insatiable curiosity of the French military regarding every aspect of the newly annexed territory. Once the country was secure the business of colonization could begin. Once reconnaissance was complete, the mysteries of the new dominion would be eliminated and the knowledge thus gained would enable better control. Military reconnaissance, in the strict sense of the term, was not widely practised in Algeria. As Bugeaud explained, reconnaissance, like all wartime operations, needed a useful, well-defined aim, otherwise it should not be undertaken and, as far as Africa was concerned, he felt reconnaissance was hardly ever useful.[1] None the less, reconnaissance as exploration and as a means of evaluating both the territory and its population was a permanent feature of the early decades of occupation. As Carette, secretary to the 1840–42 Scientific Commission, was to point out, in Algeria the compass always followed the flag.[2]

The role of the officers of the Ecole Polytechnique in these activities was considerable. The army engineering corps was in charge of reconnaissance and the officer engineers included specialists in hydrography, topography, geography and geology. The geographical service of the army was in charge of cartography and most of the major physical, geological and demographic maps of Algeria were the work of military men. Henri Fournel, a civilian graduate of the Polytechnique and director-general of the Services des Mines in Algeria, undertook the most extensive early geological and mineralogical study of Algerian resources.[3] The early pioneering work of these engineers left a permanent imprint on the services that emerged in the colony in these fields.

Scientific exploration of the sort carried out by these officers, either under the aegis of government commissions, such as in the case of Algeria the Scientific Commission of 1840–42, or as an extension of their administrative duties, was an essential process in the imposition of colonial power structures and the legitimization of the colonial presence in overseas territories. The role of science and natural scientists in stimulating imperial expansion and in encouraging notions of European supremacy was an important one.[4] To begin with, the geological, botanical, topographic and demographic classification of a colony and the resultant maps, charts and statistics meant that a vast amount of information became easily accessible to both officials and laymen alike. This material enabled the coordination of administrative, developmental and defensive activities, provided the means of organizing exploitation of resources in the colony, and underlined the emerging conviction of the superiority of European power.[5] While the codification of the accumulated data was symbolic of the advances of European technology and science, further reinforcing the notion of European supremacy, it was also a way of reconstructing the geological, geographical and historical space of the colony in the legal and intellectual terms of the colonizing power. The impact of such scientific activity, furthermore, far exceeded its initial motivations. As an example, in the nineteenth-century empires as a whole, geology, over and above its prospective function, helped to form racial and cultural attitudes by extending the notion of 'landscapes of the past' and 'fossilized regions' to the people living in the areas so described.[6] Archaeology was to play a similar role in Algeria, where interest centred on Roman ruins. By linking the Roman tradition to the French in Africa and encouraging the notion that the ensuing civilizations in Algeria, until that of the French, had never been capable of matching Roman achievements, an essentially European historical space was created for North Africa.

Quite apart from the role scientists and engineers played in reconnoitring resources in the colonies and stimulating their exploration, their expertise made them valuable advisers to government policy makers.[7] The impact of science was not restricted to academic circles, therefore, but was extended into political ones. Furthermore, organizations established by scientists in the metropolis in response to the scientific activities in the colony institutionalized the data collected, thus endowing it with a sacrosanct aura, and provided an instrument by which to orchestrate public reaction to colonial activity.[8] The ramification of science within colonial activity and imperial adventure was extensive, and if it can only be touched upon here should none the less be borne in mind when considering the implications of the 1840–42 Scientific Commission, under whose aegis much of the early scientific exploration of Algeria took place. While the influence of the Scientific Commission was primordial and long-lasting, especially where the elaboration of categories was concerned, it was the initial preoccupation with security that established an essential framework around which elaboration could take place.

The problem of security: nomad vs. sedentary

Security was the *sine qua non* of successful colonization in Algeria. Bugeaud put it plainly enough when he contrasted the situation in Africa to that of France. Civil, municipal and individual liberties are undoubtedly greatly appreciated in France, he wrote, for there there is no ever-present enemy. In Africa, however, there was something more important than individual liberty, and that was security, namely the assurance that one's head remained on one's shoulders, that one's wife would not be raped, and that one's children and harvests would not be scattered.[9] As each successive area fell to the French army, the first consideration was the maintenance of order. Vanquished tribal leaders and local dignitaries were required to submit officially to the French and frequently some sort of tribute was exacted. The military, however, was under no illusion about the nature of their submission. Any cooperation from the Arabs would remain conditional on French strength.[10] Bugeaud advocated a strong, paternalistic government to control the Arabs and had little time for the notion of a *mission civilisatrice* as an instrument of influence. Hope of seducing the Arabs through the imposition of French civilization alone was, he believed, a delusion.[11] Bugeaud's conviction that force was the mainstay of French domination had much to do with his opinion, formed early, that the Arabs were slippery and difficult to handle. It was better to fight them than to do business with them, he stated, for even in a fight they managed to steal away.[12]

To the perceived elusiveness of the Arab character was added the transient nature of his habitat, the tent. The word *nomad* in itself implied changeability and irregularity, the very opposite of stability and order. As nomads, the Arabs of the plains were difficult to control numerically and hard to contain geographically. Their errant lifestyle created a potential hazard in that they could melt away or regroup without the French being fully aware of what was going on. Added to this was the belief, popularized by the pharmacist-in-chief of Val-de-

Grâce, Julien-Joseph Virey, in his successful work, *Histoire naturelle du genre humain*, that their fanaticism was intensified by their nomadic existence, as wandering militated against progression to a higher state of civilization with its concomitant institutions and attenuation of religious fervour.[13]

Transforming the nomadic Arab lifestyle into a sedentary one, therefore, became a priority. In Bugeaud's opinion settling the Arabs by means of constructed property was the best possible policy. Although he conceded that it would be difficult and expensive, he thought that once they had been anchored to the soil, they would be less ferocious, less bellicose and easier to govern.[14] As early as 1836 he had written to Thiers concerning his project of creating military villages, for defensive and cultural purposes. When these had served their initial purpose, they would be handed over to reliable Arabs in order to sedentarize them.[15] Bugeaud was not alone in believing in the beneficial effects of 'attaching the Arabs to the land'; the idea of introducing sedentary habits to the nomadic tribes was widespread. In addition to encouraging agricultural pursuits, there was also the possibility of including them in the extensive public works that were envisaged for the colony under the guidance of military engineers. Only by embracing the type of lifestyle that characterized the French people, namely a sedentary one, could the Arab hope to achieve a modicum of civilization. In 1850 d'Hautpoul, then minister of war, addressed a report to President Louis-Napoleon on the progress to date in this area in which he stated that the notion of civilization was slowly filtering down to the Arabs. Some had already given up their nomadic existence for a sedentary one, replacing the tent, which made them so elusive, with mortar and brick, thus placing them permenantly within the controlling sphere of French administrative policy.[16]

It was but a short step from encouraging a sedentary existence to considering those who would not or could not adopt one to be beyond the pale. Thus in 1864, Lieutenant le Baron Henri Aucapitaine could speak of 'the nomadic and *still* fanatical Arab population'.[17] An amateur ethnologist and something of a scholar closely involved with the Société Historique Algérienne, Aucapitaine was moderate in his approach. There were those, however, such as Dr Eugène Bodichon, a civilian physician with a practice in Algiers, whose views, even at an earlier stage, were more extreme. If, he declared, the Arabs remained impervious to being civilized they should be dealt with as the Indians had been by the Anglo-Americans. That France, on occasion, exceeded the limits of vulgar morality in political conduct was subordinate to establishing a lasting colony which would restore the Barbary coast to European civilization.[18] Bodichon's may not have been a wholly representative view, but it is an interesting one on two counts. Firstly, it was an example of the open ambiguity of attitudes in the nineteenth century. Bodichon was a moderate republican who was once put forward as a candidate for the legislative elections by the democrats of the *Le National*.[19] He was something of a philanthropist, who advocated reform for the workers and underprivileged in France. His philanthropy, however, was restricted to the underprivileged of the civilized nations.[20] Second, in the context of Algeria his views are a sample of some of the more extreme attitudes present in the colony; attitudes indeed that persisted to the end of the century.[21] For Bodichon, and others like him, the Arabs were the 'real enemy' and it was the duty of the French to rid the colony of their influence either by absorption or through the policy of *refoulement*.[22] None the less, if Bodichon's vituperations were not universally echoed the relegation of nomad to a lower rung in the ladder of civilization was already current. Lamartine explained it to the Chamber of Deputies thus: 'Bedouins ... are a race apart ... predatory men who cannot be tamed by any civilization'.[23] In the context of colonial Algeria to be nomadic was in itself a disadvantage; to be incorrigibly so was prejudicial.

Once Kabylia had been subdued, for purposes of security the Kabyles appeared to pose far fewer problems than the nomadic Arabs. Their sedentary lifestyle meant that 'anchoring to the land', that essential first step to secure and educate, was not necessary. In theory the process of assimilating, and hence civilizing, could start immediately. Even before conquest was complete, the idea was being voiced that the Kabyles could be 'tamed' more easily. As Dureau de la Malle was to put it, the sedentary, agricultural and industrial tribes of Kabylia held more promise for the effective action of French civilization. After all, a people who had the same habits and morals and needs analogous to those of the peasants living in the French mountains could only be easier to control, and would surely submit without too much resistance to French domination.[24] Technically speaking, as a sedentary population the Kabyles could be subjected to census-taking and close examination more readily than the nomads. Control was potentially easier than with the nomads. As important, however, was the fact that their sedentary nature provided an element with which the French could identify in a way they never could with the nomadic Arab. The Kabyles might have been considered primitive but the rudiments on which to build a society along French lines were present, and that could only be viewed as positive.

From this first evident advantage issued further favourable points. Unlike the Arabs who, Bugeaud noted, had no merchants and labourers and lacked all but a subsistence industry or craft, the Kabyles had developed both their agriculture and their industry.[25] In a report published in 1850 by a member of the Chamber of Commerce of Algiers on the olive oil industry in Kabylia, considered to be among the most important potential contributors to the colony's future prosperity, it was stated that from an agricultural point of view little needed to be improved in Kabylia. On the other hand, if agriculture in Kabylia was very advanced in comparison with that of the other indigenous peoples, the industrial methods and processes used for extracting produce and creating consumable products still had to be established.[26] The possibility therefore existed of eventual cooperation between the French and the Kabyles to ameliorate the process for the benefit of both parties. Whether or not this type of cooperation was actually envisaged (and it was by some, as will be demonstrated below) its possibility provided a link, however tenuous, between the French and the Kabyles which did not exist with the nomadic tribes. With the Kabyles the French were able to look beyond the immediate imperative of security to some sort of positive interaction in a less distant future than with the nomadic Arab. This too shed a more benevolent light on the Kabyles. It also led to Kabylophile claims that within a century the Kabyles would be French.[27]

Reconnaissance and the elaboration of categories

The negative and positive connotations attached to the Arabs and the Kabyles received further amplification as a result of the activities of the numerous projects and commissions set up to examine the new colony. Over and above the concern for security, the reconnaissance, exploration and evaluation, which formed such an important part of the early decades, were undertaken with three principal objectives: as purely scientific exploration, as reconnaissance for potential colonial exploitation, and as a tool for the comprehension of local populations and uncharted territories. All three objectives served, in some way, as vehicles for the refinement of the recently established categories. The outcome of these reconnaissance forays into the Algerian hinterland and of the localized expeditions during which officers, in the capacity of scholars, produced numerous *mémoires* were the works that supplied the basis for future assessment. Many of these documents ended up in the general depot of the War Ministry, where they could be consulted by authorized personnel. (Carette, for example, used the *mémoires* and reports of expeditions from Dellys to points in and around Kabylia in the years 1842, 1844 and 1845, as supplementary sources to his own research in the preparation of *Etudes sur la Kabilie.*)

Others were published as articles in scholarly reviews or appeared in book form, often to popular and academic acclaim.

The Scientific Commission of 1840–42

Among the most significant works in this genre were those published as a result of the Scientific Commission for the Exploration of Algeria. Conceived by the Ministry of War in 1837, and eventually set up in 1839 under the leadership of Colonel Jean-Baptiste Bory de Saint-Vincent, the Commission comprised numerous artists, biologists, archaeologists and ethnographers, many of whom were *Polytechniciens*.[28] It also included a number of Saint-Simonians, the most illustrious of whom was Prosper Enfantin, engaged in the capacity of ethnographer. The *Polytechniciens* brought to the enterprise the cachet of science and Cartesian thought; the Saint-Simonians the philosophy of progress through efficient technological and industrial development and, to achieve these ends, the need to reorganize society in a paternalistic hierarchy of ability. The Saint-Simonians also had an extraordinary sense of publicity. This urge to disseminate their views found its outlet in a rich variety of journals and newspapers, and through copious correspondence.[29]

Although the final results fell short of the anticipated project, due to the renewal of hostilities with Abd-el-Kader, 39 volumes were eventually published, of which the first five were by Ernest Carette and included his *Etudes sur la Kabilie proprement dite*.[30] Carette, a Polytechnicien and one of the colony's leading Saint-Simonians, was the prototype of the officer-scholar in Algeria. He took an active part in the intellectual life of the colony, which, in the early stages of the colony, meant the establishment of and involvement in scholarly societies and institutions. The leader of the Commission, Bory de Saint-Vincent, a naturalist who was to become one of the best known and popular ethnologists of the day, expressed the hope that the exploration undertaken would clear up the woolly thinking concerning the colony and present the French public with an accurate picture of Algeria.[31] The information gleaned during the three years of research gave rise to a body of work whose components were uneven and, in some cases, incomplete. None the less its value was uncontested and several of its volumes became standard works.[32] In a collection of essays compiled on the occasion of the centenary celebrations in 1930 Stéphane Gsell, Professor at the Collège de France, commenting on the members of the 1840–42 Commission, wrote that seemingly unsuited to the task by education or employment (as officers) they had combined extensive knowledge, precision and exactitude, with a sense of reality, a lively intelligence and a very sound judgment to produce scholarship of great worth.[33] The impact of the Scientific Commission on ideas regarding the indigenous population occurred at three different levels.

The Scientific Commission as a scientific enterprise

As a scientific enterprise the Commission served a twofold purpose with regard to the French conceptions of the Kabyles. The first was less tangible than the second. The use in the texts of the various dichotomous categories into which Arab and Kabyle were being slotted elevated them from convenient but imprecise divisions to scholarly classifications. To the positive and negative connotations that were beginning to emerge around these categories, as a result of warfare and concerns for security, was added the weight of science. To find the terms *nomade* or *homme des plaines*, *sédentaire* or *montagnard* consistently linked to the Arab and the Kabyle as qualifying adjectives produced the effect that one was inseparable from the other. This in turn generated a stereotypical vision of all Arabs as nomadic and men of the plains, and all Kabyles as sedentary and men of the mountains.

Second, and more substantially, not only did the production of the Commission contain volumes, such as Carette's work on Kabylia, that would serve as a cornerstone of future work, but issues were raised that had begun to preoccupy scholars and would form part of the prominent intellectual debate on race in the second half of the nineteenth century. Two of the most important questions were interrelated and concerned language and origins. The role of language in the determination of race was already a subject of speculation in the early nineteenth century. The German philosopher Herder had introduced the idea that a shared language linked communities in the past but eschewed the notion of racial classification. The French naturalist and professor of natural history at the *Collège de France*, George Cuvier, went on to use language to bear out his classification of mankind. The English anthropologist James Prichard also used comparative linguistics in both his *Researches into the Physical History of Mankind* and his *Natural History of Man*. Later scholars and philologists, such as Eichhoff, Grimm, Renan and Bopp, focused more sharply on language and its significance to origins and race.[34]

With the disappearance of Latin as the universal European language of the educated elite and the emergence of vernacular languages as the vehicles of both written and spoken communication, language as a bond cut across hierarchical lines and became tied to the concept of nationhood. In the nineteenth century the activities of intellectuals involved in philology, linguistics and lexicography were central to the shaping of European nationalisms.[35] Once established as an integral part of the panoply of a nation, language became a milestone along the path of its evolution. The richness of a language, its structure, its grammatical complexity and its literature were considered to be a means of evaluating the degree of a nation's civilization. Not to have developed a concept of nationhood could only place a community at a lower level of political-cum-intellectual development than one that had, no matter how well other linguistic criteria stood up to the test. In compiling and collating lexicons and grammars of the languages spoken throughout their empires, European scholars contributed to an evolutionary categorization and classification of their subject peoples.

The Berber language had received attention in the years prior to and immediately following conquest. A certain Dr Walter Oudney had compiled a Berber alphabet during his travels in North and Central Africa in the period 1822–24. In the decade following the French invasion several articles on the subject appeared in scholarly journals, including one by Jean-Honorat Delaporte, an official interpreter in Algeria and son of Jacques D. Delaporte, ex-consul in Mogador.[36] In 1844 Jacques Delaporte published a work, *Spécimen de la langue berbère*, of which 175 copies were sent by the War Ministry to Bugeaud for distribution among the officers of the Bureaux Arabes.[37] Jacques Delaporte had been a member of a five-man commission set up to research a French–Berber dictionary. Headed by Amédée Jaubert, the commission produced the dictionary as well as revising and up-dating a Berber grammar and dictionary originally compiled by Venture de Paradis, who had since died.[38] On publication in 1844, they were well received, especially the latter work as its appearance had, for some time, been considered overdue. The philosopher and travel writer, Volney (who died in 1820), and the interpreter Langlès had, in particular, lamented the absence of such a work.[39] It was inevitable, therefore, that these early beginnings would be extended in the scholarly research carried out in the colony.

In his *Etudes sur la Kabilie* Carette dwelt at length on the problem of linguistics, and he assigned a chapter to the general characteristics of the Berber language and its origins. In a second chapter he discussed the linguistic differences between Arabs and Berbers, highlighting the contrast by the introduction of a simile, namely that of the differences in France between Northerners and Southerners resulting from their origins as speakers of the *langue d'oil* or the *langue d'oc*. Reminding his readers of the time France was divided into these two great regions he added that the separation, above all one of language, also encompassed needs, interests, ideas, passions, morals, customs and finally all aspects of communal life. The *langue d'oc* had its spirit (*génie*) as did the *langue d'oil*.[40] At the outset this difference of 'spirit' between North and South was both political and social. Carette went on to discuss the forces that eventually overtook the binding 'spirit' of the community or *volksgeist*, as Herder had put it, of the North and the South and subordinated them to French nationhood.

For Carette, Algeria was at the stage France had been in the Middle Ages before this unification had taken place. It was divided into two languages that corresponded to the *langue d'oil* and the *langue d'oc*, and thus the two *volksgeists* they represented.[41] It was, of course, this that separated the Kabyles from the Arabs; they represented the *génie de la langue d'oil* and the *génie de la langue d'oc* respectively. What distinguished the French past from the Algerian present was the concept of nationhood. Carette argued that in France, during the Middle Ages, a similar rudimentary concept of nationhood, that of the province, was shared by the areas of the *langue d'oil* and the *langue d'oc*; in Algeria the Kabyle and the Arab did not share such a similarity, for with the Arab it was always the patronymic name that dominated in any concept of a nation. Citing the hypothetical example of 'Ali', he stated that should his descendants leave their home territory and move far away for a century or more, they would always remain the descendants of Ali. In contrast, among Berber appellations the family occupied less space. It was to the soil that the concept of a nation, or the city, was attached. On this point, as indeed on many others, the Berbers were far closer to the French than were the Arabs.[42] Through his analysis of nationhood, Carette implied that the *génie arabe* offered little scope for integration with the French, whereas the Kabyles, as part of the *génie berbère*, had evident potential for being similar, on so many points, to the French. A 'scientific' context was therefore used to reinforce positive and negative connotations with regard to Kabyle and Arab.

Carette's comparison of the duality in the two countries is ambiguous and confusing. His overall argument, however, was that two intrinsically different communities existed in Algeria whose essence derived from their language. Although he did not define the difference between Kabyles and Arabs in racial terms, his use of linguistics as an analytical tool was pertinent. Language and its origins were to form an important part of the racial debate. As a *Polytechnicien* and an active Saint-Simonian, Carette had a good scientific and intellectual grounding. He was therefore well aware of contemporary scientific, sociological and intellectual trends. While his professed aim was to draw up 'an *inventory*' of a defined portion of Algeria, thus allowing for a better understanding of Kabylia and its potential, his approach was a scholarly one in that he discussed the Kabyles in the light of contemporary intellectual arguments.[43] By doing so he entered the Kabyles into the arena of an emergent scholarly debate concerning race. Although the primary motivation for *Etudes sur la Kabilie* was reconnaissance of an inventorial nature and not detached research, it was none the less an initial and relevant reference in ethnographical, anthropological and sociological circles, where racial questions would be most frequently raised. Its influence was lasting and Carette was frequently quoted in future works on the Kabyles.[44]

The Scientific Commission as reconnaissance for colonial exploitation

By 1840 the supporters of the idea of an *occupation restreinte* had been overruled by those who advocated total conquest and colonization. In essence the debate, which lasted nearly a decade, was whether the French presence in Algeria should be restricted to commercial activity along the lines of the *comptoirs* in West Africa at that time, or whether it should become a settler colony. Successful settler colonization rested on two prerequisites: land and labour. There were, therefore, two dominant questions in relation to reconnaissance for colonial exploitation. The first concerned the actual potential of the country, mineral, agricultural, industrial and commercial, as seen through an examination of its past experience and its present state of development. Determination of this potential would lay the groundwork for future colonial policy, most especially with regard to land. The second was the character the relationship between colonizer and colonized would eventually assume if and when exploitation took place. The former was directly addressed in such works as Henri Fournel's *Richesse minérale de l'Algérie* and Carette's *Recherches sur la géographie et le commerce de l'Algérie méridionale*; the latter obliquely so through observations on the local population as incorporated in works overtly about other subjects or, as in the case of Carette's study on Kabylia, through a focused look at a particular area and its inhabitants. If the future wealth of the colony depended on putting its natural resources to good use, this presupposed the presence of a viable labour force.

When it came to Kabylia, quite apart from the fact that the area had not yet been subdued, any consideration of the exploitation of its potential would always have to take into account the density of its population. Extermination, one of the possibilities actually aired (always with reference to the example of the Anglo-American treatment of the Indians) as a solution to the *problème indigène* was not considered for Kabylia, nor, at the time, was the policy of *refoulement*. Furthermore, sequestering land from the Kabyles would obviously pose far more problems than taking land from the nomadic tribes of the plains. Kabylia and the Kabyles had to be examined in a different light. Kabylia's potential for colonization rested therefore on some form of cooperation with the French or on the use of the area as a source of manpower.

The fourth book in Carette's two-volume work aimed at elucidating the distribution of labour and the riches of Kabylia. The book is divided into two sections, of which the first is concerned with the products manufactured or grown in Kabylia; the second with the specific wealth of each commune. This Carette gauged through the state of public and private buildings, reminding his readers that the art of building is inextricably linked to the notion of progress in civilization.[45] For Carette, Kabylia was a patchwork of two types of zone: the active and the inert. In the active zone inhabitants linked their livelihood to the land: cereal growing, forestry, and arboriculture predominated. The inert zones, on the other hand, were characterized by artisanal pursuits such as metal-working (including arms and jewellery) and wood-working, the peddling of goods (*colportage*) and itinerant labour. Together they offered considerable industrial potential. The methodical and geographically precise exposé in Carette's fourth book was intended as a tribe by tribe directory of such potential thus pointing to the important role the Kabyles could assume in the future of the colony. Listing 27 professions and the villages that specialized in each, he concluded the section by stating that in this information would enable specific branches of French industry to know both where to knock and which doors would open when they were looking for specialized workers. Just as the agreements of 1844 had avowed the fact that the domination of the Sahara was a commercial affair, so for analogous reasons it was possible to say the domination of Kabylia was an industrial affair.[46]

Labour posed an acute potential problem for the colony. European settlement in the first two decades and a half was as yet insufficient and did not provide the necessary manpower to make the colony viable. (In 1840 the European population was 25,000.[47] Although by 1855 this figure had reached 155,606, the agricultural population was only 45,847.[48]) This was aggravated at the time by disease, which took a high toll among the European population. The solution to the problem was either to import labour or to find it *in situ*.[49] Kabylia was the obvious answer to the latter solution. Carette pointed out that the area distinguished itself by the presence of established professional crafts, by the desire and habit of hard work amongst its workers and by the stability of its sedentary lifestyle. Basing themselves on these three criteria, the French could only encounter resistance and antipathy among the pastoral Arabs and the ravaging spirit of the conquering Turks. On the other hand, in the presence of the French, who knew how to honour hard work and put it to good use, the Berber artisan and town-dweller could only find reasons to integrate and associate. Kabylia, Carette concluded, had to become France's most intelligent auxiliary and useful associate.[50] Dexterity, hard work and stability were the resources the Kabyle could offer the French. All three were among the solid values vaunted as part of the meritocratic ideology which prevailed in France in the nineteenth century; all three were qualities the French identified with; all three were an essential part of the Saint-Simonian doctrine. Once again the Kabyle was opposed to the Arab, for if the Kabyles were an admirable potential source of labour the Arabs, with their propensity to err, their unstable disposition and their lack of any recognizable economic achievement, were not.

The Scientific Commission as a tool for the comprehension of local populations and uncharted territories

The lively political debate that took place during the period 1844–45 about the pros and cons of conquering Kabylia had thrust the area into the limelight as never before. Carette's study, published in 1848, was therefore very timely. One of his declared intentions was to put straight imprecise notions about the Kabyles and to situate Kabylia squarely on the map, thus eliminating the widespread misconceptions about its whereabouts. Equally important was his desire 'to reconcile, as far as possible, local affinities and customs with French exigencies'.[51] This, in fact, was the underlying aim of any close look at the indigenous population by the Scientific Commission and, indeed, of those works that did not form part of it. In all of them the prevailing theme, whether openly stated or not, was an attempt to answer the question of how the indigenous population would fit into the French scheme of things. To this end the objects of study, be they general categories such as Arab or Berber or individual tribal entities, were subjected to a scrutiny whose yardstick was measurement in relation to the values and standards of French society.

In examining the indigenous population the attraction of the sedentary tribes of Kabylia went beyond the administrative and political advantages of law, order and control. The readily (and rapidly) compilable tribe-by-tribe inventories of political, economic and social factors provided a database from which a variety of disciplines could draw. A momentum to research was initiated and continued to grow. The facility of study was valuable initially on a reconnaissance level, when it was necessary to discover the potential for revolt against the French, and later on a ethnographical and anthropological level. (From an anthropological point of view the inaccessbility of Kabylia made them of even greater interest as they were perceived to be relatively unaffected by outside influences.) The French inclined towards study of sedentary tribes because it was less complicated to do so. If for reconnaissance purposes it was potentially easier to keep tabs on Kabylia, from the 'scientific' angle the area was an admirable object of study for both tribal and inter-tribal relations. By its geographic and demographic situation, therefore, Kabylia was pre-eminently attractive. This is not to say that other sectors of the country were neglected entirely, only that the literature that emerged on Kabylia and the Kabyles far outweighed that on any other area or on any other ethnic group. Of the numerous volumes produced by the Scientific Commission, the only ones to deal exclusively with a particular area of Algeria and its inhabitants were Carette's on Kabylia.

The second volume of Carette's *Etudes sur la Kabylie* is basically an inventory of the tribes and villages of Kabylia. It is divided into 16 sections, the first dealing with the capital, Bougie, and the subsequent 15 with the 'cantons' of Kabylia, areas that were not officially designated but whose limits Carette had established. The descriptions of each tribe vary in detail and length; the tribes that had brushed with the French for one reason or another are dealt with in greater detail. Carette emphasizes the geographic position of each, drawing attention to those living in the most inaccessible areas and signalling the various tribal alliances and feuds. At the end of each section is a numerical recapitulation of the canton and the number of armed men in each village. In appearance the volume is no more than a detailed catalogue of tribes, but underlying nuances are perceptible; nuances that endorse French attitudes towards indigenous behaviour. It is interesting to note, for example, that the Oulâd Tamzalt, members of which perpetrated the assassination of Salomon de Mussis, comes in for exceptional opprobrium. Among other things, Carette states that this tribe, situated on the river Bougie, hindered peaceable relations developing between surrounding riverain tribes.[52] On the other hand one of the distinguishing features that Carette dwells upon regarding the Flissa tribe is the attractiveness of their villages, whose buildings are constructed out of stone, roofed with tiles, and mostly have more than one storey.[53] This approval of well-built edifices, which in themselves were indicative of an established sedentary development, was, of course, a subtle endorsement of the idea that the greater the degree of sedentarization the higher the level of civilization.

Carette's study of Kabylia was undertaken as a preliminary exploration of a relatively uncharted area and its inhabitants. Unlike Lapène, to whom he made reference, he did not rely on the classics. As Kabylia was still independent at the time the Scientific Commission was in operation, Carette turned to 'reliable' second-hand information. His sources were military district reports, verbal reports from officers stationed in and around the area and verbal accounts as transcribed from travellers.[54] What Carette achieved was to present the area to the public in a quasi-scientific light. His was the first work on the area to have been completed as the result of commissioned research rather than having been penned as a scholarly sideline to military duty or civilian activity.[55] In that capacity, whatever its actual merits, it remained fundamental to future research and debate on the Kabylia and the Kabyles.

The wider impact of the Scientific Commission

The net result of the Scientific Commission was to stimulate existing interest in Algeria. Its very existence and the nature of its undertaking were indications that the controversy over whether or not Algeria was to be fully colonized had been resolved in the affirmative. Its members would henceforth take an active role in promoting colonial ideology either in the colony itself or in France. Among the published works of its members, two of the most reviewed were Carette's *Etudes sur la Kabilie* and Enfantin's *La Colonisation de l'Algérie*. Both works reinforced the positive and negative connotations surrounding the categories into which Berber and Arab were being slotted.

Enfantin's work was not accepted for publication by the commissioning ministry and therefore never formed part of the final 39 volumes. As the official ethnographer of the expedition, Enfantin had chosen to study the Chaouia (Berbers from the Aurès) but the finished product was a Saint-Simonian treatise on how Algeria should be colonized. As a dispatch from the office of Field Marshal Soult, then minister of war, explained, his views were too idiosyncratic to be considered official.[56] Official or not, Enfantin's *La Colonisation* was published and the ideas it contained were widely discussed.[57] The importance of the work with regard to the Kabyles lay as much in its theories of colonization as in its geographical and sociological analysis of the indigenous inhabitants. Mountain, plain and desert; sedentary and nomad: these were the categories Enfantin made most use of. To his theory of colonization it was the latter two that were most relevant.

Enfantin's vision for Algeria was an embodiment of the Saint-Simonian doctrine of the achievement of well-being through economic endeavour under the paternalistic guidance of a natural elite (the French). He transposed this Saint-Simonian belief in a social revolution achieved from above through the agency of superior men to a colonial setting. Colonization would thus be a beneficial force for humanity, and he foresaw its success in Algeria through rational economic exploitation and the acquisition of a higher degree of civilization by the local populations. (For Saint-Simonians *civilisation* was more closely tied to technological and scientific achievement than to cultural perfection.) This presupposed a sedentarization of the nomadic Arab population, which could be achieved only through wise government. Certainly, it would be very satisfying if the Arabs constructed houses and laid out plantations, Enfantin wrote, for it would stimulate a love of the land, make them abandon their nomadic character and increase their productivity. If they did not plant and did not build, it was due, in most places, to the fact they were governed by a power that did not inspire their confidence and failed to guarantee their security. Enfantin was in no doubt that with a regular, fair government which was not bent on despoiling and a civil authority that maintained order and peace among the tribes, the Arabs, who were very self-seeking and who liked their comfort, would plant and build.[58] He advocated winning over the Arabs by extensive public works, another tenet of the Saint-Simonian doctrine. Most specifically he suggested the construction of the 'sheik's residence, the mosque, the cadi's court, the fountain and the creation of gardens'. With regard to the differences between nomadic Arabs and sedentary Kabyles, Enfantin declared that the concept of divide and rule, which had been used by the Turks, was a destructive one. It would be more profitable, he argued, to use differences between Arabs and Kabyles to stimulate constructive economic competition between the two rather than to encourage vengeful animosity.[59] This would naturally hasten the process of creating a wholly sedentary society.

The necessity to sedentarize, which underpinned Enfantin's theories, reinforced the concept as a positive attribute when considering traditional life styles. Although *La Colonisation de l'Algérie* did not deal extensively with the Kabyles, it none the less disseminated to a larger public, and in an ideological context, the dual categories that were emerging regarding the indigenous population. Enfantin's subject matter and approach were different from Carette's, but both works had common ground in their attitudes to nomadic and sedentary populations of Algeria. In this domain, Enfantin's work was more schematic than Carette's, but the differences between nomad and sedentary were hammered home and these differences were seen as applying to Arabs and Kabyles.

Conclusion

The theories and activities that evolved out of the need for security and the desire for reconnaissance served to imbue a different set of categories with the type of positive and negative connotation that had become linked to *mountain* and *plain* as a result of warfare and conquest. *Sedentary* and *nomad*, when attached to Kabyle and Arab, would henceforth bear an implied moral evaluation. Reconnaissance forays into the interior were the earliest means of gathering much-needed information regarding the indigenous population; under the aegis of the Scientific Commission this activity was amplified. The Scientific Commission was the first step towards the institutionalization of data-gathering on the colonies that began to flower with the creation of the Société d'Anthropologie de Paris and the numerous scholarly societies set up in Algeria. It was also fundamental to the spirit of scientific association that Berbrugger, president and founding member of the Société Historique Algérienne, claimed first took root in Algeria around 1851.[60]

With regard to attitudes towards the Kabyles the Scientific Commission had a sixfold effect. Firstly, on a 'scientific' level it contributed the cachet of scholarship. The elaboration of new categories and the confirmation of existing ones therefore acquired an important new dimension. Second, in this same context, it raised to the level of an intellectual problem those issues that had always proved intriguing regarding the Kabyles, such as language and origins, thus clearing the way for the purely theoretical, and in fact hypothetical, debates on race. Third, on the more prosaic level of reconnaissance for colonization, it presented the Kabyles as potentially valuable auxiliaries to colonization through their suitability as a labour force. Fourth, and in this same vein, it stressed the potential for cooperation between the French and the Kabyles as a result of the basic, albeit unequally developed, similarities in their values and lifestyles. The fifth point is that the very choice of the Kabyles as the only population group of Algeria to be officially studied in depth by the Commission added weight to their importance in the colony and was an early indication of what could almost be described as the French obsession with the Berbers. Finally, the works that emerged as a result of the Scientific Commission, whether they were official publications like Carette's or unofficial one's like Enfantin's, disseminated greatly enhanced stereo-types to a more extensive public.

Additionally the following needs to be stressed with regard to the two works arising out of the Scientific Commission discussed above. There was nothing original about Carette's ideas. They were a synthesis of prevailing military attitudes presented in a 'scientific' context and having more pronounced intellectual overtones. Enfantin's more unorthodox work, although not explicitly about Kabyles and Arabs, made use of existing categories, but did so on a more theoretical basis than Carette's. The uniting thread was a subtle reinforcement of the notion of the *good Kabyle* and the *bad Arab*, a thread which was discernible in the majority of contemporary works be they, or not, products of the Scientific Commission. Whether or not the authors were Kabylophiles, or merely Arabophiles, or even non-partisan, was immaterial. The very fact of using categories which had acquired such heavily positive and negative connotations to present their case invigorated the emerging colonial mythology surrounding the Kabyles and the Arabs.

3

Security and reconnaissance part 2: Islam and society

Islam proved to be an intractable problem for the French. They reacted to it as an ideological system rather than as a religious creed and, in Algeria, this reaction influenced the formation of Kabyle and Arab stereotypes. At the time of conquest Islam was perceived to be an obstacle in the path towards the pacification of Algeria. The memory of Abd-el-Kader and his *djihad* against the French invaders was never expunged from French minds. However much Abd-el-Kader's qualities were acknowledged by Arabophiles and officers, who recognized in him a fine warrior, for most he remained, as Tocqueville described him in 1841, unusually dangerous, 'a sort of Muslim Cromwell', who used the shield of religion to further his own interests. The religious hatred inspired by the French was the vehicle of his power; to destroy it would be to renounce that power so, overtly or covertly, he would always fight the French.[1] The spectre of Islam as a belligerent religion was ever-present throughout the 130 years of French occupation, and the French invariably imputed to Islam all forms of opposition to their rule. This delusion had a direct bearing on the evolution of French attitudes towards the indigenous population.

Once Abd-el-Kader was vanquished the worry of Islam persisted and, if security was to be achieved, a better understanding of its nature was essential. To this end a concerted effort was made to create links between French administrators and their Muslim subjects. Officers of the Direction des Affaires Arabes and later the Bureaux Arabes were obliged to speak Arabic; many spoke Kabyle as well. Communication was thus a vital first step. From this would flow the means to understand what was seen, right from the start, as an impenetrable society. The role of these native language-speakers acquired a significance over and above their official functions, for it was the Arabists who were deemed qualified to provide the most penetrating studies of Islam. Through their knowledge of the Arabic language

53

alone they were elevated to the rank of expert, regardless of how learned they actually were. The opinions these Arabists expressed on Islam, whether they were penned by scholars or not, were inevitably deferred to by those who did not understand the language. In this way much subjective reaction, dressed up as scholarship, was absorbed into the canon of thought on Islam.

Islam: An impregnable religion

Reconnaissance in its wider sense, therefore, encompassed a close scrutiny of Islam. In 1844 the government published a pamphlet, entitled *Exposé de l'état actuel de la société arabe, du gouvernement et de la législation qui la régit*, for distribution among all commanding officers and officers involved in Arab affairs.[2] The work, which was sanctioned by Bugeaud, was intended as a directive. The opening paragraph of its preface contained the reminder that the Koran, which incorporated both religious law and the most important aspects of civil law, had so closely linked the interests of religion and state that, without profoundly upsetting the population, it would always be difficult to substitute an entirely French administrative system for the one which had developed in Africa and was shaped by its customs, morals and beliefs. If the Koran served as the epicentre for the potential administrative difficulties of the French, the arcane nature of Muslim society presented further problems. For future well-being both had to be elucidated. The administration was well aware of the gaps in knowledge on Islam in the colony, which were due not only to lack of documentary material but also to the inaccessibility to the French of the Muslim family unit. To redress the situation the government appealed to both scholars and laymen, whatever their fields of interest, for assistance in studying this important subject.[3] The call to come to terms with the indigenous population through an understanding of their religion and their society, whether or not it was couched in the language of the *mission civilisatrice*, was in fact motivated by the need for security. To this end it was vital to permeate the recondite recesses of Islam.

In Algeria French interest in Islam focused on religion as an institution. An understanding of Islam as a theological creed seldom progressed further than a dismissal of it as fanaticism; an attitude as current in France as in the colony. Tocqueville, who studied the Koran with the aim of better understanding the French position in Algeria, avowed that it had convinced him that few religions were as baneful to man as that of Mohammed.[4] While the literary aspects of the Koran were often appreciated, its moral tone and ideological message were

54

condemned. The Arabist officers of the occupying army, preoccupied with security and imbued with anti-clericalism, made little of the opportunity to verify or even question the received canon of thought on Islam.[5] The belief that it imparted an infallible doctrine served as justification for their own methods of government. Therefore in Arab eyes French authority had to be infallible and the head of state had to be as infallible as the Koran, for in Islam the head of state was also the head of the church (*sic*).[6] It was better to stick by a mediocre measure than to alter it for a better one, thus showing indecision. French policy towards the indigenous population was to rest on 'force and justice', for it was this that the Muslims would best understand, and it was this that would permit true pacification.[7] The doctrine of Islam thus served as a pretext for French policy towards the local population, and was dwelt upon only in so far as it provided the rationale for such policy.

Religion as an institution, on the other hand, received close attention. In the first place there was the question of the religious leaders who, because of their great influence on the people, needed to be studied with great care.[8] French interests in the institutions of the Islamic religion arose out of their desire to secure the country and maintain stability. If the religious hierarchy could be understood and even penetrated, security would be easier to achieve, for the seditious impulse provided by the more fanatical of these leaders could thus be hampered. Attention was therefore centred on those Islamic institutions that contained the potential to undermine the security of the colony. In this respect the two deemed most important were the *khouan*, or secret brotherhoods, and the *marabouts*, or living saints.

The khouan

The earliest attempt at a serious study of the *khouan* was undertaken by another Saint-Simonian officer and member of the Scientific Commission, Edouard de Neveu. De Neveu served in the Bureaux Arabes for 25 years, of which eleven were spent in Kabylia. Married to an indigenous woman, although it is not clear whether she was Kabyle or Arab, he was considered to be a 'specialist' on the Kabyles and on Islam. His *Les Khouan. Ordres religieux chez les musulmans de l'Algérie* was first published in 1845. When the book first came out it was well received in army circles. Field Marshal Soult, who was particularly impressed, urged de Neveu to continue his research and, as encouragement, the government covered all publicity costs and ordered the publication of an enlarged edition a year later. It was an instant success, running into three editions and becoming a standard reference work on the subject.[9] Using as his sources information gathered from members of the six different brotherhoods in the Constantine area, de Neveu set out to shed light on the significance of Islamic religious orders in Algeria. Also included was one religious 'congregation', the Derkaoua, in which, he inclined to believe, politics played a substantial role. De Neveu described the hierarchical make-up of each, the significance of entering each, and pointed out that the orders were distinguishable by their rituals and religious endeavours. None the less, the essential questions de Neveu sought to answer concerned the influence of the *khouan* and their leaders (*khalifa*) within the Muslim community: which had links with known rebellious leaders, which were the most subversive and hence the most dangerous from a security point of view, and whether use could be made of their leaders to assist in the implementation of French policies. The work, therefore, was not a study of the institutional significance of these brotherhoods in relation to Islam, but an exposé of their potential as a cover for sedition.

Comparing them unfavourably to the Freemasons, one of the first points de Neveu stressed was the religious exclusiveness of their membership.[10] Short of conversion, the French were unable to penetrate the ranks of the *khouan*. Later in the book de Neveu candidly introduces the age-old concept of an Islamic–Christian conflict, thus adding incompatibility to the notion of impenetrability. It was the French providential mission to rekindle the spirit of civilization on the soil of Algeria which the barbarian Muslim hordes had devastated and kept at bay for so long. To achieve this end, de Neveu advocated cooperation: the use of French enlightenment to shape Arab ideas to solve a potential social problem and smooth away difficulties.[11] The sense of conferring honour and benefit was crucial to the French imperial approach.[12] It was an effective way of distancing themselves from the local population and underlining their control through an implied superiority, be it social, cultural, moral or indeed all three. By suggesting that their Islamic subjects were incapable of attaining French heights, de Neveu relegated Islam to an inferior position, adopting a tone that was to become characteristic of French attitudes. By implying that the barrier to progress was the religion of Islam he was adding credence to the idea elaborated by Vico, Saint-Simon and his disciples, and, more specifically to North Africa, by d'Avezac, that the nature of man's religion was the most characteristic index of his mentality.[13]

With regard to the Kabyles de Neveu had little to say, probably because only the westernmost fringes of the Constantine area bordered on Kabylia, although the *khouan* discussed in his book were active throughout Algeria. What he did contribute to the subject stressed the differences between Arab and Kabyle, including the prevalent view that the Kabyles were less zealous. Citing the order of Ben-Abd-er-Rahman, which included both Kabyles and Arabs, as the only existing link between two races always politically divided, he stated that Abd-el-Kader, unaware that the love of land was a much stronger force for the Kabyles than religion, had made the mistake of assuming that the Kabyles would rally to the call of the order and unite with the Arabs to fight the French.[14] In his conclusion, de Neveu returned briefly to the subject of the Kabyles, to explain why Abd-el-Kader had not succeeded in drawing the Kabyles into his *djihad* against the French. The industrious and commercially minded Kabyle relied on barter to dispose of his manufactured goods and to obtain his food. If, in the past, to fulfil these needs he had converted from the religion of his forefather to that of the victorious Arabs, it was to ensure that his livelihood was not disrupted. The same reasons and needs motivated the present-day Kabyle, so that when he realized that French domination was complete commerce would finally subdue him. From this interpretation of Kabyle faith emerged de Neveu's belief that in spite of the belligerence of the Ben-Abd-der-Rahman brotherhood towards the French, its members were not as formidable as their behaviour implied.[15] Thus, in the realm of religion, de Neveu reinforced the conviction, growing elsewhere, that the potential for cooperation with the Kabyles was greater than with the Arabs.

Overall, however, de Neveu emphasized the need for wariness. Associations of this sort represented an undeniable force and, for those who knew how to manipulate them, a powerful weapon. The members of the Khouan formed part of a unit whose various elements comprised a ready-made network which, with the right guidance, could be made to function as a whole. The Khouan already had a hierarchy and well-established means of communication. Meetings took place at which secret conspiracies could easily be hatched, bursting into the open when it was too late to prevent them. Constant surveillance was necessary. By means of spies the secrets of these brotherhoods could be unearthed and thus any potential moves to insurrection thwarted. De Neveu's ultimate solution was to replace the 'fanatical impostors' serving as leaders, who exploited the ignorance and superstition of the local population, by French educated chiefs for, being Muslim, they would gain the confidence of the people while propagating French values.[16]

No further major work was published on the *khouan*, or indeed any other aspect of Islam, in Algeria until the appearance in 1884 of *Marabouts et Khouan*, the work of another scholar-officer of the

Bureaux Arabes, Louis Marie Rinn.[17] For 40 years, therefore, the ideas expressed by de Neveu in *Les Khouan* prevailed; ideas that were formulated at a time of conflict and in the interests of security. A year after its publication a potted version of these same ideas appeared in an article by André Cochut in the *Revue des Deux Mondes*.[18] Cochut's tone was more patronizing than de Neveu's and the presentation more anecdotal, but the article dispersed de Neveu's views among a wider readership. *Les Khouan* thus became a standard work of reference. (Carette for example, who believed the Kabyles' materialism overrode their spiritualism, relied on de Neveu for his information on Kabyle attitudes to religion.[19]) With this as the starting point the notion of Islam as a quasi-impenetrable fortress for subversive ideas soon passed into French colonial mythology. By being presented as impenetrable, Islam in the colony was in fact being relegated to a limbo from which it would never be recovered. Linking the Kabyles to less fervent religious practices meant that the positive Kabyle–negative Arab divide was once again being reinforced.

The *Marabouts*

Of the two Islamic institutions the French showed most interest in, the phenomenon of *maraboutism* appears to have been the more difficult for them to make sense of. The *marabouts*, living descendants of saintly lineages possessing magical powers (*baraka*), although present in some Arab tribes, were primarily associated with Berber areas, where they were venerated. These holy men could and did attain positions of influence and power within the communities in which they operated, and as such were potentially threatening if they remained hostile to the French. Unlike the leaders of the brotherhoods, however, they did not function within the perimeters of a specific order which could be countrywide; their considerable influence, for all but the most charismatic, was geographically limited. The French approach to the *marabouts* was different from their approach to the *khouan*.

In the first place no study comparable to de Neveu's was attempted. This can partially be explained by the late date at which Kabylia was subdued, although interest in *marabouts* manifested itself early enough. More likely, they posed a more manageable security threat than the brotherhoods. The first volume to appear dealing exclusively with the *marabouts* did so in 1881, and then the discussion of *maraboutism* was restricted to the introduction, containing little that had not already been raised.[20] It was only three years later with Rinn's *Marabouts et Khouan* that a more substantial study appeared, but even here the *marabouts* received considerably less space than the *khouan*. Until this time discussion was limited to one or two perfunctory articles and the short passages appearing in the works on Kabylia and the Kabyles.[21] None the less, the *marabouts* did arouse interest. In 1838 Dr Baudens, a military surgeon and professor of medicine, suggested that because of their 'great quasi-magical influence' they might be useful auxiliaries to French rule.[22] What the French could not reconcile with this immense influence of the holy men in Kabyle territories was the religious indifference they perceived to be characteristic of the Kabyles. Daumas elaborated on the phenomenon in his work on Kabylia.[23] Although he was the first to do so with such clarity, it was a puzzle the French had sought to elucidate from the very start. Lapène traced its origins to the Arab invasion of the seventh century, when *marabouts* were placed among the Kabyles by the conquering Arabs to further their interests. For this reason the Kabyles did not really have any dogma of their own. They paid lip-service to a sort of *marabout* cult, respecting and consulting *marabouts* while they were alive and revering them as saints when they were dead. Lapène rationalized the blind faith which the Kabyles placed in the *marabouts* as the result of crafty exploitation and audacious use of their 'saintly' power to insinuate themselves into the heart of the tribes. It was the *marabouts* who preached holy war, and this made them France's most implacable enemy.[24] Lapène's analysis was the cornerstone of what was to follow. The *marabout* as an outsider, and Kabyle religious subservience due to influence exerted on them as opposed to true faith, became the pillars on which French ideas on the religious proclivities of the Kabyles were based.

Whether or not the maraboutic influence was considered deleterious remained a matter of subjective judgment. Carette, for example, saw the *marabouts* as a moderating force. Their influence was incontestable and their consultative role universal, he said, but it was important to note, and only fair to admit, that the spirit in which they acted was sometimes more measured than that of the secular authorities.[25] What was a widespread idea among the French was that the *marabouts* were not of the same stock as the Kabyles. The evidence on which this conclusion rested was always hypothetical. Aucapitaine, for example, in the only article to deal with the origins of the *marabouts*, concluded, like Lapène, that they were of Arab origin, basing his theory on the most dubious of reasoning. As the Kabyles had no written records, Aucapitaine had 'sought the opinion of the public' and found it 'unanimous in distinguishing between the Kabyle element and the *marabouts*'. This conclusion was reached as a result of asking the question 'Is this man a Kabyle' and receiving the response 'No he is a *marabout.*[26] Other arguments may have been somewhat less spurious, but whatever the tack there was no hard evidence to prove the theory. In spite of this, the idea of the *marabout* as an outsider took hold. Making this distinction between *marabouts* and Kabyles allowed for the growth of the idea that the Kabyles could be weaned away from any noxious influence these 'priests' might have on them and brought into the French camp. Furthermore, it served as confirmation that Islamic fervour was essentially an Arab trait and suggested that the 'mentality' associated with the Islamic religion, inferior to that associated with the Christian one, was alien to the Kabyles.

Unlike the *khouan*, which were viewed as potentially subversive cells, permanently closed to the French and hence assailable only by subterfuge if at all, the *marabouts*, as *agents provocateurs*, for thus they were often deemed to be, provided a seemingly more accessible target in that the Kabyles could be educated away from the 'superstitions' that served as the binding ties. The robust French tradition of anti-clericalism no doubt played a hand in these attitudes. The *marabouts* were equated with the ignorant parish priests of the *ancien régime*, who had been done away with during the Revolution to be replaced by the state-salaried clergy of Napoleon's Concordat. Parallels were drawn between the two based on their manipulative and socially 'para-sitical' tendencies, as well as their awe of the supernatural, their reverence of religious talismans, and their use of these devices to instil fear into their followers.[27] Loosening the hold of religion on the indigenous population was seen as imperative. As might be expected, the solution presented as the most plausible for Algeria had its own parallel with that adopted in France. Whether it was de Neveu, Rinn, or one of the authors whose theories flowed from these two works, the policy proposed was to replace the troublesome religious leaders by ones in the pay of the state (French-educated).

The drive to secularize, which repeatedly waxed and waned in France during the first half of the nineteenth century, progressed steadily in Algeria. This was due to a number of reasons. In the first place, under military occupation there was the preoccupation with security. Second, French society in Algeria, for the first three decades in particular, was much more homogeneous ideologically than it was in France, being predominantly military. Religious indifference, anti-clericalism and republicanism were the prevalent military attitudes.[28] (Republican officers who found promotion difficult in France asked to go or were sent to Algeria. The result was a largely republican officer corps.[29]) The patterns of thought established under military rule with regard to Islam were picked up by the civilians in Algeria after 1870 and used for their own ends, but by then the trend to secularize the state had gathered momentum in France anyway and during the Third Republic no allowances were made in the colony for what were seen as the theocratic tendencies of Islam.

Concerns for security and the desire to secularize in the colony militated against any outspoken enthusiasm for Islam. The unconventional brilliance of a Burton would have accorded ill with the institutionalized discipline of the military. Officers did marry Muslim women but their sympathy and understanding of Islam was tempered by their allegiance to France, the *mission civilisatrice*, and their belief in the superiority of the Christian tradition. Even the most renowned enthusiast of Islam during the civilian regime, the fervent and unconventional Isabelle Eberhardt, herself a Muslim and married to one, was an apologist for French rule, sharing her insider information with the authorities to the detriment of Muslim agitators.[30]

Misconstruing Islam

The French preoccupation with security blurred their comprehension of Islam in Algeria. One the one hand their vision of Islam as impenetrable and potentially subversive led them to conclude that attenuating and eventually eradicating its hold on the population was the only way to achieve harmony in the colony. On the other hand there was a tacit acceptance of the fact that this goal was impossible, at least in the short term. The impasse caused by these conflicting conclusions led to a false analysis of the significance of Islam to the indigenous population, in that the French were sensitized to any possible breach in religious behaviour and were inclined to see irresolution and indifference when in fact none existed. Such was their interpretation of the Kabyle faith. What in fact the French did not appreciate was that maraboutism was not indicative of a weakness in identifying with Islam. On the contrary, the cult of the saints was a means of achieving such an identification among rustic, largely illiterate, populations whose approach to religion was more easily made through the Word as flesh rather than through the Book.[31]

This misinterpretation had far-reaching consequences. In the first place it allowed for the emergence of the blanket categories of fanatical Arab and impious Kabyle. Having established these categories, reasons were sought to substantiate them. Origins provided the key to these differences for the French, provoking the image of the Arab as an outsider and the Kabyle as truly indigenous. Societal variations between the two groups further served to inculcate the notion that they were quintessentially different, even irreconcilable. In the works dealing with Arabs and Kabyles, these basic misconstructions were nuanced and embroidered upon in accordance with the author's personal convictions, but the overriding anxiety felt by the French when confronted with Islam led to a general acceptance that zealousness in any form was reprehensible.

From French misconceptions regarding the religious faith of the Kabyles and Arabs arose the erroneous assumption that the Kabyles would be ready subjects for conversion to Christianity.[32] Such was the strength of these ideas that Cardinal Lavigerie, who as a rule considered the conversion of Muslims to be inexpedient, was to act on them (see below). The notion of Kabyle convertibility had its roots in French ideas of their origins. Daumas had suggested that the Kabyles, partially of indigenous and particularly of Germanic origin, were formerly Christians who had not been completely transformed by the new religion.[33] Dr Auguste Warnier, one-time military surgeon and Saint-Simonian, who served with Daumas in Mascara and later became a leading *colon* spokesman, elaborated on this to include all Berbers.[34] A variety of Kabyle singularities, considered anomalous by the French, were traced to vestiges of this Christianity, the most visual of these signs being the cross-like design tattooed on the chin or forehead of many Kabyles. The evidence of Christian roots among the indigenous population (Berbers), as indicated by the individuality of their traditions and customs, was eventually set down in a work published in 1875 by the head of the Catholic mission in Kabylia, Father Charmetant.[35]

Thus not only were the Kabyles, as Berbers, considered to be the original inhabitants of the area, a fact which in itself segregated them from the outsider Arabs, but they had also possibly been Christians and would therefore be receptive to French ideas in a way the Arabs could never be. The rationale behind this reasoning can be imputed to the belief, also elaborated by Vico, Saint-Simon and later Comte, that the history of human intelligence was a history of religion. Added to this was the influence on French thought of the Christian tradition of religious antagonism against Islam. Hence the Kabyles, as former Christians, were historically both better equipped mentally to absorb Christian-based ideas and better candidates for redemption than the Arabs, who were entrenched Muslims. Considering the Kabyles in this way put them on a different plane from the Arabs. The desire to assimilate the Kabyles to Christianity was just another facet of the growing tendency to view Kabyles in a more favourable light than the Arabs by attributing French values to them.

Islam, an impenetrable society: The mechanics of marginalization

The unease the French felt regarding the Muslim religion was exacerbated when they contemplated Muslim society. The inaccessibility of Islamic theology to French thought was underlined by the apparent incompatibility between the two societies, French and Muslim. This incompatibility was essentially evaluated along moral lines, although broadly speaking it was presented in terms of social structures such as the family, the governing framework and the law. Underlying themes of licentiousness, deceit, indolence, violence, intransigence and immutability served as the touchstones for comparison with French society, themes which by their moral tenor could only exacerbate French feelings of alienation. The mysteries inherent in the Muslim religion were extended to Muslim society, resulting in an unwarranted obfuscation which served to entrench existing differences and magnify perceived ones. The implication that Muslim society was really beyond French grasp was reiterated both by presenting it as mysterious, that is, essentially incomprehensible, and by the adoption of a high moral tone which distanced it sufficiently to make it seem irredeemable to French influence.

The French stumbling-block when considering Muslim society was the Koran, source of both religious and civil law.[36] While the notion of a theocratic society in itself posed difficulties to French secular administrators, it was the immutability of Koranic law that was the heart of the problem for, by extrapolation, as far as the French were concerned, the practising Muslim was incorrigible. Only a deviation from strict Muslim practice could provide the possible opening for the introduction of French modes of thought. Here again, therefore, there was a heightened sensitivity among the French to seeming aberrations and divergences, and Kabyle society provided them with notable examples.

While studies of Kabyle society inclined to a comparative approach with the Kabyles being examined favourably against the Arabs, studies of Arab society avoided such comparisons. The two most comprehensive chroniclers of Arab society were Daumas and Richard, but contributions from other officers and from civilians substantiated or elaborated many of their conclusions. Both Daumas and Richard were officers of the Bureaux Arabes. Daumas had arrived in Algeria with Clauzel, served as consul in Mascara and was appointed the first director of Arab affairs. He rose to the rank of general, took over the directorship of Algerian affairs at the Ministry of War and entered politics as a senator. He became a well-known author, contributing regularly to scholarly journals on Algeria.[37] In contrast, Richard had a less illustrious military career in spite of being a graduate of the Ecole Polytechnique and having been numbered among the most brilliant of his year. He served as commanding officer in Bougie and later in Orleanville, but never rose above the rank of captain. In the domain of letters, however, he had greater success, for he was both imaginative and original – a fact which may have hindered his progress in the military, where conformity was the valued norm. He was greatly influenced by the ideas of Considerant and Fourier, well versed in philosophy, and one of the colony's best Arabists, and not only did his writing on Algeria show signs of his erudition but his literary talent extended beyond his interests in Algeria.[38] Both Daumas and Richard were motivated by the desire to enlighten their compatriots regarding the indigenous population. Daumas, who studied both Kabyles and Arabs, believed that the Arabs should not be fashioned in the image of the French but left to their own devices.[39] Unlike Daumas, Richard concentrated exclusively on the Arabs. Fluent and well-written, his works used to great effect that instrument of marginalization, the high moral tone. The portrait he painted of the Arabs was relentlessly pessimistic and he saw the French mission as one of ameliorating the Arab lot.[40] From his early conclusion that 'the Arab people was in a state of moral and physical degradation' he deviated little, although in a later work, based on the notion that 'the measure of man was his morality', he allowed that over time some improvement was possible.[41] While Daumas believed that no serious progress could be achieved with the Arabs because of an innate religious hostility to the French, Richard pointed to the prolonged decadence of their religion, as a civilization.[42] In different ways, therefore, both men perpetrated the idea that Islam was the insuperable barrier to assimilation and Islamic society incompatible with French. Substantiation for these conclusions was sought in Islamic social and legal codes of behaviour.

Domesticity and the family

In considering the domestic situation of their indigenous population French authors singled out two features for special attention: polygamy and the condition of women. Both were used as a gauge with which to measure Arab and Kabyle society against French. While neither Arab nor Kabyle came up to French standards, the Kabyles were well ahead of the Arabs in both respects.

As far as polygamy was concerned, the practice was considered reprehensible and was invariably condemned. Calls were periodically made for its eradication, as it was seen to be the root of the deplorable condition of women.[43] It was considered impossible for a monogamous society to coexist with a polygamous one without perpetual friction.[44] Abolition of this practice was therefore a practical as well as a moral necessity.[45] Although polygamy was often attacked head-on, it was as frequently assailed through innuendo. In *De la Civilisation du peuple arabe*, for example, Richard accused Arab men of orgiastic behaviour and total disrespect for women.[46] Although his description was unusually vitriolic, it is only an extreme example of a generalized attitude which viewed the Arab as lascivious and immoral, polygamy being a symbol of these pernicious propensities. The deleterious impact of polygamy on the basic social unit, the home, was another lament, 'covering the most disgraceful immorality with a legal mantle'.[47] In contrast the Kabyle was seen to be more moderate, for although polygamy was legal in Kabylia it was seldom seen in practice. Maffre elaborated on this, stating that the Kabyle man preferred only one wife to whom, together with his children, he was genuinely attached and with whom he created a perfectly harmonious union.[48] Thus interpreted, Kabyle family life corresponded more to the idealized French family unit than to the stereotype of Islamic harem life.

The condition of women received wider attention than the issue of polygamy. Their participation in the battles during the conquest of Kabylia had already impressed the French. Lapène was the first to draw attention to the status of Kabyle women. They benefited from a particular, mysterious, almost providential esteem which gave them enormous influence both in the family and the tribe, he said, and this was evidenced by the fact in addition to following their men into battle they were exempt from the heaviest labour[49] (the latter assertion would certainly have surprised most Kabyle women). Maffre, who spent 13 years in Bougie before publishing his *La Kabylie*, confirmed the moral authority Kabyle women enjoyed within the tribe.[50] Shortly afterwards, in his *magnum opus* on Kabylia, Daumas declared that not only did Kabyle women have greater freedom than their Arab counterparts, but they were valued more. He went on to contrast Kabyle and Arab women, stating, among other things, that the presence of unattached women in Kabyle society preserved it from the type of unnatural debauch (i.e. sodomy) which was so frequent among the Arabs. Daumas concluded his passage on women by stressing that in addition to their other advantages, Kabyle women could aspire to the same honours as men, as well as the power vested in sainthood.[51]

Once conquest was complete the possibility was occasionally raised that women could play some sort of role in the colonization process. Aucapitaine, who advocated that the Kabyles be used as auxiliaries to the French, saw the role of Kabyle women as positive role models for their Arab counterparts. They could, by the proximity of their living habits, raise Arab women out of the terrible situation in which polygamy had placed them.[52] The position of the Arab woman was seen as abject: at worst she was no better than a beast of burden, at best reduced to domestic intrigue as the sole means of exercising her will on a society in whose iron control she was from puberty to death. Not only did this strike the French as dishonourable but, in terms of French society, it was unnatural, an impediment to social creativity. As the sphere of Arab women was restricted to the tent, they could never, unlike French women, be a formative force in the development of society and civilization.[53] Some, like Richard, suggested that this had a deplorable moral effect on the women themselves.[54] The degree to which Arabs were condemned and Kabyles lauded for their treat-ment of women was, of course, subjective and therefore varied con-siderably.[55] The common thread was that women received more consideration in Kabyle society. The degree of respect for women was, in effect, an indication of the regard in which the family unit was held and, as a microcosm of society, of society as the French knew it.

Even when the distinction between Kabyle and Arab women was blurred, the esteem conferred on them by their respective societies was seen to be greater among the Kabyles than among the Arabs. In one of those articles synthesizing prevailing ideas on Algeria that appeared from time to time in the *Revue des Deux Mondes* this was explicated in some detail. While the position of the Kabyle woman was stressed, it was concluded that the morality of women was none the less much greater in Kabylia than in Arab territory.[56] The heroic and moral images which appeared in such journals were essential in bolstering nascent racial stereotypes. Indirectly, they also furthered the notion that the Kabyles were more inclined than the Arabs to progress towards a civilization along French lines.

Indignation over polygamy and the condition of women was a convenient entry into the moral arena. It never went further than armchair criticism for no affirmative action was taken, it being acknowledged that the family unit was inaccessible to the French. Rather, such indignation was used as a moral stick with which to beat Islam and the Arabs. The fact that on occasion, when convenient, it was also used against the Kabyles merely underlines the nature of the argument. These French attitudes must be considered in a nineteenth-century context, when the lot of many French peasant women was little better in practice than that of Arab women. The French were not examining the sophisticated urban Arabs, but were making their comparison between rural, largely illiterate, populations and the French middle class. It was a totally unjustifiable comparison. In doing so the French were, in fact, seeking out rudiments of French middle-class values to assess the degree to which progress towards them could be assured. As far as the French were concerned the Arabs proved totally lacking, whereas the Kabyles provided considerable scope for improvement.

Considered from a wider viewpoint, French attitudes to polygamy and women were of interest because they fed into a debate on socio-cultural evolution which was beginning to gather strength in Western Europe, in which the relations of the sexes and the question of sexuality were fundamental issues. These criteria, among others, were used to gauge the stage of development of a given society. Marital forms and the position of women were widely discussed, studies were made in non-European societies of polygamy, 'primitive promiscuity' and the treatment of women, and conclusions drawn as to their significance in terms of human development. In 1859 a British missionary, Thomas Williams, published a monograph on Fijian society, where polygamy was normal practice.[57] The monograph raised the tone of discussion on the subject in Great Britain, a discussion which was also in progress on the continent. On the whole polygamy was viewed as a barbarous custom and a social manifestation of primitive promiscuity. Monogamy, on the other hand, was seen to have evolved from a prior promiscuous state and the monogamous family was deemed by many scholars to be the culmination of the social evolutionary process. In a similar vein, the position of women in a society was an indication of, in the words of the British social philosopher Herbert Spencer, its 'moral progress'.[58] How a society treated its women and the respect in which they were held was primordial, for it was women who had control of the social education of children. If women had little respect or, worse, were treated as beasts of burden, not much could be expected of them in their function of schooling future generations which, in the circumstances, could only be morally and socially lacking. Sexuality and the relation of the sexes were thus positional indicators on the ladder of civilization and in this relegating capacity they became important factors in the formation first of social and then of racial categories.

Democracy vs. feudalism

The question of how to govern their newly acquired territories was a pressing one. For a brief period the French left the structures of Turkish rule in place, but as they progressed further into the interior, conquering areas untouched by the Turks, they were obliged to rethink their strategies. Furthermore, the notion of Turkish despotism held little appeal for the French, who preferred to look to Roman imperialism for guidelines. The second decade of French rule saw a spate of works on why and how Algeria should be colonized.[59] Naturally enough, indigenous hierarchical structures came under scrutiny in the effort to pinpoint how they would fit into the scheme of things. Here again Kabyle was opposed to Arab, with a picture emerging that fuelled incipient positive and negative images.

In his *Annales Algériennes* Pellissier de Reynaud had praised the democratic tradition of the Kabyles, stating that there was no government as completely democratic as theirs.[60] He pointed to the fact that Kabyle leaders were elected, and that these elections were held at regular intervals. Pellissier de Reynaud, who owed his information on the Kabyles to the ubiquitous Lamoricière, made no contribution as to the merits or demerits of this tradition, nor did he attempt to compare Kabyle to Arab.[61] With the publication in 1845 of extracts from the *Exposé de l'état actuel de la société arabe*, in the *Revue de L'Orient*, the contrast between Arab and Kabyle social organization was presented to the public for the first time. Here the Arab tribe was compared to a 'commune of the Middle Ages'. It was hierarchical, with a hereditary nobility assuming a vital role in social and political affairs. Arab society was a class-conscious one where the nobility comprised the nobility of birth, the military nobility and the religious nobility.[62] The 'lower classes' were a homogeneous stratum, with no evidence of any division of labour. What was most striking about Arab society was the total lack of proper merchants and artisans. Industry was non-existent in the tribes. While Arabs loved to indulge in petty commerce, they hated getting involved in any type of industrial work. In contrast Kabyle society was a confederation made up of a collection of tribes, each headed by an entirely democratic government. These formed numerous small warring republics, whose regularly elected chiefs had little authority. The aristocracy, so strong among the Arabs, was insignificant in the Kabyle mountains although the *marabouts* did have unlimited power.[63] From these early beginnings the notion of an aristocratic, feudal Arab society and a democratic Kabyle society took flight.

Carette, in his much longer work, had the leisure to be more nuanced about the Kabyles. He detected aristocratic and theocratic elements in Kabyle society. These, he claimed, were the remnants of governmental forms that had been introduced into the area during revolutions occurring in the Middle Ages.[64] He pointed to the decline of hereditary authority in those areas where it had once existed, noting the presence of only a handful of villages with feudal structures, some of which also had traces of democratic forms. For Carette, Kabyle society was essentially democratic, as was their spirit.[65] To the impact of the democratic spirit on Kabyle society, he devoted a complete section.

Daumas's contribution was to popularize an image of Kabylia that likened it to Switzerland: as a federation of tribes similar to the Swiss federation but lacking its permanence.[66] With regard to Arab society, he elaborated on the conclusions of the *Exposé de l'état actuel de la société arabe*, stressing the fact that 'class consciousness was deeply engraved in their minds'.[67] Daumas's works, less specific than Carette's, were more devastating in their conclusions as he used, with a singular disregard for accuracy, the stylistic device of contrast by juxtaposition (Kabyle vs. Arab) to emphasize his points. He dwelt on the Kabyle love of independence, adding that contrary to the usual consequences produced by the Islamic faith, equality, fraternity and Christian compassion were intrinsic to many Kabyle customs.[68] The social, political and moral differences between Arab and Kabyle, which Daumas was at such pains to highlight, led him to stress an idea that had already gained some credence, namely that the two groups were agreed on only one point: the Kabyle detested the Arab and the Arab detested the Kabyle.[69] How could the democratic, freedom-loving Kabyle be anything but opposed to the hierarchical, feudal Arab?

Henceforward the conception of Kabyle democracy gained stature. In his evaluation of Kabyle society in 1864, Aucapitaine introduced the notion of the power of the people. A 'stormy, defiant, public opinion' kept Kabyle dignitaries in check and determined the way in which their administration exercised its power.[70] Aucapitaine acknowledged the presence of a few 'important families' in Kabyle society, at the same time pointing to the excesses of republicanism. He concluded that they were 'municipalities with elected magistratures, an exact replica of the French communes of the fifth and sixth centuries, dubbed *Respublica* by the historians'.[71] To be sure, Aucapitaine's parallel between Kabyle and Merovingian government, while spiritually linking Kabyles and French, suggested an even earlier governmental form than feudal. That he should have linked the Kabyles to the Franks (literally 'enfranchised men') is interesting, none the less, in view of the ongoing debate in France over French racial origins revolving around the Franks and the Gauls. (François Guizot had reanimated the old debate, which also contained the implications of noble and commoner, in his *Du gouvernement de la France depuis la Restauration et du ministère actuel* (Paris, 1820), by stating that France comprised two nations: the conquering Franks and the conquered

Gauls).[72] It was not, however, the nuances concerning Kabyle society that persisted but the generalizations and the catchwords, and it was these that were picked up when the material was presented to a wider public. In his article, appearing a year later in the *Revue des Deux Mondes*, Bibesco categorically declared: 'that the form of government was simple; it was democracy in its purest form.' His description of the Kabyle commune was couched so strongly in French terms as to imply a parallel between the two. The Kabyle village, he wrote, consisted of a truly independent commune, presided over by an elected leader who was the equivalent a mayor. As for the Kabyle, he was voter, councillor, judge, and active participant in the public domain all rolled into one. In short, it was the egalitarian regime *par excellence*.[73]

The need to compartmentalize every aspect of indigenous life, better to understand it, led to the loose use of adjectives, evocative but inappropriate, which were quickly adopted as totally representative, hence becoming blanket categories. Arab society, more hierarchical than Kabyle, but as we now know no less democratic, thus became *feudal*; the very word rattling pejorative images in the mind.[74] Richard was among the first to elaborate on this concept. He presented Arab society as the inverse of French society and the Arab as the antithesis (*antipode*) of the Frenchman.[75] Having stated that the traditions of the two societies were totally opposed, he then went on to define Arab society as the image of French society during the feudal era which marked the end of the tenth century. Thus it would take the Arabs eight centuries to catch up with the French.[76] The argument is somewhat inconsistent, as such arguments often were, but these inconsistencies should not be interpreted as bad faith on the part of the author, who was no doubt sincere in his beliefs, nor should they be mocked for the dubious scholarship they certainly represent. Rather, they should be seen as an indication of the extent to which the acceptance of history as a single linear progression and, above all, the use of French references to describe indigenous situations led to a total distortion of reality. Such distortions, in turn, contributed to the emergence and amplification of the notion of French superiority and Arab inferiority.

In a later work (1850) Richard developed his initial hypothesis further, stating that the indigenous population was a mixture of *barbarie confuse* (representing those tribes not subjected to French rule) and *féodalité indigène instable* (tribes subjected to French rule). Arab feudalism had to be countered by French feudalism, the latter being further up the ladder of civilization than the former. 'French feudalism was the lynch-pin of the edifice that had to be constructed.'[77] The idea of a ladder of civilization was tied in to the concept of historical evolution as one of progressive social harmony and increased political and scientific development (complexity). Hegel, Condorcet, Saint-Simon and Courtet de l'Isle had all broached aspects of the subject. Later, Gobineau was to tie race to civilization, constructing a hierarchy which effectively eliminated the notion of progress.

Although *feudal* became the convenient catch-all adjective to describe Arab society, generally acknowledged to be hierarchical and class-conscious, it was not used in its correct sense of a social hierarchy with military obligations arising out of a well-defined system of land tenure but in a negative sense of archaic and unjust. Similarly, *democratic*, as used to describe Kabyle society, symbolized French values of equality and a consideration for the claims of all members of the society. The superiority of the latter over the former was also one of political progression in European terms, the advanced European countries, such as France, having cast off feudalism and embraced more democratic forms of government. The Arab political framework was thus considered less advanced than the Kabyle, an indication not only of the Arabs' position in the political chain of being but also of their more 'unenlightened' mentality.

Napoleonic law vs. Islamic law

The question of the legality of the colonial regime in Algeria was invariably by-passed for the French by invoking the civilizing mission with its implications of French superiority, but the problem of the acceptance of the regime by the local population was still a preoccupation. For all the rhetoric, the imposition of French morality was not just a matter of 'civilizing' barbaric practices, it also implied an acceptance of the French legal system; and here the impediment of the Koran loomed large. Just how to substitute the secular Napoleonic Code for Koranic Law and Customary Law left plenty of room for debate.

There were several options. One possibility was to replace completely the existing Muslim system of justice by a French one. Another was to try to reconcile existing legal structures with French ones. A third was to let the two legal traditions function side by side. As it turned out, none was applied to the exclusion of another, as can be seen by the fact that no coherent judicial policy emerged in the early stages of French occupation. Instead, measures were taken and, according to their viability, amended or stopped. Hence an early policy of replacing the Muslim judges (*cadis*) by the wholesale introduction of the Napoleonic Code floundered. None the less, by 1842 French law was being applied to criminal cases. It was, however, civil law that was the most vexatious, meeting, as it did, with recalcitrant resistance to change from the Muslim community and, most important, being inextricable from the question of land tenure. For even a glimmer of understanding from their Muslim subjects, the French had not only to comprehend the intricacies of Islamic law but, having done this, to streamline it in such as way as to dovetail it with French law. The codification of Islamic law was not achieved until 1916 (*Code Morand*); in the interim French reforms were grounded in ignorance.[78]

Although the complexity of Koranic law (*Sharia*) was such as to elicit no systematic analysis, customary law did arouse interest, if only because of the land question. What the French discovered was that the Kabyles had a different customary law from the Arabs. Although the Kabyle customary law varied from tribe to tribe and even from village to village, each *kanoun* (or *quanoun*), as the penal code of the differing tribal or village units was known, had to a considerable degree escaped the dictates of Islam. Before the imposition of the French legal code, Kabyle law was regulated by three sources.[79] The first of these was the Koran, which dictated religious practice and those aspects of civil law for which no tribal regulation existed. This varied considerably, and the extent to which the Koran regulated customary law was seen to be indicative of the measure to which the tribe in question had escaped foreign domination. The second source was the *aâda*, or customary law proper, which was passed down orally from generation to generation. This applied principally to personal status, property and all forms of legal contract. Finally there was the *ârf,* which was the individual tribal or village modification of the *aâda*. Unlike Koranic law, which was of divine revelation and hence immutable, the *aâda* and the *ârf* were decided by general consensus and could thus be altered. Potentially, therefore, both could be manipulated by the French without the disturbance such action would cause in the case of the *Sharia*. The *kanoun*, which became the symbolic term for Kabyle law, was in fact the penal code or system of fines imposed by the tribe or village on transgressors of penal and civil law laid down in the *aâda* and the *ârf.* Some *kanoun* also contained regulations pertaining to civil law that were not sanctioned by fines. Studying the Kabyle *kanouns*, therefore, not only showed up the legal and social differences between the Kabyles and the Arabs but the extent to which a particular Kabyle tribe or village deviated from Koranic law and, by extrapolation, how 'pure' it was. Originally this notion of purity was construed in terms of power, namely as an indication of having never been submitted to foreign domination;

ultimately it was construed in terms of race, that is to say as having largely escaped the effects of miscegenation.

As the period of French occupation lengthened, from cursory observations on criminal justice in Kabylia, such as those made by Lapène, interest in the law of the region inclined more to the *kanoun*. Daumas, in his earliest work on the area, had declared that the Kabyles were alone among Muslim 'nations' to have a legal code of their own which owed nothing to the Koran, having been passed down from time immemorial.[80] A decade later he was suggesting Christian origins for the phenomenon, which he footnoted as deriving from the Greek word for rule.[81] Aucapitaine picked up this notion in an article he wrote for the *Revue Africaine*, adding that analogies to Etruscan and ancient Roman law could also be found. More importantly, he attached a high moral value to the *kanouns*, which accrued to the Kabyles, and contended that because of this the Kabyles would make admirable allies for the French and be among the most fruitful and strongest elements of French Algeria. Aucapitaine added that it would not be difficult to reconcile Kabyle *kanouns* with French law, the latter having numerous articles that accorded perfectly with Berber custom.[82] These ideas made a further appearance in the *Revue des Deux Mondes*, where it was stated that Kabyle custom was the nearest thing to French legislation that could be expected from a primitive people. Above all, when it came to property rights the Kabyles were withdrawn from the Islamic camp and placed alongside the French.[83] Such legal compatibility as there appeared to be gave rise to the impression of potential for a harmonious resolution to the colonizer/colonized situation; a potential the less perspicacious colonialists were eager to exploit.

If on the one hand the security-conscious French manifested the desire for conciliatory solutions to irksome problems, on the other they continued to use Algerian society as a mirror in which to glimpse French images. Thus in 1865 Warnier could claim that Berber institutions, like French ones, had emerged from Roman law and were much closer to the principles of 1789 than those of the aristocratic Arabs.[84] More revealing was the conclusion, drawn from French cogitations on the *kanouns*, which saw the Kabyle as a citizen first and a Muslim second, while seeing the Arab as a Muslim, nothing more. If the French were 'to encourage the worker and citizen' in the Kabyle, 'the Muslim in him would steadily recede'. The Kabyles resembled the French 'in the very aspects that distanced them from the Arabs', so it was possible to conclude that 'he was assimilable and perfectible'.[85] It appeared the impenetrable barriers of Islam could be breached in Kabylia.

Law, like the family and society, provided yet another opportunity to praise the Kabyles at the expense of the Arabs. Although Islamic law was not systematically denigrated as was the condition of Arab women, or Arab society, it was considered to be immutable and too complex, even confusing, to be compatible with French law. While French criminal law was quickly imposed throughout the colony, customary law was reformed gradually. The discovery that the Kabyles had a customary law which, unlike that of the Arabs, was not laid down by Islam allowed for the emergence of notions linking them to a morality whose nature was essentially Christian. On the one hand their unique version of customary law could be assimilated more readily into the French legal system and, on the other, their superior morality linked them to the French in a way the Arabs never would be. In every respect the Kabyle showed more promise than the Arab.

Conclusion

The images of Arab and Kabyle society, formed in the decades of conquest and pacification, proved to be extremely resilient. Thus at the end of the nineteenth century the attack on Arab polygamy as morally untenable was as vigorous as it had been 40 years earlier, as was exposing its noxious impact on women and hence society. As can be seen from the work of Paul Leroy-Beaulieu, colonial theorist and economics professor at the Collège de France, a new rationale was sometimes used (in this case economic), but the metaphors were the same. The monogamous woman was the linchpin of the successful domestic economy prevalent among civilized peoples; without her the soul of the family and the prosperity of the home was absent. The economic stagnation of Arab society was caused by this absence. Likewise, Arab society was still classed as 'feudal', although it was stressed that Arab feudalism was infinitely simpler and more rudimentary than feudalism proper.[86] With regard to the Kabyles, their 'democratic society' and the *kanouns* came in for closer scrutiny in the works first of Hanoteau and later of Masqueray (see below), but these works were exceptional for their methodology rather than their unconventional ideas. The Kabyle was always seen to be inherently closer to the Frenchman.

The resilience of these images had a great deal to do with the patterns of scholarship established during military occupation. The need for security, which was at its height during the years of pacification immediately following conquest, led to an emphasis on rooting out subversive elements and seeking positive points of contact between French and indigenous society which could be exploited as the basis for a harmonious relationship. At every turn the French were confronted with Islam, about which they knew little. Any analysis of the subject in the colony emerged from an intellectual and practical standpoint that hindered an unbiased approach. Natural tendencies to view European civilization as universally superior were exacerbated intellectually by three factors, namely, the received ideas that had first been elaborated during the Middle Ages and had undergone little subsequent modification, the commitment to secularization on the part of an essentially anti-clerical officer corps, and the awareness, on the part of Saint-Simonian officers in particular, of the nascent ideas connecting religion to human development. In the field, the preoccupation with security and reconnaissance determined the types of information that was sought about Islam. This information, informed by intellectual trends from France but conditioned by the special exigencies of a colony in the throes of pacification, became the accepted basis of future scholarship. The underlying questions in any of the works on the indigenous society arose out of the threefold problem, administrative, cultural and ideological, posed by Islam. Whether they were directly articulated or not, these problems were: *Could the French administrative framework be substituted for the existing one?* (and here the crux of the argument rested on the Law); *Did the differences in mores and culture form an insuperable barrier between the French and their subjects?* and *Was secularization possible?* The Kabyles appeared to provide the correct answers to all these questions and they therefore basked in a positive light. The Arabs, on the other hand, appeared recalcitrant in their attachment to forms offering little scope for improvement. The resultant positive and negative attributes, with their concomitant moral overtones, which were attached to Kabyle and Arab served to elevate the Kabyle and marginalize the Arab. They were largely based on a negative evaluation of Islam.

Algeria did much to stimulate an interest in Islam and trigger the rise of Orientalism in France but, for most of the nineteenth century, in the colony itself studies of Islam and Islamic society remained wedded to reconnaissance.[87] Valid though this may have been for colonial purposes, it was hardly relevant to mainstream scholarship. None the less, works emerging out of colonial concerns made a significant contribution to the evolution of ideas on Islam in France.

4

The 'Royaume Arabe' (1860–1870)

The decade of the 1860s has been dubbed the period of the *Royaume Arabe* in commemoration of the Arabophile policies of Napoleon III instigated during this period. Until his first visit to Algeria in September 1860, Napoleon III had manifested little interest in the colony. Thereupon his somewhat ambiguous aims were set out in two 'letters' appearing in 1861 and 1865. On the one hand he declared that Algeria should be an 'Arab kingdom' rather than a colony, in which the practices and religion of the Arabs (and Kabyles, for he made no distinction between the two) were respected, thus suggesting that the French role was one of administration rather than colonial exploitation. On the other hand he countered any inherent suggestion of cultural autonomy by stating the need to live amongst the Arabs in order to 'mould them to our laws, accustom them to our domination and convince them of our superiority'. It was necessary to reconcile the settlers and the Arabs so that the former could serve as guides and initiate the latter to French law, morality and justice as well as teach them to exploit the natural riches of their country through commerce and an extensive public works programme. A skilful colonial policy was the soundest way of furthering French commercial interests.[1] Napoleon III was undoubtedly influenced by the ideas of the Saint-Simonians, especially those in the colony, some of whom, like Ismaël Urbain, became personal advisers. Tolerance tempered by strong paternalism, the belief in a strong power (or individual) acting as a moral guide and civilizing mentor to a weak one, and the emphasis on encouraging commerce and public works were all characteristics of Saint-Simonian thought. For all their utopian vision, and however much the colony seemed an ideal setting for putting such a vision into practice, their aims were a contradiction in terms of the colonial situation. For the civilian settler, whose prime motivation in settling in relatively inhospitable surroundings was to further his own economic interests, it was impossible to put the interests of the indigenous population, economic or otherwise, ahead of his own. Although the military, whose essential motivation was not economic, was better qualified to implement such policies, and the institution of the Bureaux Arabes thus came to stand for Napoleon III's policies and its officers became their perpetrators, the notion of guiding the Arabs into the path of French civilization counteracted any potential or actual tendency to encourage cultural autonomy.

It was a paradoxical decade, in which policies instigated for the benefit of the indigenous population turned out in the end to be harmful to them.[2] Practically this was most evident in the major land law passed at that time, the Sénatus-Consulte of 1863. This law, which was designed to clarify land tenure and thus benefit the indigenous population by providing them with the necessary legal rights to hang on to their land, had the reverse effect in that it facilitated land expropriation by providing the settlers, better versed in French law than the indigenous population, with a lever to prise the Arabs away from their land. Morally it was evidenced by an increase in racial tensions. This was the result of the intellectual climate created by an acrimonious battle between *arabophiles* and *arabophobes* becoming enshrined, along the way, in a power struggle between military and civilian rule. As pressure to oust the military administration increased, the civilians, who had settler interests at heart, lumped all the military personnel together and collectively labelled them *arabophiles*, in this way suggesting that to be so was to be anti-settler. Although the two camps were the symbols of the debate, arabophilia or arabophobia did not run along clear-cut military/civilian lines. Nor, as its name might suggest, did arabophilia signify pitting the Arab sections of the population against the non-Arab sections. Rather *arabophile* was the term loosely applied to those who believed that France had a lasting commitment to the indigenous population, Arab and Berber, to ameliorate their lot and involve them comprehensively in the process of colonization. By the end of the decade, in certain circles, it had acquired the connotations of a term of abuse. The *arabophobes*, on the other hand, were those who opposed Napoleon III's *Royaume Arabe* and, in general, did not admit to any meaningful political or social role for the indigenous population. The most extreme amongst them, such as Bodichon, advocated 'extermination'; the more moderate a subservient position to the European in perpetuity. In the intellectual mêlée neither side lost sight of the distinctions between Arab and Kabyle. To be sure, the more virulent *arabophobes* dismissed both Arabs and Kabyles as unworthy of consideration, but others championed the Kabyles at the expense of the Arabs. While the *arabophiles* were intent on promoting indigenous society it was often openly acknowledged that the Kabyles were in a position to make much faster progress than the Arabs. Both camps therefore fuelled the stereotypical images that were to crystallize into the Kabyle Myth.

In France the most significant consequence of the political and intellectual ferment that arose out of the clash over Napoleon III's policies was a heightened awareness of Algeria and its inhabitants. As Algeria captured the French imagination, French culture looked eastwards for stimulation. Flaubert, de Nerval, Daudet, Fromentin, Delacroix and later Loti are only a few of those who flirted with the Oriental muse. The attraction for the exotic was felt well beyond literary and artistic circles, however. The decade opened with the establishment of the Société d'Anthropologie de Paris and closed with the foundation of the Ecole des Langues Orientales. In between the groundwork for modern French Orientalism was laid, and new avenues for racial debate were opened. These developments were to impinge directly on the evolution of ideas concerning the Kabyles and the Arabs.

In Algeria, the decade witnessed an acceleration of the dissolution of traditional Arab society resulting in a pauperization exacerbated by cholera, locusts and famine and culminating in the crisis of 1867–69. The period was punctuated by indigenous protest in the form of forest fires and uprisings. Land was the central issue and its seizure the principal reason for the Arab tragedy. Kabylia, on the other hand, was largely unaffected. Final subjugation having been completed only in 1857, existing structures remained more or less intact. An administrative penetration of the area continued, but Kabylia rode out the Crisis of 1867–69 and was spared major land sequestration until 1871. These factors were also to have a bearing on attitudes towards Kabyles and Arabs.

Paradoxically, therefore, it was during the period of Napoleon III's *Royaume Arabe* that the image of the Arab took its greatest battering in Algeria; a battering from which it never recovered. Although studies of Kabylia and the Kabyles continued to appear, the accentuation of the negative Arab image did as much to enhance the Kabyle Myth as any new material from these studies. The denigration of the Arab occurred on two levels. The first was a direct attack by means of polemical literature in the context of the *arabophile/arabophobe* conflict. The second was more subtle, occurring as a result of colonial policies that proved detrimental to Arab society. Ironically, into this second category falls the work of the Bureaux Arabes, the officers of which were regarded, often quite rightly, as the champions of the indigenous population.

Resistance and reaction

The Bureaux Arabes

The Bureaux Arabes were military administrative units set up as a link between the French central government and indigenous leaders.[3] In the years immediately following the conquest Arab affairs had been the responsibility of a single individual, the Agha of the Arabs. Originally these aghas were chosen from amongst local dignitaries, but this system proved unsatisfactory to the French and they were replaced by a number of officers. La Moricière, one of the only Arabists at that time, was placed in charge. In 1837 the office of the Aghas was abolished and three years later a Directorate of Arab Affairs was established, headed by Daumas. It was only in 1844 that the Bureaux Arabes acquired their definitive form when a ministerial order officially setting out their organization and objectives was drawn up. Accordingly, each Bureau administered a limited geographical area, or *cercle*. A number of *cercles* were grouped together into sub-divisions, which were in turn grouped into divisions. The Bureaux were in the charge of an army officer, who headed a team of varying size depending on the Bureau's geographical importance. In addition to the Bureau chief, some Bureaux had one or more subordinate French officers; others had non-commissioned indigenous military personnel only. Medical officers and interpreters also formed part of the Bureaux in certain areas. Bureaux chiefs were only accountable to the *commandant supérieur* of the *cercle*, usually a colonel, but the latter was essentially concerned with military matters so tribal administration was left wholly to the Bureaux Arabes.[4] This included judicial proceedings, taxation, selection of candidates for official positions, drawing up statistical records and writing regular reports on the political, social and economic situation of the tribes being administered. Policies were evolved by officers out of past experience within the *cercle* rather than emanating from Paris in the form of directives.[5] Indigenous policy, therefore, bore the imprint of the Bureaux Arabes officers.

Career officers in the French army who did not rise through the ranks were graduates of one of four schools: the Ecole Polytechnique, St. Cyr, Saumur and the Ecole d'Application de Metz. In Algeria the overall percentage of such graduates was high; among the officers of the Bureaux Arabes the figure was proportionately higher still.[6] These officers, *arabophiles* par excellence as the civilians would have it, would have been conversant with the ideas of Saint-Simon and his disciples having either graduated from the Ecole Polytechnique or the Ecole de Metz, both centres of Saint-Simonian thought, or having been in close contact with those that had. Some were in fact self-professed Saint-Simonians with a mission to implement their belief in the civilizing effects of commerce, the doctrine of *doux commerce,* and their faith in benevolent paternalism. Freedom, to the Saint-Simonians, was the ability to develop one's potential within a framework of social guidance.[7] It was a notion easily applicable to the colonial situation. The progressive ideas of the officers of the Bureaux Arabes differentiated them from their colleagues. As one of their number stated with hindsight, 'they were nearly all motivated by a very liberal spirit.'[8] With regard to local administration, this 'liberalism' translated into a desire to find the least abrasive method of keeping the indigenous population pacified. Security was to be achieved by means of a radical transformation of the indigenous lifesyle, namely anchoring the nomadic tribes to the soil; it was a concept dear to Enfantin. For the more idealistic officers, such as Azéma de Montgravier, who served in the Oran Bureau and produced several archeological and historical studies, this process was a part of France's civilizing mission.[9] For the more pragmatic, improving the indigenous lifestyle was a way of diluting hostility. The role of the Bureaux Arabes was as 'interpreter of the conquering nation's thought and institutions'.[10] As time progressed the officers of the Bureaux Arabes saw themselves as the 'link (*trait d'union*) between the European race and the native'.[11] (It was this attitude that caused so much hostility on the part of the European settlers.)

The extent to which the doctrine of the Bureaux Arabes was put into effect depended on the inclinations of the commanding officers of the individual bureaux. None the less, in the period up to 1858 a concerted attempt was made to sedentarize the nomadic population through the construction of houses and public utilities, such as fountains, wells, public baths and markets (but not mosques or Koranic schools), and the development of a more sophisticated agrarian economy through the introduction of new crops and agricultural methods.[12] By the mid-1860s it was obvious that the Bureaux Arabes had achieved only limited results in their endeavours. Overall security was achieved. The lid was kept on large-scale revolt until 1864 and a unified uprising was prevented, but this was a result not of increased well-being due to sedentarization and a better agrarian economy, but rather to the inevitable social dislocation such policies engendered and the resultant reduction of possibilities for political mobilization.[13] Richard, one of the most prolific authors of the Bureaux Arabes, relied on architectural metaphors in *De la civilisation du peuple arabe* to get across his message of France's mission in Algeria and that attempted by the Bureaux Arabes. He divided his work into two sections entitled 'The Hammer' and 'The Trowel' and used a quotation from the Roman architect, Vitruvius, to sum up its contents: 'to build on ruins it is first necessary to demolish ... having demolished it is then possible to build.'[14] Unfortunately, 'having demolished' the old structures the new proved somewhat lacking and Arab society bore the brunt of this shortfall.

Yacono attributes the failure of the Bureaux Arabes programme essentially to insufficient financing; Perkins to the fact only a few of the officers had the agricultural expertise necessary for the successful implementation of their programme.[15] Both factors undoubtedly contributed, but resistance to French methods was equally important. The Arabs did not want the buildings the French foisted on them nor indeed Western 'well-being', for which they had little understanding. On the whole, the Arabs reacted to the Bureaux Arabes techniques passively, adopting refractory behavioural patterns, as the regular references to Arab indolence and resistance to the civilizing mission testify. For many of the officers the Arab character had numerous redeeming features (and the length of the list was proportional to the officer's benevolence). Similarly the quantity of 'faults' was subjective. One cannot help but be struck by the regularity with which certain of these 'faults' appeared in reports and published works alike, eliciting universal condemnation. In the words of Captain Ferdinand Hugonnet, whose *Souvenirs* claimed to attempt a balanced view of the Arabs by stressing their qualities rather than their faults, these were: 'laziness ... an aversion for all progress towards our civilization ... lying and deceit'.[16] If one reflects on these 'faults', which through frequency of use in written texts were eventually accepted as traits endemic to the Arab character, it is strikingly evident that they are all characteristics of reluctance stretched to its limits. If indeed they did on occasion characterize Arab behaviour towards the French, it is a measure of the extent of Arab resistance to French rule. In their assessment of Arab behaviour the only allowances the officers made for possible resentment of French rule was an acceptance of the eventuality of revolt. Passive resistance to the imposition of French culture and rule was never considered, hence behavioural patterns that are indicative of this type of resistance were merely written off as inherently Arab defects.

The situation presented by Kabylia was different. In the first place, subjugation of the area was completed at a time when the institution of the Bureaux Arabes in Algeria was well established. Results in the Tell had fallen short of expectations, idealism was on the wane among officers and innovative public works projects were less enthusiastically undertaken. Second, the methods employed by the Bureaux Arabes for the Arab tribes were not applicable: the Kabyles were already 'anchored to the soil'. In 1850, the commanding officer of the Bougie *cercle* stated that it was unnecessary to oblige the Kabyles to build, as they all resided in houses.[17] Similarly, among the Kabyle tribes settled in the Cherchell *cercle* established in 1842 within the Algiers Division, new construction was deemed superfluous because of the existence of stone houses and well-developed orchards.[18] The Kabyle economy, however primitive it might be, elicited approval from French officers who were impressed by Kabyle industriousness.[19] As early as 1841, General Duvivier had drawn attention to this and its implication for French rule by stating that Kabyle sedentariness, and the love of work which was an attribute of their race, could make them the sturdiest pivot of a policy for settling the French in Africa in an orderly, successful and stable fashion.[20] Their agrarian lifestyle had already given rise, on numerous occasions, to comparisons with the French peasant. These agrarian resemblances were not picked up by officers of the Bureaux Arabes, who were more inclined to discuss such similarities as existed between the French commune and Kabyle municipal organization.[21] In fact, whether the comparisons were agrarian or administrative is irrelevant; both were made in an attempt to illustrate Kabyle 'perfectibility'.[22] Be it in the field or from a distance, the idea of potential for progressive change inherent in Kabyle society was a strong one.

The dictates of security and the civilizing mission were modified to accommodate the circumstances in Kabylia. During the 1860s progress signified ameliorating existing structures, not radically changing them. Security did not mean sedentarization but ensuring that the 'fiercely independent' Kabyles were kept happy by maintaining the status quo as far as security allowed. Inculcating ideas of well-being through the imposition of a *Pax Gallica* was the preferred method among Bureaux Arabes officers of drawing the Kabyle population into the French fold.[23] They were accepted as being protesters (*reclameurs*) by nature and attention was paid to their grievances.[24] Officers in the newly pacified area were more concerned with the legal and administrative side of their task than with public works and agriculture. Preoccupations centred around Kabyle reaction to any legal and political structures that were to be imposed on them. This involved taking a stand on Kabyle *kanoun* and the question of the village *djemâa* (council of elected elders arbitrating in matters of customary law).

After the conquest of Greater Kabylia in 1857, in the interests of security, Field Marshal Randon had requested and obtained permission from the Ministry of War to allow the Kabyles, in this newly pacified area, to preserve their traditional administrative structure.

The Kabyles kept their *kanoun* and continued to elect members to their *djemâa*. In the *cercles* which administered both Arab and Kabyle tribes, the Arab tribes had their own administration with *caïds* and *cadis* and the Kabyles theirs, with the institution of the elected *djemâa* and their dignitaries, the *amins el oumena* and *amins*.[25] Those *cercles* which had no Arab tribes in their jurisdiction had no *cadis*.[26] In *cercles* where Kabyle tribes had come under French rule prior to 1857 and where the French had nominated Muslim judges or *cadis*, the *djemâa* was allowed to take precedence over the *cadis* in civil matters.

Those changes that were introduced in Kabylia were done so in the name of progress or security. Thus attempts were made to eliminate aspects of the *kanoun* considered to be retrograde and introduce new social ideas.[27] Nonetheless the *kanoun*, or *Code Kabyle* as it was some-times called, was considered to be the only viable code for the area and was seen as evidence of a different and more advanced civilization than that of the Arabs.[28] As for the *djemâa*, the main grievance was the disturbance caused by the annual elections of members.[29] Officers sought to circumvent the problem by introducing tri-annual elections and by using their influence to purge the *djemâa* of 'subversive' mem-bers. Some, who felt too much judicial power was concentrated into the village *djemâa*, suggested a three-tier system to dissipate their powers.[30] Resistance to such measures was deemed to be minimal. As the end of the decade approached it was estimated that the ferocity with which the Kabyle defended his independence had given way to an avid desire for peace and tranquillity.[31] Such delusions left the French unprepared for the amplitude of the 1871 Kabyle insurrection, on the eve of which it was still possible for an officer to claim that the Kabyle 'submits willingly and of his own accord to our authority, and is less rebellious than the Arab in adopting our ideas of civilization and progress'. Wherever the French and the Kabyles were in contact the former noticed remarkable improvements in the latter, 'as much in the transformation of ideas and morals as in the partial adoption of our methods of agriculture and perfected tools'.[32]

Kabyle resistance never needed to be passive. Kabyle society was not disrupted in the way Arab society was, and when the Kabyles took more readily to French agricultural methods it was because they were well served by them. Acceptance of agricultural innovations varied from area to area: some tribes took to the French plough, the French scythe and the use of natural fertilizers, others did not; vines were a success in Drâ-el-Mizan, but not elsewhere. Cotton was a general failure. Ameliorations in arboricultural techniques, such as the grafting of olive trees, were more readily accepted. The only innovation universally adopted was the cultivation of the potato.

The Kabyles were in a better position to mobilize when the time came than the Arabs, as the 1871 insurrection demonstrated. Kabyle resentment had no need to manifest itself by means of sullen hostility. It could be and eventually was channelled, erupting in a full-scale revolt. Not only did the French overlook the build-up of this resentment, but the lack of significant passive resistance meant that behavioural patterns continued to appear normal and therefore called forth little criticism.[33] The Kabyle was not 'devious', because he did not need to be: he voiced his dissent and was heard. He 'accepted progress' when it suited him to do so. He was seen to be perfectible and therefore presumed progressive.[34] He survived the tribulations of the 1860s because his society had not been ripped apart, as yet. For these circumstantial reasons he was held to be superior to the Arab. It was a superiority that encompassed his intellect, his morality and his politics. It was a superiority that created irreconcilable differences with the Arab, who did not share his aspirations and whom he 'profoundly detested'.[35]

The role of the officers of the Bureaux Arabes in the propagation of the Kabyle Myth was, with few notable exceptions, a passive one. This did not make it any less significant; quite the contrary. Their indirect contribution was considerable. The very fact that they advocated and encouraged the maintenance of a different administrative system in Kabylia fuelled the notion of radical difference between Arab and Kabyle that had already taken hold. In their *cercle* reports, some officers actually did compare the Kabyles to the Arabs, favouring the former in each case. For example, the Kabyles were seen to be more receptive to French medical ministrations than the Arabs.[36] Their agricultural produce was seen to be more varied than those of the Arabs and their use of agricultural land more intelligent.[37] Agriculture was considered to be more advanced in Kabylia than in the rest of Algeria and the degree of perfection achieved by the Kabyle in spite of primitive tools was a source of surprise.[38] Kabyle industry, too, was more satisfactory than Arab industry and showed promise of rapid amelioration.[39] Of course, there was also the difference in customary law. No analysis or explanation was ever proffered regarding such disparities. These observations, however casual or well-intentioned they might have been, merely served to enforce the idea of Kabyle superiority.

The *cercle* reports were a source of information for other officers and for the administration in general. For those who did not have access to these documents but were in need of information concerning indigenous affairs and in particular Arabs and Kabyles, there was always the possibility of personal exchanges with the Bureaux officers themselves. Many of these officers used knowledge gained in the field to establish links with scholarly societies and publish in their journals. Then too there was their personal correspondence to recipients both in France and in Algeria. In the nineteenth century letters, it will be remembered, were discussed and even passed around. In this way ideas were propagated. In their reinterpretation and re-presentation distortions occurred; such distortions could only increase the mythological proportions of the lore on the Kabyles.

The land question and the crisis of 1867–69

Property encroachment by the French started with the 1844 Land Law. Uncultivated land within specified areas was classified as vacant unless valid title deeds were provided to prove ownership. As most of this land was collective property and title deeds were not always available, the French authorities had ample room to manoeuvre. Furthermore all purchases made by Europeans were declared valid *ex post facto,* which eliminated possibilities of redress on the part of the Arabs.[40] A second major law in 1851 provided the French with even more leeway and the squeeze on Arab property was intensified.

Ironically, it was the 1860s which marked the beginning of major land sequestration in the colony.[41] Legal foundations were laid that would turn existing land tenure and property rights inside out. The Sénatus-Consulte of 22nd April 1863, with its articles establishing the *Douâr-Communes,* commenced the process of imposing French land tenure structures, sometimes dubbed the *kabilization* of Arab property, namely the conversion of collective property into individual holdings.[42] In fact it was a misnomer, for *melk,* which constituted the bulk of Kabyle property, although designated private property was not bought and sold as an exchange commodity and any change of ownership was regulated by restrictions.[43] None the less the notion that Arab property was being *kabylized* is significant. It is an example of the effect of category formation and its assimilation into colonial terminology. Furthermore, a popular misconstruction was that Kabyle tenure resembled the French. Henri Verne, author of several books on Algeria, wrote that 'in Kabylia individual property was constituted in the same way as in France, in accordance with laws that appeared to have been borrowed from the Romans'.[44] Verne, was in fact quoting a report written by the Count of Casabianca concerning the Sénatus-Consulte, but he thus popularized a simile that had been used on more than one occasion to clarify the implications of the new Land Laws. The similarity was also stressed by Dr Warnier, who was instrumental in promulgating the 1873 Land Law bearing his name, the Loi-Warnier, which took the institution of individual property tenure even further than the Sénatus-Consulte. The Kabyle tribes, Warnier declared, did not need a Sénatus-Consulte at all. Nor did they need commissions to mark out and attribute property, for land continued to be managed as it had been in Roman times and as it was in France. All that was necessary was to send surveyors to carry out a cadastral survey and compile an inventory of private property. Once this had been done property tax could be applied without delay or difficulty in Berber areas.[45]

Warnier contrasted the ease with which the concept of individual property could be absorbed in Kabylia with the difficulties that would be encountered in Arab territories, and concluded that the essential quality that set the Arab apart from the Berber was the 'non-individuality' of tribal members. Warnier footnoted his statement, adding a 'few' of the numerous other distinctions between Berbers and Arabs and stressing that these were mainly of a moral order.[46] The introduction of morality to the argument was a potent way of emphasizing worth, especially where institutions were concerned. By favourably comparing French and Kabyle institutions, linking them morally, and then contrasting them to Arab ones, not only were the contenders of these ideas adding to the myth of Kabyle superiority over the Arab and in the process re-informing their categorization, they were also providing a moral justification for the imposition of French institutions in the place of existing ones.

Through the creation of local administrative units, the *douar-communes*, the Sénatus-Consulte took the differentiation of Arab and Kabyle a step further. The division of tribal (*ârch*) and state-bestowed (*makhzen*) lands into easily administered units was to be applied throughout Algeria with the exception of Greater Kabylia, where Randon had undertaken to leave the existing organization intact.[47] In Kabylia the *douar-communes* were nearly always established respecting tribal boundaries; elsewhere boundaries were completely redefined.[48] The 1863 Sénatus-Consulte, by enabling the division and commercialization of *ârch* lands, struck at the foundations of tribal structure.[49] Not only was the first step taken to legalize the dispossession of tribal lands but the new boundaries split up Arab tribes. Furthermore, *djemâas* were to be set up in each *douar-commune* following elections organized by land commissions. In Kabyle areas this did not constitute a radical change in established patterns; in Arab tribes it involved a direct attack on the hierarchical structure of tribal life.[50] Thus during this period Kabyle society retained its identity; Arab society disintegrated.

When, in Kabylia, the clauses of the Sénatus-Consulte were applied, the *cercle* reports suggest that certain officers tried to cushion the Kabyles from possible ill effects. Some did express confidence that the Kabyles would have few problems coming to terms with the new system and would pose no difficulties to the authorities.[51] Others were less sanguine. It seemed to be preferable to wait a few years before penetrating Kabylia; to concentrate on the areas of the Tell rather than Kabylia where they would certainly not be opposed but where their work would be less useful.[52] As the end of the decade approached the Kabyles, as yet, had been spared the major disruptions of the colonial land policies.[53]

This relative stability allowed the Kabyles to weather the economic crises of a decade which brought locusts, cholera, poor harvests and famine on an unprecedented scale. The crisis of 1867–69, the climax of these disasters, was the final blow to rural Arab society, whose dislocation was to provide the *colons*, particularly in the Mitidja, with the labour, hitherto lacking, to enable European agriculture to flourish.[54] The Kabyles, as if to rebut the French conviction of Arab–Kabyle animosity, succoured the starving Arabs giving, in the sub-division of Dellys at least, 'a brilliant demonstration of their charity'. What appeared even more remarkable, notched up as 'a point in favour of Kabyle institutions', was that no disorder was caused by the pro-longed presence in Kabylia of 'so many totally bereft strangers'.[55]

The pauperization that followed these natural and administratively induced catastrophes for the Arabs, who were now stretched to the limits of their tolerance, led them to adopt more extreme patterns of refractory behaviour than had previously been the case. Criminal acts increased: forest fires, theft and even assault were perpetrated against a regime which had held the promise of reconciliation but had failed to deliver the goods.[56] In 1868 the 600 colons of Médéa were robbed on average four times each; annual losses through theft rose to half a million francs.[57] In response the *colon* press rounded on the Arabs. An article appearing in the newspaper of the province of Oran, *L'Avenir Algérien*, in March 1868 'exposed' the thefts, and seized the op-portunity to attack the army for 'defending the Arabs who were systematically robbing the *colons*'.[58] Articles of this nature became a staple of the *colon* press, which jeeringly referred to '*MM les Arabes*' when denouncing 'yet another' criminal offence.[59] The Arabs were even accused of cannibalism, an accusation which found its way into the metropolitan press.[60] The stridency of the *colon* press, which stripped the Arab character of all claims to morality, found no echo among the officers of the Bureaux Arabes. None the less, some officers harboured the conviction that Arab agricultural incompetence con-tributed to their inability to cope with the economic crisis.[61]

The tragedy of the Arab was manifold. Not only had he been dispossessed and his traditional rural society disrupted, but he was deprived of all hope of acceptability into the new society that was forming around him. Unlike the Kabyle, who suffered inconvenience but little dislocation, his only recourse, until new societal forms evolved, was to sink into apathy or indulge in criminal acts to alleviate his grievances; thus he could only perpetrate the stereotypes that had been formulated about him. To extricate him from this unfavourable position would require more effort and time than his supporters could possibly provide.

Ismaël Urbain and the voices of reason

From Algeria's inception as a colony, voices of moderation tried to warn against the excesses inherent in colonial practice. Such was the case of Pellissier de Reynaud, who had attempted to dispel his compatriots' prejudices regarding Islam and elicited criticism as a result. The paternalism which most of these voices expressed strove, at its best, to treat the indigenous population with as much justice and benevolence as the situation allowed. As the colony evolved so too did the tenor of these voices. Instead of merely warning, they questioned the anomalies and injustices in the colony in the vain hope of redressing the situation. Among the most influential of these was that of Ismaël Urbain. Urbain, who was largely responsible for the *arabophile* policies of Napoleon III, was an Arabist and leading interpreter in the colony. He was a Saint-Simonian who had at one time been secretary to Gustave d'Eichthal, with whom he had written an exchange on the significance of race.[62] Following voyages to Egypt and the Near East he converted to Islam. His considerable intelligence and knowledge of Islam led to his participation in the Algerian administration at a high level: he became a member of the advisory council attached to the governor-general and was involved in most of the major decisions taken concerning Algeria.[63] He was also a prodigious letter-writer, corresponding with many of the leading political, military and cultural personalities in Algeria at the time.[64]

Urbain first took up his pen in defence of Islam and the Arabs in the colony in 1847.[65] In a letter of response to an article on the struggle between Christianity and Islam, Urbain lamented the historical inaccuracies of the article and the misrepresentation of Islam. He went on to signal the dangers arising out of such attitudes, and stressed the danger, when two people lived in close contact, of trying to determine which was superior.[66] Similarly, he warned against the direction France's civilizing mission was taking. Although an examination of the moral and political situation of the tribes showed that much improvement was necessary, 'what the Arabs certainly did not want was the refined vices of French civilization.' What they did require was a favourable administrative organization to enable them to develop their agriculture and commerce, an organization of their religion and their judicial system and a network of schools.[67] Urbain emphasized the error of introducing radical changes where they were not absolutely necessary or where there was no organizational void to accommodate them.

Urbain's desire to set the picture straight as far as the Arabs were concerned could not fail to encompass the question of the Kabyles. In 1857 his only article on the Kabyles appeared in the *Revue de Paris* with the opening words: 'From the first years that followed the conquest of Algeria by France, the Kabyles were accorded a special place among the population of the country.'[68] Urbain argued that this should not have been so, concluding that the Kabyles of the Djurdjura mountains were neither a separate race nor a separate people. He paid tribute to Carette and Daumas and drew attention to the recent translation (1852) by the Baron de Slane of Ibn Khaldun's fourteenth-century treatise on the Berbers. Concerning contemporary works on Kabylia he pointed out that authors were especially inclined to gather details of Kabyle customs for their curiosity value and their picturesque quality, and then compare them to the Arabs. As the notions of history and ethnography of the indigenous Algerians were very sketchy at the time of publication of these works, regrettable confusions and errors emerged.[69] Urbain denied the racial dichotomy between the peoples of the mountains and those of the plains and rejected the hypothesis of Christian antecedents to the Kabyles. Urbain admitted having no access to the considerable information collected by the Bureaux Arabes on Kabylia, stating that his opinions had been formed after careful perusal of published documents on Algeria and ancient and modern works dealing with such matters.[70] As for the word Kabylia, it was, he rightly pointed out, a French invention, Kabyles being present in other areas of Algeria. A product of the French systemizing mind, it was used by neither the Arabs nor the Berbers.[71] Urbain wrote his article without ever having visited Kabylia. Five years later, in a letter to his friend Frédéric Lacroix, Director-General of Civil Affairs in Algeria and author of numerous studies on the Mediterranean basin, in which he also picked up his attack on anti-Islamic tendencies, he expressed his desire to visit Hanoteau in Kabylia, no doubt to be able to vindicate his beliefs. He poured scorn on de Neveu's bolstering of the Kabyles at the expense of the Arabs and criticzed his 'hatred' of Muslims and the Koran. Too many people were inclined to see Romans and Christians in the Kabyles when all they should be doing was what Carette had attempted, namely to study the Berber race.[72] A few months later, however, while lamenting the formation of a pro-Kabyle clique in Algiers, he was less charitable about Carette's work, stating that from it originated the belief that the Kabyles could be more easily civilized than the Arabs and that the Kanouns were worth more than the Koran. It was necessary to combat such trends, which would only work against the civilizing mission.[73] Shortly afterwards Urbain met Hanoteau, who had received the Prix Volnay in 1860 from the Académie des Inscriptions for his work on the Berber and Tuareg languages. The meeting appears to have confirmed, in Urbain's mind, the travesty of the growing canon of thought on the Kabyles for he informed Lacroix that 'an imaginative novel had been created about Kabylia'.[74]

Urbain's rational approach to the Kabyles and Arabs, and his attacks against anti-Islamic tendencies, found little whole-hearted support in colonial society. Unfortunately his indignation regarding the elevation of the Kabyles to a higher status came too late, if indeed it ever could have made an impact. The publication, using the pseudonym Georges Voisin, of *L'Algérie pour les Algériens* in 1861 and *L'Algérie française: indigènes et immigrants* in 1862, in which his ideas on Islam and the indigenous populations were amplified, set off an uproar in the colony, polarizing opinion on indigenous and colonial policy between the *arabophiles* and the *arabophobes*.[75] Urbain attacked the notion of a republican democracy in Kabylia; he declared that Islam, like Christianity, was a religion of equality; and he asserted that Muslim Algerians could be assimilated into French civilization. He also supported the army in Algeria, which had been the instigator of a civilizing mission whose results were satisfactory enough to warrant the continuation of army rule, both in the interests of the local population and of France.[76] Feelings about his two brochures rose so high that their rational content was completely overshadowed by the controversy surrounding them.

In many ways, Urbain's was a singular voice. He was awakened to the prejudices of European society early, being the illegitimate son of a Frenchman and a mulatto woman. His intelligence and erudition allowed him to channel any resentment he might have felt into a crusade on behalf of all those who suffered racial opprobrium at the hands of others.[77] The pro-Arab inclinations of other *arabophiles* were tempered by their overriding allegiance to French civilization and culture. One of Urbain's closest friends and a leader in the *arabophile* camp, Dr Auguste Vital, who practised in Constantine for most of his career, expressed his reservations. Although he admitted sharing some of Urbain's ideas regarding the indigenous population and was, like Urbain, convinced that nothing could or should be done about the Islamic religion, he went further, for he believed equally strongly that there was no hope of a rapprochement or a fusion. 'It is not only their profoundly and actively hostile religion that separates them from us, it is their inferior morality.'[78]

The strong paternalism of the age militated against a bias-free attitude towards the Arabs. This is at the root of the paradoxical nature of a decade which appeared to take away with one hand what it gave with the other. *Arabophiles* could and did regret the unfortunate situation of the Arabs and many genuinely strove to improve existing conditions but, sufficiently distanced from them by their paternalism, they could also adopt uncompromising attitudes that were in no way pro-Arab. Furthermore, the military *arabophiles* were always constricted by the dictates of security. Hence staunch *arabophiles* like Desvaux, Yusuf, Lapasset and Margueritte were pitiless in their repression following the 1864–66 revolt.[79] Indeed, Lapasset was promoted to the rank of general as a result of his crushing the Flitta tribe during the revolt and preventing an uprising among the Dahra. As long as the pro-Arab stance was subordinated to the demands of the French state, be they cultural, social, political or in the greater context of French culture as the vehicle for civilization, there was no possibility of pro-Arab arguments, however rational, leading to cultural pluralism. It was a dilemma that could only lead to disillusion on both sides. It pushed the most sensitive elements among the *arabophiles* to learn the local idiom, to steep themselves in local culture, and in some cases to take indigenous wives, in an endeavour to mitigate, consciously or unconsciously, the pressures created by a situation in which their humanitarian instincts were overshadowed by their commitment to French colonization. The situation could never be clearcut and numerous authors were sufficiently aware of its complications to stress, in their introductions, that theirs was a quest for 'the truth'.

Anonymity was an easier way to launch a broadside against injustice, but anonymity was not sacrosanct, as Urbain found out to his cost. None the less anonymous works appeared throughout the colonial period, often in response to a particular issue. Hence in a pro-Bureaux Arabes work devoted to the causes of the crisis of 1864–66, the author reminded his readers that 'those Arabs who are today labelled cannibals, often lent a willing hand in settling in our *colons*.'[80] He went on to explain that the areas in which the Arab had suffered most were those in which the Europeans had already taken over the most fertile, well-irrigated lands which yielded a good variety of crops. Kabylia had resisted best because the Kabyles still retained all their lands.

History had shown that the Arabs had had great moments in their civilization. Their fanaticism, the author believed, was greatly exaggerated and he had faith in their perfectibility. However, he stressed that in the Ladder of Being, the Arab was a child and the Frenchman his tutor, who thus had to take charge of Arab interests until they could manage for themselves.[81] (Racial paternalism of this sort was a characteristic of Saint-Simonian thought and was very much in evidence among the officers serving in the colony.[82]) If the Arab people was dying, the author concluded, it was due not only to the succession of scourges which assailed it, but also to the wearing away and inferiority of its living standards compared to those of the Europeans.[83] The impact of these topical works was limited in that once the issue had blown over or been resolved the resulting commentaries were shelved and usually forgotten.

The Arab was not without his champions. His defenders were, however, too hampered by the circumstances of the colonial situation to be truly effective. Unlike the *kabylophiles*, who were manifestly pro-Kabyle, nearly always to the detriment of the Arab, the pro-Arab element never strove to elevate the Arab over the Kabyle. *Arabophiles* were all pro-*indigènes;* some were markedly pro-Arab; none was anti-Kabyle. Being pro-Arab was often more indicative of an exceptional tolerance of Islam than a particular penchant for the Arab people. These pro-Arab sentiments were neither of the calibre, nor focused enough, to resist the racial myth-making that was beginning to take hold in the colony. Furthermore, in the controversy over the *arabophile* policies of Napoleon III, which crystallized into a power struggle between the military and the civilians, the interests of the local population were submerged. The polarization which occurred, causing 'civilian' to become synonymous with *arabophobe* and 'military' synonymous with *arabophile* (a spurious dichotomy), served to obfuscate genuine pro-Arab arguments which were merely treated as *arabophile* polemics, and subsequently ignored.

The Oriental muse

The question of Orientalism and the way France viewed the Orient was affected by the Algerian experience and in turn affected attitudes in Algeria. Edward Said has devoted much research to this topic and in his book on the subject has shown the way in which the West and, during the nineteenth century, France and Great Britain in particular, assumed an intellectual authority over the Orient, creating a body of theory and practice which formed an integral part of European material civilization and culture.[84] The image of the Orient and, by extension, the Arabs who resided there as romantic and exotic could, logically, have counteracted the attitudes to the Arabs formed in the colony. This was not, however, the case. There was a clear distinction between the illusory Orient of art forms and the reality as perceived in the colonies. Said has extensively considered the perception of the Orient in literature and Monneret has visually suggested the evolution of the image of the Orient in painting, but it is none the less useful to touch briefly on the topic to demonstrate why the Orient in art did not and could not counterbalance the categorization of the Arab taking place in the colony.[85]

France's involvement in Algeria stimulated a nascent interest in the Orient. Prior to the conquest, in 1829, Victor Hugo had drawn attention to the trend, in artistic circles, away from being Hellenist to being Orientalist.[86] Nearly 40 years later de Nerval made a similar observation concerning the French attraction for the curious, the eccentric and the paradoxical.[87] By the early 1860s, Théophile Gautier, the Goncourt brothers, Flaubert, Feydeau, Daudet and Fromentin were among the better-known authors who had visited Algeria. These visits produced only one novel on Algeria, Daudet's *Tartarin de Tarascon*, whose comical hero confronts the mysteries of the colony with aplomb.[88] In spite of its humour the novel met with little success on its initial serialization in 1869.[89] Its lack of exotic romanticism may have contributed to its initial unpopularity, for as yet Algeria was too unfamiliar to be captivating. If Algeria did not serve as a direct literary stimulus, it did serve as a visual one as the canvases by Fromentin, an artist as well as an author, and Eugène Delacroix, show. Delacroix visited Algeria in 1832. The experience transformed his paintings and placed him in the vanguard of an artistic revolution. He stressed colour and imagination over draughtsmanship and knowledge, thus eschewing the values of the Academy. Whether it bore direct fruit or not, intellectual curiosity about the colony was increasing. Artistic curiosity about Algeria reflected a wider curiosity about the Orient; a desire to enter different worlds in order to augment creativity and enhance imagination.

Be it via paintings, such as those of Delacroix, or prose, such as that of Gérard de Nerval, Gustave Flaubert and later Pierre Loti, the Orient is viewed from a distance and imbued with an exoticism that divorces it from reality. De Nerval's *Voyage en Orient*, with its passages of great lyric beauty, does attempt to dispel some Western misconceptions about the Orient, but the work is so dreamlike that all sense of immediacy is lost.[90] There is a marked difference in the Orient as seen from above, or afar, and the Orient as seen from below. Thus, on the one hand de Nerval could express the conviction that, if handled correctly, the contact between East and West, long-standing enemies though they were, had the potential of bearing great fruit.[91] On the other he could describe the Arab as little better than a dog.[92] Flaubert too used the canine metaphor, describing Arab huts as dog kennels and, when actually confronted with Arabs for the first time in Constantine, recoiling from the 'long white dirty floating masses', cursed and poor in the extreme and smelling of 'the pariah'.[93] Yet on leaving the area he would evoke the charm of a 'masked ball'.[94]

The Orient was a place of mystery, of illusions and dreams, peopled with the unfamiliar. De Nerval's Orient was 'Egypt, serious and pious ... land of riddles and mysteries'.[95] His passage through Cairo resembled a 'dream voyage in a city of the past, inhabited by phantoms that fill but don't animate it'.[96] For Flaubert it was life on the Nile that epitomized the Orient: 'here is the real Orient, a melancholic and soporific effect ... a vast and pitiless thing in the midst of which you are lost.'[97] For these artists the Orient shimmered, mirage-like, before them, challenging their imaginations with myriad permutations of reality. Actually, the Orient held few surprises, for they found in it what they desired. For de Nerval it was the tissue of dreams.[98] For Flaubert and Loti there was the added attraction of the lubricity of the Orient. Kuchuk Hanem, the Egyptian courtesan and dancer Flaubert encountered during his travels, served as the prototype of female voluptuousness portrayed in his heroines, Salammbô and Salomé.[99] Loti's first novel, *Aziyadé*, published in 1879, is the sexual idyll of a British officer and the young Muslim girl of the title amid the exoticism of Constantinople. The prose is as sensual as the plot, with intimations of homosexual as well as heterosexual desire. After all, when it comes to sexuality: 'in the old Orient everything is possible'.[100] Loti, for such is the officer's name, and Aziyadé have been united 'to sample together the heady charms of the impossible'.[101] (Loti was so enamoured of the Orient that he even transformed his house in Rochefort into an oriental residence, complete with miniature mosque.)

However strong the attraction of the Orient, and however well it was presented in the various art forms, the fact remains that it was essentially a contrived image reflecting the personal obsessions or desires and the artistic needs of the individual author or artist. Their portrayal of the Orient failed to dispel its mystery and in many ways reinforced existing stereotypes, particularly where sexuality was concerned. Oriental sexuality was used as an artistic device. As wantonness in the Orient was a received idea, it allowed the author to present sexual licence or be more sexually explicit without undue censure. (When Zola used a French heroine, Nana, to do the same, in spite of the fact that Nana was a prostitute, the book was attacked for its blatant salacity rather than its depiction of corruption in Napoleon III's Empire.) Similarly a new dimension could be added to painting; one need only consider *The Odalisque with the Slave* or *The Turkish Bath* of Jean-Auguste Ingres (1780–1867). Shifting the setting of female nudity from Olympus, where hitherto it had been most firmly ensconced, to the East altered the connotations surrounding sexuality. The sexuality of the gods implied inaccessibility, capriciousness and even retribution; that of the harem held the promise of submission, intense eroticism and endless pleasure without cost or obligation. In the arts, the Orient became glamorous, romantic and exciting; the Arab did not. The perfumes, colours, noises and sensuality of the Orient were evoked; its significance was not. It was the senses these artists and authors sought to assail, not a sensibility towards its culture or even its peoples. The penchant for the Orient, as manifested by French authors and artists in the nineteenth century, in no way dispelled misconceptions about the Arabs, Islam or the Islamic world. At best it presented an exotic image that was hardly in line with reality; at worst it only reinforced existing stereotypes.

Conclusion

The skein of pro-Arab and pro-Islamic sentiment in France and Algeria is tangled, and teasing out the strands can be as frustrating as it is edifying. Nor is it easy to try to pinpoint the ideological framework out of which these sentiments arose. To be sure, in Algeria, being pro-indigenous signified 'being liberal'. But this encompassed attitudes as varied as mere benevolence of treatment to a belief in the eventual success of assimilation. Furthermore, for all the revolutionary terminology of equality and fraternity, notions of civilization and human progress were still fettered to the hierarchical paradigms of the past: the Ladder of Being with the Aborigines and Hottentots at the base and the Aryans at the top was the simplified framework, perfected during the nineteenth century, for these ideas.[102] Hence in Algeria Captain Richard, one of the best Arabists of the colony and a disciple of both Fourier and Considérant, and thus a 'liberal' in the terminology of his contemporaries, could be relentlessly derogatory concerning the Arabs, whose civilization he considered to be on a lower rung than that of the French. Similarly, in France, a scholar and Orientalist such as Ernest Renan could devote years of research and make an appreciable contribution to the study of Semitic languages and yet indulge in such unscholarly generalizations about Muslim society as: 'every Muslim society soon attains the most bloody absolutism.'[103] Both men would have been shocked to have been considered retrograde. The point to be made is that 'liberals' and progressive thinkers both in Algeria and in France could be as involved in the process of racial myth-making as the overtly anti-indigenous or anti-Islam elements. There is even a case for arguing that theirs was the more potent contribution, being anti-polemical in nature, and emerging as it did from 'rational' and respected minds.

The *Royaume Arabe* achieved little for the image of the Arab. Prejudices and stereotypes, which logically the *arabophiles* and Orientalists should have dispelled, accumulated and were reinforced. The economic and political situation in Algeria counteracted progress in this direction, as did the nineteenth-century climate of paternalism. All pro-Arab sentiments were inevitably subordinated to the received ideas of a European heritage. In Algeria passive resistance to French methods led to further denigration of the Arab. The tarnishing of the Arab image burnished that of the Kabyle. In France interest in Algeria spread from political to intellectual circles. Although literature looked further afield for its inspiration, the debates surrounding the colonial policies of Louis-Napoleon had succeeded in stirring the imagination of social scientists, who were awakened to the potential for research the raw material of Algeria could provide. Ethnology, anthropology and eventually sociology would each consider the Arabs and the Berbers. It was via these disciplines that Kabyle imagery was to acquire its most mythological dimension.

PART II

Social sciences and
military men

In the section above it has been demonstrated how the pragmatic concerns of conquest and military occupation focused on the Kabyles and the Arabs in a way that drew attention to certain categories and prompted their positive/negative evaluation. We have seen which circumstances were involved in the formation of categories and what received information influenced this process. There were, however, intellectual, ideological and methodological factors that also came into play and were to form part of a framework which endowed what were basically socio-geographical categories with racial connotations. Furthermore, by their nature these factors made the categories culturally specific, that is to say looking beyond the general Eurocentricism of their viewpoint they were definably Gallic. This had to do with the way in which the French army differed sociologically from other nineteenth-century imperial armies. To begin with, the officer corps was no longer fundamentally dynastic and endogamous, with entrance into and promotion within the corps being based on the purchase of commissions; rather it was meritocratic, with entrance and promotion based on educational or military performance.[1] Then too, officers no longer deferred to superiors from a hereditary class-defined social hierarchy with a monarch as titular head of a state religion; rather they deferred to superiors from a meritocratic class-defined social hierarchy which was essentially secular, as state and religion were linked together throughout the century in an increasingly uneasy compromise. These differences nurtured viewpoints that could and did, with the right encouragement, open new conceptual doors in social evaluation and hence in category formation. If the social structure of the French army sensitized its personnel, consciously or otherwise, to an evolutionary progression of society, it was the intellectual traditions of the officers that created a setting which enabled category formation in the colony to assume the importance it did.

97

The following section will try to discover what it was about the intellectual traditions of the French army that caused category formation to take place in the way it did during their regime and, beyond that, to indicate the directions in which their distinctive analysis of indigenous society was to lead. The three chapters in the section are thematic, of necessity looking back to and overlapping with certain aspects of those above, while laying the groundwork for explicating developments under the civilian regime in those that follow.

5

The Ecole Polytechnique, Saint-Simonianism and the army

For the first half of the nineteenth century the Ecole Polytechnique, embodied the educational reforms arising out of the French Revolution and the Napoleonic period and, until the rise of the Ecole Normale Supérieure as a rival force, dominated the French intellectual scene with its ideas and the eminence of its faculty. It was the institution which forged the link between science and the military, provided many of the leading officers who served in Algeria, and created the intellectual framework on which the scientific evaluation of the country proceeded.

The Ecole Polytechnique was founded during the Convention in 1794 as the Ecole Centrale des Travaux Publics, acquiring its definitive name a year later, and taking as its motto *Pour la Patrie, Les Sciences et La Gloire*. The criterion for entrance was merit, not birth, and its professed aim was to produce engineers and educated officers, capable of properly managing and perfecting public, civil and military services.[2] It amalgamated and replaced the preparatory institutions of the *ancien régime* which led to scientific careers and aspired to serve as 'the muse of all sciences and types of engineering'.[3] In this aim it was to succeed, foreshadowing what became one of the tenets of Saint-Simonianism. It was, furthermore, to be central to the diffusion of Cartesianism throughout French society.[4] During the years 1830–42, for example (an important period with regard to developments in Algeria) 21 *Polytechniciens* were elected to the various sections of L'Académie des Sciences in France.[5] The First Republic and Empire revolutionized educational practice by making science an essential part of the national curriculum.[6] The Ecole Polytechnique, as France's premier scientific institution, thus became an arbiter as much of ideas as of the methodology of their application.

The changes wrought on the Ecole Polytechnique during the Napoleonic period had far-reaching implications with regard to Algeria and, less directly, to French colonization in general. On 16 July 1804, by imperial decree, Napoleon ordered the militarization of the school, thus creating the first institutional link between science and the military and establishing a long-lived trend. The emphasis the First Empire placed on scientific education for its recruits was further stressed when, in 1812, the best students in mathematics started to be requisitioned by the Ministry of War. The pursuit of a scientific education, therefore, became 'tantamount to enlisting'.[7] Although during the Restoration this latter notion diminished, the correlation between scientific endeavour and the military remained strong.[8] A further repercussion of this development, not without relevance to Algeria, was the perception by certain officers of a social role to be assumed by its educated elite in the context of the *mission éducative* of the army.[9] This notion persisted throughout the nineteenth century.[10]

Candidates for the Polytechnique were expected to be well behaved, to adhere to Republican values, to have a sound grounding in arithmetic and algebra, and to be between the ages of 16 and 20.[11] Once accepted they received a high-quality education, being taught by many of the best mathematicians, physicists and chemists of the day.[12] While the curriculum was essentially one of pure science, there were aspects of the instruction given that influenced the way students perceived the world about them and approached subjects extraneous to their field of study. In the first place it fostered the idea of European superiority by linking the concept of advancement in civilization to that of science and technology. Thus, for example, an article on the history of algebra which appeared in one of the school's journals in 1816 declared the mid-eighteenth century as the beginning of European pre-eminence in the subject and, of pertinence to subsequent perceptions in Algeria, not only drew attention to the negligible contribution of the Arabs but also suggested that their very mode of thought was different from that of the Western tradition. A comparison of the algebraic texts of the Greeks, the Arabs, the present-day Europeans and the Persian translations of Indian texts showed that those of the Arabs 'differed greatly' from those of the Greeks, such as Diophantus. Furthermore the Arabs had made no progress since the time they had acquired their texts from the Indians who, until the mid-eighteenth century at least, were more advanced in many aspects of the science than the Europeans.[13] With regard to the Greek (and Latin) classics the magnitude of the legacy ancient Greece and Rome bequeathed to mathematics (and the fact it was more accessible in its original form than that of Egypt, India, China or the Arabs) reinforced their importance, in the minds of the students, both as source material and as the sovereign antecedents to French civilization.[14] Second, that the Ecole Polytechnique was the font of so much innovation in the sciences encouraged its graduates to think of themselves as an elite destined to disseminate new ideas and help mould society into an improved, or even radically different, form. Third, the innovations themselves created new patterns of thought. Among the farthest-reaching was the contribution of the Marquis de Laplace, an astronomer and mathematician who gave his introductory lectures at the Polytechnique in 1795. Laplace's *Philosophical Essay on Probabilities* opened the door to the doctrines of natural laws and the espousal of statistical science. The close connection between mathematics and philosophy allowed for the emergence of a style of reasoning that was essentially mathematical in nature. Deductive analysis, calibration and statistics became the tools used to define society and evaluate human beings. The laws of probability became entwined with statistics and as the use of statistics increased so too did its impact on society. First of all it gave rise, in the 1820s, to the concept, as we know it today, of *normal* meaning regular or typical.[15] What was not normal was therefore deviant or irregular. This type of comparative analysis, with its connotations of correct and incorrect, used in conjunction with statistics was integral to racial reasoning. Statistical laws, originally used to describe large-scale regularities, were eventually turned into laws of nature and society dealing with underlying truths and causes by statisticians such as the Belgian Adolphe Quetelet. (Quetelet, who was very popular in France, was one of the greatest international propagandists for the values of statistics. In his *Sur l'Homme et le développement de ses facultés, ou essai de physique sociale*, first published in 1835 and revised in 1869 he used statistics to back up his concept of the average man (*homme type*), the nearest one could get to perfection. The average man of each race was calculated by measurement of physical and moral qualities.[16]) The Ecole Polytechnique was one of the leading institutions contributing to such developments which formed part of the scientific mode of reasoning that was to characterize so much of nineteenth-century, and indeed twentieth-century, thought.

On leaving the school, those who did not enter the military found employment in governmental agencies or as engineers involved in public works. Whether they ended up in the army or in the private sector, *Polytechniciens*, like graduates of other *grandes écoles*, kept in close touch with each other, forming an extensive 'old boys" network. The camaraderie established during the two or three years at the school was carried forward into later life through social and intellectual associations. Furthermore, the notions of leadership and the unabashed elitism in which the school immersed its students ensured the dissemination and reinforcement of its ideas and values across society and across generational levels. The fact of having earned one's silver spoon, rather than having been born with it, stressed the intellectual rather than the social aspect of elitism, and facilitated the process even further.[17]

The associations of the Ecole Polytechnique with the First Republic imbued it with progressive ideals, accentuated under the Restoration and the July Monarchy through ties with Saint-Simonianism. Officers emerging from the Polytechnique, therefore, either actually were, or were perceived to be, more 'liberal' than those schooled at St. Cyr and Saumur. While the French army of the early nineteenth century was undoubtedly more progressive structurally and socially than its counterparts in other European countries, due to the experience of the French Revolution and Napoleonic expansion, republican elements and other manifestations of intellectual 'progressiveness' were not always appreciated in its midst. First Corsica, then Algeria and later the outposts of the French Empire became repositories for these nuisance factions; thus many a republican officer found himself sent abroad to work off his 'liberal' fervour.

The Ecole Polytechnique and the Napoleonic expedition to Egypt

The testing ground of the capabilities of the *Polytechniciens*, beyond their role of combat, was to be the Napoleonic expedition to Egypt. Here, for the first time, the scientist and the soldier came together in a working relationship that extended beyond strategic science. In the overall European experience of the Orient, the expedition played a decisive role. According to Fück, it was this event more than any other which produced the conviction that: 'the prevailing superiority of Europe over the Orient was axiomatic and absolute.'[18] For Said, the Napoleonic invasion of 1798 and the subsequent foray into Syria had 'by far the greatest consequence for the modern history of Orientalism.'[19] Similarly for Algeria and the emergence of the Kabyle Myth its impact was crucial.

Forty students and five professors from the Ecole Polytechnique accompanied Napoleon to Egypt as part of the officer corps and the scholarly contingent of the expedition. It was the first major campaign in which officers graduating from the Polytechnique took part and it provided them with 'a brilliant occasion' to focus attention on themselves.[20] This they apparently did, both on a military and on a scholarly level, to the immense satisfaction of the school.[21] The novelty of their endeavour, and its importance with regard to Algeria, lay in the accumulation of large quantities of valuable material on ancient history and geography 'in the arena of war'.[22] Within the precinct of the battlefield, therefore, the role of officer and scientist became interchangeable. The statistics and *mémoires* compiled and written by the *Polytechniciens* formed part of Napoleon's master-plan to record and chronicle every conceivable aspect of Egyptian society past and present, thus laying bare the country for its deeper understanding and assimilation by the French. The legacies of this ultimately abortive expedition were embodied in the Institut d'Egypte and the monumental 23-volume work *Description de l'Egypte.*[23]

The Institut d'Egypte was the prototype for the ethnological institutes that sprang up as a result of French colonization. The two leading institutions eventually established along these lines in North Africa were the Comité d'Etudes Berbères and the Institut des Hautes Etudes Marocaines, but the Institut d'Egypte was also an influence in the emergence of the numerous scholarly societies of the colony, associated with its major cities, in which scholar-officers were not only closely involved but often founding members. Napoleon created the Institut d'Egypte as the learned division of the army.[24] In this way the army became inexorably linked with the scholarly research of an occupied territory, be it historical, biological, archaeological or medical. The work carried out under its aegis served as the precedent for Algeria, where officers conducted detailed studies on every aspect of the country, providing posterity with an overwhelming quantity of material, some of the most noteworthy being penned by officers of the Ecole Polytechnique. While such studies were undeniably part of the panoply of reconnaissance, the scholarly approach with overtones of scientific analysis ensured a readership which extended beyond official circles. Their high degree of formal education stimulated officers to occupy their leisure hours with scholarly pursuits beyond the direct requirements of their military service. This was especially so in the more remote Bureaux, many of which were in the mountainous region of Kabylia. None the less, if completed works caught the attention of the establishment, even when not officially commissioned, a wide circulation was guaranteed as publication of further editions was then facilitated either by defraying publication costs or by governmental sponsorship. (Such was the case for de Neveu's *Les Khouans.*) This meant that officers never lost sight of military objectives: a fact which restrained unorthodoxy.

If the Institut served as a blueprint of sorts, so too did the *Description de l'Egypte.* A series of scientific expeditions in Algeria produced a number of multi-volume works which became the standard reference books for background research into the colony.[25] These were very obviously based on the type of material to be found in the

Description de l'Egypte. In perusing this *magnum opus* of Napoleon's expedition, several points emerge which are of relevance to Algeria. The first has to do with colonization and the role of such studies in its perpetration. It defined the nature of such studies as a combination of science and reconnaissance. Scholarship, more than official dispatches, became a vehicle for the pragmatic concerns of colonization such as the need to ascertain colonizing potential and the necessity of keeping tabs on the inhabitants. De Chabrol, one of the expedition's ethnologists, was quite candid about the importance of the expedition's role in gathering statistical information to this end, over and above any services rendered to the sciences, arts and archaeology.[26]

For those taking part in the expedition, the concept of civilization, past and present, took on a new meaning. The officers were, by their own admission, 'struck by the sight of the huge monuments of a lost civilization still standing in the middle of the desert and Muslim brutishness', and most probably metaphorically linked the desert to Muslim culture and the lost civilization as represented by the monuments to their own.[27] The presence of archaeological ruins, of civilization in the midst of barbarity, was a revelation. It awakened a realization of the role the French occupying officer could assume in relation to the occupied *indigène*. The extent of this ideal is apparent from the *Description de l'Egypte* and is visually presented to great effect. The volumes of plates which illustrate the texts are masterpieces of detail and seeming archaeological accuracy. What is of interest to the researcher, however, are the human touches, undoubtedly added to lighten the overall scholarly effect. The foreground of many of the plates contain figures of French officers and Egyptian civilians. In one, a French soldier has his arm on the shoulder of an Egyptian and is pointing didactically towards the ruins of ancient Egypt with his *képi*. In another, a Frenchman is sketching the ruins with an Egyptian lying prone behind. A third shows a French soldier indicating the grandeurs of an interior to yet another interested Egyptian.[28] The implication is striking: the French soldier assumes his role as an agent of the *mission éducative* by instructing the hapless *indigène* not only in the glories of his past but in the importance of *civilization* as a whole. The *mission éducatrice*, which remained a mere suggestion in Egypt, was openly transformed into the *mission civilisatrice* in Algeria, eventually becoming the justification of France's presence in Algeria and one of the principal arguments in undertaking colonial expansion elsewhere.

The expedition prefigured attitudes in Algeria in other ways, for it aroused an awareness of the importance of Rome as France's exemplar in the enterprise of colonization. The grandeur of the archaeological ruins impressed the officers, who saw them as palpable evidence that Roman culture had echoed down the ages, as France's civilization surely would in the future, a fitting testimony to its power and glory. Rome excited admiration both as an innovator of an architectural style and for the speed at which its newly created urban centres surpassed existing ones in importance.[29] By the time the French embarked in Algeria, not only was France's connection to Rome entrenched in military attitudes, but the next logical step in the argument had also taken shape, namely that France was about to redress the calamity of the demise of Roman civilization in North Africa by wresting the area from Islam and the Arabs.

Of course it was not just archaeology that stimulated this awareness. Roman and Greek texts formed an important part of the source material on Northern Africa. To be sure the Ecole Polytechnique, as an institution of higher education, turned out science-oriented graduates but the basis of French secondary education was still the classics. Officers who undertook research were usually better versed in Latin and Greek than in Arabic. The sources for the *Description de l'Egypte* were essentially Latin and Greek texts, with only the occasional reference to an Arab scholar. In Algeria, particularly in the early years, the tendency continued of relying on the classics as the most noteworthy primary sources. (In the case of the Kabyles, Lapène is but an early example.) There were relatively few Arabists in the early decades of the century and Arab works in translation were limited. (Ibn Khaldoun's fourteenth-century work on the Berbers was only translated in 1852, for example.) The textual approach that a classical education stressed, and the intellectual admiration of the classics that such an education conferred, led to unintentional ambivalence on the part of these scientifically trained officers. While they pursued their goals by means of 'scientific' methodology the reliance on the classics as sources could be, and often was, an obstacle to proper objectivity. Not only were the classics on occasion a source of empirical error but, more important, it proved difficult for many of these officer-scientists to divorce themselves from their textual training, as evidenced by quasi-verbatim transcriptions of text from one work to another. (Hence in Algeria, for example, Daumas's description of Arab and Berber as a catalogue of negative and positive attributes was not only presented without question in many subsequent works, but in some cases embellished.)

The success of the *Description de l'Egypte* ensured that it would be emulated elsewhere where circumstances were similar. Among the numerous *mémoires* were several concerned with the ethnology of Egypt's inhabitants.[30] Two of those, by Larrey and Jomard, receive a special mention in the correspondence of the Ecole Polytechnique, which was published at the time for the benefit of its students. Thus in addition to the overall importance of the expedition, *Polytechniciens* were made aware of the types of study, ethnological and otherwise, that should be undertaken on the occasion of comparable expeditions in the future. This is evident in the case of Algeria, where the Scientific Commission initially served as the 'learned division' of the army and where the *Description de l'Egypte* obviously served as the model for the 39 volumes officially published as a result of the research carried out by its members. *Polytechniciens* were prominent among the Commission's members and it is of more than passing interest to note that the only work to which ethnological significance can be imputed was by a *Polytechnicien* about the Kabyles, namely Carette's *Etudes sur la Kabilie.*

The final point to be made with regard to the Napoleonic expedition to Egypt concerns the army's intellectual preparation for the campaign. It was the first expeditionary campaign outside Europe in 'modern' history. It was also the first 'exotic' battleground to which the new army, forged from the intellectual traditions of the Revolution, was dispatched. Officers prepared themselves by reading what was available in contemporary works on the area, mainly travellers' accounts and geographical works. Two books on travels in Egypt were published shortly before Napoleon's expedition and both were widely read by officers in his army.[31] Volney's *Voyage en Syrie et en Egypte* and Savary's *Lettres d'Egypte* had each run into three editions by the end of the revolutionary decade and the latter had been translated into English. Both were relevant to the development of ideas in Algeria.[32] Both books emphasized the 'fanaticism' and 'barbarous nature' of Islam. Savary dwelt on the destruction by the Arabs of the Ptolemies' library in Alexandria, suggesting that it was this act that initiated the veil of ignorance which spread over the Middle East and North Africa.[33] Volney stressed the anarchy inherent in the Islamic tradition and its lack of natural morality.[34] He also discussed the differences between sedentary and nomadic Arabs, stating that these were so great as to make Arabs raised in these separate lifestyles virtually foreign to each other. The sedentary Arab, Volney continued, had a social organization reminiscent of 'our own'.[35] Volney believed a people's morality was determined by the social framework within which it lived; not only was behaviour influenced by this factor, but also physical appearance.[36] The mental preparation which officers sought from works such as Volney's and Savary's served in the first instance to acquaint them with the peoples they were to encounter in their campaigns abroad and, in the second, as the source of ideas from which any analysis of the occupied people was to proceed. The use of such material set the standard for what followed in North Africa.

Intellectual preparation for the North African campaign

At the time of the Algerian conquest the number of such works had increased but was still small enough to ensure the universality of their use as source material. Volney and Savary therefore remained important. It is interesting to note that the sources mentioned in the anonymous *Journal d'un Officier de l'Armée d'Afrique*, published one year after the conquest, included, in addition to the standard Latin classics, such diverse references as the works of Malte-brun, Shaler and Gall. Konrad Malte-brun was a Danish geographer best known for his *Précis de la Géographie Universelle*. William Shaler was the American representative in Algiers from 1815 to 1827. During this time he wrote his *Sketches of Algiers, Political, Historical and Civil*, a work acknowledged as full of interest by his contemporaries, in which he stressed the importance of Sidi Ferruch as an embarkation point along the coast, the site finally chosen by the French.[37] Franz Joseph Gall was a German physician and phrenologist, who believed that the back of the head served as a measure of the brain and hence as an indicator of human accomplishment. In time his ideas were adopted by the Société Ethnologique de Paris and permeated literary and political circles, influencing the likes of Balzac, Taine and Proudhon.[38] He lived in Paris, where he was a popular medical practitioner, serving Saint-Simon and other progressive thinkers.[39] Gall's presence as a source would suggest that the author, if not a 'liberal' himself, was at least familiar with progressive trends.

Shaler, along with Dr Thomas Shaw and Abbé Raynal, was among the notable references for officers about to embark for Algeria, all three being regularly quoted in works written after the conquest.[40] Abbé Raynal, some of whose works were among the most popular in the eighteenth century according to Cohen, was an anti-slavery campaigner who, with Rousseau, encouraged the notion of the Noble Savage, a concept containing a moral message for sybaritic Europeans, which pointed out that a virtuous existence could flourish in a simple, natural environment.[41] In his posthumously published work on North Africa Raynal discussed the Berbers, drawing attention to their love of liberty, their sedentary lifestyle and their 'superficial' attachment to Islam. Raynal made no explicit connection between the Berbers and the concept of the Noble Savage; Tocqueville, it will be remembered, did. Unlike the classics, these eighteenth-century and early nineteenth-century works were seminal for attitudes in the colony regarding Islam and as the source of contemporary ideas on human kind, society and civilization. The sort of intellectual preparation that was initially undertaken by officers partaking in the expedition to Egypt was amplified in Algeria, where conquest gave way to a military occupation lasting 40 years. Its imprint on the subsequent works emerging from the colony was therefore marked.

Important though it was (and although it is now considered a seminal work on North African History), it is unlikely that Ibn Khaldun's fourteenth-century work, the *Kitab al-Ibar* (Universal History), formed part of the general intellectual preparation for the Algerian campaign. Slane's translation, the first in French and a partial one at that, only appeared in 1852.[42] None the less Arabist officers, limited though they were at the actual time of conquest, may have been aware of its existence and even familiar with its contents.[43] Just how much influence Ibn Khaldun had on late nineteenth-century works is difficult to evaluate. An appraisal made at the time of the centenary celebrations by Emile Gautier, a professor at the University of Algiers, suggests that in colonial Algeria his work was not taken into the consideration it is today. 'For all his genius,' Gautier wrote, 'he had an oriental brain which does not function like ours. He cannot be read like Titus-Livius or Polybius, or even Procopius. He has to be interpreted, transposed.'[44] When classical sources were required it was to the Latin and Greek ones that French scholars turned and not to the Arabic.

Utopian socialism and the army in Algeria

Three of the leading institutions that provided army personnel for Algeria were closely connected with utopian socialism, in particularly Saint-Simonianism: the Ecole Polytechnique, the Ecole d'Application de Metz and the Ecole de Médécine de Paris. In this respect the former had a national significance which the other two lacked but with regard to Algeria all three combined constituted an intellectual bed-rock of considerable solidity.

Saint-Simonianism and the Ecole Polytechnique

The Saint-Simonian connections of the Ecole Polytechnique are sufficiently well known not to require extensive recapitulation here. Saint-Simon himself was a close friend of Le Grand Monge (Gaspard Monge, Comte de Péluse), one of the founders of the Polytechnique, and soon after its inception he moved into a house opposite the school where he presided over gatherings of faculty members and students, from whose ranks some of his leading disciples were drawn. Most notable were Prosper Enfantin, Augustin Thierry and Auguste Comte. Of importance to Algeria, in addition to Enfantin, can be added the names of Louis Juchault de La Moricière, Carette, Prax and Fournel. It was only after Saint-Simon's death in 1825 that what is now known as the Saint-Simonian Doctrine was formulated, thanks to the close collaboration of his disciples, namely Enfantin, Bazard, Buchez, Chevalier and a number of students from the Polytechnique.[45] The link established between Saint-Simon and the school was maintained and the influence of Saint-Simonianism was extended to Algeria.

In 1830 the foremost liberal newspaper of the previous decade, *Le Globe*, became an organ of Saint-Simonianism, due to the conversion of its manager, Pierre Leroux, to the movement.[46] The paper was a great success and widely read among the students at the Polytechnique.[47] It was equally widely disseminated in Algeria, as a letter from one of the officers serving there indicates: 'Other friends with whom I am in daily contact read it ... talk about it; they love talking about and discussing the New Doctrine which is important as interest is awakened in it.'[48] Saint-Simon had little place for the army in his scheme of things to come, but his disciples, headed by Michel Chevalier, editor-in-chief of *Le Globe*, saw the role of the soldier as an important one, with the army even serving as a model of the new society. This was to be achieved by wrenching the soldier from his past servitude and making the whole of the army an annexe of the Ecole Polytechnique, to enable it to learn the new industrial and scientific methods.[49] *Soldiers as builders* was added to the concept of *soldiers as scientists*. 'Building' was used in its literal meaning of construction (*travaux publics*), but also in its abstract connotation of the creation of a different society. The Ecole Polytechnique, therefore, was to be the hub of the distribution of Saint-Simonian ideas throughout society. Certainly, this is the way Enfantin envisaged things. It was, he said, 'the milk imbibed at our dear school' that had to nourish future generations. The positive language, methods of research and demonstrative techniques learned there were the means of making the political sciences function.[50] Saint-Simonian centres were organized in leading towns in the provinces including Metz, and in the army in Algeria. Bigot, an officer in the engineering corps, took it upon himself to go to Algeria and disseminate the Saint-Simonian doctrine, first introduced to the colony by two other *Polytechniciens*, Lamoricière and Chabaud-Latour.[51]

Of the voluminous writings of the Saint-Simonians the leading aspect retained from their doctrine was the idea that the social revolution, which would eradicate the last vestiges of feudalism and replace it with an industrial and scientific system, would come from above 'through the leadership of superior men'.[52] The new society was to be characterized by order and unity and its social hierarchy was to be determined by ability. Industry (with its double meaning of diligence and manufacture) and science were the keys to progress, and every effort was to be made to encourage their development. The intellectual impact of Saint-Simonianism was considerable. According to Iggers, the movement claimed 40,000 adherents, was familiar to every educated person in Europe, and had one of the most profound influences on the development of social philosophy in the nineteenth century.[53]

In Algeria, an actual 'Saint-Simonian revolution' was no more in evidence than it was in France. There was, none the less, an important nucleus of disciples, of whom Enfantin was the guiding force and the *Polytechniciens* the most numerous.[54] But the connection of army officers to Saint-Simonianism, however tenuous, was of import. The idea of building a new, non-feudal society, and the intrinsic paternalism of the Saint-Simonian doctrine, found definite echos in military Algeria. Richard, it will be remembered, actually used the concept of building a new society as a straightforward analogy for colonization in one of his theoretical works and, along with other officers of the Bureaux Arabes, attempted its practical application.[55] The officers of the Polytechnique, even if they were not themselves Saint-Simonians, were therefore exposed to these ideas and consciously, or unconsciously, transmitted them to their subordinates through their suggestions and directives, and to their fellow officers through the network of scholarly institutes and societies that were gradually set up in Algeria, of which they were active members. The soldier-scientist, the soldier-builder and the soldier-educator were attractive concepts for officers involved in the conquest and occupation of a difficult, hostile and alien territory, whatever their personal philosophy. The ideas of Saint-Simon and his disciples were the intellectual props around which these concepts could be built.

The significance of Saint-Simonianism to the development of the Kabyle Myth was as an intellectual preparation. Viewed from the standpoint of utopian socialism, however diluted, the differences between Arab and Berber were magnified. The value placed by Saint-Simonians on economic endeavour, dexterity, hard work and stability, the belief that religion was a characteristic of man's mentality, that civilization was tied to technological and scientific achievement, and that the progression up the ladder of civilization was measured in terms of the extent of social harmony, the complexity of political institutions and the degree of scientific development meant that only those aspects of indigenous society that suggested the possibility of progress in these directions would be singled out as worthy of consideration. A sedentary existence, however basic, was closer to this ideal than a nomadic one. Into this conceptual framework the Kabyles appeared to fit more readily than the Arabs. Some of these concepts, including the notion that one climbed to higher states of civilization or the idea of a hierarchical society under the leadership of superior men, gave rise to mental patterns which pointed in the direction of racist thought. It is one of the ironies of history that utopian philosophies can lead to reprehensible realities. The colonial situation in Algeria is a case in point.

Ecole d'Application de Metz and the Ecole de Médecine de Paris

Saint-Simonianism in the Ecole de Metz was a by-product of the Ecole Polytechnique. *Polytechniciens* entering the artillery corps usually attended the school on completion of their studies at their Alma Mater.[56] While all officers graduating from Metz were not necessarily *Polytechniciens*, the presence of the latter in the school was a further avenue for the transmission of their ideas to Algeria. Saint-Simonian proselytizing did take place, but its students were also exposed to other novel sociological ideas of the epoch. Victor Considérant, a *Polytechnicien* who stepped into the shoes of Charles Fourier when he died, preached another brand of utopian socialism at Metz. His conferences there were so successful that he submitted his resignation to the Ministry of War, becoming a full-time disciple spreading Fourier's ideas.[57] Richard was greatly influenced by these ideas, adapting them to suit the Algerian situation. Where the Fourierists sought to replace the evils of the *ancien régime* with their brand of socialism, Richard sought to replace the 'evils' of Islam with those of French civilization. An offending civilization, Fourierists believed (capitalist in this case), had to be destroyed before a new one (Fourierist) could take its place; it could not be amended.[58] This, of course, Richard adapted to suit the *mission civilisatrice* in his *De la civilisation du peuple arabe*, suggesting that the civilization in existence in Algeria had to be destroyed before French civilization could be put in its place. Richard, whose ideas did not adhere completely to any one utopian socialist doctrine, acquired a reputation in nineteenth-century academic circles as a philosopher and his body of thought, albeit little known today, was dubbed *la philosophie synthésiste*.[59]

Metz provided the artillery in Algeria with many officers, who had not attended the Polytechnique but who had, none the less, rubbed shoulders with *Polytechniciens*, Saint-Simonians and other utopian socialists. They were, therefore, aware of the directions in which these schools of thought were leading and could grasp the implications, if not the details, of their respective philosophies. Even if they in no way adhered to the doctrines, their horizons had been broadened by the proximity of these 'progressive' ideas.

The Ecole de Médecine, which provided officers for the medical corps in Algeria, was the third institution of higher learning closely involved in Utopian Socialism. In his later years Saint-Simon left the 'mathematicians' to his disciples and sought out the company of 'physiologists', moving from the vicinity of the Ecole Polytechnique to that of the medical school. When he died his disciples took up where he left off, spreading their doctrine among its students. Auguste Comte, once a Saint-Simonian but later founder of the school of positivism, also had close connections with the Ecole de Médecine, using it as a forum for his ideas.[60] The school therefore acted as a further channel for progressive ideas into Algeria.

The Ecole de Médecine was, however, more than just a forum for the ideas of utopian philosophers. During the revolutionary era radical reforms to medical education were introduced, whereby medicine and surgery were bracketed together as the same science. These reforms were institutionalized with the transformation of the medical school of Paris in 1794 and those of Montpellier and Strasbourg shortly thereafter. Among the chairs established at the Ecole de Médecine was one of medical physics and hygiene.[61] Public hygiene thus became a focus of attention for medical students and qualified practitioners. Under the influence of the Paris hygienists, diagnosis moved away from the examination of mere disease symptoms, seeking pathological changes in the human body as well. This had an impact on public health investigation, which in time ceased merely to describe phenomena and created a 'social pathology'. The burgeoning of public health interest in France during the first half of the nineteenth century had much to do with the fact the Ecole de Médecine was initially so closely tied to the army. Most medical graduates in the early decades of the school went straight into military service, an experience that was invaluable to surgeons and physicians alike, for there they were confronted with every conceivable medical situation, became accustomed to dealing with large numbers of people and established a tradition of preparing comprehensive reports on their activities.[62] The need to process such large quantities of information in a short space of time encouraged a reliance on numerical analysis. Diagnostic therapeutic and sanitary problems were all analysed in this way. The

accumulation of data that ensued as of a result of the reigning preoccupation with numerical analysis inexorably led medical practitioners
and hygienists to look beyond the confines of medical analysis to an
analysis of the ills of society, and by analysing the available statistics
attempts were made to uncover the characteristic patterns of society.
Using numbers as their shorthand, socio-medical investigators identified factors that distinguished one social group from another. In
France, distinctions were drawn between the rich and the poor; in the
colonies between the 'races'. The hygienic implications of these socio-
economic distinctions, while formulated in economic terms, were
generally linked to moral differences between the various groups.[63]
Morality thus became a factor in category formation.

The innovations in medical practice married well with certain
aspects of the newly emerging utopian philosophies. Hygienists and
medical students were attracted by the notion of progress inherent in
these philosophies, seeing their sound economic enquiries and the
seeming rationality of their solutions to complex social phenomena as
a solid basis for a science of society.[64] The medical and philosophical
ideas that came together in the Ecole de Médecine de Paris had a
profound influence throughout Europe and the Americas.[65] Although
the Paris school's influence began to wane in the 1840s, it was to be
another generation before the German universities rose to replace its
prominence. Methodologically and philosophically, therefore, the impact of its ideas lasted longer, especially in Algeria, where so many of
its early graduates practised.

The *Polytechniciens* in Algeria

Of France's four military establishments the Ecole Polytechnique was
the only one to provide a consistently high-quality education; certainly
it was the only one that emphasized science above all else. *Polytechniciens* in Algeria were graduates of one of four sections of the
school: the engineering corps (*génie militaire*), the artillery corps, the
civil engineering corps (*ponts et chaussées*), and the mining corps
(*mines*), of which the first two were the most important. For all these
officers the conquest of Algeria represented 'a civilizing mission full
of weariness and danger'.[66] Once the country was pacified, furthermore, it provided the additional attraction of being 'a vast field of
study'.[67] Leaving aside their actual combat duties, the *Polytechniciens*
were closely involved in every aspect of military endeavour in the
conquest. This was particularly so in the case of the engineering corps.
Africa had been a 'wonderful school' for the army and especially for
the engineering corps, who had played a leading role from the time

they disembarked in 1830 until pacification was achieved.[68] A leading advocate of the expedition and, symbolically, one of the first to land at Sidi Ferruch, was the commanding officer of the engineering corps, Valazé, but others such as de La Moricière, Duvivier, de Cavaignac and Carette made more lasting and varied impact on the Algerian scene. The final military *éclat* of the corps came during Randon's expedition on Kabylia, the last and most arduous campaign of the conquest, but its Polytechnique-trained officers continued to play a major role in the prolific statistic-gathering that was an integral part of French colonizing methods.

It was a *Polytechnicien*, Raffeneau de l'Isle, who was called upon to study the length of the Algerian coastline for suitable port sites. He not only accomplished this task but also drew up the plans for the drainage of the Mitidja, which eventually became the colony's biggest money-spinning area. Henri Fournel, who explored the geological and mineralogical potential of the colony, was another *Polytechnicien*.[69] His research lasted three years and resulted in the two volume *La Richesse minérale de l'Algérie*. Two others, de Coq and de Ville, followed in Fournel's footsteps, producing similar studies, while *ponts et chaussées* engineers, such as de Poirel, de Bernard and de Béguin, undertook the construction of the port of Algiers and other strategic sites. Several *Polytechniciens*, including Enfantin and Carette, were members of the 1840–42 Scientific Commission. When a geological cartography department was set up, the chief cartographer was the 1853 graduate, *Ingénieur en chef* Pouyanne.[70]

While building, reconnaissance and statistical research were among the foremost practical achievements of the *Polytechniciens*, their involvement in learned societies and their role in the scholarly studies of the colony was also striking. Of the four most quoted books on the Kabyles published in the first 50 years of occupation, two, considered to be the most erudite, were by *Polytechniciens* and a third was written in collaboration with one.[71] Ethnology had another regular contributor in the person of Louis Faidherbe, perhaps the most illustrious of the colonial *Polytechniciens*.[72] Faidherbe spent three years in Kabylia before being sent to Senegal, where he eventually became governor-general. Not only did Faidherbe carry out research in his own right, he was an elected official of the Société Anthropologique in Paris, corresponding member of several journals such as the *Revue Africaine*, and co-author, with the anthropologist Dr Paul Topinard, of the instructions as to the methodology to be employed for anthropological research in Algeria.[73] Furthermore, he was an advocate of the belief that the Kabyles were of non-Semitic, pre-Aryan origin, attributing this assumption to the results of linguistic research carried out in this domain.[74]

Another focus of research that arose out of the Algerian conquest was that of archaeology. The contemplation and compilation of Roman ruins may have provided enjoyable intellectual stimulation in an otherwise harsh environment, but they were also a means of studying Roman colonization. Général Creuly, another *Polytechnicien* and commander of the engineering corps in Constantine, was struck by the abundance of ruins in the area and, once Constantine was taken in 1837, he could concentrate his attention on this phenomenon. From Roman ruins his interest spread to those who had indomitably resisted Roman colonization, and among his works to appear in the *Revue archéologique* was a study of the Kabyles: 'Etudes sur les Quinquegentiens, ces peuples si souvent rebelles du Djurdjura, et sur les Berbères'. The development of his work is noteworthy, demonstrating the ramifications of scholarship which led to interest in the Kabyles. Creuly was not alone in his preoccupation with Roman ruins. His interest was shared by numerous other *Polytechniciens* and set the precedent for what became one of the liveliest disciplines in Algeria, giving rise to several societies of which the Société archéologique de la Province de Constantine was probably the most renowned.

Polytechniciens had links with most of the learned societies that were set up in Algeria. Creuly was a founding member of the Société Archéologique de Constantine, Captain Boissonnet, a Berber-speaker and director of *Affaires indigènes* in Constantine, was the founder of the Société Historique d'Alger; Carette, Faidherbe and Hanoteau were regular contributors to the *Revue Africaine*, journal of the Société Historique Algérienne, while others concerned themselves with geography, philology, and the etymology of place names. The works of these officers served as the role models of much that was to follow and was the practical confirmation of the marriage between military conquest and scientific endeavour.

Finally, of course, the *Polytechniciens* made their presence felt in the domain of colonial theory and in the actual administration of their subject peoples. From the early years of the occupation the debate regarding the methods and extent of colonization was clamorous. Theoretical studies, such as Enfantin's *Colonisation de l'Algérie*, appeared alongside more practical expositions by serving officers, like de La Moricière.[75] Such was the interest generated among *Polytechniciens* regarding Algeria that contributions to the literature were made by officers who had never even set foot in Algeria, but were 'strongly desirous to do so'![76] Certainly, the *Polytechniciens* in Algeria had much to say about the question in the early days, arousing the ire of Bugeaud, who strongly disapproved of the ideas of de La Moricière and his followers, considering them to be too progressive for practical application.[77] As for its application, the 40 years of military administration, first by the officers of the *Affaires indigènes* and then by those of the Bureaux Arabes, left its mark. Of the 248 officers who held the position of *cercle* bureau chief in Algeria, 170 graduated from a military school.[78] One of the first such officers was de La Moricière (Polytechnique) and, with Marey-Monge (Polytechnique) and Daumas (Saumur), is considered to be one of the prototypical bureau chiefs.[79] The relative freedom enjoyed by Bureaux Arabes officers not only enabled them to interpret official directives with a certain elasticity, but the nature of their office permitted enterprising officers to undertake research in addition to their administrative work. Four such examples are Boissonnet, Devaux, Hanoteau and Richard. Boissonnet's interests were essentially archaeological, Devaux and Hanoteau made notable contributions to the literature on the Kabyles, and Richard produced a variety of works on colonization and the Arabs. All were *Polytechniciens*; all served in or around Kabylia.

Polytechniciens in Algeria were a motivating force in the initial process of colonization. Their ideas, initiatives and research contributed to the creation of an infrastructure on which colonial practice was based. Their methodology or, more accurately, their style of reasoning was emulated, even when their ideas were not completely assimilated. As graduates of a *grande école*, the camaraderie which they shared amongst themselves provided an excellent network through which to swap and reinforce their ideas. As commanding officers, they were in a position to impose their methods and implement their ideas. And, finally, the education they received at the Ecole Polytechnique provided them with the versatility necessary to fit the multiple roles of the colonizing soldier.

Conclusion

The Ecole Polytechnique fashioned and reinforced a new image of the officer, an image which extended beyond that of the soldier-warrior to include the soldier-scientist, the soldier-builder and the soldier-educator. It created an officer prepared to assume a social role but it did not provide him with a proper outlet in France for these newly acquired talents. With the military occupation of Algeria this changed. The new versatility attached to the role of the officer transformed him into an ideal agent of colonization. Bugeaud's concept of colonization 'by the sword and by the plough' was a derivative of the idea of soldier as colonial agent, and for all his dislike of the *Polytechniciens*, they, in fact, were well suited to carry his project through.

The concept of the soldier-scientist is not as paradoxical as it seems.

It was the practical expression of an acknowledged link between two abstract concepts: control and understanding. The studies emanating from the colonial officers were efforts to lay open the country intellectually and hence to find the best way to control it, socially, politically and economically. Most officers made no pretence that it was otherwise; they merely went about it in a 'scientific' manner. The scholarly dimension was a response on the one hand to this 'scientific' approach, but also a spontaneous reaction on behalf of the public reading them, to the elitism of having emerged from one of France's premier educational institutions. Thus the initial objectives of such studies were often obscured and the scholarly aspect came to the fore. This tendency was exaggerated by an avid desire for first-hand material on the part of the scholarly societies in France, created at that time in response to the exploration fever that characterized the nineteenth century.

The ranking of the Ecole Polytechnique in the early half of the nineteenth century as the foremost school of science in Europe ensured that its imprint was discernible, to some extent, in most of the 'scientific' endeavours undertaken in Algeria. It is no coincidence that the body set up to reconnoitre Algeria was called the 'Scientific Commission'. In the 40 years between the publication of the *Description d'Egypte* (1809–28) and the *Exploration scientifique de l'Algérie* (1844–67) the notion of science and its concomitant methodology had begun to permeate society. Indeed, the difference in the two titles is in itself an indication of the progression science was to make throughout the nineteenth century. Science suggested cut-and-dried methods with clear-cut solutions, valuable tools in the uncertain terrain of the colonial situation. Science implied logic and rationality, necessary concepts in creating an illusion of stability and strength in a society founded on the quicksands of the irrationality and paradox of an occupation. The *Polytechniciens* serving in Algeria created the network through which 'science' became a useful tool of colonial endeavour, and scientific reasoning a metaphor for colonial rule.

6

Race and scholarship in Algeria: the impact of the military

Military scholarship in Algeria laid the foundation for the development of the Kabyle Myth by indirectly contributing to the emergence of racial patterns of thought. It was an empirical, a methodological and, on occasion, an ideological contribution. Military scholars shared a contemporary vision, propagated by philosophers such as Condorcet and Saint-Simon, of the growing importance of science and were aware of the prestige attached to the individual scientist. (It was the latter's contention that 'the individual scientist was the seminal historical force'.[1]) It was their 'scientific' approach, a necessary ingredient in creating the illusory "science of race', that led to their scholarship being so well received in those academic circles exploring this dubious new science.

Military scholarship functioned on two levels. Military personnel acted as scouts and gatherers of material, which then found its way into the hands of scholars in France for use for their own ends, or they researched and produced works of their own, considered to be *bona fide* pieces of scholarship in academic circles in France. The relationship between military men and scholars and academics in France was, therefore, often a close one. The anthropologist Quatrefages, one of many academics to do so, testified to this effect in 1867 when he paid tribute to the military role in furthering French anthropology. 'The scholar', he wrote, 'walked alongside the soldier, and the alliance had been fruitful, as was well known. In Algiers the example set by the Scientific Commission produced sedulous followers from the ranks of the Army' and numerous works had resulted from 'the momentary association of scholars and men of war'.[2] The combination of genuine intellectual curiosity demonstrated by military men serving in Algeria and the military exigencies which shaped their work had various results. First, it motivated them to take an active role in the intellectual life of the colony. This helped the spread of their ideas within the colony. Second, it led them to establish and participate in scholarly societies in Algeria, which then forged close links with those in France. This enhanced the exchange of ideas between France and the colony. Third, it acted as the tinder-box for kindling interest in a variety of disciplines, notably linguistics, archaeology, history, ethnology, anthropology and the natural sciences. The willingness of these scholars and researchers to venture into and show competence in more than one area of scholarship, and the necessity dictated by circumstance to do so, served as a catalyst in bringing together a number of disciplines crucial to the formation of racial thought.

The role played by military scholarship in the actual creation of racial concepts was indirect but complex. While it certainly encouraged the cross-disciplinary examination of the indigenous population necessary to the development of racial scholarship, provided the ethnographical and anthropological societies in France with the material on colonized peoples which served as the basis for racial evaluation, and adhered to a scientific framework which was to be the essential culture in which racial theories were to grow, it also had an ideological dimension. Military personnel came to their research with certain presuppositions and prejudices. Some, such as the concepts of the utopian socialists, were 'modern' and progressive. Others, such as the attitudes towards Islam, were an echo from times past. Prejudices from the past were modified to suit modern circumstances, and together with progressive concepts were woven into the fabric of nineteenth-century racial thought. Then too there was the military as an institution. Its innate paternalism and the conditioning to hierarchical allegiances that military training produced, encouraged patterns of thought well suited to racial dialogue. In isolation no one factor was significant; in aggregate they were so.

The medical corps, imperialism and the concept of race

The question of medicine, disease and imperialism is an intriguing one, the complexity of which has only recently begun to be broached.[3] While the approach to the history of medicine has been divided for some time between those who see it as a succession of scientific achievements which have decreased mortality and increased longevity and those who see it as a reflection of society at large where disease can be used as a social metaphor and where medical practice mirrors social values, prejudices and fears, it is the former interpretation that has usually been favoured in the case of colonial medicine. Lyautey's claim that medicine was the only excuse for colonization found an echo in the work of numerous historians of imperialism.[4] Certainly this has been the case for Algeria, where the examination of colonial medicine has been limited. Turin, who has looked at the areas of contact and conflict and the ensuing 'dialogue' between the colonizer and the colonized and examined the resistance of the latter to the innovations of the former, saw the confrontation between the two in the realm of medicine in nineteenth-century Algeria as a clash between modernity and tradition.[5]

A more critical approach with regard to imperialism in general has been adopted latterly by writers who stress the deleterious demographic and social consequences of European contact and the health hazard to the indigenous population posed by colonization.[6] Relevant to what follows has been the recent appreciation of disease as a factor in the conceptualization of indigenous society. Europeans prided themselves on their scientific understanding, denigrating indigenous medicine and responses to disease as barbaric and superstitious. Disease became a tool with which to condemn indigenous society and medicine a symbol of racial and technological superiority. The emergence of the discipline of 'tropical medicine' at the end of the nineteenth century gave scientific credence to the notion of the tropics as underdeveloped and dangerous, in contrast to the developed and safe temperate zone.[7] Beneath the language of scientific objectivity, therefore, medical attitudes were often subjective, expressing current social and cultural prejudices. Medical pluralism was thus eschewed in favour of the conviction that Western medicine was both superior and unique.[8] Historical research along these lines has concentrated on the end of the nineteenth century, when the bulk of the European colonies were acquired and medicine reached its apogee in imperial ideology, but Algeria was in the vanguard of the process. This was due, on the one hand, to the large number of physicians that were present in the colony as of its inception and, on the other, in spite of the enormous progress medical science and especially epidemiology was yet to make before the end of the century, to the pre-eminence of French medicine and science throughout the first half of the century.

Physicians and the propagation of racial ideas in Algeria

One hundred and seventy-six surgeons arrived in Algeria with the army of conquest.[9] The number of medical personnel was further augmented as civilian hospitals, run largely by military doctors, were successively set up in Algerian towns as they fell to the French.[10] By

1840 nine such hospitals were in existence. As conquest proceeded and the Bureaux Arabes were established, a military physician was assigned first to each administrative division headquarters and then to the *cercles* themselves. As of 1867 even the remote tribal regions were regularly assigned doctors.[11] Although the majority of the medical personnel in Algeria, both military and civilian, were caught up in the pressures of their daily duties, some found time to pursue their own research.

The value of the physician in colonial terms was never underestimated by the administration. In addition to their medical services, which were essential due to the high incidence of disease and epidemics, they were considered to be indispensable agents of the civilizing mission. Once the French had convinced the indigenous population it was incapable of resisting them, they could then demonstrate the extent to which France could help it. In this the physician would become the most useful missionary of French authority and civilization. But it was not just a question of services rendered to the local population; it was also a matter of spreading French and Christian culture through their access to the indigenous home, normally taboo to the French.[12] This ability to penetrate into restricted areas made physicians valuable scientific scouts in the early decades of occupation. The material they gathered during their research found its way back to scientific institutions, mainly the medical academies of Paris, Marseille, Lyon and Montpellier, or was published in scholarly reviews and in the form of *mémoires*. Their methodology was analytical, sometimes statistical, their style of reasoning deductive, and prior to 1850, by concentrating on the effects of disease, lack of hygiene, climate, and rates of morbidity among the French, they sought to contribute to the debate about whether Algeria could be colonized by Europeans. Among the first to do so was Dr Trolliet, head physician of the civilian hospital in Algiers.[13] Trolliet discussed the problem with Tocqueville, with whom he was acquainted.[14] Their involvement in the colonial debate and their interest in human anatomy, physiology and even physiognomy inevitably led to a curiosity about the indigenous population, which they sought to assuage by comparison and contrast to human types of which they had experience. Theirs were the initial steps in institutionalizing the view of humanity from a racial standpoint.

An early contribution to the evolution of such patterns of thought was that of Dr Baudens, principal surgeon and medical professor of the army and member of the medical academies of Marseille, Lyon and Montpellier. Baudens, who arrived in Algeria with the conquering expedition, divided humanity into castes, implying a rigid hierarchy with little possibility of movement. In his *Relation de l'Expédition de Constantine* he stated that there were five Muslim castes in Algeria, which included the Arabs and the Kabyles. Baudens did not contrast the Arabs negatively to the Kabyles nor in any way favour the Kabyles, whom he was inclined to see as barbarous, but he did dwell on their physiognomy. With regard to the Arabs, Baudens observed that they were inclined to be full of guile and extremely lazy. Cruel and cupid, they spread bloodshed and stole with equal pleasure. They were nearly always too thin and most had rags for clothing. Nothing was as ugly as their traits and slovenliness. The Kabyles, on the other hand, were tall and athletic. They had a bold, firey look and an assured gait. They had a proud, masculine expression, a result of their innate traits of which courage and perseverance were the most distinctive.[15] Although Baudens went on to enumerate three defects of the Kabyle character, namely avarice, distrust and duplicity, his linking of positive moral characteristics to physical appearance bore too strong a message to diminish the Kabyles, who in his writings appear more attractive physically and morally than the Arabs. The connotations arising out of Baudens's observations speak for themselves and are, on the one hand, precursors to the more pointed contrasts that were to follow and, on the other, intimations of a more strident racial approach.

In 1845 Dr Eugène Bodichon published *Considérations sur l'Algérie*, a work setting out his views on the situation in Algeria. It contained a chapter on the indigenous population, which was a much more obvious step in the direction of such an approach. Bodichon believed in the force of heredity. The fundamental and differentiating character of human families was determined through the generations, he wrote. Provided miscegenation did not occur, it was incontestable that intellectual and moral aptitudes, as well as character, passed from father to son.[16] Bodichon devoted more space to the Arabs than to the Kabyles, no doubt because Kabylia was as yet unconquered and contact was restricted to itinerant Kabyles. None the less he did declare that the Kabyles formed part of a pure race. He also provided the anatomical model of the Kabyle type together with a character sketch which concluded that Kabyles had an honour, honesty and integrity unknown among African nations.[17] In spite of his more detailed treatment of the Arabs, Bodichon had little good to say about them. He dwelt at length on their physiognomy, linking, in the manner of Baudens, physical appearance to moral characteristics. The expression of the Arab face and the general demeanour of his body revealed the existence of brutal instincts, he wrote. The best analogy that could be made was to the dromedary. Morally and physically there were similarities between the two. Both originated in the desert, had long legs and necks, large feet and hairy skin, and admirably resisted fatigue and prolonged deprivations.[18] The Arabs too were a pure race whose moral and intellectual traits had altered little down the ages. The present-day Arabs, more than any other branch of the Caucasian family having reached the same degree of civilization, were pillagers and thieves. A lack of cross-breeding with other races meant that their love of thieving and raping, traits which had characterized their ancestors, had developed and had been passed down the generations. These were now the dominant passions of their race. Bodichon was insistent on the hereditary nature of these particular vices. A European who stole committed a calculated act which contradicted an innate instinct of honesty; an Arab who stole indulged an innate instinct. The Arab propensity to theft was underscored by indolence, cupidity and fanaticism. Bodichon saddled the Arabs with two other 'major' hereditary characteristics: over-excitability and unreliability. He explained all these hereditary features as being the inevitable result of their physical and moral make-up. Their social organization into nomadic tribes provided further reinforcement.[19]

Bodichon's racial interpretation of indigenous society led him to champion the Kabyles. It was obvious, from the main traits of their character, that they were totally different physically and morally from the Arabs, and were graced with qualities that predisposed a race to understand and adopt European civilization. As agriculturalists they did not disdain work. They had regular habits and that eminently social sentiment, the love of one's country. They had a community spirit and a marked aptitude for the mechanical arts. Last but not least, not being steeped in the dogma and morality of the Koran, they would be quickly civilized once they had embarked on the path of civilization.[20] Bodichon pitted civilization against barbarity and did not stop short of suggesting the elimination of the uncivilizable elements in indigenous society.[21] To the modern reader, his work is just a shrill anti-Arab polemic; in fact the chapter on the indigenous population, from which the above quotations are taken, is a faithful reflection of contemporary ideas on race as applied to the Arabs and the Kabyles. That Bodichon, having established these essentially racial distinctions, used them to further his personal political views regarding the Arabs and the Kabyles is irrelevant; what is relevant is that his arguments in favour of the Kabyles were founded on racial concepts.

While Bodichon's preoccupation with anatomical and physiological characteristics can be imputed to his training as a physician, his overriding theme of civilization versus barbarity, his linkage of physical appearance to moral characteristics and his dismissal of the Arabs as less civilizable because of their physiognomy, inherited traits and social organization were all evidence of prevailing ideas on race. Physiognomy had first been developed by the German theologian and mystic, Johann Kaspar Lavater. Lavater had stressed the importance of facial features in determining human accomplishment and had ranked human species in accordance with classical ideas of beauty. This preoccupation with physique and morality was very much 'in the air' at the time. The French physiologist and professor of legal medicine and the history of medicine, George Cabanis, elaborated at length on the connection between the physical and the moral in a two-volume work of 'physiological psychology' entitled *Rapports du physique et du moral*, in which he claimed that the former determined the latter. (Cabanis was one of the four principal sources for Saint-Simon's *Mémoire sur le Science de l'Homme*; he considered Cabanis to be among the thinkers who did most to encourage the progress of the 'science of man'.[22]) These ideas, especially those of Lavater, were popularized in France by Julien-Joseph Virey.[23] Virey had linked moral values to physical traits in his two-volume *Histoire naturelle du genre humain*, published in 1800.[24] Going further than Lavater and Cabanis, he had also tied beauty and morality in a race to the presence of advanced social institutions.[25] Beauty as an index of superiority was further developed by the Saint-Simonian Victor Courtet de l'Isle in his *Science Politique*.[26] In a much later work Courtet went on to declare that the more beautiful the race the more advanced the civilization, concluding that the most brilliant civilization and most beautiful physical type belonged to the European race.[27]

In terms of contemporary thought, stressing the agricultural lifestyle of the Kabyles, their industriousness and their sociability was a means of pointing to their capacity to progress up the ladder of civilization. Virey had suggested all three as essential for the advancement of civilization together with an ability for commercial activity (extensively practised by the Kabyles). He had also stressed the importance of the evaluation of a people's laws and customs. On the other hand, little could be expected from a nomadic existence. Demographically it was less successful than a sedentary existence for, in general, nomads had low fertility rates. Civilization, therefore, could never develop as the principal element from which the process drew its strength was stunted. Furthermore, nomads could not even be civilized in the same way as the sedentary, for only barbarians allowed their lands to remain uncultivated and wild.[28]

Bodichon was a civilian doctor and a member of *colon* society, but his *Considerations sur l'Algérie* was more polemical than that of the average military doctor, who was inclined to restrict himself to the production of monographs and reports. His work, along with that of Dr Auguste Warnier, served to vulgarize racial notions in a way monographs and reports did not. None the less, military doctors were invaluable to the development in France of interest in racial questions. Many were members of scholarly societies, especially the anthropological societies. Their research provided the first-hand information necessary to confirm or refute racial hypotheses, and was therefore discussed and often published. As one military doctor put it, on the floor of the Société d'Anthropologie de Paris: 'It is not our intention to debate the great questions of ethnology on the unity or plurality of human races ... our work is only to set down what we have seen, an overall groundwork on which more detailed research can later be carried out.'[29]

In fact these doctors were more than mere gatherers of material. Their ministrations in Algeria brought them face to face with an unusually high mortality among Europeans due to epidemics and malaria and introduced them to diseases they had not been accustomed to in Europe. This situation produced a preoccupation with hygiene and acclimatization, first with regard to Europeans in Algeria and then, more broadly, with regard to human races in general. In 1851 Bodichon produced two pamphlets in which he discussed the acclimatization of Europeans in Algeria and elaborated on the concept of moral hygiene.[30] Climate had an effect on human beings, he claimed, and races had environmentally specific characteristics. The European was likeable, sociable and intellectually curious. The Asiatic was antisocial, organized into well-defined castes, stationary, religious and credulous. The African was hostile, violent and instinctive.[31] Fair races adapted with difficulty to Algeria and although Europeans from the Southern Mediterranean made an easier transition, the climate of Africa had a corrupting influence on all non-Africans who lived there for any length of time, which manifested itself in a 'disturbance of intellectual and moral faculties'. To counteract these ill effects among the settlers it was necessary to encourage them to leave the towns and settle in the countryside, for an agricultural population was healthier and had higher moral standards than an urban population. For this reason too he vaunted the qualities of the Kabyle over those of the Arab, urging his compatriots to favour Kabyles rather than Arabs, for they were sedentary, less volatile in character and represented greater interests. In spite of the problems Algeria appeared to pose to European physical and moral health, Bodichon did not advocate their departure from the continent for he believed that, left to its own devices, the continent would revert to being the accursed land (*terre maudite*) it had been of old.[32]

The climatic debate in Algeria, which was grounded in genuine anxiety regarding the potential for colonization by the French because of their initially high mortality rate, foreshadowed a lasting preoccupation with climate that characterized colonial communities in general. Even when scientists began to uncover the microbiological basis for tropical diseases at the end of the nineteenth century, the preoccupation with the climatic influences on Europeans continued. 'Climatic neurasthenia' had a wider resonance, giving metaphorical form to fears about loss of European supremacy and reinforcing, symbolically, the need to maintain social and racial barriers between the colonizer and the colonized. A resurgence of the climatic debate, in a more sophisticated version, occurred in the early twentieth century throughout the colonial world.[33] Algeria, by this time, had a well-established settler population and was less inclined to use climate as a way of expressing colonial anxieties. None the less, the climatic debate found its first strong voice there and set the tone for its future evolution.

The linking of disease and race was another area in which physicians in Algeria played a role. In a pamphlet entitled *De l'Humanité*, Bodichon raised the question, stating that each race had its specific diseases.[34] Among the most repellent diseases and afflictions prevalent among Europeans many had been acquired from contact with other races: syphilis from the red races, skin diseases such as leprosy and scabies from the brown races, transmitted at the time of the Crusades, lice from the yellow races. The Europeans, on the other hand, had spread scrofula, also known as the king's evil, a tubercular condition affecting the lymph glands. While it is incontestable that there are regionally specific diseases and that these were spread by the migration to or from these areas, such diseases and afflictions are not racially determined. In Bodichon's day bacteriology, virology and immunology were unknown disciplines, for it was only in the last two decades of the nineteenth century that the relation of bacteria and viruses to disease began to be unravelled. Racial explanations for such phenomena, therefore, could seem plausible. Linking disease to race and demonstrating that some races were able to overcome their innate deficiencies by proper hygiene and care opened the door to the notion of superior and inferior races. Certainly Bodichon believed that such a hierarchy existed. Inferior races were unable to raise themselves up because they lacked the necessary attributes, while superior races had them and were therefore able to progress steadily upwards. The lot of mankind had been placed in the hands of the fair races, for they had conquered the 'tree of science' which would make them god-like. Five nations from among the fair races were to be the tutors of mankind and on them would depend all humanitarian progress.[35] As for the Arabs and Berbers, in *De l'Humanité* Bodichon classified them as two separate races within the white-brown type. The Berbers, who were of the *race Atlante*, were capable of advanced civilization and, due to innate patriotism and xenophobia, were characterized by a stubborn resistance to any unifying religious or political system. Among the traits of this race Bodichon also listed sedentariness and democratic tendencies. The Arab race, on the other hand, was characterized by its migratory, bellicose, proselytizing spirit, its changeable character and its pride.[36]

Disease and acclimatization in Algeria were among the starting points for a racial determinism that would eventually lead to a racial polarization of European and non-European. Acclimatization, which so preoccupied doctors under the military regime, continued to receive attention during civilian rule. As settlement increased and disease was better controlled, especially among the European population, the concept of artificial acclimatization (*acclimatement artificiel*) was introduced. The Europeans from the Mediterranean shores – Spaniards, Maltese, southern Italians – were seen to be better adapted to life in Algeria than those from the north. Intermarriage between these two groups of Europeans, to create a new race eminently adapted to Algeria, was the essence of artificial acclimatization.[37] Disease, or rather its control and containment, served to reinforce the European and non-European divide by fostering the idea of an innate European superiority. The scientific and technological advancement of the Europeans was transfigured into physical and racial superiority.

Two other doctors renowned, among their contemporaries, for their interest in and contribution to racial questions were Boudin and Périer. Both served in Algeria and were active members of the Société d'Anthropologie de Paris. Boudin was senior physician at the Vincennes Asylum, but spent four years in Algeria, first in Constantine and then in Algiers, followed by seven years as senior physician at the military hospital of Marseille, which dealt with all severe cases from Algeria. It was Boudin who first insisted on the importance of gathering information on the races of Algeria.[38] He was especially interested in the results of inbreeding, inter-racial breeding and, like so many other doctors in Algeria, the morbidity of races transposed from one area to another.[39] The research he carried out with regard to the latter, and his conclusions that human races had difficulty adapting to climates unlike their own, led him to opine that the colonization of Algeria by the French was not feasible. His *Traité de géographie et de statistique médicale* (a good example of the way the discipline of statistics was developing into a social tool) contained, in the words of the anthropologist Paul Broca, 'a fund of precious anthropological information' and was an important landmark in racial studies.[40] Although he did not publish any work specifically about the Kabyles and the Arabs, he kept abreast with developments in the racial studies of Algeria by regular attendance at the Société d'Anthropologie de Paris and through his close friend Joanny-Napoléon Périer.

Périer pursued a successful career in the military medical corps, entering as a student in 1829 and progressing to the post of senior physician at the Hotel des Invalides. He first went to Algeria as the member of the Scientific Commission in charge of hygiene and produced a two-volume work on the subject.[41] He shared many of Gobineau's convictions on race, including the belief that pure races were superior to mixed ones as miscegenation weakened a race, and showed an early interest in the Kabyles, to whom he devoted considerable research. His nomination to the Scientific Commission of Algeria had first kindled this interest, which had then led on to a more general preoccupation with race. For 20 years he was a regular contributor to the Société d'Anthropologie, both on matters concerning the Kabyles and on racial questions in general. His *mémoire, Des Races dites Berbères et de leur ethnogénie*, became an acknowledged reference on the subject.[42] In his funeral oration Broca paid tribute to Périer for having devoted such close attention to the Kabyles and the Arabs, two radically different races so unequally receptive to European influence. Périer's work, he went on, had enlightened colonial administraters who, as a result, were in a position to distinguish between the two and use their respective aptitudes.[43] In his discussion of Berber races and their ethnology, Périer referred to over one hundred authorities. He mentioned every author of note who had contributed something to the question of Berber origins and race, considering their work in the light of his own arguments.[44] Périer's research was concerned with the purity of the Berber race, and more specifically with the disparities between two of its branches, the Tuareg and the Kabyles. His conclusion was that Berbers stemmed from two ancient races, the Libyans and the Getules – the Kabyles having descended from the former, the Tuareg from the latter. The significance of Périer's work lies over and above its overtly racial approach. What is inescapable is that he, and in this he resembled many a contemporary theorist on race, incorporated material which was not manifestly about race; works such as Carette's, Daumas's, Devaux's, Bibesco's and Duprat's which, to be sure, contained rudimentary elements of racial theory but which were not arguing an essentially racial case. As early as 1848 the journalist and pamphleteer, Alphonse Esquiros, had pointed out the grip of this new ideology on the well-informed.[45]

From that date it spread steadily, with scientists or, more accurately, scientifically trained men, playing an important role. As Finot was drily to remark in the opening decade of the twentieth century: 'From the time Gobineau and his disciples permitted themselves to be hypnotized by the size of the human brain, science has made some singular findings.'[46]

The scientific credentials of a physician were, in theory, beyond reproach. Medical students, then as now, were creamed off the upper layers of the school achievement roll. The training was long, often arduous, and the drop-out rate high. Qualification brought with it a certain prestige, enabling the fledgling doctor immediately to assume a significant role in society. In spite of the distancing effect such prestige can engender, the physician, more than any other 'scientist', remains in touch with the lay person. This was even more accentuated in colonial society, where anybody with an official position was known and deferred to by all. Physicians acquired an authority over and above their medical role, and it was this that made of them such efficient vehicles for the propagation of racial ideas. They were admirable professional and social communicators. It comes as no surprise, therefore, that members of the medical profession swelled the ranks of the anthropological societies, or that the more articulate among them served as the vulgarizers of the ideas that were making themselves felt in more select circles.

Dr Auguste Hubert Warnier (1810–75)

Among the most influential disseminators of ideas concerning the Kabyles was Auguste Warnier. Warnier had arrived in Algeria as a military surgeon in 1834, and served with Daumas in Mascara while the latter was consul there from 1837 to 1839. Daumas found in him a congenial and talented collaborator, and expressed his appreciation to his commanding officer in Oran.[47] Warnier's medical capabilities, humanity and growing reputation as a practitioner also won him praise.[48] Initially one of the colony's Saint-Simonians, he was an activist with as many detractors as admirers. For some, like de Neveu, he was a petulant latter-day 'Danton'.[49] For others he was one of the best-informed members of the colony on Algeria and its peoples.[50] By the early 1860s Warnier had left both the military and the Saint-Simonian camps and assumed the role of *colon* spokesman. He was closely involved in land evaluation and the 1873 Land Bill bears his name.

Warnier divided the indigenous population into three majority groups: 1 million Berber-speaking Berbers *(Berbères berberisants)*, 1.2

million Arab-speaking Berbers *(Berbères arabisants)* and 500,000 pure Arabs, and various minority groups such as the Turks, Moors, etc.[51] Although he stated that the majority of the indigenous population was Berber he drew a distinction between the Berber-speakers and the Arab-speakers, claiming that the former had totally escaped the demoralizing influence of Arab culture. The Berber was the autochthon of the area; the Arab the invader, a 'devastating torrent' and element of disorder who had never been able to establish anything of value. Warnier believed that the Berber civilization, together with all Western European civilizations, had evolved from Roman and Christian traditions and would therefore prove more adaptable to French civilization than the Arab.[52] The Arabs, incorrigible nomads that they were, could never be drawn into the French fold.

Warnier distinguished between Arab and Berber on the grounds of origin, language, culture, social organization and morality. It was the latter three headings that provided him with the opportunity to draw his sharpest comparisons. Among Warnier's claims were that Cordoba and Seville were the works of the Berbers, not the Arabs, that Berber social organization bore a promising resemblance to the French, and that the Berbers had a sense of justice that was lacking in the Arabs.[53] Warnier's works were indisputably polemical but this served to draw attention to them, making his views well known. His material was not overly 'scientific' and his prose was accessible to the lay person. He used racial arguments to political ends, and by doing so assisted in popularizing the notion that the Kabyles were racially superior to the Arabs.

Military ethnologists … military anthropologists

The question of who was an ethnologist and who was an anthropologist in nineteenth-century Algeria is vexing, as distinctions between the two are often blurred. Stocking, in his work on Victorian anthropology, suggests that the difference, in England at least, was one of intellectual orientation, social and political background, style and tone, rather than choice of subject matter.[54] According to his research, 'ethnologicals' were inclined to be Darwinians from dissenting middle-class backgrounds with a university education or an established profession. They were also predominantly Liberal in their politics and their humanitarian concerns. 'Anthropologicals', on the other hand, were inclined to be anti-Darwinian and to come from traditionally established social backgrounds. Fewer were university educated and more were Conservative in their politics and social concerns.[55] The conflict and recriminations that characterized the relationships between the Ethnological Society and the Anthropological Society in Great Britain, especially throughout the decade of the Darwinian revolution, were absent in France. To begin with the French Ethnological Society of Paris had ceased to exist by the time the Anthropological Society of Paris was founded in 1859 and, second, the reaction to Darwinian ideas was slow in France and the debate never reached the pitch it did in Great Britain.[56] None the less, the hardening racial attitudes that were to characterize the stance of the 'anthropologicals' of Great Britain was reflected in French anthropology. French officer-scholars cannot be classed as 'ethnological' or 'anthropological' in Stocking's terms, for whatever their political agenda, in the first half of the nineteenth century the number of scholarly institutions available for the dissemination of their work was limited. At this stage, therefore, the possibility of institutionalizing ideological *cum* intellectual factions was circumscribed. What is certain, however, is that as the century progressed the racial tone in France was raised and a more overt racial approach made its appearance in research.

Anthropology, as a discipline in its own right, came into being in France with the formation of the Anthropological Society of Paris, and concerned itself, in the nineteenth century at least, almost exclusively with physical anthropology. Strictly speaking, therefore, the majority of the works on the Kabyles emerging from Algeria were ethnological. Pure physical anthropology was limited to works such as those by Gillebert d'Hercourt, Topinard and, in the twentieth century, Bertholon and Chantre.[57] (Even then it could be argued that some aspects of these were ethnological.) After 1859 military ethnologists became closely involved with the Paris Anthropological Society, and later with similar societies. Faidherbe, for example, was considered to be an anthropologist although he did not limit himself to physical anthropology; so too was Hanoteau. They were adopted into the anthropological fold because of the value their work held for anthropologists in France. They responded to this need by keeping abreast with anthropological developments and by maintaining close communications with anthropological societies. After 1860 anthropology dominated the sciences of man until the emergence of the French school of sociology led by Emile Durkheim at the end of the century. During this time it was natural that military scholars studying indigenous societies tended to gravitate towards anthropological societies; to this extent they were anthropologists rather than ethnologists.

However eminent these early ethnologists and later anthropologists became in circles concerned with the social sciences in France, it is important to bear in mind that they were military men first, social scientists second. Carette was not commissioned by the government to produce an ethnological treatise on the Kabyles but to situate them, in as much detail as possible, from a reconnaissance point of view. The question he was asking was not *What is Kabyle society all about?* but *How will Kabyle society fit into the French scheme of things?* That his endeavours became a foundation stone in Kabyle ethnology was a tribute to his formal education, not to his approach nor indeed to his methodology which was, by his own admission, 'an inventory' of a certain area of Algeria.[58] The works of other military scholars such as Aucapitaine, Daumas, Devaux, Lapène, de Neveu, even Hanoteau, all bore the imprint of military thought but none the less went on to become substantial sources for nineteenth-century ethnology and anthropology. It is necessary, therefore, to take a closer look at why their work was so valued and how the lens through which these military scholars viewed indigenous society shaped future ideas.

Obviously enough the primary value of the work produced by these military scholars lay in the fact they were detailed, first-hand accounts of little-known societies. As such they were hitherto unmatched primary sources. It was not merely a question of the military being able to penetrate where the civilian researcher could not, which of course was the case during the initial stages of conquest. The situation in Algeria, greatly enhanced by the institution of the Bureaux Arabes, enabled officers, whose term of duty in a given post extended to many months or even years, not only to observe the local population closely but also to do so for long stretches at a time. This is of course the basis for any anthropological study, and this is what made their work indispensable to social scientists and scholarly societies in France. For the first time, here was a wealth of detail which could be sifted for relevant material but, most important, could be cross-checked. Unlike the travellers and geographer-explorers of the past, on whose material scientists had relied up to the nineteenth century, these military scholars remained on site, so to speak, and could be consulted to elucidate aspects of their work that continued to puzzle scientists in France or be prodded to research into matters of contemporary interest. The Société d'Anthropologie de Paris wasted no time in issuing instructions for anthropologists in areas where France was flexing its expansionist muscle. The first of these saw the light of day in 1860. It is no coincidence that the formal instructions for anthropological research in Algeria, when they appeared over a decade later, should have been the collaboration of a military man, Faidherbe, and an anthropologist, Topinard.[59]

The layout of these instructions was in itself symbolic of the wider relationship between the military and the social sciences. The first part was by Faidherbe, who presented his contribution as an enumeration of the races and peoples who had successively made up the population of North Africa. In the second part, Topinard paid tribute to the 'honourable reporter' of the first part and proceeded to set out the requirements for anthropological research as well as the primary criteria for determining race. These comprised social organization, language, all possible information on history, origins, local traditions and genealogies, and moral and physical characteristics. It was of course the Berbers who stimulated the most interest and it was here that more precision was needed. The instructions stated that after determining the characteristics of the present-day blond Berbers, what was needed was to continue the excavations so successfully carried out by Féraud, Bourguignat, Faidherbe, Berbrugger and Bourjot, and to collect sufficient quantities of skulls and bones for examination. Craniometry substituted rigorous methods for more imaginative ones, and was a totally new branch of anthropology which required the calm of the laboratory and endless comparison with other series of skulls.[60] Topinard's adherence to scientific methods prevented the flights of fantasy that had characterized some work on the Berbers, but it did not preclude placing his faith in what had gone before. To begin with he was in no doubt that all nomadic tribes were Arab, while all sedentary tribes were Berber.[61] His elaboration of the differences between the Arabs and the Berbers owes everything to the military ethnologists who had devoted themselves to the subject to date.

Anthropologists and scholars in France picked up on the military interest in the Kabyles, but the focus of enquiry was shifted. As we have seen, early military observers were interested in Kabylia and the Kabyles for reasons of reconnaissance and security. They were intrigued by the impenetrability of the area and the success with which the Kabyles had resisted conquest. Their interest in the indigenous population lay in their potential to be incorporated successfully into colonial society. However obliquely it was presented religion, or rather the perceived lack of it, was the crux of their preference for the Kabyles. The French then, as now, recoiled before the excessive manifestations of Islam and the Kabyles remained untainted by such zealousness. In the face of conquering armies, they had withdrawn into their mountains and retained their individuality. The attraction the military ethnologists felt for the Kabyles was transmitted to scholarly circles, where it was transposed into a scientific interest. In the jargon of the scientists it was converted into a desire to discover the enigmas of an unspoilt people. The absorption with the study of unspoilt societies was a spill over into the methodology of anthropology of the idea that what was 'pure' was good, an idea itself later subsumed into racial ideology.

If the impetus behind military research was reconnaissance and security, military ethnologists none the less brought to the task certain mental impediments that had a bearing on the way they approached their subject matter. In the first place, the concept of cultural pluralism was an alien one; in its stead was the conviction of European superiority, which engendered the fallacy of the *mission civilisatrice*. An idea dear to Saint-Simon, it had found expression in his most successful pamphlet, *De la réorganisation de la société européenne*, produced in collaboration with the historian Augustin Thierry in 1814. In it Saint-Simon had stated that populating the globe with the European race, superior to all other human races, ensuring ease of travel around it and making it as habitable as Europe, was an endeavour the European parliament should oversee and keep constantly in its sights.[62] Saint-Simon's futuristic and, as it turns out, prophetic vision of Europe encompassed a general parliament that would legislate and direct the educational, social and moral affairs of its members and, by extension, their spheres of interest. Saint-Simon's conditions for religious practice were also pertinent and presage even the most 'liberal' attitudes to Islam in the colony.[63] The conviction of European superiority, which for Saint-Simon would find its apotheosis in a sort of pan-Europeanism, was one of the most pervasive concepts to emerge in the nineteenth century.

Methodologically this implied a comparative approach. In ethnology the researcher, consciously or unconsciously, sought out similarities to European society and issued value judgements concerning the object of study using European norms as the yardstick of evaluation. This led to a skewing of reality. For example, in the egalitarianism of the Kabyle *djemâa* early military observers were quick to see a rudimentary republican democracy when in fact it was an egalitarianism arising out of the defence-intensive nature of Kabyle society. If the concept of democracy was to be used at all, it was a structural rather than ideological democracy or, as Bourdieu put it, a *démocratie vécue* without an inalienable right to political participation.[64] By giving a sociopolitical interpretation to an essentially organizational phenomenon, it was easy to assume that Kabyle institutions could be more easily adapted to the French than those of the Arabs. In the family sphere, it was monogamy that attracted the attention of French observers. Here too Kabyle society seemed to strike a harmonious chord with the French, causing observers to focus on the morality of Kabyle family life rather than educing a more pertinent socio-economic analysis. Suffice it to cite just two of the many possible examples. This *are they like us/aren't they like us* attitude was, naturally enough, greatly exacerbated by the colonial mission, which was to dissolve and absorb societies indigenous to the occupied territories. The transmission to scholarly societies of material with this inevitable bias, however attenuated, greatly assisted the development of the classification of races into a meritorious pyramid of being. So too did the tendency to conceptualize in hierarchical terms, which came all too easily to these officer-scholars as they were themselves part of a rigidly imposed hierarchical system. If there were social and political hierarchies so too could there be racial ones. It is easy to understand how, out of a compulsion to conceptualize in this way, the notion emerged that the Kabyles were not just different from the Arabs, they were better.

The other important notion that impinged on the work of the military ethnologists was that of *progress*. Saint-Simon advocated the reorganization of European society in order that it would, among other things, be better placed to aid other peoples to progress. The concept of progress was a recurrent theme among intellectuals during the first half of the century and one which could be admirably woven into the tissue of the *mission civilisatrice*. The optimism of the early half of the nineteenth century may have engendered the idea of a will to progress among humanity, but it fell short of suggesting any universality in the phenomenon. In the words of Courtet de l'Isle, progress was dependent on the dual influences of heredity and environment.[65] The suggestion that an entire people could fall short due to inherent aptitudes, or rather a lack of them, left the door wide open to more prejudicial standpoints. Renan was one who adopted such a view, in a passage that stressed the Arab component of the Semitic race as much as, if not more than, the Jewish component. He was, he said, the first to recognize that in comparison to the Indo-European race, the Semitic race was really an inferior combination of human nature.[66] In Algeria, Daumas followed suit by stating that European and Semitic races progressed at an unequal pace. Europeans built on ancestral knowledge; Arabs remained wedded to ancestral tradition. One marched onwards; the other stayed still.[67] Comparisons between the Semitic and European races had a further relevance with regard to the Kabyles as a philological debate was carried on at some length as to whether or not the Kabyle language was a Semitic one. There was an ineluctable direction to these debates for they all led to the same underlying question, namely, could the indigenous population progress, and in the case of Algeria, were the Kabyles more apt to progress than the Arabs or were they not.

The received ideas of European superiority, of the hierarchical nature of the human condition and of the conviction that progress was possible, albeit unevenly, coupled with the dictates of security and reconnaissance, affected the focus of research and the structure of the ensuing work. Of paramount importance to the military was the organizational structure of a society, its judicial system and its potential for progress, for these were the indicators of its capacity to absorb French civilization. Transposed into scientific circles, the focus shifted only slightly. What assumed importance was the organizational value of a society as evidenced by its political and administrative institutions; its morality as evidenced by its judicial and domestic conventions; its potential to obscurantism as evidenced by its religious practices. Thus distinguishing features of indigenous society for military scholars became the criteria by which ethnologists and anthropologists in France evaluated a society and placed it on the pyramid of civilization.

General L.J. Adolphe C.C. Hanoteau (1814–97)

The high point of military scholarship came with the publication of *La Kabylie et les Coutumes Kabyles*. Although the work was a collaborative effort between Adolphe Hanoteau, a graduate of the Ecole Polytechnique and an officer of the Bureaux Arabes for 13 years, and Aristide Letourneaux, a judge at the Appeal Court in Algiers, it is Hanoteau who is best remembered as its author. Both the scholarly career of Hanoteau and the work itself demonstrate how military concerns impinged on scholarship, blurring with it to make separation of the two indistinguishable. Hanoteau first interested himself in the Berbers through their language. In April 1842 the Ministry of War had set up a commission for the compilation of a dictionary and a grammar manual of the Berber language; the decision arose out of a pragmatic desire to enable officers serving in Berber-speaking areas to master the language in order to understand and control their subjects without the aid of an interpreter. The commission produced the dictionary but not the grammar manual, and 15 years later Hanoteau took up the unfinished task by tackling the Berber grammar.[68] But Hanoteau set out to do more than just the initial task set by the Ministry of War; he also hoped to elucidate the nature of Berber origins, which were proving so elusive to establish. Only philology, he believed, could throw some light on the question, and it would then be possible to link the Berber race to one of the great divisions of the human family.[69] When other evidence was lacking language could be a decisive indicator of a people's past. He felt certain that in some past era the Berbers had been masters of the whole of North Africa. Without the historical traces necessary to prove it, recourse to language was the only way of justifying this opinion.[70]

But there was more to the Berber than his widely spoken language.

Hanoteau drew attention to the persistent way in which the Berber race had preserved its own physiognomy, its language, its individuality and its independence in the midst of all the vicissitudes it had been subjected to. As one of the most remarkable aspects of African history, its people deserved to be studied.[71] Hanoteau was encouraged in his work by de Neveu and on its completion in 1858 he submitted it, together with a similar work on Tuareg grammar, to the Académie d'Inscriptions. Two years later he was awarded the Prix Volnay for his work on Berber languages, a distinction he shared with Ernest Renan.

Philology was often closely linked to a preoccupation with race. That race was an ever-present consideration for Hanoteau is given credence by his opening sentence, which stressed the racial nature of the North African population and the fact that of the two races, Arab and Berber, the former had been implanted by conquest. Hanoteau's work aroused considerable interest in scholarly circles in France. Renan, in his review of *La Kabylie et les Coutumes Kabyles*, assessed Hanoteau's oeuvre on the Berbers and praised him for his contribution to this branch of linguistics. Hanoteau's Kabyle and Tuareg grammars, he said, had 'objectively laid down the outline of this great linguistic system, prudently leaving any conclusions to comparative philologists.'[72] Hanoteau may not have drawn definitive conclusions concerning the Berbers, but Renan had no such scruples. In the first place he declared that Berber was profoundly different from the Semitic languages. He went on to say that thanks to Hanoteau a shaft of light had appeared on the obscure history of Africa. That the Kabyle language was almost identical to the Tuareg, which in turn was linked to all the Saharan idioms, had clearly determined the ancient stock of this North African race.[73] Thus what had started out as scholarship primarily for military consumption had attained a much wider and more significant readership.

Hanoteau's *Essai* was the beginning of a lengthy commitment to the study of Kabylia and its people. In his *magnum opus*, researched in the final years of military rule in Algeria, Hanoteau picked up some of the themes of his earlier work. While he left to others the amplification of deciding to which branch of the human family the Berbers should be attached, he did acknowledge the importance of race and its implications in a short chapter devoted to the subject. The question of race in Kabylia, he said, deserved serious study but, due to its ramifications, was too time-consuming to undertake at present. None the less he noted its importance and the need for further study in the area at a future date. As far as Hanoteau was concerned, miscegenation had been a feature of Kabyle society over the centuries. Unlike Gobineau and Périer, who believed in the force of racial purity (and who, in any case, had a minority following in France), he was inclined to support those who believed that miscegenation regenerated a race. Hanoteau said that if it was true that the more cross-breeding a race had been subjected to the more likely it was to be receptive to civilization, at present the prospects for the Kabyles were perfect.[74] For all this *La Kabylie et les Coutumes Kabyles* did not seek to answer questions on race, yet its importance as a work made it an indispensable reference in this area.[75] Presentation was more significant than information; how it was said more important that what was said. In his review, Renan evoked its stimulating effect, declaring that he knew of no more thought-provoking overall picture on the conditions of human societies.[76]

La Kabylie et les Coutumes Kabyles was the most thorough treatment of Kabyle society to date. The work is not a catalogue of comparisons with the Arab race but that Hanoteau was a Kabylophile, and an ardent one at that, is evident throughout its three volumes. So too is his belief that Kabyles were the most promising candidates for assimilation. It was their willingness to accept innovations in their daily life that distinguished the Berber race from other Muslim peoples and would prove advantageous for the French civilizing mission.[77] Although Hanoteau relies heavily on what went before, there is much innovation – he was, for example, the first to recognize the defence-intensive nature of Kabyle society.[78] But instead of starting from that premise and working outwards in an attempt to grasp how the customs and institutions of Kabyle society evolved, he latches on to recognizable structures and institutions, primarily the administrative and judicial systems characterized by the village (*thaddart*) and the penal code (*kanoun*), presenting them in all-encompassing detail but failing to analyse them in a meaningful way. Such an empirical approach leaves the door open to personal interpretation on the part of the reader. Instead of being led to view Kabyle society in its own right, the reader has free rein to make comparisons with what he knows best: his own society.

It is also useful, when assessing Hanoteau's work, to bear in mind the post-revolutionary (1789–99) developments in France which occasioned a reorganization of the French judicial system with the introduction of the Napoleonic Code and the emergence of a heightened awareness of new concepts: political (democracy; egalitarianism), social (individualism), and administrative (*départements*; *communes*). Such concepts (and innovations) become value-laden in a society which has been submitted to the sort of social trauma provoked by a revolution, acquiring positive or negative connotations depending on from which side of the political spectrum they are viewed. Interpreting indigenous society in their light would naturally lend itself to the distortions of approbation or disapprobation. Hanoteau, it would seem, was unable to resist this inclination.

Hanoteau dwelt at length on the Kabyle village, on Kabyle democracy and on Kabyle law (to which he devoted over 400 pages). For Hanoteau, if the village was the cornerstone of Kabyle society, it was the streamlined version of self-rule found in the mountains of Kabylia that most stimulated his imagination. The political and administrative organization of the Kabyle people was among the most democratic and straightforward imaginable. The ideal free, low-cost government that utopian philosophers had long strived for had been a reality for centuries in the Kabyle mountains, and it resulted from the Kabyle community spirit and their love of solidarity.[79] Hanoteau may have seen his personal political utopia reflected in Kabyle society, but he was aware that others might not share his views. He stressed the importance of focusing on Kabyle institutions none the less, however rudimentary and imperfect they might be. It was in French interests to understand them well; if they could not serve as institutional models they could at least be the subject of interesting studies. Hanoteau did not try to evaluate the Kabyle passion for egalitarianism and independence as manifested in Kabyle democracy in the light of his prior assertion as to the defence-intensive nature of Kabyle society, but put it down to an intrinsically racial trait. There follows one of those paradoxical conclusions that is the salt of the work and would seem to indicate that its author had not altogether come to terms with the innovations of his own era. Having lauded the will to egalitarianism inherent in the Berber race, he then proceeded to read into it the seeds of their political decline. It was 'just in principle and, within limits, good for a restricted society but it was fatal for the masses'. Furthermore, by the encouragment of unbridled fragmentation resistance had been sapped and the formation of a strong homogeneous nation had been prevented. Perhaps, he concluded, no other explanation was needed for the successive collapses of Berber dynasties.[80] Whatever the outcome of this egalitarianism, the message that it was inherently Berber was not lost. It led Renan to declare the democratic nature of the Berber constitution unique, setting their law apart from that of other traditional peoples.[81]

It was of course on Kabyle law that Hanoteau dwelt at such extreme length, and it was this very insistence that provoked Renan to include legislation in his original enumeration of the five essential attributes in the determination of a race from the standpoint of the social sciences.[82] In Hanoteau's treatment of Kabyle law one is again aware of the impact of military concerns on a larger scholarship. Hanoteau's aim was threefold: to record for posterity Kabyle legislation as it was prior to French conquest and before it was swallowed up, at some future date, by the Napoleonic Code; to show the ameliorations brought to the system to date by the imposition of the French code (primarily in penal law); and on a less pragmatic level to assuage an interest 'in the philosophy of history and the laws regulating human development'. A study of Kabyle criminal law would be of particular interest because of its originality, whereby primitive private law was juxtaposed with a relatively liberal progressive social law as defined by the village.[83] A society's legislation could thus be an indication of its progress and Hanoteau, whenever appropriate, compared and contrasted Kabyle and French law in order to stress this point. Indeed, in his extensive footnotes, although cross-references to the Napoleonic Code predominated, he also alluded to articles in, among others, Germanic, Hebraic, Muslim and Ancient Greek law which were relevant to his text. Kabyle customary law was, for Hanoteau, the most vital manifestation of the original ethos of the Berber race (*l'esprit primitif de la race*), an ethos that was especially well developed due to the absence, until the arrival of the French, of foreign domination.[84] Hanoteau's meticulous handling of Kabyle law and the acclaim with which the book was met had a wider implication. In the study of a given society or a given race, its morality was elevated to a central position. Henceforth *race* would have more significance. In Renan's words, race was 'a mould of moral education more than a question of blood'.[85] Hanoteau's work may not have been overtly concerned with questions of race but his methodology, along with that of other military scholars, contributed to the evolution of the patterns of thought on which racial ideology was founded.

Scholarly societies in Algeria

The first scholarly institution of Algeria, the Bibliothèque d'Alger, was founded in 1835. In 1839 the creation of the Scientific Commission for the exploration of Algeria served as confirmation of the fact that scholarship, military and civilian, would be intricately tied up with the conquest and exploration of North Africa. In 1847 a certain Charles Texier started to compile a list of the historic monuments of Algeria.[86] The same year Bugeaud established in Algiers the colony's first society to concern itself with arts, sciences and letters. It was, however, in the 1850s that scholarship in Algeria really took flight with the foundation of two of the colony's leading societies, the Société archéologique de Constantine in 1853 and the Société historique algérienne in 1856.[87] These societies served as the meeting point of civilian and military scholarship and the channels for exchange of ideas with similar societies in France. Both show a strong military presence among their members. The establishment of the Société historique algérienne was encouraged by Field Marshal Randon, who became its first honorary president, but it was Dr Louis-Adrien Berbrugger who was its guiding force until his death in 1869. Berbrugger, a Saint-Simonian and a *kabylophile*, first arrived in Algeria in 1834. He was an Arabist, married to a Muslim, who became a well-known personality in the colony. Involved in every aspect of scholarship in Algeria, he helped found the Bibliothèque Nationale d'Alger, later becoming its chief librarian. He was editor-in-chief of the *Moniteur Algérien*, wrote regularly for the *Revue Africaine* and published various works on the colony, of which *Les époques militaires de la Grande Kabylie* is the best known.[88]

Berbrugger's presence was exceptionally evident in scholarly circles but, like him, many officer-scholars made the most of the scholarly facilities available to them in the colony. It was through their journals, the *Annuaire de la Société archéologique de la Province de Constantine* and the *Revue Africaine* in the case of the Société archéologique and the Société historique, that the ideas formulated within the precincts of Algerian scholarly societies were disseminated most widely.[89] Both the Société archéologique and the Société historique sought to shed light on the history of North Africa, the former through its study of ancient ruins and inscriptions, and the latter by analysing unpublished material and authentic historical documents.[90] An area of particular interest was Kabylia. According to the *Revue Africaine* everything about it, past or present, would now fascinate readers.[91] Initial interest was stimulated, of course, by the impending conquest of the area, but Kabylia and the Kabyles remained eminently researchable throughout the colonial period. The scholarly societies in Algeria took up the gauntlet thrown down by d'Avezac, the geographer and researcher into race, when he reminded scholars that 'it was in national traditions and the archaeology of language and monuments that the vestiges of African origins and revolutions should be sought.'[92] It was in the *Annuaire* that the first forays into ancient inscriptions were published, leading to the development of Libyan epigraphy. It also contained the first articles concerning the allegedly Celtic monuments in the area of Constantine, curiosities that were to side-track scholars in their search for the origins of the Berbers. It was the *Revue Africaine*, however, that did the most to encourage the quest for Berber origins, primarily through the study of ruins, inscriptions and history (mainly with reference to the classics). The one attempt to do this through oral reports, made by Alphone Meyer, an interpreter with the army, was published but scathingly received by the journal's editor, Berbrugger. He warned his readers that nothing could be less historical than Meyer's work but added that it was interesting none the less, for it showed that Kabyle oral traditions concerning their origins completely ignored their history during 'ancient times'.[93]

It is significant that French scholars dismissed local traditions regarding Kabyle origins, preferring to rely on the classics. On the one hand it was evidence of the tendency to pit the West against the East: the sources of Western civilization must be more reliable than those of Eastern tradition. On the other hand, by relying so heavily on the classics many scholars started with a premise and then tried to prove it, rather than the other way around. In this way the Libyans became the ancestors of the Kabyles.[94] They were not content to let it rest there, and a debate ensued as to whether or not the Libyans were of Aryan origin.[95] Colonel Louis Rinn, who owed much to Faidherbe, spent considerable time studying the origins of the Berbers and contributed a lengthy work which was serialized in the *Revue Africaine*. He concluded with the statement that 'the Berbers who actually formed the majority of the indigenous population were of the Indo-European race and language.'[96] Using a theory, derived from the Book of Genesis (Chapters 9 and 10), which attributed racial ancestry to the three sons of Noah – Japheth, Shem and Ham – Rinn claimed that the Berbers were descended from the former.[97] According to this theory Japheth sired the white race, Shem the Asiatic and/or Semitic and Ham the black.[98] However, not everyone was partisan to Rinn's theories. The debate as to whether or not the Berbers were of Aryan or Semitic descent had extended over several decades, had had a considerable following and had aroused interest in France. Mercier, one of the colony's leading interpreters, argued that the Berber language had too many similarities to Semitic languages for it to escape such classification.[99] Faidherbe, using Libyan inscriptions and the examination of dolmens to bolster his case, claimed it did not and that Berbers were not of Semitic origin.[100]

Whether it was in the esoteric terminology of race or by direct comparisons, the yardstick was always Western civilization. Once again the presentation of the material was fundamental. In a discussion of Hanoteau's *Littérature orale des Touareg*, Berbrugger stressed the Rabelaisian quality of Berber fables. It was easy to see the connection between the stories of the Saharan fabulists and the fables of the classics, he said. Not only was the resemblance in the basic plot striking but certain sentences appeared to have been penned by a European author. As for those Berber fables that began with the words 'in the time when beasts spoke', the temptation to complete this familiar Rabelaisian sentence was irresistible.[101] Such comparisons were an inexorable compulsion and few scholars resisted them; they were inaccurate rather than false, and distorted the picture by what they left out. Berbrugger would have shown more objectivity had he pointed to the quasi-universality of talking animals in ethnic myths and legends. By linking Berber fables to French literature he was not making a false analogy but a spurious one, which was more misleading than it was informative. Berbrugger was no doubt lending credibility, subconsciously or otherwise, to his belief that across the ages 'from a social point of view, the Berber is closer to civilization than the Arab'.[102] Whatever lay behind the analogy, its selective nature reinforced misconceptions about the Kabyles. In another domain, the preoccupation with archaeology and Roman ruins, especially in the *Annuaire*, and the parallels drawn between the Roman colonization of North Africa and the French reinforced the notion of civilization versus barbarity; of Christianity versus Islam.[103] This again worked in favour of the Kabyles who, it will be remembered, often had Christian antecedents attributed to them.

The channels for the exchange of ideas functioned on several levels. In the first place connections between scholarly societies in Algeria and similar societies abroad were close. Such links were established by the nomination of members of the Algerian societies to honorary memberships, usually as correspondents, by the societies abroad. In 1864, for example, Berbrugger, Faidherbe and Duveyrier received such nominations from the Royal Geographical Society in London.[104] Second, members of the Algerian societies also held membership of French societies. Faidherbe, for example, was not only a member of the Anthropological Society, but also served as its vice-president for a year (1873). Hanoteau, de Neveu, Sabatier and Devaux were members of numerous societies, both in Algeria and in France. Then too French experts in relevant disciplines were appointed members of the Algerian societies and were actively engaged in the debates. Such was the case of Renan, de Slane and d'Avezac. Finally, the societies served as repositories of contemporary monographs, studies, complete works and journals, in short the corpus from which ideas on race were plucked and developed.

Conclusion

Race as a dogma is dependant on the validation of a metaphysical concept of identity by 'scientific' means and ultimately its vulgarization into easily accessed images. Military scholarship in Algeria contributed to this process at different levels. The rudimentary concepts necessary for the development of racial thought were part of the intellectual baggage military personnel brought with them to the colony. Medical practitioners in particular had much to contribute in this domain. They were familiar with those eighteenth-century and early nineteenth-century physicians, prestigious in their day, whose works contained theories essential to the creation of the edifice on race. Equally they had knowledge of the leading zoologists and biologists involved in debates on subjects such as the mutability and evolution of species, debates which were to impinge on the development of racial ideas.[105] Non-medical military personnel, although they too were often familiar with the general outline of thought of these scientists, were more conversant with the philosophical concepts, particularly those of the utopian socialists, which lent themselves to an analysis of society along racial lines. In Algeria these two strands of thought were brought together in an unprecedented way. On a theoretical level this allowed for a necessary convergence of ideas.

The contribution of the medical corps was especially significant to the scientific validation of racial concepts as well as to their vulgarization. The medical practitioners' interest in anatomy and their preoccupation with disease drew attention to physique and endurance, acting as a stimulant to the emerging interest in physical anthropology. The statistical analysis characteristic of their methodology gave their work, for the lay reader especially, that aura of infallibility which statistics seem to endow and contributed to the development of social statistics. Their contribution to the gathering of material and its dissemination through scholarly societies in France was also significant. Furthermore, the involvement of the medical corps in the lives of the *colons* and the participation of some of its members in *colon* politics greatly enhanced the acceptance of their ideas. They were thus well positioned to popularize racial ideas and, as the activities of Bodichon and Warnier demonstrate, availed themselves of the opportunity to do so. Military ethnologists and anthropologists extended this scientific validation beyond the realm of pure science to that of the social sciences, an arena in which race became well established.

The military scholars of Algeria provided France with a corpus of work on the indigenous population informed by the 'progressive' ideas of the time but confined by the institutional and operational framework of the military. In France this was analysed and reinterpreted by scholars and intellectuals in the light of contemporary academic trends. The exchange of ideas that occurred between military scholars in Algeria and academics in France and the links established between scholarly societies in the colony and the metropolis accelerated the spread of 'new' ideas and encouraged a tendency to apply them to the indigenous population in Algeria. This could occasion futile endeavours and much wasted ink, as can be seen in the attempt to apply the Aryan–Semitic dichotomy to the Kabyles and Arabs, but it did serve a purpose. On the one hand it endorsed the idea that the Kabyles were racially superior to the Arabs and, on the other, it was instrumental in entrenching racial concepts in the colony. In academic circles in France consideration of the Arab–Berber dichotomy was a theoretical exercise. In a climate sympathetic to racial interpretations of the human condition it was perhaps inevitable that differences between Arab and Berber should be seen to be basically racial ones. It is to this, therefore, to which attention is now turned.

7

Scholarly societies in France: the Kabyle Myth as a racial paradigm

Throughout the nineteenth century French scholars followed the flag. The precedent was established by Napoleon in Egypt but developed first in Algeria and later in France's Black African and Far Eastern colonies. With their rich variety of flora, fauna and humanity, these colonies provided perfect laboratories for scholarly research. In response to this challenge of unlimited primary sources, and abetted by governmental encouragement of reconnaissance and research within the colonies, scholarly societies flowered. The interest generated by Algeria, and other colonies, was by no means impartial. The debates which were conducted in the precincts of these learned institutions not only reflected colonial concerns but were often a direct response to them. This was especially true of the ethnographical and anthropological societies, concerned as they were with the study of ethnicity and race. Scholarly societies were the forums at which contemporary colonial issues were debated, couched in scientific language. Issues such as miscegenation, the morbidity of semi-tropical and tropical (colonial) territories, the significance of racial differences, all of which had begun to stir the imagination of scholars in the eighteenth century, now acquired a new urgency, for they lay at the heart of the 'indigenous question'.

Furthermore, interest was roused in new disciplines, spawned by the colonial enterprise. Such was the case of Libyan epigraphy, an offshoot of archaeology and an early example of what was to develop into the larger discipline of Berber Studies. In a retrospective article on Berber Studies appearing in 1874, J. Halévy stressed the importance for the discipline of French occupation of a part of North Africa, adding that 'all documents pertaining to this area now available to Orientalists were thanks to the indefatigable activities of French scholars.'[1] The interest in Libyan epigraphy reflected the nineteenth-century scholarly preoccupation with language as one of the keys to unlocking a people's past and situating it on the ladder of civilization. Cuvier (1769–1832), professor of natural history at the Collège de France, who dominated the natural sciences in France for the last three decades of his life, used linguistic arguments to support his classification of mankind. This was picked up by Ernest Renan (1823–92), the most renowned French philologist of the century, for whom language was one of the five distinguishing criteria of a person's race.[2] Its study, he said, would always be the most effective means of understanding the origins of the human mind.[3] Léopold de Saussure, colonial theorist and opponent of assimilation, also tied language to race.[4] De Saussure, together with the majority of contemporary philologists, emphasized the superiority of Indo-European (Aryan) languages over those of Semitic origin (which of course included Arabic). Philological concerns also stimulated the new discipline of Orientalism. With the creation in 1869 of the Ecole des Langues orientales French Orientalism gained stature and by the end of the century it had acquired an unrivalled intellectual power.[5] These developments were pertinent to Algeria, for the Berbers appeared to provide an ideal case for study in a variety of ways.

Scholarly societies in early nineteenth-century France

The first society of import to scholarship in the colony was the Société de Géographie de Paris. It embodied the geographical movement which, it has been argued, was so instrumental in colonial expansion.[6] The society was founded in 1821 and drew its initial membership mainly from the military and the aristocracy.[7] Its stated aim was to achieve a greater knowledge of the globe and its inhabitants and to establish communication among scholarly societies, travellers and geographers.[8] Membership was small to begin with, only increasing in the second half of the century: from around 250 in the 1820s it reached nearly 600 after 1871.[9] None the less its early significance should not be underestimated. The society's journal, the *Bulletin de la Société de Géographie de Paris*, was particularly important, serving a twofold purpose as far as Algeria was concerned. In the first place it drew together some of the threads that were to make up the fabric of racial ideology. Thus among its first issues appeared articles and letters on the origins and languages of diverse peoples, including the Berbers. These pre-conquest contributions by travellers and geographers were soon to be elaborated upon by on-the-spot military ethnographers and anthropologists, such as Carette, Aucapitaine, de Neveu, Duveyrier and Faidherbe. Second, the journal was one of the earliest vehicles for the publication of material by officers with scholarly inclinations.[10] It thus provided an important channel for the exchange of material and ideas between Algeria and France.

The role of the Société de Géographie de Paris in the dissemination of ideas about Algeria in the early part of the nineteenth century established a pattern that persisted into the twentieth. Throughout its history it brought together amateur and professional science in an unprecedented way: initially, when the distinction between the two was blurred, it served as a useful forum for their encounter, and latterly as an indispensable link between the two. After 1870 geographical societies proliferated in the provinces, a phenomenon which closely coincided with the development of public and press interest in the colonial enterprise, and geographical studies moved forward in tandem with the objectives of French businessmen.[11] From the earliest days of conquest, therefore, the society was a focus for scholarly work from the colonies.

The early intimations of racial ideology, as expressed in the journal of the Société de Géographie de Paris and similar publications, became more pointed during the second decade of conquest and after the formation in 1839 of the Société Ethnologique de Paris. Founded by Dr William Frederick Edwards, out of the direct interest shown in a paper he published ten years earlier, *Des caractères physiologiques des races humaines considérés dans leurs rapports avec l'histoire*, the society was established as 'a scientific association' to study human races by means of their history, language, and physical and moral characteristics.[12] Its vice-president was the geographer Avézac and among its members it counted many who also belonged to the Société Géographique de Paris, including the Saint-Simonians Gustave d'Eichthal and Victor Courtet de l'Isle. The geographer Sabin Berthelot, the historian Michelet, and Amédée Jaubert, who presided over the compilation of the 1844 French–Berber dictionary, were also members, as were a number of naturalists and scientists both foreign and French such as Prichard, Lawrence, Ritter, and Isidore Geoffroy Saint-Hilaire. Thus the interdisciplinary exchange of ideas was considerable. In spite of its purely scientific intent, the Société Ethnologique became closely associated with the slavery debate and closed its doors in 1849, one year after abolition. However, its relatively short existence served as a stimulus for the foundation of similar societies in London and New York and encouraged new trends in racism.[13] More important, in France it was the first institution concerned primarily with race and as a result Edwards's legacy was a powerful one. In his paper, which was a response to Amédée Thierry's *Histoire des Gaulois*, Edwards had suggested that physical characteristics were retained over long periods of time.[14] He believed that the most important of man's physical attributes was the form and proportion of the head and facial traits.[15] Races could thus be distinguished in spite of political upheavals. Like that of the Thierry brothers his racial vision had a historical dimension, but to the moral and social frames of reference, previously suggested as criteria in racial determination, he added the physical. Edwards's reasoning was pertinent to the debate on the Kabyles, who were seen to have altered little over time. Numerous attempts were made to establish the alleged physical differences between Kabyle and Arab, but none was conclusive. While Edwards's views pointed to the direction French anthropology would take later in the century, the debates on race at the Société Ethnologique were dominated by historical, philosophical, linguistic and environmental considerations.

Among the first exhibits donated to the society was a portrait of two Kabyles, a man and a woman.[16] Contributions from qualified personnel from overseas, be they specimens or reports, were welcomed and at the monthly meeting of April 1841 a military surgeon from Algeria, M. Lacger, presented a paper on the indigenous inhabitants of the colony. He divided them into five classes, describing the Kabyles as the aboriginal population and separating them from the *race blonde* (also Berbers), which he believed was of European origin. Lacger attributed the depopulation of the area since Roman times partially to endemic and epidemic diseases, but principally to the 'depravity of Muslim customs and morals'.[17] The presentation of the paper is significant not for any contribution it made to the Kabyle Myth but for the fact it was the first of its kind to be presented by one qualified in science on the floor of an institution dealing with matters of race. It is also an illustration of the prevalent tendency to provide moralistic answers to social, economic or political questions and, in the case of Algeria, to moralize about Islam.

Pascal Duprat: race and the Kabyles in the 1840s

Four years later a much broader reflection of existing trends concerning race was published by Pascal Duprat, editor-in-chief of the *Révue Indépendante* at the time but later professor at the Lausanne Academy.[18] His *Essai historique sur les races anciennes et modernes de l'Afrique septentrionale* was in the mould of the Thierry brothers, whose interpretation of history had been in the light of race.[19] Duprat was an environmentalist who believed that establishing the origins of the peoples of North Africa was imperative for a better understanding and administration of the area. For Duprat it was the Libyans, now known as the Berbers, who were the original inhabitants, having come to the area from Asia in some antediluvian epoch. Using classical, Arabic and contemporary sources, he concluded that in spite of the successive conquests to which the Libyans had been subjected there was little trace of the ancient conquerors who had inhabited the area, namely the Phoenicians, Greeks, Vandals, etc. Only the Romans had left their mark, but this was due to the genius of Roman civilization, the spirit of Rome (*le génie de Rome*)[20] – in other words the impact of what Herder had dubbed the *Volksgeist*, rather than any noticeable migration of the Roman race. The Libyans, or Berbers, had remained impervious to conquests thanks to the Atlas mountains, the 'spinal cord of North Africa'. Being an environmentalist, Duprat believed that the mountains had endowed the Berbers with their qualities: the fusion of this race with the mountains had created its rock-like temperament and superb immobility.[21] While the Berbers had drawn their strength from the mountains, other races had not done so and were thus absorbed or swept away via subsequent conquests. When it came to the Arabs Duprat attributed their continued presence, an anomaly in his thesis, to the fact that they had been followed by another Islamic race, the Turks.

At the time of the French conquest five races were discernible: the Libyans or Berbers, the Arabs, the Turks, the Koulouglis and the Jews (who had never been conquerors but had come to North Africa to escape persecution in Europe). Of these the most permanent were the Berbers and the Arabs. Both were necessary for the vitality of the colony, but the Berbers were more so. For Duprat the Arabs of North Africa were not of the calibre of the Caliphate Arabs when the star of Arab civilization was rising, rather they were the 'degenerate sons of the Orient'. Duprat emphasized the physical differences between Arab and Berber. The Berber was remarkable due to his 'rugged looks and proud, abrupt manner', while the Arab had a 'dry, thin constitution'.[22] Duprat contented himself with overall appearance rather than facial angles (prognathism) and skull calibrations (cephalic indexes). (Both were deemed important components in racial determination and were adopted by French anthropologists after the establishment of the Société Anthropologique de Paris in 1859, the former having been devised by the Dutch anatomist, Peter Camper, in the late eighteenth century, the latter by the Swedish scientist Andreas Retzius in 1845.) But he did link both appearance and character to the environment. 'With his nervous, active disposition the Arab was a man of the bare, dry plains,' he wrote, 'a man of vast spaces and open horizons, while the Berber with his strong coarse complexion was a man of the rocks and mountains.' Duprat continued in this vein, paraphrasing Hippocrates to make an analogy which was later to be used in the Aryan–Semite dichotomy of the *Volk* and the Jews in Germany. The Berbers or Kabyles showed great variety, like forest-covered mountains; the Arabs, who were meagre in temperament and sparse in build, were like bare, arid plains.[23] In 1890 Julius Langbehn, in his best-selling *Rembrandt als Erzieher*, coupled race with creativity, claiming that every race had its landscape. For the Aryans it was that of the forest, symbolizing their richness and vitality; for the Jews that of the desert, expressing their rootlessness and the aridity of their souls.[24] Renan too used the desert as a metaphor and a reason for a lack of spiritual fecundity among the Semites.[25] It is interesting to note that Duprat continued the above passage by linking the Jews and the Turks (two less important races in his scheme of things) to the swamps and the prairies, respectively, a fact that would suggest that in the semantic symbolism of the environment it was the *forest* and the *desert* that best evoked positive and negative attributes. In a wider symbolism the forest represents life in all its richness; the desert, the starkness of death. The connotations arising out of these latter associations are unlimited, thus endowing these two words with considerable semantic power.

Duprat's research led him to conclude that the Berbers were a 'great' race. Having survived the vicissitudes of countless conquests they were also an 'immortal' race. Duprat called for an alliance with the Berbers, for the past had shown that of the dominating powers that had established themselves in North Africa those that had created alliances with the Libyan or Berber race had prospered, while those that had opposed them had been bedevilled with misfortune and disaster. Duprat's work was published twelve years prior to the conquest of Kabylia, at a time when the debate was animated as to whether invasion should take place. He believed that armed intervention in Kabylia was an error, although he argued that without the mountains of Kabylia Algeria could never be considered wholly under French domination. He was convinced that the Berbers would 'give their mountains to the French' so it was imperative to cement a Mediterranean–Atlas alliance as soon as possible as it would be the only lasting security against outside attack.[26] In spite of Duprat's inability to resist alluding to his political concerns, and in this respect he resembled many a contemporary ethnologist, anthropologist or social scientist, his work was essentially one of non-polemical ethnology. His sources were varied and good, by contemporary standards, and he was a respected intellectual. The pro-Kabyle sentiments discernible in his work were metaphysical rather than political and arose out of the conviction that theirs was a noble race. Duprat's *Essai* was the first substantial work in a field that was to preoccupy French scholars well into the twentieth century, namely the origins of the Libyans or Berbers and their role in North African history.

Duprat's environmentalism, his linkage of physical beauty to environmental influences, his discussion of mixed races and his racial classifications were symptomatic of contemporary arguments regarding questions of race, all part of the larger debate which opposed the doctrine of *transformisme* to that of the *fixité des espèces* and sought to determine whether or not characteristics of race (or species) were immutable. The monogenist naturalist Buffon was among the first to classify man physically and to point to the environment as having the most pervasive influence on his physical appearance. He divided human beings into six races, distinguishing them by their skin colour, stature and bodily form, and physical traits. The link between aesthetics and environment was developed further by the German physiologist Blumenbach, also a monogenist. Blumenbach believed that the most beautiful faces were to be found in the most moderate climates.[27] He classified human beings into five racial groups and coined the word Caucasian.

Duprat's classification of the five races (or peoples, for he used the two terms interchangeably) in North Africa was far from precise, as indeed was the case for most such contemporary classifications. He did, naturally enough, err towards an environmental classification. Of the ancient Arabs he concluded that residing as they did in the midst of ever-shifting sands, they were accustomed to an errant, vagabond life, subject to constant change.[28] Thus the Arabs, people of the desert, flat-lands, plains, were a different race from the Berbers who, in their sheltered mountain range, had assumed its attributes and remained unsullied by outside influences. This line of thought corresponded to Lamarck's argument, presented in his *Philosophie Zoologique* (1809), that a species could maintain its continuity provided the environment remained constant; under such circumstances acquired characteristics became hereditary.[29] It also reflected an early tendency to categorize environmentally which had originated during the Enlightenment. Among the first to do so was the Swedish naturalist Carolus Linnæus (also known as Carl von Linné) who had divided *homo sapiens* into American, European, Asiatic, African and one non-environmental category, the Monstrous, into which he slotted the regional anomalies.

The standards for racial classification were vague; so too was the nomenclature. Buffon and Blumenbach dubbed their human groups *races* but the French naturalists at the turn of the eighteenth century were more inclined to the term *espèce*. An *espèce* could be, and sometimes was, sub-divided into *races*, which in turn could be broken down into *variétés*.[30] Bory de Saint Vincent, who presided over the Scientific Commission in Algeria, devised 15 different classes (*espèces*) of man. Although he called Linnæus to task for using an environmental classification, his own, which was somewhat inconsistent, included one such class.[31] It also included two, the Arabs and the Hindus, whose classification was made on grounds of religion, with a salient feature for the former class being the practice of circumcision. The point of this little digression is to suggest that while hard-and-fast standards cannot be extricated from a perusal of the numerous approaches to racial classification, the fact of classifying at all was in itself an initial commitment to this type of reasoning. By taking this classification a step further and contrasting one category positively or negatively to another, a firmer commitment was being made. Duprat was not a theorist of race but he shared a view, which was beginning to prevail by the mid-nineteenth century, that race (whatever that signified, and it signified different things to different people) was a defining feature of the human condition. His *Essai* was a contribution to the emergence of racial themes within the Kabyle Myth and his ideas a precursor to more dogmatic theory in this regard.

The Société d'Anthropologie de Paris

It was with the foundation of the Société d'Anthropologie de Paris in 1859 that interest in the Kabyles as a race acquired a new dimension. The society was founded by Paul Broca, professor at the Faculty of Medicine in Paris and member of the Medical Academy. As a student he had attended the lectures on polygenesis of Professor Bérard Snr. at the Faculty of Medicine, but Broca could also be Lamarckian in his arguments. He was, in his own words, inclined to 'polygenic transformism'.[32] The influence of Broca and the society he founded was to extend beyond the limited circles of anthropologists. As early as 1864 his society was officially recognized as an *établissement d'utilité publique*, a legal term which bestowed it with official status and endowed it with certain privileges. Thirty years after Broca's death, Jules Harmand, a colonial theorist of the Doctrine of Association, acknowledged his debt to Broca, stating that Broca's positivist school of ethnological research, which had so felicitously coincided with renewed French expansionism, had had an enormous influence not only on colonial policy but also on matters of administration.[33] At its inception, membership of the society was heavily weighted towards the medical profession. Of the 19 founding members, ten were professors of medicine or physiology.[34] Anatomical considerations therefore assumed an added importance in French anthropology, and physical anthropology was its mainstay for most of the nineteenth century. The presence of so many doctors also influenced methodology. The meticulous and systematic presentation of the *mémoires*, the result of diagnostic reasoning acquired from medical studies, added an unequivocal scientific weight to arguments concerning race.

The foundation of the Société d'Anthropologie heralded a movement, occurring throughout Europe, towards new assumptions regarding race. Unlike the Société Ethnologique, whose political parameters had been shaped by philanthropic concerns about enslaved races and against the backdrop of a national debate as to whether the colonization of Algeria should proceed, the internal debates of the Société d'Anthropologie occurred within a political framework which accepted colonization, of Algeria at least, as an irrecusable fact. By the nature of its power structure, colonization introduced into national parlance (whether it was directly articulated or not) the concept of superior and inferior in relation to different peoples in a given society as opposed to different classes, as had hitherto been the norm. This new type of hierarchical concept, initially one of power but by implication one of civilization and race, having once been released from Pandora's Box was ever present in the national discourse. Whatever an individual's political agenda, therefore, it became increasingly difficult to avoid taking some sort of stand on race and its hierarchy. The Société d'Anthropologie, concerned as it was with the science of 'the nature of man' inevitably became a forum for the elucidation of questions on race. In effect it was seeking the metaphysical confirmation, through the scientific medium of anthropology, of a political fact. The overall enquiry may have been about the distinguishing attributes, physical, social and moral, of the different peoples and races of the globe in order to come to grips with the 'nature of man'; but the subliminal question was which of these attributes made for superiority and domination.

Unlike Germany, where purity of race was the pinnacle to which a people could aspire, in France mixed racial origins could also signify greatness. In his *Histoire des Gaulois*, Amédée Thierry had put forward the theory that two races, the *Galls* and *Kymris*, were the original stock of France.[35] Edwards had elaborated on this. Broca introduced the question to the Société d'Anthropologie at its fourth session by reading a paper on the subject, and with it the debate on the viability of mixed races. Anthropologists, he reminded his listeners, were divided into two camps: those who believed that all races had been subjected to miscegenation at some time or other so that pure races no longer existed, and those who believed that only pure races could prosper down the ages. These included in their number de Gobineau, Knox, Nott and Gliddon.[36] It was a debate that was relevant to Algeria on several counts, as the discussion concerning the paper at the following session indicates. In the first place there was the question of colonization and the impact on indigenous races that the colonizing army or settlers might have.[37] Then, as an offshoot of this train of thought, there was the idea of a mixture of races begetting a new race. The concept of a racial 'melting pot' flourished in Algeria towards the end of the nineteenth century when it was argued that a new white Mediterranean race was being formed through the amalgamation of the various immigrant stocks.

Third there was the question of the Kabyles. Were the 'blond Kabyles of the Aurès' descendants of the Vandals? (In fact the Berbers from the Aurès are the Chaouia, a fact that was only clarified later. In these early days 'Kabyle' was often used interchangeably for all the Algerian mountain Berbers.) Broca was inclined to think not.[38] None the less, it was a question that was to worry anthropologists for many years to come. A session in February 1860 was devoted to these blond enigmas from the Aurès.[39] Dr Périer, who later produced a paper on the ethnology of the Berbers, agreed with de Gobineau in doubting the Germanic origins of the blond Kabyles. Others, including Bory de Saint-Vincent, Dr Lacquer and Broca's former professor, Bérard, believed in such origins.[40] The blond Kabyles were destined to remain an enigma, but interest in the Berbers and the Kabyles did not abate.

In August 1860 a commission of the society, which included de Quatrefages, drew up a questionnaire and instructions for anthropologists relating to the study of races in Algeria, the Sahara, the Sudan and Senegal. Dr Boudin, a leading member, initiated a discussion on these instructions by insisting on the importance of gathering material on the races of Algeria, in particular the blond Kabyles.[41] This call for information met with the desired response. One of the first specimens to arrive at the society was the mummified head of an Algerian called Abdullah, who had perished in a fight with a French soldier and whose severed head had been preserved in salt.[42] Although it was allegedly that of an Arab, after careful examination it was decided that in all probability it was a Kabyle, due to its shape. A discussion ensured on the Arabs and Kabyles, leading into another on differences between Aryans and Semites, in which one member, Dr Pruner-Bey, ethnographer of Egypt and former physician to the Viceroy of Egypt, concluded that 'the Arab was certainly the most characteristic Semite and the most different from us'.[43] Although

Pruner-Bey, who was greatly interested in craniometry, did not claim Aryan origins for the Kabyles, the inclusion of the Arabs and the Kabyles in such a discussion signalled the trend towards their racial categorization. Henceforth, the Arabs and the Kabyles would be frequently included in the principal debates concerning racial questions, namely those on linguistics, origins, perfectibility, acclimatization and the permanence of physical characteristics.

In 1865, the society's Prix Godard was awarded to Dr Gillebert d'Hercourt for work carried out in Algeria. His *Etudes anthropologiques sur soixante-seize indegènes de l'Algérie* was pure physical anthropology including such contemporary preoccupations as skin colour, hair definition and cephalic indices. With regard to the latter, Gillebert d'Hercourt reminded his readers that on average the lowest cephalic index was that of the blacks, who were very dolichocephalic. He concluded that both Kabyles and Arabs were generally dolichocephalic, but stated that tribal Arabs were much closer to the blacks than were the Kabyles, although town Arabs showed higher indices.[44] Gillebert d'Hercourt's work was the first of several studies that sought to define the Berber or Kabyle race through calibration, culminating in Bertholon and Chantre's *magnum opus* in 1913.[45]

While the attempts to differentiate Arab from Berber by means of physical criteria were a sign of the extent to which the two groups were considered to be racially different, research in this direction was factually inconclusive in spite of being tenaciously pursued. That no concrete proof was forthcoming and that, with hindsight, such pursuits seem absurd should not detract from their importance in contributing to the nineteenth-century racial edifice. Measurements provided data which scientists then used selectively, usually unconsciously, to confirm their expectations about racial differences.[46] Analogy-guided research, of which this was an integral part, created and disseminated hypotheses and technical vocabularies which encouraged reasoning oriented to hierarchical classification of human groups and sought to establish what it was about them that was problematic.[47] The debate as to the physical differences between the Arabs and Berbers continued, therefore, for over seventy years, during which time the Kabyle Myth was institutionalized.

Major Emile Duhousset, an officer stationed in Kabylia for many years, took a major step in the direction of its institutionalization when he read his *Etudes sur les Kabyles du Djurdjura* to the society in 1868. He paid careful attention to physical characteristics and devoted a chapter to craniology, another to social organization and one to a character study of the Kabyle who, he declared, were hard-working, industrious and hospitable. M. de Jouvencel, an attentive auditor to

Major Duhousset and enthusiastic phrenologist, it would seem, extrapolating from Duhousset's exposé linked skull shape and lack of religious fervour among the Kabyles, suggesting that the depressions on the Kabyle skulls corresponded to that area of the brain that dominated religious sentiments and comparing them to similar observations made on Germans linking skull shape and religious sentiments.[48]

By 1873 there was a commission in charge of Algeria at the society and in July of that year two of its members, Faidherbe and Topinard, presented detailed instructions as to how anthropologists should tackle Algeria.[49] The instructions, which ran to 55 pages and contained all the current wisdom on the Arabs and Berbers, linked moral and physical characteristics, stating that the impact of the former on the latter was such that few people travelling in Algeria could not distinguish the Arabs from the Berbers almost at first sight.[50] Physical and moral man were inextricable in racial terms. Topinard later elaborated this concept in one of his own works, concluding that separating the two was impossible.[51] In the same work he summed up the typical physiological Kabyle and contrasted him to the Arab:

> The Kabyle has a fixed abode. His communal administration is highly liberal. He is active, hardworking, honest, dignified, open-minded, honest and good humoured. He has elevated sentiments of equality, honour, human dignity and justice. He is courageous and attacks his enemy frontally. The exact opposite of the points enumerated in the summary correspond to the physiological type of the Arab.[52]

The passage is an example of the extent to which the method of contrasting Kabyle to Arab and drawing favourable moral conclusions regarding the former had penetrated scientific circles, a method that was essentially a device used in the elaboration of racial ideology.

Topinard, like many of his colleagues, was closely involved with the anthropology of the colony. In 1881 a convention was held in Algeria by the French Association for the Advancement of Sciences. Several delegates from the Anthropological Society attended, and took the opportunity of travelling around the country to promote an interest in anthropology and underline the influence it could have on the administration.[53] Topinard summed up the event and presented his conclusions on indigenous types in Algeria. As if to underline just how anthropology could be beneficial to the administration, he turned to the question of the perfectibility of races. The Arab race had run its course, he said. It had held its place in the history of human evolution, had rendered services to humanity and indeed still continued to do so to some inferior negro civilizations of Central Africa, but compared to the European civilizations it was moribund. On the other hand the Berber race, of which the mountain Kabyles were the perfect example, had ceased to develop many centuries ago. France could either kill it or resuscitate it, develop its qualities, adapt its institutions to the French ones and transform it into the strength of Algeria and the security of France.[54] Topinard was alluding to two contemporary racial postulations. The first was Renan's hypothesis that the mission of the Semite race to humanity, crowned by the efforts of Islam, was to spread monotheism and having made this contribution they had exhausted their creativity, ceding their place to the Aryans.[55] The second, Broca's, was that some races were eminently more perfectible than others, the most perfectible being capable of creating their own civilizations.[56] (Broca was elaborating on Virey's contention that the majority of European nations demonstrated the highest degree of perfection.[57]) Topinard was suggesting that the Kabyles could be 'civilized' and moulded to French colonial needs in a way the burnt-out Arab could not; in short they were more perfectible.

Topinard's interest in the Kabyles and Arabs persisted throughout his association with the society and evolved over time, reflecting attitudes in the colony. By 1881, having identified several different physical types among the indigenous population, he admitted that the Berbers and Arabs could not be considered as pure races. This did not prevent him from arguing that the Kabyle, untouched by outside influences in his mountain stronghold, was the consummate example of the Berber race nor from suggesting that the Kabyles' most striking trait, sedentariness, was intrinsically racial.[58] Topinard was cautious in his conclusions, refraining from overt negative/positive contrasts, a stance which elicited considerable criticism from Duhousset, who lamented at not having been presented with a 'Kabyle Topinard', which he had anticipated as an updated version of his own research.[59] Nor did Topinard use anthropology to promote his political agenda in the strident manner of the coterie of young radical anthropologists headed by Gabriel de Mortillet.[60] (With regard to Algeria, for example, in an article on colonization Mortillet echoed Ferry's sentiments that European domination was an inevitable part of the development and modernization of humanity.[61]) Topinard's political circumspection may have been a result of 'scientifically diplomatic' habits developed by Broca and his followers during the early years of the society, when its activities were closely monitored by a disapproving government or by a conviction held by some anthropologists that scientific objectivity could only be maintained by avoiding the social ramifications of anthropology and concentrating on measurement and its analysis.[62]

Other members, however, could be and were both less reticent politically. Such was the case of Camille Sabatier, whom Topinard acknowledged as 'the most erudite and best informed man on the question of Algerian races I have ever known'.[63]

Camille Sabatier: race and the Kabyles in the 1880s

Sabatier was a colonial administrator who took anthropology seriously. Having had experience at all levels of the administration, first as administrator of the *commune mixte* at Fort National (Kabylia), then as a judge in Tizi Ouzou (Kabylia) and later as senator of Oran, he believed that 'the Algerian question was in part a question of anthropology'.[64] His contribution to anthropological research on the Berbers was acknowledged both by contemporaries such as Topinard and Gabriel de Mortillet, representatives of the Broca School and the Radical School of Anthropology respectively, and by latter-day anthropologists such as Ély Leblanc, writing at the time of the centenary celebrations in 1930.[65] In his first paper presented to the Paris Anthropological Society Sabatier raised the question of nomadic and sedentary lifestyles, stressing the respective negative and positive aspects of each. Nomads, having always had to submit to the rule of the chieftain, had developed the most imperfect of social forms, patriarchal despotism. This was characterized by an absence of property rights, of culture and of any industry other than a pastoral one. It encouraged the pillaging instinct, physical paucity, intellectual sterility and social oppression. In contrast the sedentary existence, to which the climate and natural production of mountain regions were so well suited, was practically the key condition for economic, political and moral progress.[66] It was this sedentariness that was the cornerstone of Sabatier's arguments in favour of the Kabyle race, for a year's research with callipers in Kabylia had led him to similar conclusions as Topinard, namely that physically there were two types of Kabyle.[67] Evidence of the progress that characterized sedentary peoples was already present in Kabylia, namely the 'existence of absolute equality among its citizens, individual liberty, and protection of minorities against oppression by the constitution and the federation of the *çofs*'. Until the arrival of the French, furthermore, the Kabyles had managed to safeguard the originality of their race, keep the entirety of their civil law and maintain their moral integrity.[68] It was the legislation and institutions arising out of sedentariness that linked the Kabyles to France, for 'the unknown Lycurgus who dictated the Kabyle *kanouns* was neither of the family of Mohammed nor of Moses, but of that of

Montesquieu and Condorcet. More than the skull shape of the mountain Kabyles, this work bore the seal of the French race.' They were
'a sister population' who had not allowed the spirit of their common
ancestry to degenerate. In addition to the *kanoun* Sabatier also lingered
over the *çof*, 'a unique institution which safeguarded the population
from the abuses of power'. Religion, or rather the total absence of it,
was a further distinctive feature of this people. For Sabatier could see
no trace of it either in their political constitution, their family structure, their property rights or indeed in their conceptualization of good
and evil. Even if the Kabyles outwardly professed to be Muslims,
their *kanouns* were the complete negation of the basic principles of
the Islamic code. The Kabyle, he concluded, was essentially anti-
clerical. Sabatier singled out ten distinctive traits, essentially social
and moral, as characterizing the Kabyles.[69] The qualities of freedom,
equality, an elevated morality and anticlercialism were embodied in
their institutions and were thus inherently Kabyle.

Sabatier's conceptualization of race was in line with late nineteenth-
century ideological trends. The above passages reflect a number of
contemporary attitudes towards race and racial hierarchies which
borrowed the restricted clinical definition of the physical anthropologists and endowed it with a more cosmic approach where history
and culture, in the broadest sense, were as relevant as anatomical
structure. Sabatier's description of sedentariness as a positive lifestyle
was one of these attitudes. Max Müller, for example, claimed that
'Aryan' meant 'tillers of the soil'. The Aryans were a virile peasant
race endowed with all the attributes Europeans held dear, namely
honour, nobility, courage and a pleasant countenance.[70] The association
of sedentariness with the Aryan race automatically elevated it in the
hierarchy of social organization. By way of contrast, it was contended
that a nomadic lifestyle lacked order and showed few redeeming
features. In Renan's words, 'the Orient, especially the Semitic Orient,
has never attained an equilibrium between the complete anarchy of
the nomadic Arabs and bloody despotism. The notion of public service, of the common good, is completely lacking among these peoples.
True freedom and the great institutions of the State are completely
foreign to them.'[71] The nomadic lifestyle, characterized as it was by
pillaging and disruption of the status quo, caused too much apprehension to be readily acceptable. Sabatier's insistence on the importance
of Kabyle commitment to freedom and equality, and evidence of a
well-developed morality as testified by existing institutions, was a
second such attitude. Müller maintained that freedom was an intrinsic
part of the Aryan world of self-reliance.[72] The love of freedom among
European peoples also occupied historians, who sought to discover

the origins of free institutions as an explanation of this phenomenon which was perceived to be essentially European. Freedom came to be especially associated with the Germanic and Celtic tribes, whose rudimentary institutions were considered to have practised a primitive form of equality. This is additionally relevant in view of the stubborn persistence of the idea that the Kabyles were of Germanic or Celtic origin.

Sabatier's enumeration of religious sentiments and type of legislation as distinguishing the Kabyle are further examples of such attitudes. Renan, for example, included religion and legislation among his five primary factors in racial differentiation. For Renan religion was a key to the lack of progress of the Semitic people, for they had bequeathed not only monotheism to mankind, but also intolerance.[73] On the other hand Indo-European peoples, having, before their conversion to monotheism, never considered religion to be an absolute truth but rather to be an inheritance from family or caste, were strangers to intolerance and proselytism. This analysis of Renan's bears an uncanny resemblance to comparisons between Arab fanaticism and Kabyle tolerance. Furthermore Renan believed that Islam was a religion that manifested virtually no republicanism.[74] There was also 'the dreadful simplicity of the Semitic mind, constricting the human brain, closing it to any sensitive idea, to all fine sentiment, to all rational research'.[75] A race's religious proclivities could therefore situate it on the Ladder of Being.

Finally, the fact of researching into the origins and evolution of a people was in itself an indication of a preoccupation with collective identity, which in late nineteenth-century parlance translated into nationalism and a preoccupation with *race*. It stemmed from the commonly held assumption that a major distinction between one people or race and another was their journey through time.[76] Sabatier's *Essai sur l'origine, l'évolution et les conditions actuelles des Berbers sédentaires*, in common with other such papers on the Berbers, reflected this assumption.[77] Race and history had first been connected in a systematic way by the Thierry brothers. Victor Courtet de l'Isle went further, linking history to the superiority of the European races for, he claimed, their history had shown that everywhere the Europeans went they always achieved pre-eminence over other races. It was therefore certain that by their personal worth alone, Europeans were superior to all other races.[78] Courtet de l'Isle, a Saint-Simonian, participator in *Le Globe* and an active member of numerous scholarly societies, was the first in France to theorize on the hierarchy of races and was thus a precursor of de Gobineau, who picked up many of his ideas.[79] Later in the century Renan, who paid scant attention to physical attributes but was one of the most articulate exponents of the view that culture and civilization were paramount components of a people's racial identity, listed history as the fourth of his primary factors of race.[80] An elucidation of the Kabyle past would lead to a clearer understanding of what the contemporary Kabyle race was capable of and what its role could be in French colonial society. For Sabatier there was little doubt on this score. 'Thanks to the Kabyles France would play a great role in the future of Africa, while thanks to France the Kabyles would play a great role in humanity.'[81]

As an anthropologist in the field who was also a colonial administrator, Sabatier could not help but be influenced by the pressures of the colonial situation. Like other administrators working in Kabylia he was heartened by the absence of Koranic law in everyday Kabyle life and felt that this would make it easier to integrate the Kabyles than the Arabs into French society. Like so many of his colonial colleagues, he believed the Kabyles were infinitely perfectible.[82] He backed up this conclusion by interpreting other anomalies in Kabyle society in the light of contemporary anthropological and sociological reasoning on matters of race. Sabatier's appropriation of science to convey political convictions did not invalidate his anthropology in the eyes of his contemporaries; quite the contrary. It was seen as an indication of the possible practical application of theoretical concerns. Indeed the lack of such practical applications caused many an anthropologist to lament the obtuseness of the Algerian government in their refusal to recognize the findings of ethnological science concerning the differences between the Arabs and the Kabyles and to act on these findings.[83] The distinction between the two races was considered by anthropologists to be anthropologically and politically of paramount importance.[84] By the 1880s, when Sabatier presented his papers to the Anthropological Society, the Kabyle Myth had already been incorporated into the canon of anthropological thought and acknowledged as axiomatic in other intellectual circles. As one scholar with no political axe to grind had said as early as 1871, it was now no longer necessary to mention that the Kabyles and Arabs were two entirely distinct races and that the essential and fundamental differences between the two were all to the advantage of the Kabyle race.[85] By the end of the 1880s Sabatier's role in the Myth's dissemination to governmental and administrative circles was an acknowledged fact.[86]

Just how superior the Kabyles were to the Arabs still left scope for controversy. Renan, for example, was ambiguous about the Berbers, whom he placed behind the Arabs with regard to their contribution to world civilization but not in the general line-up of humanity.[87] From an early date he was fascinated by their origins, their resistance to outside influences and their language, which he did not class among the Semitic languages.[88] Furthermore, their anthropological importance was undeniable, for the Berber race 'had become a scientific topic in its own right'.[89] The Arabs, bearing the twofold burden of the stigma of Islam and belonging to the Semitic race, had had their day, but a question mark hung over the Berbers. Ambiguity was the hallmark of all racial ideology, it being impossible to lay down hard-and-fast guidelines as to what a race really was. In fact it was not what a given individual said about a race that was particularly important, for the emphasis could vary depending on personal convictions, but the general context in which it was being said. This, for the Arabs and Berbers, was more than just suggestive of the language of race. The use of physical criteria as a determinant of race, so precious to French anthropologists, was in fact a tool by means of which it was sought to prove the dubious cultural and moral criteria that were also used to differentiate races. While scholarly societies continued to carry on discussions around these factors without coming to any definite conclusions, in popular circles less attention was paid to precision. Syllogisms containing moral, cultural and physical premises with racial conclusions formed an integral part of racial theory. The role of the scholarly societies in the development of a racial ideology was to provide the premises from which these syllogisms were formulated.

The dissemination of ideas

Scholarly societies sanctioned the Kabyle Myth, thus endowing it with its power. Geographic, ethnological and anthropological societies did not have a monopoly in its dissemination. Numerous other scholarly societies concerned with history, archaeology, linguistics, ethnology or anthropology involved themselves to some degree in the Arab–Berber differentiation. After all, since the French conquest of Algiers, North Africa had become a subject of supreme interest.[90] The Société Asiatique and the Société Orientale de France, both of which had a significant number of members from Algeria, were among those whose role was especially significant. They printed numerous articles on subjects related to the Arabs and the Berbers, and membership itself also provided an outlet for ideas. If a membership diagram of a given society had been drawn up, it would have shown a series of concentric circles. At the centre lay a nucleus of specialists and internationally renowned scholars (Renan, de Sacy, Broca, for example) surrounded by a wider ring of acknowledged experts in their fields (Aucapitaine, de Neveu, Daumas, Duhousset, Hanoteau, Sabatier, in the case of the Kabyles). This in turn would be surrounded by a much wider ring of full, honorary and corresponding members from all corners of the globe, whose common denominator was a certain erudition and an interest in the subject in hand. The most frequent exchanges within the society occurred between the first two rings of membership. The third ring was involved in the casual distribution of the societies' ideas and in this the societies' journals were of considerable importance. Membership overlapped substantially among societies, especially among the first two categories, further guaranteeing the spread of ideas.

During the second half of the nineteenth century there was a burgeoning of cultural, ideological, professional and economic associations, both in Paris and in the provinces, a witness to the intellectual ferment and intensity of the epoch. Revues and journals had an extensive readership in both specialized and non-specialized circles. The best known acquired exceptional importance in the spread of ideas through their unimpeachable respectability on the one hand and their servicing of a variety of schools of thought on the other.[91] This was the case of the *Revue des Deux Mondes*, the *Revue Indépendante*, the *Nouvelle Revue*, the *Revue de Paris*, and the *Revue politique et littéraire*, all of which were among the numerous journals, specialized and non-specialized, in which articles appeared on the Kabyles or the Arab–Kabyle dichotomy. While these journals formed a significant channel for the spread of such ideas, the emphasis on scientific methods as the most legitimate means of social analysis prompted a need to vulgarize the sciences. In 1859 a society with its own park, going by the suggestive name of Jardin d'Acclimatisation, was set up to do just this. In the last quarter of the century it organized a series of ethnographical exhibitions to present the environment of overseas peoples to the French public, thus providing visual proof of what had hitherto appeared only in print.[92] Situated in the Bois de Boulogne, it had the additional attraction of being a pleasant venue in which to pass a few hours.

By the end of the century the Kabyle Myth had found its way into popular works about North Africa, regardless of whether the content was pro-Kabyle or not. Hence Charles Farine's *Kabyles et Kroumirs*, an illustrated travelogue with an easy-to-read, lilting style consecrated several pages to the contrast between Kabyle and Arab using all the accepted stereotypes and including the assertion that there was evidence of Germanic blood among the Kabyles.[93] Similarly, an author of a book on brigandage in Kabylia, who was not overly sympathetic to the Kabyles, could introduce his subject with the throwaway line that the Kabyles were of Aryan stock, the Arabs of Semitic.[94] Potted ideas on the Kabyles and Arabs in popular works were the norm rather than the exception. Sometimes, as is the case in *Sous les Figuiers de Kabylie*, a text would be full of contradictions arising out of the author's difficulty in reconciling his own observations with the received wisdom on the Kabyles.[95] Such works had no original contribution to make on the Kabyles or the Arabs; they often reflected the author's standpoint with regard to the indigenous population but, above all, they were indicative of the extent to which the Arab–Kabyle dichotomy was a received idea which had become a racial cliché.

Conclusion

The academic response in France to the Algerian conquest was a thirst for information; a desire to live the exploration and occupation of the colony vicariously through intellectual discovery. Scholarly societies sprang up and material emanating from the colony was avidly snapped up. It was natural that in the colony itself the indigenous population should so preoccupy the French occupational force – it was, after all, the only obstacle to immediate victory and unhindered occupation. Once the regional topography had been established, by the awkward fact of its presence the indigenous population inevitably became the principal obsession. This interest in the indigenous population within the colony foreshadowed a similar interest in France, an interest which became institutionalized with the establishment of ethnological and anthropological societies, as of 1839.

However, the motive for this interest was not the same. In the colony it was practical: a derivative of military exigencies and colonial preoccupations. In France it was intellectual: a quest for answers to the metaphysical and scientific conundrums of the time. That material gathered in response to the former should be accepted as suitable for use in response to the latter could only create distortions. Bearing this in mind, it is easier to understand the dogged determination with which scholarly societies in France continued to amass documents, each as inconclusive as the one before, on the size of Arab and Berber skulls, on their physiognomy and on their anatomy. If the moral and social superiority of the Kabyle was accepted as a given it was logical to try and seek endorsement physically and racially. As the debate on the implications of race amplified, the Kabyles and Arabs became points of reference in the larger debate on race and discussions on the extent of their 'racial differences' continued.

There was more to the process than merely drawing the Kabyle Myth into, and including it in, the racial dialogue in France. Echoes of the discussions and debates concerning the racial origins of the Kabyles and the Arabs bounced back and forth across the Mediterranean. The colony was kept abreast with the 'scientific' developments of racial theory, while the metropolis bore witness to its practical implications in the multi-racial society of the colony. Both fuelled the belief that race was a primary factor in defining the human condition. Paradoxically, the growing importance of racial theories did not, in the long run, further the Kabyles' cause. Rather it shifted attention away from the Kabyles and the Arabs onto the European settler, enabling the development of the notion of a Mediterranean race emerging from the 'melting pot' of settler Algeria. The positive/negative images of Kabyle vs. Arab were replaced by the more powerful one of European vs. the *'indigène'*.

PART III

Algeria 1871–1900: The eclipse of the Kabyle Myth

As a result of a series of decrees passed in the autumn of 1870 and culminating in 1871 with the appointment of Governor-General Vice-Admiral de Gueydon, the colonial administration of Algeria passed out of military hands. The most tangible long-term changes that occurred under civilian rule were demographic, political and economic. The European population increased significantly: in the first three decades alone, it tripled from 236,000 to 621,000.[1] Colonial policy shifted from assimilation to association. The transformation of the economy, from an indigenously controlled subsistence economy into a European-controlled capitalist one, was greatly accelerated. Land sequestration and the subsequent growth of labour-intensive capitalist agriculture on the sequestered lands played an important part in this transformation. So too did the clearing of the mosquito-infested swamps of the Mitidja and its subsequent development into Algeria's principal wine-growing area. The transformation of the economy enriched the settlers and accelerated the pauperization of the indigenous population in rural Algeria, driving it off the land into the cheap labour market, first in the colony and then in France. The Kabyles, who had hitherto escaped this process, now found themselves caught up in it. These were the most obvious transformations, but there were also intangible changes, which were as important to the relationship between the settlers and the indigenous population and what happened to the Kabyle Myth under civilian rule as were the tangible ones.

Civilian rule did not bring about the spontaneous generation of new ideas; rather existing ones were refashioned to accommodate its needs. While the section below will concentrate on the specific factors that affected the impact of the Kabyle Myth it is necessary to mention, very briefly, four intangible changes which occurred in the shift from military to civilian rule, significant to the development of the mental framework of the colony or, for want of a better phrase, to its collective psychology. Three of these occurred at the inception of the new regime and had to do with the nature of power, society and control. One took place more gradually and had to do with intellectual influences. All contributed to the process that modified French attitudes towards the indigenous population.

In the first place the nature of the power structure in the colony changed. The nature of military rule had been custodial, necessitating a certain political and administrative cooperation with the indigenous population and providing an atmosphere conducive to the emergence of paternalistic utopian concepts such as the *mission civilisatrice* and assimilation, in which progress towards a higher (French) state was the acknowledged aim. Civilian rule, on the other hand, was proprietorial, initially straining cooperation and eventually disrupting it and creating an atmosphere better suited to ideologies which maintained the status quo.

The second change concerned the nature of the occupying society. Military society was enclosed and masculine, with a hierarchy based on meritocratic achievement of an endogenous nature. The indigenous population, therefore, could only enter it through predetermined selection and progress, if at all, was under strict institutional control. The nature of the hierarchy, furthermore, transformed deference and respect into a veritable system that automatically distanced the occupying power from the indigenous population. This gave rise to a paradoxical situation in which, for as long as the military held the reins of power and remained numerically strong, the ultimate goals of the *mission civilisatrice* or of assimilation were in effect practicably unattainable. Algeria under the military was a never-never land of assimilation and as such could tolerate its theory and even initiate its practice without fear of upsetting the colony's Eurocentrism. Under civilian rule these institutional barriers to social integration disappeared and full assimilation became technically possible. Over a period of time this stimulated latent fears of the loss of European superiority, eliciting compensatory action in the form of racial attitudinizing.

The third change affected the nature of control. Under military rule the mechanism of control was the army as a monolith: an institution which not only put domination into practice by force when necessary but, by its very presence, permanently symbolized it. With the advent of civilian rule the ability to dominate through a monolithic institution disappeared. Its place had to be filled in such a way as to promote minority interests without negating the Declaration of Rights on whose values the Third Republic was based.[2] The spontaneous response was racial determinism, the theories of which could justify applying those restrictions to indigenous rights, when and where they were made, that would have accorded ill with the Declaration of Rights.

Finally, the nature of the intellectual currents emanating from France changed. The utopian socialism of the early nineteenth century, with its optimism and emphasis on the progress of mankind, gave way to a strident pessimism that was to characterize much late nineteenth-century French thought. Its premonitory obsessions with demographic, cultural and national decline and the espousal of Darwinian concepts such as the survival of the fittest coalesced into deterministic ideologies of class and race. These ideas intensified existing notions on race in the colony, working to the detriment of the indigenous population.

With these developments in mind, the circumstances, events and influences which affected the evolution of attitudes to the indigenous population will now be examined.

8

Civilian rule

Towards the end of the nineteenth century French colonial theory started to shift from assimilation to association. The concept of assimilation, whereby colonial practice was geared to ensuring the complete integration of a colony into France, thus bestowing French status on it and its inhabitants, was superseded by the idea that it was more desirable to form an association, cooperating with the indigenous populations and respecting their institutions. The will to improve the 'condition' of the indigenous population remained, so the notion of the *mission civilisatrice* did not disappear. But 'civilizing' now meant improving on what was already there, rather than refashioning it in the image of France.

As far as the indigenous population was concerned both doctrines had inherent theoretical defects. Assimilation, while presupposing human equality, was none the less essentially a paradigm of vertical thought based on the premise that civilizations formed a hierarchy, with that of the French at the top. Even accepting the patronizing assumption that the indigenous population wanted to be assimilated, full social assimilation was virtually impossible in the short term, as it would require several generations to be achieved successfully. This time factor, aggravated by inconsistent policies adopted towards the indigenous population, opened the door to the argument that its members were not susceptible to the 'civilizing' process and hence could never really be Frenchmen. It only needed a few short steps along this line of thought to attribute such resistance to race. At first glance, association could be seen to be a less intransigent policy for the indigenous population than assimilation for, rather than impelling a conformity to an alien culture, it held the promise of the tolerance spawned of cultural pluralism. In fact, because its basic premise did not arise out of a notion of equality but, on the contrary, out of one of racial inequality, it marginalized the indigenous population even more than before.

In practice too assimilation fell short of its goals. Immediately following the installation of civilian rule in 1871, the political and administrative changes that occurred were motivated, for the most part, by a desire to assimilate the colony to France. Assimilation became the driving force of the Republican settlers but the concept was not all-encompassing: it remained institutional and organizational, never attaining the ideological and social dimension of a universal doctrine. If the theorists in the colony believed that by assimilating the institutions and administrative organization of the colony to those of France ideological and social assimilation would follow in the longer term, the practitioners soon realized that the long-term goals of assimilation could be dispensed with as far as the indigenous population was concerned.[3] Furthermore, the measures adopted to assimilate the administrative organization and political and cultural institutions of the Algerian colony to those of France inexorably led to an exclusion of the indigenous population from positions of power and to their alienation due to their unfamiliarity with the new system.[4] Ignorance of the French system led to confusion on the part of the indigenous population, which was then attributed by the *colons* to incapacity or innate stupidity. Paradoxically, therefore, the steps taken to assimilate on one level created an atmosphere that militated against assimilation on other levels. This situation was amplified by a strong anti-indigenous sentiment on the part of many of the settlers who, for a variety of reasons, had no desire for integration. Indigenous discontent at the new measures also came into play, exacerbating existing tensions. Indeed, that the indigenous population might not care to be assimilated was never even considered.

Islam proved to be a further barrier to the proper application of assimilation. Muslims were required to repudiate their statutory rights to Islamic law in order to become French citizens, a step few were prepared to take. The partiality of the doctrine and indeed its paradoxes can be appreciated if one considers the collective naturalization of the Algerian Jews in 1870 as a result of the Crémieux decrees. To be sure, the personality of Adolphe Crémieux, an influential metropolitan Jew, and the volatile political situation in France and Algeria at the time, greatly enhanced the successful outcome of his crusade on behalf of his Algerian 'brothers' but, unlike those who proposed collective naturalization of the Muslims, he met with little opposition to his plan.[5] The Jewish population was, of course, smaller than the indigenous population, a factor which may have mitigated settler antagonism. None the less, that the Jews, who were also bound by civil and family law within their religion, should renounce their rights to Mosaic Law was never even raised.

Out of assimilation's inherent theoretical defects and its ideological

and social denial by the settlers was to emerge the concept of association, based on the premise that the indigenous population was too
different or, worse, too inferior to be assimilated and should therefore
be allowed to maintain its institutions and culture and co-exist with
the French. Politically and administratively this implied autonomy
from France; ideologically and socially this meant a separation of 'the
races'. In North Africa the doctrine of association found its purest
expression in the protectorates of Tunisia and Morocco, but neither
doctrine ever really functioned to the exclusion of the other. In
Algeria, the traditional testing ground for administrative policies,
colonial practice was always a hybrid, creating seeming paradoxes and
a confused skein of ideas that can be difficult to unravel. Certainly
the progression from one doctrine to the other was not linear. The
two were synchronic, for a time at least. Not only was this so on a
practical level but, as will be demonstrated below, evidence can also
be found in the ideas expressed in works concerning colonial matters
written in the first three decades of civilian rule.

These developments had an impact on the Kabyle Myth. Its logical
conclusion of a global pro-Kabyle policy was never attained. Kabylophilia seemed to come to a head in a flurry of works published in the
1870s and early 1880s, but it was not strong enough to counteract the
rising tide of settler society. Three factors were especially significant
in the evolution of attitudes that shifted attention away from the
Kabyles: the Great Kabyle Insurrection and its aftermath, Lavigerie
and the Catholic Church, and the rise in importance of racial ideas in
the colony. The first provided a stick with which to beat the Kabyles
and allowed for the punitive confiscation of their land. This had a
levelling influence in that it politically equated the Kabyles with the
Arabs for the first time. The second articulated the old concept of
civilization versus barbarity in a manner the settlers found appealing.
It was to assume considerable importance in the climate of civilian
rule. The third polarized society into the settlers on the one hand and
the indigenous population on the other. For all this, Kabylophilia did
not dry up. It continued to fuel the mythology surrounding the
Kabyles but its potency waned and with it interest in the Kabyles.

The 1871 insurrection of Kabylia and its aftermath

From January 1871 to January 1872 the French African Army, the
French navy, the *colon* militia and loyal indigenous contingents were
involved in 340 encounters with an insurrectionary force of 200,000
fighting men and an insurgent population of 800,000.[6] Although

casualties were low on the French side it was, in Louis Bertrand's words, a 'formidable insurrection that nearly flung us back across the Mediterranean.'[7] So formidable was it that colonial society had difficulty comprehending from where it had obtained its impetus; nor could it believe that the insurgents had been acting alone. It was said to have been triggered by the Crémieux Laws, to have been fomented by the Bureaux Arabes, to have been abetted by Prussian meddling.[8] Vital, who wrote regularly to Urbain from Constantine keeping his friend abreast of events, raised the latter two hypotheses as early as February 1871.[9] Three months later, however, the voices raised against the Bureaux Arabes were not so hushed and once the insurrection had been quelled they became vociferous.[10] As for the hypothesis of the Crémieux Laws, there was no Jewish population in Kabylia, where the insurrection occurred. Furthermore, Mokrani, the leader of the revolt, did not oppose the naturalization of the Jews whereas he did oppose that of his fellow Muslims, believing that espousing French citizenship was inferior to adhering to the Islamic faith.[11] A more logical explanation of this accusation would be that it was grounded in settler anti-Semitism.

Civilian inability to comprehend the reasons behind the insurrection was transmuted into savage anger channelled, on the one hand, into virulent anti-militarism and, on the other, into reprisals the cruelty of which was in no way commensurate with the insurrectionary events. At the time Vital lamented to Urbain that the French had killed many of the indigenous population, had caused even more to flee and had disorientated the entire mass of the population. Furthermore, to pay for the enormous war contributions demanded of them, the tribes sold most of their beasts of burden.[12] The most far-reaching measure was the confiscation of land. From the outbreak of the insurrection the Thiers government considered land sequestration as an appropriate punishment.[13] In the end 324,000 hectares of collective land holdings and 250,000 hectares of individual land holdings were confiscated and a total of 31,500,000 francs of reparations was exacted from the insurgents.[14] In Kabylia the land sequestration proved catastrophic and had a lasting effect on Kabyle society. In an area where arable land was at a premium almost all the fertile lands were seized.[15] Land was even taken in areas untouched by the insurrection.[16] Kabyle despair at the retribution meted out to them found its expression in poignant ballads composed by itinerant Kabyle songsters.[17]

The 1871 insurrection halted any possibility of an overall Kabyle Policy evolving out of the Kabyle Myth. Randon's Organisation Kabyle was abandoned; so too was a project for a uniform Kabyle legal system devised by Letourneux and Hanoteau for which the former was assiduously seeking approval from the Ministry of War.[18] A clean sweep of Kabyle institutions followed, enabling French legal structures to be imposed for civil as well as criminal law.[19] In short, the insurrection was deemed to exonerate the civilians from the continuation of any preferential treatment the Kabyles may have enjoyed under the military. Vice Admiral Gueydon, governor-general from April 1871 to June 1873, stated the fact plainly enough, adding that all immunities granted to the Kabyles at the time of their submission could now be disregarded.[20]

If the insurrection provided the settlers with an opportunity to avail themselves of hitherto inalienable lands it also increased their wariness towards the Kabyle population. Unlike the 1857 conquest of Kabylia, when the French had moved in on the Kabyles, the 1871 insurrection was an 'unprovoked' Kabyle revolt against the French. This allowed for the development of two lines of thought that were to be consequential with regard to the future impact of the Kabyle Myth. The first was to view the French suppression of the insurrection as a victory for modern civilization. It was described as a clash between forces of the past and those of the present, in which the triumph of the latter could only benefit the former.[21] The theme of civilization versus barbarity, which had been evident at the time of conquest, was now reintroduced in the colonial intellectual repertory and found expression in a variety of ways, often with strongly racial overtones. The net result was to pit European civilization against indigenous civilization and in this the Kabyle, for all his potential, could not measure up to the European. Auguste Pomel, a believer in Kabyle superiority who set out the aptitudes of the different races of Algeria in his *Des Races Indigènes de l'Algérie*, interspersed his version of the Kabyle–Arab dichotomy with just such reservations. For all their affinities to the French, their understanding of French ways and the inherited subtlety which allowed them to accommodate the improvements of civilization, he wrote, they were more 'barbarous' than the French, with all the social defects which that implied.[22] The second notion of import challenged the idea of the Kabyles as supremely suitable for assimilation. Here too Pomel was somewhat hesitant. Assimilation, he said, was probably not a vain hope as far as the Moor and especially the Kabyle were concerned, although present events did not favour such a hypothesis, but as far as the Arab was concerned 'it was utopian'.[23] Such doubts were intimations of the trend towards association that would effectively exclude the indigenous population from all hope of achieving complete equality of opportunity either socially, politically or economically.

With the Kabyle insurrection the punitive mentality, which was to be so characteristic of settler attitudes to the indigenous population, flared into being. Had these events been the only manifestation of Berber discontent settler antagonism might have abated, but outbreaks of violence continued. In 1876 there was a revolt in the M'zab; in 1879 in the Aurès; in 1881 in the *Sud-Oranais* and in 1881–82 and 1887 there were further troubles in Kabylia. Attitudes to the Kabyles were aggravated further in the 1870s and 1880s by arson in the forests of Kabylia. The most devastating occurred in 1881, when 169,056 hectares of forest were burned.[24] The damage was estimated to be between 9 and 10 million francs.[25] Guy de Maupassant who spent two years in Algeria writing for *Le Gaulois*, captured the unease in the area at the time. The whole country was aflame, he wrote; each night the horizon was illuminated with a multitude of new fires. It was an incalculable disaster for which the Kabyles were blamed but no culprits were found.[26] The settlers were disoriented by the experience. As fast as they extinguished the fires, new ones appeared. The ensuing unease gave rise to the sentiment that the Kabyles were trying to 'evict them by fire'.[27] De Maupassant advocated radical treatment for the culprits; as arson was punishable by death he suggested that the heads of the culprits be nailed to the charred trees with a placard 'Arsonist' underneath. Within eight days, he confidently predicted, not so much as a bush would remain alight in Algeria.[28] In spite of this outburst de Maupassant was sensitive to the grievances of the Kabyles and the inconsistent treatment they received at the hands of the colonial administration. He pointed out that whereas in principle the forestry commission allowed the Kabyles access to the forests, in practice they did not. The Kabyles, furthermore, were still treated as the vanquished and not as working associates. The French, he went on, were too arrogant, too hostile and had not created any worthwhile relations with the Kabyles. Had the Kabyles been allowed to tend their forests themselves, as their ancestors had done, the present unfortunate situation would have been averted.[29] The settlers, however, were on the defensive and in this mood positions towards the Kabyles could only harden. Attitudes towards the indigenous population in 1881 were such that pro-indigenous elements deemed it necessary to set up a society for their protection. In July of that year the Société française pour la protection des indigènes was founded, with the economist Paul Leroy-Beaulieu as its president.

Watersheds in intellectual history are impossible to pinpoint, for the evolution of ideas is never diachronic. The 1871 insurrection was not, for the Kabyle Myth at least, the sort of watershed it has been said to be by latter-day social, political and economic historians.[30] It none the less contributed to the impetus for change by initiating a punitive pattern of behaviour on the part of the settlers. The myth of the superior Kabyle persisted, however. Ideas may be discredited as a result of major events but they do not disappear. Under civilian rule the Kabyles had numerous champions: Warnier (very briefly; he died in 1875), Sabatier, Pomel (for all his reservations), Caix de Saint-Aymour and Liorel were in the vanguard of those who attempted to further the Kabyle cause in the colony after 1871. But theirs was, in effect, an assimilationist swan-song. For all the attractiveness of their theories, for few took it upon themselves to deny the Kabyle Myth outright, the voices of the *kabylophiles* were hard pressed to compete against the vindictive outbursts of the settlers and the mounting conviction that the only sector of the population, the only race, worth sustained consideration was that which the metropolis was soon to dub the *pieds-noirs*.[31] In the shift from military occupation to settler domination, it was the focus that changed, not the ideas themselves.

Lavigerie and the Church

On 12 January 1867 Charles Martial Allemand Lavigerie was appointed Archbishop of Algiers. Algeria was, in his own words, 'the door opened by Providence onto a barbarous continent of 200 million souls'.[32] Lavigerie wasted little time in taking up the challenge offered him by Providence and until his death in 1892 he worked indefatigably to introduce 'Christian civilization' to the 'dark continent'. His legacy to Africa and Algeria was considerable. Within two years of his appointment, in October 1869 to be precise, he had established what was to become Africa's most ubiquitous missionary society, the Pères Blancs. The Soeurs Blanches followed eleven months later. Lavigerie also concerned himself with the eradication of slavery in Africa, launching a personal campaign in 1888. Two aspects of his vision of the Church's work in Algeria and Africa are of importance to the impact of the Kabyle Myth. The first was his desire to restore the Church in North Africa to its former Augustinian glory; the second was the question of Islam.

Lavigerie's role in the evolution of the Kabyle Myth is an interesting one. He was a confirmed *kabylophile*, having been exposed to the more subtle aspects of the Arab–Berber dichotomy before arriving in Algeria. His Pères Blancs were most active in Kabylia, and Lavigerie was convinced that proselytizing there would be successful due to the Christian antecedents of the Berbers. Their inveterate hatred of the Arab, the (tatooed) image of the cross, the Christian (monogamous) marriage, the creed or *canon* of civil law, were the indelible traces of a past now forgotten but none the less present beneath the ruins.[33] In spite of all evidence to the contrary, nearly twenty years later Lavigerie was still making similar claims.[34] Lavigerie's efforts in Kabylia won him few friends among the indigenous population. In fact, missionary zealousness in the area may well have been a factor in triggering the 1871 insurrection.[35] Nor was his proselytizing zeal appreciated in governmental circles. A dispute soon flared up between Lavigerie and Mac-Mahon, governor-general of the colony from 1864 to 1870. It was centred around Lavigerie's indictment of Islam, which he was convinced received the protection of the Bureaux Arabes, and his attempts at indoctrinating Muslim children orphaned by the 1867–69 famine.[36] Paradoxically, Lavigerie's Kabylophilia did nothing to further the Kabyle cause. The tenacious persistence which characterized the Church's efforts in Kabylia alienated the Kabyles and resultant manifestations of Kabyle discontent merely provided fodder to nurture anti-indigenous sentiment among the settlers which then worked to the detriment of the Kabyles.[37]

Lavigerie's most important contribution to the intellectual climate of the colony during the first decades of civilian rule and, ironically, to the erosion of support for the Kabyles was, on the one hand, his evocation of the early Christian Church as personified by Cyprian (200–58), Bishop of Carthage (in present-day Tunisia) and Augustine (354–430), Bishop of Hippo Regius (in present-day Algeria) and, on the other, his attitude towards Islam.[38] In a rousing pastoral letter delivered on taking up his duties as Archbishop of Algiers, Lavigerie reminded his flock of the Church's former grandeur in Africa, with its multitude of saintly heros and bishops. An example to the Christian world of the time, this period of glory was none the less followed by centuries of 'mourning'. The catastrophe that had befallen the ancient Church was the invasion of the barbarians (the Vandals, whose Kingdom of Africa lasted from 429 to 534) and, of course the fanatical armies of Islam. These 'armed apostles of a sensual religion' massacred the Christians of North Africa *en masse*. France (*la France libératrice*) would lift the veil of darkness from this historically Christian land and bestow on it a renewed grandeur. Algeria would once again become the cradle of a great Christian nation, a second France which would spread the Christian civilization with the ardour characterized by the French race and faith.[39] If Lavigerie's sentiments were merely the religious adaptation of the *mission civilisatrice* they were no less potent for that. No matter how bothersome the authorities found Lavigerie, this message of his would be relayed, in some form or other, from pulpits throughout Algeria. This made of it a more powerful version of the *mission civilisatice* than that confined to the works of colonial theorists and administrators, hitherto the most sedulous purveyors of the word. It was also potentially a more hostile variety vociferously pitting, in the manner of the crusader-officers of the conquest years, Christianity versus Islam, civilization versus barbarity, but now to a European audience of significant size. (Whether they were churchgoers or not, Lavigerie's status in the colony ensured that they were aware of both the man and his ideas.) Whereas, in the early decades of occupation the *mission civilisatrice* envisaged civilizing the indigenous population and, at however far-removed a date, turning it into a French one, Lavigerie's *mission civilisatrice* held out promise only to those who were willing to convert, and even then he was categoric that they were not to be turned into Frenchmen. Addressing an audience of missionaries and physicians, Lavigerie declared that missionaries were to be the initiators, but the lasting work had to be done by the Africans themselves, as Christians and apostles and not as Frenchmen and Europeans. Their souls must be transformed but their external appearance must remain indigenous.[40] Not only did such a message prefigure the ideas of association, but the morality that was at the core of Lavigerie's apostolic mission reinforced, on a spiritual level, the notion well established on a material level, of European (Christian) superiority.

Islam, a regrettable religion in Lavigerie's eyes, proved also to be an incorrigible one. The proselytizing of the Pères Blancs met with limited success in Algeria, as a report written at a mission in Kabylia indicates. The Muslim, it stated, was a being full of self-importance and corruption. The few notions of religion Muslims possessed led them to imagine they were the most enlightened of men, a fact that made conversion difficult.[41] Lavigerie had always been aware of the problem Islam posed for the Church. It was for this reason he so relentlessly promoted the mission orphanages as a major undertaking of the Church. Orphans were the *tabula rasa* on which the Word could best be inscribed, and the only hope for achieving any sort of assimilation. Such youthful converts would ensure regeneration and true assimilation, as they would have escaped the deleterious and indelible influence of the Koran.[42] This insistence on regeneration and the moral assimilation of the indigenous population again fuelled extant notions of European superiority and suggested, short of conversion, an insuperable gulf between the two. The 'moral depravity of Islam' was reiterated in the campaign Lavigerie waged against slavery in the late 1880s. Acknowledging that Islam treated its slaves with kindness in the Orient, he none the less affirmed that in Africa (Morocco and the Sudan were examples cited) its cruelty and horror was immeasurable.[43] It was Lavigerie who did the most to promote the concept of the African slave-trade as essentially Islamic.[44]

Throughout his apostolic career Lavigerie made few concessions to Islam, nor did he relinquish his attachment to the importance of the early Christian Church. As late as 1883 in a pastoral letter to his clergy he set out its history and instructed them to learn it and teach it to their flock.[45] These twin concerns, which he managed to link inextricably by promoting the concept of civilization versus barbarity, encouraged the deterioration of the relationship between the Europeans and the indigenous population. This was more significant when it came to attitudes towards the Kabyles than it was for the Arabs, who were already viewed with varying degrees of disdain.

The impact of Lavigerie's message arose principally from the fact he was a controversial figure who carved out a niche for himself in colonial history, becoming a *colon* spokesman in the process, rather than from the religious significance of his message. In the words of a contemporary, he was 'steel-willed with a rare energy, reminiscent of those bishops of the Middle Ages who were as much men of war as ministers of the Word. Profoundly attached to Africa, like Faidherbe he dreamed of a French territory stretching from Algeria to Senegal.'[46] His colonizing ambitions and his proselytizing missions were viewed with mixed feelings but his influence was indisputable, as Paul Bert, who was to hold the posts of minister of education and governor-general of Indo-China, discovered in his conversations with *colons* and administrators while travelling through Kabylia in 1885. Some sung the Cardinal's praises to Bert. Others saw him as an ambitious blunderer, who placed France in the thrall of Catholicism, incited Muslim fanaticism, and caused more harm than good in the colony with his boisterous personality. Detractors and supporters alike agreed that as far as indigenous relations and internal policy were concerned, the administration accorded Lavigerie far too much importance.[47] By the last decade of the nineteenth century the sociological climate of the colony had deteriorated sufficiently to cause the economist and theorist of colonization, Paul Leroy-Beaulieu, to comment that while the economic rise of Algeria in the last quarter of the century may have been rapid, the same could not be said of the moral situation. Here Algeria seemed to have taken a step backwards for the colony's moral state was less healthy than it had been before 1870. The various elements of the population – the colons, the indigenous people and the Jews – now confronted each other with hostility.[48]

Lavigerie's overriding Christian message detracted from his pro-Kabyle sentiments and encouraged the alienation of the European population from that of the indigenous one. His desire to assimilate (re-convert) the Kabyles because of their Christian antecedents encouraged the religious-cum-cultural polarization that was emerging in the colony. His re-introduction of the concept of civilization versus barbarity, with its Eurocentricism and exacerbated notions of moral superiority, invited racism. For all his claims of moving towards spiritual assimilation, Lavigerie's message did more to usher in association than to encourage assimilation. In this the Kabyles, however favoured they might be, still remained on the wrong side of the European–indigenous divide. Civilization versus barbarity was an attractive concept to the European population and it was not long before it found a champion: author and eventual member of the Academie Française, Louis Bertrand. Bertrand secularized the notion, incorporated elements from ideas prevalent in France, added his own embellishments and created an ideology which left little room for Arabs and Kabyles. Let it be said that this concept was by no means restricted to the colony. Ernest Renan, Gustave Le Bon and André Lefevre were among many who elaborated on aspects of civilization versus barbarity and who used Islam as a convenient example of the latter. It was an old notion with its foundations in medieval Christianity; Lavigerie merely redefined it in accordance with contemporary circumstance.

Some post-1871 versions of the Myth and their significance

By the time the civilians took over the reins of power the Kabyle Myth was well established. The works of military men such as Carette, Aucapitaine, Daumas, Devaux and Hanoteau were the foundation on which all further research was based but the need for reconnaissance and security, which had motivated the military studies in the past, was superseded by the dictates of a colonizing power concerned primarily with economic and social aggrandizement. The diminution of paternalism, with its underlying assumption of guiding the undeveloped to adulthood, so evident under the military, saw the emergence under civilian rule of the less felicitous 'join us or be damned' approach. This found its apogee in the question of indigenous naturalization where, with few exceptions, Muslims were denied French citizenship unless they renounced their statutory rights to Islamic law, a step which amounted to apostasy.[49] Naturalization aroused anxiety in the decades immediately following civilian take-over, for the European settlers were fearful that metropolitan deputies would instigate a movement towards mass indigenous naturalization culminating in a law similar to the Crémieux decrees for the Jews.[50] Such fear obviously failed to discriminate between Kabyle and Arab. Pomel, who raised the question in 1871 in his *Des races indigènes de l'Algérie,* sought to appease the settlers in this respect by stating that the unanimous revulsion of the indigenous population towards naturalization was a lasting cause of comfort to the French.[51] Nearly twenty years later, in 1887, when a bill for the naturalization of the indigenous population was proposed in the Chamber of Deputies by two members of the extreme left, Michelin and Gaulier, denunciation of such schemes became more forthright. The press in the colony did not mince words: 'We Algerians cannot admit that the indigenous population be French like us.'[52] No exception was made for the Kabyles. A professor of Roman and maritime law in Algiers, François Charvériat, was against all attempts at naturalization for Arabs and Kabyles alike.[53] Not only was Charvériat against naturalization, he also believed assimilation of the Kabyles to be chimerical. He based his argument on the fact that contact with the French had had few beneficial results to date. Daily contact with French civil servants, far from transforming the Kabyles' intrinsically rebellious nature, had, on the contrary, made them even more hostile. None the less Charvériat was sufficiently versed in the Kabyle Myth to make a reservation to his argument, namely that if Muslims were ever to assimilate the Kabyles would be the first to do so. Unlike the Arabs, who were full of aristocratic prejudices, they were open to modern ideas. Charvériat listed the usual gamut of attributes, compared them favourably to the peasants of France and concluded that if by nature the Kabyles were wild and uneducated they were none the less full of vigour. These were traits that would make it difficult for France to master them and bring them around to European customs, but if they managed to do so the Kabyle would do them great honour.[54] Charvériat's attitude was representative. Settlers, especially those who had immigrated to Algeria after 1871, were prepared to pay lip-service to the idea of greater potential for assimilation among the Kabyles than the Arabs while still advocating that such a policy was in the interests of none.

Naturalization was linked to another concern, that of demography. The need to populate the colony in order to make it economically viable, hitherto an essentially academic debate, acquired new urgency under the civilian regime. The majority of the European immigrants gravitated to the towns, thus creating a potential agricultural labour problem, especially as European-controlled agriculture was developing into its labour-intensive, capitalist form. Just how this problem could be resolved rose to the fore in the colonial theorizing of the first two decades of civilian rule. Looking to the indigenous population, in particular the Kabyles, was one solution. These discussions on naturalization, demography and labour took place in a milieu where racial interpretations, eventually incorporated into the larger debate of assimilation versus association, were in the ascendant. Attitudes towards Arabs and Kabyles were woven into all these debates.

Instituting settler politics, different in essence from what had gone before, usually entailed some sort of justification of the reasons former policies were being abandoned. Such justification was often presaged by vociferous attacks on the Bureaux Arabes and 'their' *Royaume Arabe*. Among the accusations levelled at the military regime was that they had promoted the Arabization (i.e. Islamization) of the Kabyles.[55] The implication that the military regime had failed to differentiate between Kabyles and Arabs, an erroneous suggestion to which the sobriquet *Royaume Arabe* lent itself admirably, was used to discredit military policy toward the indigenous population by both pro- and anti-assimilationists. The former tried to regenerate the waning theory by suggesting a new approach, the latter by advocating an altogether different policy.

In the last three decades of the nineteenth century factors such as these were evident in the works on the Kabyles. Interpretations were often frankly racial, as in the case of Pomel. The more polemical works were also noticeably ambiguous. While setting out to present a case for the assimilation of the Kabyles they contained much that suggested an affinity with the ideas of association. To illustrate the evolution of attitudes towards the Kabyles, three of the better known works of the period will be discussed below, namely those by the senator-palaeontologist Auguste Pomel, the *colon* Amédée Caix de Saint-Aymour, and the anthropologist Emile Masqueray.

Pomel and the racial division of labour

Nicolas Auguste Pomel (1821–98) was a senator from Oran with scholarly inclinations. He had over 35 titles to his credit, principally on aspects of palaeontology, geology and zoology, of which several appeared in more than one edition. In collaboration with Pouyanne, an engineer from the Polytechnique, he set up the Service de la Carte géologique détaillée, which produced a number of valuable maps of the colony.[56] Pomel was deferred to as the 'palaeontologist scholar', and his work was an oft-cited source on the Berbers.[57] In 1871 he published *Des Races Indigènes de l'Algérie et du role que leur réservent leurs aptitudes*, a work that reflects both the contemporary inclination to theorize racially and the gamut of settler preoccupations.

Pomel considers four 'racial' groups: the Arabs, the Berbers, the Moors (*Maure*) or city-dwellers (*Hadri*), and the Jews, in relation to their potential role in colonial society. Of the four he devotes most space to the Arabs and the Berbers. A cursory reading of the work suggests an exaltation of the Kabyle. Yet a closer look reveals that Pomel was not a *kabylophile* in the mould of an Aucapitaine, a Carette or a Daumas. Certainly he accepted the precepts of the Kabyle Myth. He had nothing good to say about the Arabs, and lauded those aspects of Kabyle society and physiognomy that reflected European values. He contrasted the sterility of the nomadic lifestyle of the Arab to the flourishing one of the sedentary Kabyle. His enthusiasm for Kabyle democratic tendencies, hospitality, treatment of women and propensity to work was wholehearted, so too was his appreciation of the beauty of their race.[38] Yet he was reluctant to draw them into the sphere of the European race. For all their racial differences from the Arabs and their physical affinity to the Europeans it was difficult to prove that the Kabyles had crossed the Mediterranean with the invasion of the Celts and Gauls. If these 'Atlantes', as he called them, were the true natives of the land it was hardly necessary to demonstrate the fact they had come for elsewhere.[39] Pomel acknowledged the impact of Roman occupation as witnessed by Kabyle law and their alleged Christian antecedents, but he stressed that there had been no racial assimilation and, using the Roman experience as his example, he warned of Berber resistance to foreign domination. The Kabyles merely used periods of seeming peace to regroup and prepare for renewed efforts to rid themselves of the foreign yoke. Certainly there were affinities between Kabyle and European but the Kabyles were more 'barbarous' and adhered to Islam. *If* these obstacles could be overcome, Pomel concluded, the Kabyle was the most apt for that 'utopia of assimilation'.[60]

Pomel's work was not an attempt to shed further light on the ethnology of the various sectors of the indigenous population. Rather he used the received wisdom on these groups, especially the Arabs and Kabyles, to present his case for the reorganization of indigenous society under the new civilian order. The most pertinent questions of the day, namely demography, naturalization, security, property and Islam, are evoked and discussed in relation to the four racial groups (most especially the Arabs and Berbers). The book is not merely Eurocentric, it is anti-Islamic and anti-Semitic, both attitudes for which nineteenth-century scholars and writers made no apologies. Racial imagery forms an integral part of the text, and judging from this work, Pomel's vision of mankind was a racial one: some races were better suited to certain functions than others.

As a senator with the interests of the settlers at heart, Pomel was primarily concerned with the success of colonization. This entailed finding solutions to the problems of land, labour and security, over-riding questions which subsumed those of demography, naturalization, property rights and Islam. Naturally enough these solutions had to take the indigenous population into account, especially the Berbers, who were numerically superior to the other groups.[61] *Des Races Indigènes de l'Algérie* attempted to provide answers to these questions. From a purely pragmatic point of view it was impossible to write off the Kabyles. Kabylia was densely populated, with well-established settlements. Herding the Kabyles into the Sahara, as Pomel suggested should be done with the Arabs, would be far too dangerous.[62] But Pomel was writing under the influence of the recent Kabyle insurrection. Although he inclined to blame the 'military satrapy' for these events, his enthusiasm for the Kabyles was tempered by wariness. He was aware that security had to be maintained and that under civilian rule it would have to take different forms. The overt symbol of force which the military, as an institution, represented would have to be replaced somehow to contain the impulse to rebel. The solution for Pomel was to encourage European settlement. An extensive colonial network would eradicate all illusions harboured by the indigenous population.[63] In Kabylia there was the added imperative of combatting Kabyle isolation. European settlement on lands confiscated or 'vacated' (as a result of the decimation of the tribes to which they belonged) would kill two birds with one stone: security and land for colonization. Wherever it was in French interests to maintain a strong military position the largest possible number of European agricultural and industrial centres should be set up. The imposition of direct French rule in this way would ensure that power groupings were split up and any lasting pockets of resistance destroyed. This could even lead to miscegenation, as long as the 'contamination with Islam' and dogmatic antagonism were not irreversible obstacles.[64]

Pomel, unlike his contemporary Warnier, had little to do with the actual development of the Kabyle Myth. He merely adapted it to the exigencies of the new order. Being a received idea it was difficult to ignore in any serious discussion on the indigenous population. Pomel was pragmatic enough to realize that for demographic reasons allowances would have to be made for the Kabyles, but he was also a European settler and instinctively distanced himself from the indigenous population. This led to the sort of reservations that would eventually eclipse any serious consideration of assimilating the Kabyles, let alone the Arabs.

The emerging racism in the colony, of which Pomel's work is but an 'erudite' example, was not levelled against the Islamic sectors of the population alone. Jews came in for their fair share of opprobrium. For Pomel these 'unscrupulous vampires' were 'lying, dissimulating, cheating, sordid, dirty, hypocrites' worthy only of a two-page mention.[65] Anti-Semitism in the colony exploded in ugly riots at the turn of the century and if it is mentioned here it is to stress the racial polarization that occurred in the last three decades of the colony, which pitted 'European races' (Christians) against 'non-European races' (Muslims and Jews) and affected the impact of the Kabyle Myth.[66] The racial character of Pomel's discussion also serves to underline the nature of the developing hierarchy in the colony; a hierarchy whose framework was racial above all else.

The question of the formation of a social hierarchy in the colony merits research of its own. It was more subtle than the indigenous–European divide that this work, by the nature of its subject matter, is obliged to stress. If on the one hand the Kabyles were at the top of the indigenous half, the European half was more than just a pyramid with the *grands colons* at the top and the *petit blancs* at the bottom. Spaniards, Italians, Maltese gravitated not only to specific towns, or to specific districts in the towns, but often to specific jobs (Esparto-grass gatherers in the 1880s were predominantly Spanish, for example). This led to the formation of a nuanced hierarchy, where not only employment but national origin could dictate one's place in the pecking order. Naturalization was a substantial brick in the mental construction of the new social order. It was the passport to 'Frenchness', the pinnacle to which all were presumed to aspire. According to Caix de Saint Aymour, a *colon* living in Algeria in the last decades of the century, in mixed European marriages it was nearly always the man who was French. The prestige French nationality bestowed served as an attraction to women from the southern Mediterranean shores, in particular the Hispanic-Algerian women who were gratified to marry into 'the conquering race'.[67] The 1889 naturalization law, which granted automatic citizenship to all Europeans born in Algeria (and to children of non-French fathers born on French soil), eased the way for new immigrants. The neo-French, as they came to be known, were none the less soon being derogatorily dubbed *'les Néos'* by the *'Français d'origine'*.[68] While the concept of a new white Mediterranean race, hardy, voluptuous and proud as Gide was to characterize it, did much to solder the Europeans into a bloc, providing them with an 'advantage' over the indigenous population, it must be borne in mind that the importance of race in colonial society extended well beyond that of castigating the Islamic Other.[69] It was the social fabric of this society. Pomel's work, written at the outset of civilian rule, was an intimation of the importance race was to assume in the colony.

Civilian rule

Amédée Caix de Saint-Aymour (1843–1921):
an assimilationist swan-song

By 1891, when Viscount Caix de Saint-Aymour's *Arabes et Kabyles* appeared, interest in the Kabyles was largely academic. The civilian population had not been seduced by the Kabyle Myth, remaining indifferent to Arabs and Kabyles alike. As Caix de Saint-Aymour wrote, 'for the majority of Franco-Algerians administrative mandarins, whether in the public or private sector, the native is an inferior being to be despised, taxed and worked without mercy, although unfortunately protected by law in the most ridiculous fashion.'[70] Caix de Saint-Aymour produced his work, the fruit of 'nearly ten years of research', in response to the drift away from assimilation by his fellow settlers but also to the debate, renewed in France at the time, over possible reforms to the administrative structure of Algeria. His solution to the problems confronting colonization at the time was a plea for assimilation of the Kabyles. Nothing could be done with the Arabs but everything could with the Kabyles.[71] The Kabyle, 'a keen worker', had proved himself to be a valuable asset in the colony. As labourers, Kabyles were equal to, if not better than, their European counterparts. Without Kabyle assistance settler lands would lie fallow or necessitate the unsatisfactory alternative of Sardinian, Sicilian or Spanish labourers. For this reason existing policy towards the indigenous population had to change. The French Algerians had to cease treating the indigenous population as inferior beings and grant them the dignity they deserved.[72]

In an effort to convince his readers of his arguments, Caix de Saint-Aymour presented his case by means of the most compelling example of the Kabyle Myth to date, berating the obtuseness of existing French policy. France must understand the need to apply a different policy to the sedentary, monogamous, hard-working Kabyles from the one it did to the lazy, polygamous, vagabond Arabs? Collaboration with the Kabyle, he suggested, made demographic sense for they would be the renovating force of Algeria.[73] This was a theme that had been dear to Aucapitaine, but the intervening 30 years had seen considerable change in the colony. Aucapitaine had suggested that the Kabyles would be suitable 'intermediaries' at a time when colonial theory was in its formative stages and economic colonization was virtually non-existent.[74] Caix de Saint-Aymour was exhorting an unsympathetic audience of settlers to offer part of what they considered to be their hard-won economic cake to a sector of the population who had the potential to become a serious competitor. While reproaching his audience for their tendency to consider the indigenous population as an inferior race, Caix de Saint-Aymour was sensitive enough to prevailing racial attitudes to declare that cross-breeding between the two races could only be achieved very slowly. He felt it would be foolish to try and create mixed European-Berber villages until the Kabyles were well and truly Gallicized. It was best to wait for the mingling to occur naturally. Assimilation had been unsuccessful to date, according to Caix de Saint-Aymour, because of a past failure to distinguish between Arabs and Berbers. This had been particularly evident during Napoleon III's misguided *Royaume Arabe*.[75]

Caix de Saint-Aymour, like Pomel and most other *colons*, was incapable of resisting the urge to censure the military regime when the opportunity presented itself, blaming them for a state of affairs that had improved little in the 20 years of civilian rule. If, under military rule, there had been no official policy to assimilate the Kabyles rather than the Arabs, Randon's Organisation Kabyle was an administrative policy that certainly differentiated between Kabyles and Arabs placing the former in a 'favoured status' position. This had been swept away after the 1871 insurrection and with it any tentative beginnings of an official pro-Kabyle policy. Since then piecemeal policy initiatives had been taken with regard to the Kabyles, especially in the domain of education, but no coherent global policy had been adopted and many of the initiatives had themselves soon been abandoned.[76]

Caix de Saint-Aymour's arguments reflected the viewpoint of a minority of reforming republicans who realized that the marginalization of the indigenous population could only lead to acute problems for the colony in the future. Personalities such as Paul Leroy-Beaulieu and Senator Jean-Jules Clamageran were among the *kabylophile* element adhering to this viewpoint. Theirs was a more insistent viewpoint than that of those who refrained from discriminating between Arabs and Berbers. In spite of this insistence and purported Berber superiority, the drive to assimilate the Kabyles met with little response among the settlers. Two years after the publication of *Arabes et Kabyles*, Caix de Saint Aymour's ideas were picked up by one Jules Liorel in *Races Berbères. Kabylie du Jurjura*. Liorel too was concerned with the lack of enthusiasm for the Kabyles and set out to 'vulgarize' all that had been written on them to date. Referring to every preceding work of note, Liorel declared that in spite of their excellence, it was a regrettable fact that no author had yet produced a book in which all that was known about the Kabyles was summed up in a simple and cogent form.[77] The work, prefaced by Emile Masqueray, had a wealth of ethnological detail and was indeed easy to read, but for all this it too failed to produce the desired effect. Relatively few works appeared on the Kabyles during the decade of the Nineties, and those that did were similar in tone and content to that of Caix de Saint-Aymour. They were vain attempts at fanning the embers of a fire that had ceased to glow.

Emile Masqueray (1843–1894): the viewpoint of an academic

Emile Masqueray's *Formation des Cités chez les populations sedentaires de l'Algérie,* was the only scholarly work on the Berbers (Kabyles, Chaouia and Mozabites) of note to emerge during the first three decades of civilian rule.[78] It remains, along with Hanoteau and Letourneux's *magnum opus,* one of the monuments of Kabyle ethnology-cum-anthropology. Masqueray, who was eventually appointed by Paul Bert to the directorship of the Ecole Supérieure des Lettres d'Alger, arrived in Algeria in 1872 and, until his premature death in 1894, dedicated himself to the study of archaeology (most especially the Roman ruins in the Aurès), philology (namely Berber dialects) and an understanding of the social framework of Berber society. This three-fold interest is evident in his *Formation des Cités.* Masqueray acknowledged his debt to his predecessors on Kabyle terrain, in particular Carette, Devaux, Sabatier, and Hanoteau and Letourneux, but his guiding precepts were different. His work is shaped by an intellectual deference to Roman civilization, which produced some curious convolutions in his argument and impelled him to use a comparative methodology, whether comparing France to Rome or Kabyle social organization to that of the primitive Romans, and their precursors the Greeks.

Masqueray sets the tone of the work at once by his declaration that for the second time in history Europe dominated the Mediterranean. The work of the Romans was being picked up and improved upon. The one major policy difference was that the French, unlike the Romans, were attempting to elevate the indigenous population to their level rather than keeping them in servitude, but like the Romans they were maintaining European supremacy. In contrast to many of his predecessors and all his contemporaries Masqueray did not believe in the validity of racial analysis in defining the different peoples of Algeria, but rather in the impact of the environment.[79] Nor did he elevate the Kabyles by denigrating the Arabs, and here he differed from most fellow *kabylophiles.* But he did liken Berber villages to the primitive villages of classical Rome and Greece, the seed-bed of European institutions. Berber villages were a replica of the ones out of which the French race had emerged; any differences that existed were not essential but rather developmental. Thus the Berbers showed promise of being elevated to the level of the French. The careful study of Berber villages, the *tiddar* in Kabylia, the *thaquelathin* in the Aurès and the *qçour* of the M'zab, would shed light on the institutional origins of Western civilization.[80] It was a shared heritage of sorts and, no matter how much further France had evolved along the path of civilization, it held promise for the successful assimilation of the Berbers.

Although Masqueray eschews racial characteristics in his analyses he regularly draws the Berbers into the European sphere. He describes the villages of Kabylia with noteworthy lyricism and compares them to those found in Auvergne and Savoy.[81] But his most telling comparisons evolve out of his division of the indigenous population into sedentary and nomad. Sedentary Berbers had points in common with the French. Their villages, for example, were very similar and were organized into small republics, with assemblies being regularly held. The nomads on the other hand did not. All they needed was to know in which month the grass grew on the slopes of the Tell and in the Sahara. The positive and negative connotations attached to the words *sédentaire* and *nomade*, developed during the 50 years of French occupation, were too strong not to be suggestive. The nomad as a dweller of semi-arid and barren lands was shaped by his environment, in the same way as the sedentary village dweller was by his, rich and variegated as it was by comparison. This environmental categorization held the inference of concomitant intellectual/social development in each case. Thus the Berber lifestyle, 'the perfect example of barbarous sedentarism' as Masqueray put it, offered a undeniable potential for development. It was a point he kept coming back to and was at pains to prove.[82] The nomad did not share this potential. Although Masqueray believed it was environment, not race, that was responsible for the salient characteristics of a people, in colonial Algeria the very use of the sedentary–nomad division, where the former was equated positively with the Berbers and the latter negatively with the Arabs, was suggestive of racial arguments. For all his personal rejection of racial analysis therefore, by concentrating on '*the* sedentary peoples of Algeria', three Berber groups, and stressing their potential for assimilation, Masqueray did nothing to dispel racial attitudes towards Arabs and Berbers.

Masqueray's Kabylophilia influenced his friend Jules Ferry into adopting a pro-Berber educational policy. In 1881 Ferry created eight schools in Kabylia and although only 4 were opened, ten years later a similar programme was launched following a survey by the Commission sénatoriale des XVIII, of which Emile Combes was a member.[83]

The outcome of this policy is interesting: according to Colonna it was a success in Kabylia but a failure in the Aurès and the M'zab. (*Kabylophiles* claimed that this success was due to innate Kabyle ability.[84]) Colonna, in *Instituteurs Algériens*, puts this down to economic and linguistic reasons rather than to any active encouragement on the part of the French, let alone to innate Kabyle ability. None the less, a policy was adopted and Masqueray was its *éminence grise*.

Masqueray's work is noteworthy in that it is a junction of the intellectual trends that were to affect colonial attitudes towards the Kabyles. On the one hand it promotes, in its own way, the tenets of the Kabyle Myth and on the other it provides strong evidence of an increasingly overt tendency to juxtapose France/Rome/civilization and contrast it to indigenous population/primitiveness/barbarity. Masqueray, of course, believed that the Berbers could be elevated from their 'barbarous' state; most other settlers did not. Ironically, Masqueray's denial of 'sedentary' and 'nomad' as an inherently racial lifestyle and his insistence that these were purely environmental categories had been broached in Gustave Le Bon's anti-assimilationist work *La Civilisation des Arabes*, which appeared in France two years earlier than Masqueray's assimilationist treatise on the Berbers.

Le Bon declared that the Arabs were not a pure race and that fundamental distinctions had to be made between nomadic and sedentary Arabs.[85] As might be expected, Le Bon considered the Arabs of Algeria to be a particularly inferior quality of cross-breed. He did not, however, have much sympathy for the Berbers. The Berber psychology, he believed, was very similar to that of the Arab, provided of course a comparison was made between sedentary Berbers and Arabs and nomadic Berbers and Arabs. His conclusion was in direct contrast to Masqueray's. A comparison of sedentary Berbers and Arabs clearly demonstrated, he wrote, that there were absolutely no grounds to support the theory that the former could be more easily civilized than the latter. The present-day Arabs and Berbers were equally inept at living, feeling and thinking like Europeans.[86] Le Bon did much to popularize racial ideas in France and was, according to Robert Nye, 'the supreme scientific vulgarizer of his generation'.[87] No doubt because of this, his work was frequently attacked by organized science in France.[88] None the less, he was an advocate of association and his ideas were those beginning to prevail in colonial circles. If his theories are juxtaposed here with those of Masqueray it is to illustrate that at this particular point in time there was an overlap between the ideas of assimilation and association. The categories of the former were being re-examined and repudiated by the latter. By lumping together Arabs and Berbers and declaring them to be inferior to Europeans, Le Bon was articulating the sentiments that were to triumph among the European settlers of Algeria.

Of the three principal works discussed above there is little evidence that those by Pomel and Caix de Saint-Aymour had an impact on settler attitudes towards the Kabyles. Their very nature and those of others like them such as those by Liorel and Coeur, with their exhortatory tones and their avowed desires to 'elucidate', 'convince' or 'vulgarize', suggest the degree to which their audience had lost touch with or was impervious to the Kabyle Myth. Unlike the officer-scholars, whose guiding precept was reconnaissance and whose research, for all its shortcomings, was motivated by a pragmatic need to understand better (and thus secure) the indigenous population under their control, the concerns of civilians writing after 1871 arose less out of pragmatism and more out of personal conviction. Theirs were syntheses, cemented together by their ideological or political beliefs (race, assimilation, anti-militarism) and presented as original research to convince an increasingly unreceptive audience of the merits of assimilating the Kabyles. They were not the polemics of divide and rule but arose out of a sincere, but misguided, conviction that it was possible, for racial reasons, to assimilate part of the indigenous population. (The majority for a few, as Warnier had declared that his research showed that four-fifths of the local population was to some extent Berber: the figure was subsequently adopted.[89]) The fact that they relied so heavily on racial arguments to present their case is in itself an indication of the importance racial attitudes had assumed in the colony.

Masqueray was the exception. His contribution constituted *bona fide* research and was an original and important piece of work in its genre. For all this he too found it necessary to ply the French–Kabyle connection. Masqueray was writing for a different audience. Like the scholar-officers, his research was motivated by a desire to increase understanding of the Kabyles but his work was primarily for academics and scholars (*Formation des Cités* was his doctoral thesis). He did not need to exhort his readers in an endeavour to convince them; they were familiar with the canon of thought on the Kabyles. His work was well received in scholarly circles although, interestingly enough, reservations were expressed, both by his defence committee and a number of scholars in France, as to the wisdom of his comparison of Berber villages to primitive Roman ones.[90] This itself can be construed as an indication of the extent to which classical antiquity had become an obsession in the colony. In the milieu to which it was addressed, Masqueray's work had a lasting influence. The world of scholarship proved to be a bastion of the Kabyle Myth. Here it was difficult to dislodge the accumulated ideas that had been cogently argued by two generations of scholars. In contrast, among the settlers in Algeria academic argument was irrelevant and the distinction between Kabyles and Arabs was not one they cared to dwell on.

Conclusion

The advent of civilian rule brought with it a series of ideological changes that affected the impact rather than the import of the Kabyle Myth. In the first place occupational colonization gave way to economic colonization. The paternalism of the occupying military force was replaced by settler politics with economic interests, rather than security and reconnaissance, as its fulcrum. Property, with its attendant, and oft-times pernicious, notion of ownership displaced, as the overriding concern, the desire to maintain harmonious relationships between the colonizers and the colonized. Military personnel, of course, could not and did not obtain and exploit land for personal gain. Personal interest, therefore, did not encroach on their relationship with the local population in the same way as it did with the settlers. Within the limits of their paternalism the military were inclined to sympathize with the local population when pitted against the settlers, especially over questions of property, which until 1871 only concerned the Arabs anyway. The massive land sequestrations in Kabylia following the 1871 insurrection placed the Kabyle for the first time, in a very significant domain, on a par with the Arab. For all their alleged superiority to the Arabs, when it came to land the Kabyles were *indigènes* in the same light as the Arabs.

The last quarter of the nineteenth century saw the European population of Algeria multiply. Algeria now appeared to be irrevocably French, and settling there was growing less hazardous yearly. The clearing of mosquito-infested areas such as the Mitidja, the introduction of prophylactics against malaria, and the improvement in medical facilities greatly reduced European mortality rates. These developments, coupled with the phylloxera epidemic of the 1870s which forced French peasants off the land, led to an influx of immigrants emanating from the shores of the northern Mediterranean. The majority settled in the coastal towns. Algiers, Oran, Bône, Philippeville, Mostaganem became flourishing centres of European bureaucracy, trade and commerce, activities requiring little indigenous collaboration. Such assistance as was called for was mainly in the form of manual labour. As de Maupassant had caustically noted in 1881 about the urban European settler: 'the only Arabs the Algerians of Algiers have seen are those that shine their boots: they indulge in boudoir colonialism and gandourah culture.'[91] In the social hierarchy, therefore, it was only the lower ranks that needed to be filled by the indigenous population on any significant scale. The notion of assimilating the local population into French civilization, of turning its members into Frenchmen, slowly subsided and the idea emerged of associating with it and selectively drawing such members as were required into the French labour market and bureaucratic framework. Colonial theorists began attacking assimilation and promoting association. By 1900 the theory of assimilation had been virtually eclipsed and the voices of the most influential colonial ideologues were, and would continue to be, raised in favour of association.[92]

The question of social hierarchies is an important one in the consideration of the diminishing impact of the Kabyle Myth, particularly during the last decade of the nineteenth century. Elites form part of any society, and colonial society was no exception. Colonial Algeria in the last three decades of the nineteenth century was Republican. Its colonizing element was a mixture of numerous Mediterranean nationalities, of *Latins*, a popular misnomer but an especially pertinent one in the light of ideological developments in the colony. There was no predetermined hierarchy with which these diverse sectors of the European population could identify, and the colony therefore threw up its own. The first major distinction in any society is between the *haves* and the *have nots*, and in colonial society the *haves* became the colonizers and the *have nots* the colonized. However many hierarchical nuances developed on either side, and they were many, however *evolué* the latter became in relation to the former, however many individual exceptions were made, this essential divide was never breached. It is important to stress that in Algeria this division was not merely a material one with its connotations of an *economic* social and cultural order. It was a question of civilization, with cultural, social, but above all religious implications that were deemed infinitely less surmountable than the economic divisions the two words imply. In this domain, the indigenous population as a whole was always found lacking. For all their perceived superiority to the Arabs, when it came to this essential divide the Kabyles were placed alongside the Arabs. This, of course, did not preclude advocating the advantages of Kabyle–French collaboration over that of an Arab–French one.

Taken together, these factors opened the door wide to the advent of racial ideas. Both the racial theories that were emerging in Europe and outright racism became conspicuous under civilian rule. The notion of Algeria as the crucible of a new white Mediterranean race gained credence. Overt racial attitudes made themselves felt. Violent anti-Semitism swept through the colony in response to the Dreyfus affair. Pejorative sobriquets such as *bicot, melon, bougnoul, raton* were attached to the indigenous population.[93] Race became a significant factor in the colony. The racial myth of the superior Kabyole did not diminish, it was displaced in importance by the more powerful one: that of the new dominant Latino-Algerian race.

9

Algeria, the melting pot of the Mediterranean: the impact of Louis Bertrand

Racial ideology, whose essential function is to maintain the power-lessness of certain sectors of a society, is advanced by the creation of myths. Once these myths pass into the mainstream of social consciousness they can be, and usually are, acted upon, giving rise to discrimination and even violence. In Algeria overt racism was a fact of life arising out of the creation of racial myths of which the Kabyle Myth, the myth of the nomadic Arab, and the myth of the new Latino-Mediterranean race were the principal examples. Two of these myths, the Kabyle Myth and the myth of the Latino-Mediterranean race, were positive while the third, the myth of the nomadic Arab, was negative. The racial dialectic can only function within the framework of a positive/negative juxtaposition. This reductionism, the root of the distortions and inaccuracies in racial thought, cannot satisfactorily accommodate several positive myths without completely losing what coherence, if any, it has. The rise of the myth of a Latino-Mediterranean race left no ideological space for the Kabyle Myth. The latter was therefore marginalized to a point where it could not present an impediment to the development of the new myth. In order to understand this marginalization, therefore, it is necessary to look at the rise of the new positive myth.

The 'new white race' and its attitude to the indigenous population

The idea of the possibility of a new white race being formed in the crucible of colonial Algeria was aired in anthropological circles in France as early as 1873.[1] By the mid-1880s the idea had gained a wider credence and was mentioned in many leading works on the colony. Paul Bert raised the question of this mixed race which, he claimed, would one day dominate Algeria.[2] The high birthrate among the French and *neo-French* heartened observers like Bert, who were dismayed at the demographic decline in France. Such demographic optimism, often backed up by lists of statistics, served to bolster the myth of a new white race. In this alleged racial melt-down the indigenous element played no role, as Bert somewhat regretfully pointed out. In 1886 the orientalist Octave Houdas published an ethnography of Algeria which included the *Algériens* as one of the major ethnographical elements of the colony. The *Algériens*, he claimed, were a new race whose defining traits were formed from the merging together of characteristics specific to the various Latin peoples residing in Algeria. It was an essentially Latin amalgam, for the indigenous population was in no way included in the process.[3] Houdas advocated intermarriage between the Europeans and the indigenous population, for he believed it to be the best way to eradicate the taboos and ignorance that separated the two sectors of the colony's population. Such advice was not about to be taken seriously by the settlers, who had little enough sympathy for the indigenous population on a day-to-day basis let alone in the issue of marriage.

Jules Ferry, in his booklet on the government of Algeria, saw the conflict between the Europeans and the indigenous population for what it was, namely racial, and laid the responsibility of resolving this conflict at the door of the governor-general.[4] The settlers, he declared, had no idea how to behave towards the indigenous population. The only policy they knew was one of repression. Furthermore, he asserted that assimilation was not a theory they held dear. It was very difficult for the settlers to understand that the indigenous population also had rights and was not there to be mercilessly worked and taxed. Few settlers were imbued with the notion of the civilizing, educational mission of a superior race; even fewer believed it was possible to ameliorate the conquered race. They spent their time lamenting the incorrigibility and impossibility of educating the indigenous population without ever having tried to improve their moral or intellectual lot.[5] The combination of intellectual theories concerning a new Mediterranean race and popular conceptions of the inferiority of the indigenous population created the climate which allowed Louis Bertrand's work to achieve the importance it did. Indeed, it is arguable that without these two preconditions his *œuvre* might not have taken the form it did. Bertrand's work was not the epitome of settler thought, it was its blueprint. He articulated, in a way few settlers were able to do, the intellectual ramifications and significance of being *Algérien* in nineteenth-century Algeria.

The theories and significance of Louis Bertrand
(1866–1941)

In 1925 Louis Bertrand was elected to the Académie Française to fill the seat vacated by the death of Maurice Barrès. Congratulating Bertrand on his maiden speech, Jules Cambon declared that his originality had been to discover and interest himself in the settlers of Algeria, and to understand that their efforts had regenerated the riches of the ancient granary of Rome. Bertrand had offered 'an insight into the lives of the Provençaux, the Catalans, the Maltese, and their like, who were at present merging together, as they had done in the time of Rome and Carthage, to form a resistant combination which resonated with the sounds of the Mediterranean.'⁶ But Bertrand's work was more complex than merely demonstrating the worth of the *colon* to a wider public. He himself claimed his contribution to be fourfold, namely: to have been the initiator of the idea of a Latin Africa; to have demonstrated that Latin Africa was not an accident, that is to say French Africa was a continuation of the Latin tradition; to have restored nobility to the *colon*; and to have shown that Africa (Algeria) was a school of energy from which French civilization, weary and enfeebled, could draw fresh vitality: this was his theory of *rebarbarization*.⁷ Incidental to the four pillars on which his work was erected had been another achievement, one which in fact was to have the more profound impact. He had brushed aside, as he put it, the Islamic, pseudo-Arab decor which so fascinated superficial onlookers and exposed, from under this shallow display, a living Africa which hardly differed from the other Latin countries of the Mediterranean. Bertrand's marginalization of Islam and hence the indigenous population, his *Sens de l'Ennemi* as he was to put it, was the ideological expression of primal racial animosity among the settlers.

Background and influences

Louis Bertrand, who was born in Spincourt in Lorraine in 1866, spent his youth in the political and social shadow of the Commune and the French defeat at the hands of the Prussians with the subsequent loss of Alsace and a part of Lorraine. He was educated in Bar-le-Duc and in Paris where he graduated from the Ecole Normale Supérieure. His intellectually formative years coincided with the 1880s, a decade in which the intellectual response to the above-mentioned events was one of profound pessimism and, more dramatically in some circles, nihilism. France's demographic decline, coupled with a loss of confidence in its leaders, gave rise to an obsession with social, political and intellectual decadence. The ensuing quest for personal and national vitality called for a need for vigilance against devitalizing influences and encouraged social and political polarization based as it was on strongly nationalistic ideas and well-defined notions of 'the Other'.

The first intimations of pessimistic thought and the concomitant preoccupation with decadence had appeared in the early 1850s with the publication of Claude-Marie Raudot's *La Décadence de la France* in 1850 and Arthur de Gobineau's *Essai sur l'inégalité des races humaines* in 1853, but it was the publication in 1884 of a novel, Joris Karl Huysman's *A Rebours,* that brought the notion of decadence into the limelight and pessimism into the open.[8] It caused a literary sensation which could not have escaped the notice of the young Bertrand. Huysman's hero, Des Esseintes, was the personification of decadence and the distillation of the fears of the pessimists. He was part of the 'cultured but burnt out class of an exhausted and aging civilization', as Paul Bourget was to describe it, whose members caused 'the malaise of our Old World'.[9] Huysman's presentation of decadence in so bald a form set up a cry to invigorate those elements in France that had been sapped before it was too late. The desire to revitalize France's culture, social values and elites became a significant political and intellectual force in the last two decades of the century. The literary and political response to this desire was varied, and Bertrand's solution to look to Algeria as the font of this revitalization was only a personal interpretation of what many of his contemporaries sought elsewhere. Paul Bourget (1852–1935), Gabriel D'Annunzio (1863–1938), Paul Deroulède (1846–1914) Georges Sorel (1847–1922), and Maurice Barrès (1862–1923), all of Bertrand's generation, were among the best-known participants in this movement. Of these Barrès cast the longest shadow and, as a fellow Lorrainer, shared a heritage common to Bertrand. Bertrand was not only aware of Barrès but saw in him a rival whom he was never able to eclipse and from whom he consciously delineated himself intellectually.[10] For all this echoes of Barrès are evident in Bertrand's work. It was Barrès who coined the word *barbare* as a definition of 'the Other'. In his three-volume *Culte de Moi,* first published in 1891 on the eve of Bertrand's departure to Africa, Barrès advocated an egoistical quest for self-fulfilment as a means of reconstituting the unity of the individual. The *barbare* was seen as the antithesis, as 'everything that could be prejudicial to or resist the Self'.[11] For Barrès' generation truth was to be found through race and milieu and not through intellect.[12] In this Bertrand was to remain true to his generation.

Bertrand first came to Algeria in 1891 to take up a post at the Lycée of Algiers. He was friendly with the archaeologist Stéphane

Gsell and, in 1895, visited the Roman ruins at Tipasa in his company. The excursion was seminal to his thought: henceforth, following the 'revealing trail' of the vestiges of Rome, he would go from one intellectual discovery to another. At Tipasa, he said, he rediscovered 'the men who spoke his language and believed in his gods. He was no longer a lost *Roumi* in an Islamic land.' Tipasa brought Bertrand face to face with an Africa whose existence he had hitherto only suspected. As with other Roman sites in the area it was, for him, the architectural, cultural and linguistic manifestation of the true North Africa, a Latin Africa.[13] Through its occupation and colonization of the area, France was merely picking up the threads of this vibrant past.

Three other influences moulded Bertrand's thought on Algeria: Flaubert's *Salammbô*, the works of Fromentin, and Saint Augustine. *Salammbô* revealed to him the importance of the question of the mingling of races in North Africa, principally that a master race always dominates that of the original inhabitant. The novel became a major reference. It brought together in his mind the Africa of the past and the Africa he was beginning to get to know, and confirmed that the question of race was a major motivating force of humanity. If Flaubert aroused in Bertrand the awareness of race Fromentin opened his eyes to the continued existence in North Africa of a fundamental Mediterranean being (*l'homme méditerranéen primitif*). Saint Augustine, on the other hand, contributed the religious element: a Christian Africa which had been splintered by the Donatists and usurped by Islam.[14] A Christian Africa, therefore, but also a Latin Africa; both were ideas which had been cherished by Lavigerie. Bertrand, who did much to secularize Lavigerie's religious ideas of resuscitating the Christian civilization in Africa, was a great admirer of the African prelate who had inspired him from his earliest days in Algeria. When Bertrand was still 'in search of the living Algeria', Lavigerie had set him in the right direction.[15] This admiration was founded on Lavigerie being the 'able soldier of Western civilization'.[16] Bertrand shared Lavigerie's interest in archaeology, his sense of the 'barbarian' presence in Africa, and his wariness of Islam. He felt pride at his own contribution to Lavigerie's universal goal, which was to return Algeria and then the whole of Africa to Latin and Western Civilization.[17] But Bertrand went beyond Lavigerie. His was not a religious vision but, appreciating the potency of the symbols and stereotypes present in religious rhetoric, he put religion to use in conveying his message that France was merely repossessing what was hers by hereditary right.

The impact of Louis Bertrand

Rome and France in Africa

Although Bertrand consecrated several books to exposing it in detail, his thesis that Latin civilization was the first, and true, civilization of North Africa, thus designating North Africa as a Latin Africa, permeated all his work in some form of other.[18] Its significance was extensive. First and foremost, of course, it justified the French presence in Algeria. All they were doing, he declared, was recovering a province lost to Latinity. It also elevated the settlers to their 'rightful' position as the heirs of Rome, who could lay claim to rights predating those of Islam. 'Alongside the usurping Arab and the enslaved indigenous inhabitant (the Berber), refashioned by Islam', the settlers were 'the descendants of ancient Africa, the real masters of the land'; a land whose symbol was the triumphal arch and not the mosque.[19] Then too, it served to minimalize the importance of the local population, not only by exalting the settler but also by deprecating the indigenous civilization through the denial of its originality and its labelling as undeveloped and backward. 'What I first thought was Arab or oriental', he wrote, 'is really benighted Latin, worn down and sullied by the rust of centuries.'[20] The indigenous population was such that it had been unable to use its Latin past as a springboard for progress. The Europeans had evolved so spectacularly since Roman times that when they encountered customs and structures that had not progressed for over a millenium, they no longer recognized them.[21] Like Masqueray, Bertrand saw Rome imprinted on indigenous Berber society and read contemporary meaning into the fact, but unlike Masqueray Bertrand was inclined to see primitive (Berber) and progressive (French) forms not as a bond but rather as a division. Roman vestiges among the Berbers were 'bastardized Roman, encumbered by African materiality. Islam had covered everything with its uniform chalk-like shroud.'[22] In contrast the French mind 'was a refined and aristocratic form of Latinism. It could only be hoped that the indigenous African would become more and more like it.'[23] This superior Latinism was the settlers' title deed to North Africa.[24] Had Bertrand left his thesis at that interest in it would no doubt have been limited, as it had with similar theories about Rome and France in Africa appearing sporadically from conquest onward. Bertrand's strength lay in his capacity to synthesize a number of theories attractive to procolonialists, thus creating an ideology perfectly suited to the settlers of Algeria. Into the basic concept of a Latin Africa he wove the themes of civilization opposing barbarity, the apprehension of Islam and the creation of a new Latin race. This amplitude of interconnected concepts gave his thesis a substantiality which made it difficult to ignore.

At its core, however camouflaged it may have been, lay the as yet unresolved 'indigenous question', namely, in modern terminology, what was to be the relationship between the *colonizer* and the *colonized*.

Bertrand's attitudes to the indigenous population

Bertrand's own attitude to the *colonizer* and the *colonized* was the real source of the various themes that characterized his work. His African novels, which created his literary reputation, had no place for either Arab or Berber, being primarily concerned with the 'new Latin race'.[25] The only interest the indigenous population held for him was as a 'walk-on in beautiful surroundings'. With the Latins of Africa, on the other hand, he had a 'multitude of affinities' and he was drawn to them as much by nature as by literary predilection.[26] His novels were a celebration of the virility and vitality of the settlers. In contrast he saw the indigenous population as a negation of these attributes. The old world of Islam was one of decrepitude and death, whose only revenge (*revanche*) was that of barbarism. He disliked the indigenous population for its latent hostility and its benighted barbarism and was drawn only to those of his own race, the Latins of Africa.[27] Bertrand distinguished between Arab and Berber, seeing the former as the usurpers and the latter as the original inhabitants of the area. Although he did believe that the Berbers had come under the influence of the Romans and had been Christianized, he also believed that by the time the Arabs invaded the area the Berber intellectual and social elites had fled across the sea, leaving behind only the inferior sectors of society. The Arabs brought with them poverty, endemic warfare and barbarity, all of which succeeded in destroying what remained of the civilizing effects of Carthage and Rome on the Berbers.[28]

He distanced himself from the idea that the Berbers were racially compatible with the Europeans. The idea that North Africa had in the past been the land of a Latin race (indigenous as opposed to conquering) was absurd, he said. Rather it was the melting-pot of present-day Latin races. Nor did he believe that the country had ever been thoroughly Romanized or Christianized.[29] Bertrand's Latin race was a new race being formed in the country and its connections with the country's Latin past came from the northern shores of the Mediterranean, not the southern ones. The Berbers, whatever their past may have held, did not share the common Latino-Mediterranean heritage, for the evolution of their civilization had long-since been arrested.

The impact of Louis Bertrand

Bertrand's new Latin race

That race was paramount to Bertrand's vision of the human condition is incontestable. If he had had doubts on the subject in his formative years, Algeria had convinced him of the contrary. It is evident, he wrote, that race is a reality, difficult to define perhaps but whose existence is beyond dispute. Also indisputable, as far as Bertrand was concerned, was the inequality of races with regard to moral and intellectual values and the fact that 'bastardized' races lost their special qualities and with them their capacity to defend themselves. Bertrand's experiences in Algeria provided him with two basic arguments on which to rest his racial case, namely the ineluctibility of the presence of a master race in Africa and the inevitability of the failure of assimilation. Race, for Bertrand, was a combination of environment, education and blood, and was therefore impervious to assimilation.[30] Like Gobineau, he believed that race was a metaphysical and spiritual entity that did not lend itself to miscegenation which, if it did occur, would sap its strength and render it powerless. To retain France's empire it was essential 'to remain Latin', to keep the Latin race pure.

In his African novels, Bertrand presented his image of this new race, an image formed in the close contact of travelling the roads with Spanish, Maltese and Italian waggoners, hauliers and labourers. It was a formative experience for Bertrand, and in contrast to the listlessness of the bureaucrats and government officials in Algiers he was struck by the ebullience and vigour of these Mediterranean immigrants. There was nothing like it in the whole of the Near East, he wrote. The merging of the Italians, Maltese and Spanish with the French from Provence, Languedoc and Catalan had produced a race with a zest for life, a physical beauty and a hot-blooded nature which had been a revelation to him and the inspiration for his concept of *le sang des races*.[31] He turned this concept into his first novel. *Le Sang des Races* was serialized in the *Revue de Paris* commencing in 1898, and published a year later. Its heros and heroines, like those of the African novels which followed, were the European immigrants with whom he had travelled about Algeria and whose characteristic milieu become the quarter of Bab-el-Oued. Athletic, ardent and proud, quick to take offence but generous and hardworking, unintellectual but quick-witted and pragmatic, for Bertrand, they were the colony's staff of life. Unlike the indigenous population they would, due to the vigour of their race, surmount the difficulties of their environment. It was only to be expected, he wrote, that this lotus-eating land enervated the indolent Orientals, who slid into laziness and an endless pursuit of pleasure. Active races, on the other hand, having briefly dallied with sensuality, were stimulated into action.[32] It was a race whose promise was soon being fulfilled. 'Like the effervescence of a beehive in full activity', its people exuded a palpable aura of confidence in their activities, their future and the resources of their land.[33] Their accomplishments were due to their race and the fruits of their land.[34]

There was one distinguishing feature, however, that singled them out from their counterparts across the Mediterranean: this was their veneer of barbarity. They were, Bertrand wrote, violent and complicated beings who only appeared simple to those who had not penetrated their world deeply enough. He had been shocked at first by 'these fierce men with their uncouthness and their appearance of barbarity' but little by little he had discovered the 'eternal Mediterranean being with his indomitable zest for life at its most beautiful and ostentatious', and his zest for the 'harmony of labour that neither wore out the body nor degraded the soul.'[35] Bertrand's admiration for the settlers' outward barbarity, which he saw as a font of creativity, led him to create his concept of *rebarbarisation* which, he believed, could become the indispensable ingredient for national regeneration.

Bertrand's theories of Rebarbarisation and le Sens de l'Ennemi

For Bertrand the real barbarians were the indigenous population. It was in the midst of their barbarity that the new race would be schooled. Bertrand considered Africa to be 'a school of energy, heroism and physical, intellectual, national and social regeneration. It was a good thing to be obliged to live next to people who were rough and often troubled for it aroused an awareness of the Barbarian and of the Enemy.'[36] Honed on the whetstone of indigenous barbarity, the new Latin race was thus submitted to a process, dubbed *rebarbarisation* by Bertrand, which stimulated even the most torpid of immigrants into irrepressible energy and fecundity. For Bertrand settler fecundity was vital to counterbalance the unstemmable proliferation of the true barbarian, the *indigène*.[37] The spectacle of this vigour would in turn regenerate France itself.[38] The indigenous population, rudimentary, savage, violent and impenetrable, was an ever-present psychological reminder to both the civilized idealist and the Frenchman that the universe was not always shaped in the French image.[39] It was not, however, without its uses and Bertrand urged his compatriots to make the most of the fact by means of the vitalizing process of *rebarbarisation*. 'By rebarbarizing ourselves', Bertrand wrote, 'we can successfully take on the Barbarian; we can assume the qualities that make him strong and turn them against him so he won't crush us.' It was an urgent task for essentially it consisted of regenerating the French race, enfeebled by a century of well-being and security and a weak, senseless education.[40]

The *rebarbarisation* of the settler was successfully accomplished due to the presence of an innate sense which Bertrand believed to be essential to the preservation of any civilization: the sense of the enemy within. True for France, it was doubly true for Algeria, where lives were often threatened and living conditions were different from the metropolis. The Algerians had a finely developed 'sense of the enemy' as well as the instinct and pride of conquest and the need for perpetual progress.[41] For Bertrand, as a native of Lorraine, it was a primal sense which first found its expression when he embarked in Algeria. 'My first view of ... Algiers', he wrote, 'was of the Barbarian world and I use the word Barbarian in its widest sense ranging from foreigner to savage and enemy of civilization. This vision of my youth has since expanded, taken on depth and become more focused.'[42] Vigilance was essential, for the enemy was ever-present. The barbarians were not just the menacing Asian hordes of the time but anyone opposed to civilization. Ubiquitous, they spoke one's language and constantly contrived to undo the work of education. Civilization was a never-ending struggle against evil instincts from within and the enemy without.[43] In Algeria the enemy was of course the Muslim, whose sole aim was to endure; an aim pursued with obstinate inflexibility against all odds, making it impossible to remove the religious barrier preventing integration. Citing such examples as the Greeks and the Turks in Constantinople, the French of Alsace/Lorraine and the Germans, Bertrand claimed that history had shown that a true sense of the enemy was too deep-seated to eradicate. The irredeemable nature of the enmity between the settler and indigenous population was confirmed by the very sect of Islam prevalent in Algeria, the Maliki, which was among the most retrograde of Islamic sects in Bertrand's estimation.[44] In short, Islam rendered the indigenous population impossible to assimilate.

Civilization versus barbarity: France and Islam

The notion of a barbarous Islamic tradition pitted against a civilized Roman/Christian tradition had been present in Algeria since conquest. Bertrand elaborated on Lavigerie's resuscitation of the subject, adding the rejoinder that the latter was destined to dominate the former. It was a message he never ceased to propagate, often finding its most evocative expression in symbolic form.[45] He believed that the hatred of the indigenous population for the European was endemic. It was not, however, a hatred of the poor for the rich or even the Muslim for the Christian, but rather of the barbarian for the civilized being, the barbarian who was cruelly confronted with his inferiority.[46] Bertrand, like many conservative turn-of-the-century intellectuals, was fearful of the possible decline of Western civilization and saw Islam as an obscurantist threat. It was Lavigerie who had pointed Bertrand in this direction, for he had pointed his finger at the 'obtuse, stubborn soul of Islam with its ineradicable fanaticism, and intellectual sterility; the real adversary of Western civilization'.[47] Bertrand's secular vision of a religious antagonism led him to define the clash in intellectual rather than spiritual terms. He attacked the Romantics for inventing an Orient which had nothing in common with reality and only perpetrated the current obsession with exoticism. By so doing they had anaesthetized the civilized Frenchmen to the threat of the barbarian at a time when it was essential not to let one's guard down. He warned that Western civilization had already been sullied and had thus taken a step backward.[48] Islam could never progress and Bertrand was even reticent to concur with Renan's patronizing contention that for the blacks Islam did represent a form of progress.[49]

While he did not rule out the fact that 'the barbarian' could take steps towards civilization he was adamant that Western civilization should not lower its standards by any cultural imposition from below, and in this he included what he saw as the pernicious influence of the cult of the latinized Berber.[50] Islam, for Bertrand, was not a religious thorn in the Christian flesh which with patient nurture and Christian spirituality could be alleviated by inclusion in a wider spiritual family or even removed through eventual conversion. Islam was an implacable barrier to progress for which no accommodation could be made in the process of Western civilization. Bertrand secularized the religious message and blocked its humanitarian aspects; in short he converted what could have passed, with a stretch of the imagination, as an argument for assimilation into a strident argument for association or indeed domination.

The impact of Louis Bertrand

Bertrand was not modest about his achievements. In a review essay of a collection of short stories, entitled *Notre Afrique*, he claimed with some satisfaction that everything he had striven for and predicted in the course of a quarter of a century had come to pass, namely a renaissance of Latin Africa. The word 'Africa' had regained the significance it had had in the time of Apuleius and Saint Augustine. His gratification at seeing his message picked up by young *Algérien* authors led him to declare that *Notre Afrique* was a true literary, political and national manifesto. For the first time the new race had found itself.[51] He drew particular attention to Robert Randau, as an inspiration to partake of the process of *rebarbarisation*, and to Charles Hagel and Louis Lecoq for their well-developed sense of the enemy. It was a theme central to their work and a constant reminder of the need to struggle against ever-watchful malevolent forces.[52]

Bertrand's acclaim, however, was not limited to self-satisfied observations about his own achievements. His renown was genuine. He was a staff correspondent for the *Revue des Deux Mondes* and his regular articles reached a wide middle-class public. His works, novels and essays alike, were reprinted in numerous editions. *Sur les Routes du Sud*, for example, in which his theories were most cogently argued, came out in nine. Quite apart from the fact he was elected to the Académie française for his contribution to French literature, he was a popular author both in Algeria and in France. By 1922 an American doctoral candidate could claim that Bertrand's heros were not only legendary in Algeria but that the youth of France found a source of vitality and renewal in this books.[53] In a collection of essays that appeared on the occasion of the centenary celebrations in 1930, the Dean of the Faculty of Letters of Algiers, Pierre Martino, suggested that Bertrand's *œuvre* be placed in the naturalist school and compared him to Zola for his documentary precision, his application to detail and his evocative depiction of Algerian realities, his was 'the epic of a new race'.[54] Analyses of his work continued to appear on a regular basis until just prior to the Algerian war of independence.[55] During his lifetime Bertrand secured a key situation for himself in the French literary scene.

The dissemination of the idea of a new Latin race

In Algeria the new Latin race found other champions. Some, like Robert Randau, had close personal and literary connections with Bertrand. Others just shared Bertrand's desire to present the new Latin race, with its qualities and its defects, to the French public. Many of these novels were serialized in literary or popular journals before being published. *L'illustration*, *Mercure de France*, *Revue de Paris* and the *Revue des Deux Mondes* were among the most widely-circulated journals that published short stories or serializations of novels by settler authors. Among the most distinctive of these voices was that of Musette, the antics of whose hero, Cagayous, discoursing in the patois of the *neo-français*, entertained settlers and Frenchmen alike for over twenty years.[56] In spite of achieving posthumous acclaim, Musette had no literary pretensions; his aim was to amuse by bringing to life the colourful characters that inhabited quarters such as Bab-el-Oued. But other authors, who were equally popular in their own ways, did have greater aspirations.[57] The conspicuous feature of all these novels was the role assigned to the *indigène*. If he was present at all then conflict, in some form or other, characterized his relationship with the settler. In Hagel and Lecoq's *Broumitche et le Kabyle*, for example, human wiliness was the central theme, with 'Latin' ruse coming up against Kabyle ruse and the former winning out.[58]

The one notable exception was Randau, who created space for the Berbers in so far as they could serve to 'Berberize' the settler. It was of course a more accommodating version of Bertrand's theory of *rebarbarisation*. *Evolués* Arabs are also present in his novels, but for Randau total assimilation is never really feasible. Early in *Les Algérianistes*, one of his three major novels attempting to depict the 'new race', an *évolué* Arab and friend of the hero, Cassard, asks why Cassard, who works so hard towards the creation of a nation of Berberized Frenchmen, neglects the Muslims out of hand. To this he receives the reply: 'you are ... conservative out of a taste for the mystical; we would never agree to the established social order of your religion; your virtues and your vices are not ours; we proclaim an everlasting dawn of the mind but you its twilight.'[59] Randau's two novels, subtitled *roman de la patrie algérienne*, sought to elucidate the difference between the mainland European and the *Algérien* (European of Algeria) by exposing the 'soul' of the new race.[60] Randau's settler society was more complex than that of Bertrand, but it too was shot through with sensuality and violence. Like Bertrand he saw in this new race a force for regeneration. A new race, he wrote, arose as a result of an unprecedented progressive surge from the old races. To achieve this it was necessary to extricate the disparate sections of Algerian society from the defunct ideas and atrocious ancestral sentimentalities they had brought with them from their diverse mainland metropolises.[61] To Bertrand's characteristics of physical beauty, ardour and pride, Randau added that of the entrepreneurial instinct. Paraphrasing the words of one of his characters, they were men of action disguised as poets by a veneer of education and a penchant for sentimental reading matter, but were infinitely better suited to earning money.[62] Between the two world wars Randau launched a literary movement which he dubbed *algérianisme*. In its manifesto he declared that its aim was 'to create an intellectual climate in Algeria common to the races living there and formed from their union ...'.[63] It was a call to bury religious differences and gather the Muslims into the

Algerian fold, if only in name. In this way the different races which made up the country could harmoniously coexist, even if they did not fuse. It was association at its very best, but unlike his novels, *algérianisme* was a flop. The settlers were not prepared to make concessions to Islam, intellectual or otherwise. For them the Latin race could only dominate.

Although the idea of a new Latin race was most widely disseminated in short stories and best-selling novels, be they of literary merit such as those by Bertrand and Randau, or of less exalted style such as those by Musette and other popular authors, it was not restricted to this form of publication.

The Mediterranean race in anthropology

The question of a Mediterranean race in anthropological terms was the focus of some debate at the turn of the century. In 1899 an Italian anthropologist published a work on the subject, which was soon translated into German (1897) and English (1901).[64] Sergi, whose basic aim was to dislodge the theory of the Aryan origins of the Northern Europeans, claimed that Europeans descended from a Euro-African race which had split into three great branches: the African, which had remained in the hinterland of the continent (only certain 'aristocratic' African peoples such as Nubians, Masai, Watutsi and Fulahs were included, so too were the Egyptians, but not the Arabs), the Mediterranean, which peopled the Mediterranean basin, and the Nordic, which had migrated to Northern Europe. Although Sergi included the Berbers in the Mediterranean species, he declared that successive immigrations had so diluted their race that they were no longer pure Mediterranean in the sense that the Italians, Spaniards or French were.[65] Sergi's racial theories were of little interest to the settler colony or indeed to the average Frenchman who showed an interest in Algeria. They are, none the less, of relevance as they demonstrate that there was an anthropological dimension to the idea of a Mediterranean race which could be used to reinforce the cultural and sociological conception of a new Latin race arising out of the fusion of Mediterranean elements.

The question of course arose as to whether the Berbers should or should not be considered as a potential contributor to the new race. Opinion was divided. The Orientalist and ethnographer Houdas believed they should, although he was not partisan to the theory that Berbers were superior to Arabs. Bertrand certainly did not. An examination of these different attitudes would suggest that the educational discipline out of which their exponents emerged was a decisive factor. Where culture and civilization were seen to be primordial in the attributes of a race, as they were among literary figures, the indigenous (Berber) population could not figure along with the 'Latins'. Where other attributes were given equal or greater weight, as they were in anthropology or ethnology, attitudes were more elastic. Among physical anthropologists the debate was never really resolved, craniology being the dubious science it is and anthropometry (cephalic and nasal indices and height in particular) usually providing in-conclusive results. The determination of whether or not the Berbers were dolicocephalic or brachycephalic, which presumably would have settled the question once and for all by linking them or distancing them from the 'pure' Mediterraneans, also remained in the air. Bertholon and Chantre, in their definitive physical anthropological study of the Berbers in which they examined 8,000 subjects, declared that they could be both, with the Kabyles generally falling into the latter category.[66] The only certain elements of the new Latin race were those of the 'pure' Mediterranean race.

The theory that a new racial type was being formed in North Africa from these Mediterranean elements was also raised in anthropo-logical circles. A paper read to the Paris Anthropological society in 1898 stated that 'the Algerian exists'; by this was meant 'the French of Algeria, born and bred in the colony' who 'had acquired a dis-tinctive appearance, a special physiognomy'. A group of people called Algerians was evolving and 'a typical Algerian was emerging and asserting itself more clearly with each passing day.'[67] It was not just a question of naturalization or nationality. It was a question of the formation of a new type of man. It was, as Bertrand had dubbed it, *le sang des races*.

Race and colonial theory

In theory the idea of Algeria as a melting-pot for a new race would seem to be ideally suited to the arguments of the assimilationists; in practice it became part of the arsenal of the associationists. The contradictions that are evident in some theoretical discussions on racial questions in Algeria arise out of the fact that assimilation could be seen to be commendable from a humanitarian point of view while being denounced as utopian and impracticable from a pragmatic point of view. Settler 'pragmatism' with regard to the indigenous population arose out of overtly acknowledged obstacles as well as sociological factors implicit in colonial society.

In the latter category the most obvious was demographic. A 'new race' which included the indigenous population meant intermarriage between Christians and Muslims, and while this did occasionally occur the numbers were too insignificant to create any 'fusion' of the races. There were too many taboos on both sides to make it viable on a large scale. Furthermore, in settler society there was not the shortage of marriageable women there had been in the decades of conquest when officers and civil servants (Berbrugger, de Neveu, Urbain for example) were able to marry indigenous women without social stigma. (Marriage between European women and Arab men was virtually non-existent in nineteenth-century Algeria.) The arrival of European women in substantial numbers led to a diversification of choice which allowed for the development of a social hierarchy in the marriage stakes: certain women became socially more desirable than others. The indigenous woman was thus relegated to the lower rungs of the marital ladder. There was little need for intermarriage, therefore, and the few who did intermarry had a strong enough personal commitment to allow them to surmount the psychological and social barriers that the majority were inclined to avoid.

Demography apart, the associationists believed in a hierarchy of race which excluded the racially levelling concept of fusion. Harmand, one of the most forceful exponents of association, claimed that '*the right to domination was based on moral superiority*. Therefore one had to accept the principle of a hierarchy of races and the existence of superior civilizations. The fundamental justification of indigenous conquest rested on the conviction of France's superiority, especially its moral superiority. On this was based France's right to guide the rest of humanity.'[68] To the assimiliationist proposition that fusion could take place over time Harmand countered that fusion between the inferior and superior races of a colony, if it took place at all, would benefit neither. The superior of the two had nothing to gain from such a fusion and the inferior race would not be elevated but rather would lose its specific qualities and thus sink even further.'[69] In a history of French colonial practice which appeared in 1913, the question of the formation of a new race in Algeria was raised, with mention of the possibility of miscegenation of the indigenous element. Its author, Charles Humbert, whose ideas on race and miscegenation were not excessively dogmatic, explained simply that the inclusion of the indigenous element was never deemed necessary and that their refractory attitude towards the Europeans had ensured that no attempts in this direction were made.[70] The formation of a new race, therefore, would progress without indigenous collaboration.

Conclusion

The ideology of a society, in accordance with Mannheim, is the collection of partially articulated assumptions by which it operates and the tool with which it maintains the status quo[71]. In Algeria where two different social forms, that of the European immigrant and that of the indigenous population, confronted each other across a gulf of suspicion and animosity, with the former seeking to create its own specific identity, separate from France and yet related, and the latter obdurately refusing to relinquish its own well developed identity, it was inevitable that the ideology evolved by the settlers would be one which sought to obviate and dominate all existing theologies, doctrines or concepts. Domination and control were no longer just a question of security, although of course that could still be a problem. It was now a question of creating a society in the image of the newcomer, and this could only work to the detriment of the society already *in situ*. The settler ideology that evolved denigrated and marginalized indigenous society better to anchor its own. This ensured the exclusion, with a few individual exceptions, of the indigenous population from the European social pyramid. Indigenous society evolved at its own pace, and with its own hierarchies, alongside European society but not within it. (Ironically, it was the separateness encouraged by settler ideology that allowed for the development of a cohesive social base from which to agitate against colonial rule and eventually demand independence.) It also ensured by its anti-indigenous rhetoric, again with a few individual exceptions, that the settler did not 'go native' and thus sap the edifice of his own society.

Louis Bertrand's contribution was to articulate the assumptions underlying settler society in an attractive and compelling manner. His notions of the Latin race, of civilization versus barbarity, of *rebarbarisation* and of the *Sens de l'Ennemi* were the literary expression of settler desires to create a national identity, their wariness of Islam, and their attitudes towards the indigenous population. He synthesized existing ideas into a coherent whole. The notions of France's Latin antecedents in Africa and civilization versus barbarity had been present in some form or other in the colony since conquest. But the linkage of civilization with France and barbarity with Islam was not peculiar to the colony. Renan, who denigrated Islam in numerous works, summed it up by saying 'Islam was the complete negation of Europe; Islam was fanaticism.'[72] The radical anthropologist, André Lefevre, in a work on race and language discussed the disruptive influence of Islam on the development of languages.[73] In his discussion Lefevre, who believed there be to an intelligence-linked hierarchy of language, put his finger on the most troubling aspect of Islam for the French, namely the appearance of Mohammed 'with his incoherent and inoffensive Book but also with his terrible doctrine of the confusion of powers – religious and civil.'[74] Islamic society was a theocratic society; French society was not. The secularization process which France had been undergoing since the 1789 revolution would no longer tolerate the intrusion of religion into the state. It was regressive, it was barbaric, it was the enemy within. Bertrand smoothed the sharp edges from the rhetoric and elegantly presented it as the *Sens de l'Ennemi*.

The concept of the new Latin race, and its attendant ideology, relegated the Kabyle Myth to the sidelines. It did not diminish: the Kabyles were still seen to be superior to the Arabs, but both were considered to be beneath the settler. As association took hold and assimilation was seen to be less viable, the sort of interest that had previously be shown in the Kabyles waned. The Kabyles, for all their superiority, did not need to be assimilated into settler society; they could develop alongside it. The gut reaction of the average settler was anti-assimilationist. It was this sentiment that Bertrand captured so well. The power of works such as his was their popular appeal. Unlike dry theoretical tracts on assimilation or association, they were presented in an accessible form making the ideas contained in them available to even those who professed total disinterest in colonial theories and practice. In so far as he was not a *kabylophobe*, Bertrand was not actively instrumental in the displacement of the Kabyle Myth, but his work perfectly illustrates the reasons why this occurred.

PART IV

The legacy

10

Persistent stereotypes and resultant policies

Colonial policy with regard to the indigenous population in Algeria proceeded largely by trial and error during the nineteenth century. As a result no coherent policy emerged on how to deal with the Arabs and Berbers. With the displacement of assimilation by association, so much better suited to the needs of the settler, focus shifted from the Kabyles, who had been deemed pre-eminently qualified for assimilation. In spite of this the stereotypes that had developed concerning the Kabyles and their society persisted. There was more to the legacy of the Kabyle Myth than mere stereotypes, however. The complexity of this legacy arose out of the French view of indigenous society in Algeria as one ethnic group opposed to the other. This meant that an integral part of the Kabyle Myth was the opposing view of the Arab and therefore the legacy, in the sociological domain at least, also encompassed the negative attitudes towards Islam and the Arab that had been used in the elaboration of the myth.

The documented legacy bestowed on the twentieth century by the Kabyle Myth was threefold: popular, academic, and political. Of these, in Algeria, the most powerful was undoubtedly the popular. The stereotypes of Arabs and Kabyles, the prejudices regarding Islam and the acceptance of racial ideas were intrinsic to the attitudes the settlers expressed in their daily life. Once independence was granted to Algeria, this body of thought became part of the historical memory of both colonizer and colonized. For the French the memory was a didactic one in that it served, indirectly to be sure, to inform post-independence opinion in France on Islam and on the Arabs and Berbers regardless of any negative attitude towards the colonial experience. For the independent Algerians it was a divisive memory; it was necessary to eradicate it but difficult to do so. This historical memory, selectively used by each side, was also a legacy of sorts and will be considered accordingly.

The legacy

The popular legacy

The images of Arabs and Berbers present in popular novels were the means by which existing stereotypes were most widely propagated. Unlike the early novels emerging from Algeria, where there was little place in settler society for the indigenous population and where the relationship between the *indigène* and the *colon* was always seen in terms of conflict, by the end of the second decade of the twentieth century colonial society, as depicted in novels, included Arabs and Berbers. Novelists even made them central to the plot. The colonial novel, which reached its apogee between the two world wars, was a faithful reflection of sociological trends in the colony and as such the social distinction between *colon* and *indigène* was preserved. This, however, did not preclude relationships between the two, although more often than not they fell short of actual friendship. When true friendship did develop the European was usually from France (the French from the metropolis being out of tune with the social hierarchy of the colony which, unlike the 'mother country', was dependent on race). Whatever the relationship, the *indigène* was, more often than not, an educated Kabyle.

The legacy of the Kabyle Myth in popular literature functioned on two levels. In the first place there was the explicit use of Kabyle and Arab stereotypes. Second, there was the image of colonial society as a racial hierarchy. The Kabyle Myth had been an important building-block in the construction of this image, since by viewing the Arabs and the Berbers as two incompatible races it had introduced racial configurations of thought into the colony and thus opened the way to the more dogmatic racial attitudes adopted by the settlers. With regard to the latter, the racial themes that prevailed in colonial novels where the indigenous population played a significant role were the clash of racial cultures, *le choc des races* as Charles Géniaux was to label it, and the permanence of racial attributes. These two themes implicitly suggested a third, namely that assimilation was a pipe-dream. Géniaux, who like Conrad believed in the morally corrupting influence of colonial life, introduced all three themes in his novel, *Le Choc des Races*, telling a tale of blighted love between the two races: a European woman and an Arab man and an Arab woman and a European man.[1] At the end of the novel, in the tradition of the classics, a *deus ex machina* in the guise of an assassin intervenes to prevent the alliance of each, which could only have led to disaster, and to punish the hubris of the lovers who imagined they could defy the dictates of colonial society. The novel is set in Tunisia and predates Algerian novels with similar themes, but it is none the less a potent, if Euro-centric, evocation of racial alienation.

Colonial novels emerging out of Algeria were more pointed in their themes. Ferdinand Duchêne, the honesty of whose novels his contemporary Martino extolled, gleaned his sociological insight of the *'indigène'* in the tribunals of Kabylia.[2] In a tale similar to Géniaux's, his 1926 novel *Kamir*, Duchêne's principal themes are the strength of racial heredity, the ingrained nature of Islamic traditions and the impossibility of relationships between *indigène* and *colon*. Under the stresses of such a relationship, Kamir, heroine of the novel and daughter of the gendarme Bakir, begins to lose the veneer of her French education. 'Was not Kamir, like her father, returning to her Arab roots? Was not the dismal fatalism of her Muslim heredity rising to the surface in her small mind cleared and revitalized at a French school but now troubled by deception?'[3] As the denouement approaches, Kamir's Western education is seen as an embarrassment, raising expectations which have only led her into a blind alley. Shortly before the final catastrophe, when Kamir throws herself off a cliff, she is taken under the wing of Si-Mahfoud, a Kabyle primary school teacher who is involved in improving the lot of Muslim women. Si-Mahfoud, unlike Kamir and Bakir, is a 'true *évolué*'.[4] Although Si-Mahfoud is not a central character in this particular novel the Kabyle primary school teacher was a staple of the colonial literature of Algeria, the Kabyle being deemed to be more receptive than the Arab to French education. Lucienne Favre, another popular novelist of the 1930s, made a habit of including one such character in her tales.

Favre, who felt sufficiently familiar with the indigenous population to write from their point of view in the first person singular, employed racial themes similar to Duchêne's. The shaping of one's destiny by race, making escape (social mobility) impossible, was one. Race was worse than a wet-nurse, she wrote, one was inevitably drawn back to it.[5] Unrequited love between the races was another.[6] But Favre did not restrict herself to all-encompassing racial themes. She made use of the Kabyle as an *évolué* in many of her novels to elevate him in the colonial hierarchy, albeit never as high as the European. *Mille et Un Jours, Mourad* are the 'confessions' of a Kabyle primary school teacher. The novel is well written, with much sentimental interest, and the Kabyle Myth is reinforced throughout. The Berbers, the hero Mourad tells us, have been in North Africa since the beginning of time and have always excelled in everything. The Kabyles are the Auvergnats of North Africa, whose qualities have been forged by the climatic contrasts of their mountains. On no condition are they to be confused with the Arabs, to whom they remain ever opposed.[7] Novels, however, did more than diffuse stereotypes and racial themes. They were also a useful forum for authors with a political axe to grind or as a means of attacking extant or past colonial policy. In *L'Agonie de Cosmopolis*, the author, Albert Bessières, explicitly accuses successive administrations of having Islamized the Kabyles.[8] An argument can, of course, also be made to the effect that this was the implicit root of the theme of Kabyle reversion to Islamic ways that was employed by so many colonial authors, including Favre in *Une Dimanche dans La Casbah* and *Mille et Un Jours, Mourad*.

The literary legacy was not confined to novels. Travelogues and romanticized ethnography in the form of essays penned by popular authors, such as Géniaux and Duchêne, did as much as novels to reinforce stereotypes.[9] *Ceux d'Algérie*, Duchêne's contribution to a series on the peoples of the world, was a folksy look at the ethnological make-up of Algeria. No negative feelings permeate the work but Duchêne presents the multiracial population of Algeria in terms of a hierarchy with the Europeans at the top, followed by the Jews, the Kabyles and the Arabs. The Berber was closer to the European than the Arab,[10] not only from a sociological point of view but also from a physical one. Where the stamp of the Bedouin was dominant the silhouette was long and thin. If on the other hand it was Berber blood infusing the body with mountain vitality, the face and torso, and indeed the demeanour, bore a closer resemblance to the European. Berber hair was also fairer and the eyes lighter, ranging from grey to blue.[11] Using Daumas's comparison, Duchêne likened Kabylia to Switzerland and the Kabyle to the Swiss.[12] In contrast the Arab was 'a transplanted, modified Asian who still recalls his origins and not, like Mohand, a Mediterranean cross-breed. Less spontaneous he is actually more pliant, as Orientals are.'[13] Duchêne dubbed his 'typical' Kabyle Mohand, a secular name popular among the Kabyles, and his 'typical' Arab Mohammed, name of the Prophet. The choice is significant: not only was the secular contrasted to the religious but the popularity of the names implied a stereotypical universality. (There is a cultural dimension to the name Mohand too, of which Duchène may have been aware, given the length of time he spent in Kabylia. Si Mohand (1840?–1906) was a Kabyle troubadour poet of considerable renown, a collection of whose poems was first made by Said Boulifa and published in 1900 under the title *Receuil des poésies kabyles.*[14]) Thus Duchêne condensed the ramifications of the positive and negative stereotypes into a single convenient symbol for the 'eternal' Kabyle or the 'eternal' Arab. By personifying the Kabyle Myth he endowed it with added potency. (One need only think of Stowe's Uncle Tom, a term now associated with supine black connivance with white domination, to understand the implications of such characterizations.) Encroachment of this sort on literary terrain by travel writers and popular ethnologists gave an anecdotal quality to their works, making them easy to read and digest.

The framework of the popular legacy of the Kabyle Myth was a social one: it perpetrated stereotypes and hierarchical notions of race on a social level. The good Kabyle was not explicitly contrasted to the bad Arab as he had been in past, particularly in ethnological works. Rather the contrast was implicit in the manipulation of existing stereotypes whereby the Kabyle was characterized as being more open to French culture, industrious, sedentary, etc. and the Arab incorrigibly religious, inclined to indolence, and so forth. The notion of race as a hierarchy, with the Arabs at the bottom and the Kabyle significantly closer to the European, was conveyed on occasion explicitly but more often than not implicitly. In the latter case this was achieved in a variety of ways: either by making the Kabyle character more central to the plot (sometimes as the hero or heroine); or by endowing him with a better European education, or simply by depicting him as more reliable, agreeable, etc. Paradoxically these novels were sociologically accurate, but their verisimilitude came not in their ethnic realism, as contemporary literary critics liked to claim, but in their exact, if inadvertent, depiction of the colony's social ladder, whose principal rungs were racial.

The academic legacy

The academic legacy was concerned more with concepts than with stereotypes. To be sure, the opposition between Berber and Arab could still be presented in resoundingly stereotypical tones, as for example the claim that the Berbers were Western rationalists in categoric opposition to the Arabs, who were imaginative Orientals.[15] The impulse to democracy among the Berbers was still extolled while the aristocratic tendencies of the Arabs were denigrated.[16] And, as late as 1958, Kabyle democracy was presented as the ideal democratic form, a subjective opinion, in view of the difficulty of defining such an ideal, but a very revealing one all the same.[17] It was, however, in the sociological and historical analyses of the indigenous population of Algeria in terms of sedentary–nomad, mountain-dweller–plain-dweller and indigenous population–usurping hordes that the most significant legacy lay.

By the 1930s the sedentary–nomad opposition, with regard to the Kabyles and Arabs, had acquired dimensions over and above the initial sociological analysis. 'Today', wrote Emile Gautier, renowned geographer and professor at the University of Algiers, 'Kabyles and Arabs are not just sedentary and nomadic; they have also the notion of belonging to two different races, to two different human species.'[18] Out of the sedentary–nomadic division had emerged the notion that not only did this opposition represent radically different lifestyles, it also designated fundamentally different types of people. In the case of the Berbers and Arabs the connotations surrounding the terms acquired racial significance, but the attractiveness of the opposition lay in its evolutionary suppositions, namely that the nomadic state came before the sedentary state in the march towards civilization. The tribal and nomadic character of Arab society had prevented it from attaining the degree of civilization acquired by sedentary societies.[19] This provided an easy handle by which to grasp unfamiliar territory. The analysis could be, and was, extended beyond the frontiers of Algeria to Africa at large, where as far back as it was possible to remember, humanity had been divided into the 'great nomads and groups of people that were more or less sedentarized'.[20] The nomadic state, furthermore, was the embodiment of negative political concepts that the stability of a sedentary state, such as that of the Kabyles, managed to attenuate or avoid altogether. Because of his lifestyle, the nomad 'was a communist. Politically he was an anarchist, a nihilist, who preferred disorder as the means of enlarging his horizons. He was a destroyer, a negater.' Kabyles and nomads were 'two indomitable elements', which only force could reconcile.[21] The terms of this analysis echo those of the French officers whose preoccupation with security had caused them to see nomadic and sedentary lifestyles in contrasting lights of disorder and order.

The question of whether or not a nomadic existence does in fact pre-date the sedentary form of social organization can never satisfactorily be answered. Braudel, alluding to this question, pointed out that 'things never happen as an *a priori* model would suggest. The past has been richer in catastrophes and brutal revolutions than in slow evolution.'[22] Nor is it possible to state definitively that nomadism is more primitive than sedentarism, even allowing for the Eurocentric viewpoint from which such an evaluation is made. The nomadic Arab–sedentary Berber opposition which evolved within the framework of the Kabyle Myth was the first on-the-spot analysis of sedentary and nomadic populations to be undertaken at such length by the French. That it should have become a sociological paradigm is not altogether surprising. The 'success' of defining the society indigenous to Algeria in terms heavily weighted with evolutionary meaning meant that it was logical for this sort of analysis to prove attractive enough to be applied further afield.

The mountain-dweller–plain-dweller opposition which, in the colonial ethnology of Algeria, was a by-product of the Kabyle Myth, also acquired value as a convenient geo-historical analysis. In Algeria it would always have some validity. Ongoing research seemed to bear out 'the original overall categories of Tell and High Plateau that had been established out of necessity during the first decade of the colony'.[23] It was there that the notion of the mountain-dweller as hard working, rigorous, independent and democratic was extensively elaborated and contrasted to the plain-dweller, who was inclined to be more indolent, more decadent, less independent and more autocratic. What acquired importance over and above the physical and moral types thrown up by the mountain and the plain was that geography became the bottom line for socio-political analysis. As Gautier, writing on this very subject, explained, in France geography forms part of the Faculty of Arts and is closely associated with history, whereas elsewhere in the world it stands on its own as a scientific discipline.[24] One has only to think of Braudel's extensive analysis of mountains, plateaux and plains in his *magnum opus*, first published in 1949, to realize the truth of this statement.[25] Then too there was the notion that the mountain-dweller withdrew into his domain in times of conquest and thus remained 'pure', a notion which had been amply aired in the case of the Kabyle. Anthropology, which first came into its own in the second half of the nineteenth century, made much of this notion, of course, and has since delighted in mountain communities for their homogeneity.[26] The Atlas mountains in particular became a haunt of sociologists and anthropologists.[27]

It would be rash to claim that there was a direct causal relationship between the Kabyle Myth and these academic developments, but what is undeniable was that the first-hand scrutiny to which the Arabs and Berbers were subjected by the French created a valuable precedent, reinforcing extant tendencies towards such patterns of thought. The nomad–sedentary opposition, which in Algeria was linked to concerns with securing the colony and came to connote disorder and order among the officers serving there, was interpreted as a confirmation, in academic circles, of hypotheses elaborated prior to conquest by scholars and scientists whereby it was stated that nomads could not be civilized in the same way as sedentary populations or that they were at a lower stage of development. Similarly the mountain–plain contrast, with its stress on the ennobling impact on the inhabitants of the former, found in the Kabyles and Arabs its first, and most enduring, sanction of theories concerning the power of nature's influence on man's soul and, in particular, the nobility of mountain life. Rousseau was, of course, among the most renowned protagonists of such thought and it is no coincidence that the Kabyle was sometimes depicted in the terms of a 'noble savage'.

The legacy

A more direct result of the Arab–Berber opposition arose out of the historical analysis of the Arab as the usurper and the Berber as the true autochthon of the area. Of the two waves of Islamic conquerors that swept through North Africa, the armies of the Ommayyad caliphs and those of the Hillali tribes arriving in the seventh and eleventh centuries respectively, it was the latter which was deemed to have been the basis of Islamic colonization of Algeria.[28] These Bedouins, who had swept the area with all the fanaticism of the nomadic hordes they were, had stamped the indigenous population with their mark.[29] Thus were the Berbers tarred with the brush of Islam. Once conquered by Islam, North Africa was not only cut off from its past but also became a stranger and an enemy to the other countries of the Mediterranean.[30] In the eyes of French historians, these two invasions were to assume cataclysmic proportions. For George Marçais, for example, North Africa 'would evermore resound from the effects of this catastrophe.' For Julien, never given to strident analysis, it was the most important event to take place in the Maghreb during the Middle Ages.[31] Negative interpretations of the event were, more often than not, seen in terms of civilization. Guernier, professor at the Institute of Political Science of the University of Paris, declared that North Africa was only provisionally of the Orient and while he professed the hope that the proclivities of the Arabs, as scavengers from rather than creators of civilizations, would eventually induce them to spread Western civilization, he refrained from embracing them into the Western fold.[32] Although the races of North Africa were all white, the cultural heritage that divided them was too great to bridge:

> the Asian races (Arab and Jew) and the Western races (Berber, French, Spanish, Italian) are all white races. If the Arab race brought with it the imaginative configuration of Oriental thought, the land of the Berbers saw the flourishing of Augustinian intuition, the rationalism of an Averroës and a Maïmonides, the sociological thought of an Ibn Khaldun; we are at the heart of Western territory stamped with a distinctive Mediterranean destiny where the only stranger is the Oriental, that is to say the Arab ... it is the Arab who is hostile to the West.[33]

Of course it suited conservative French historians, particularly those who reached academic maturity prior to independence, to view North Africa as rooted in Western civilization and to present its history in terms of before and after the arrival on the scene of the Orient. While this 'before and after the Flood' approach echoed the tenets of the Kabyle Myth, it also reinforced the implacably negative attitude towards Islam. French academics, in the words of Berque, inclined towards the Berber option and, by so doing, turned their sights away from Orientalism proper.[34] Western historians of the post-independence era have made no further contribution to the analysis of this event. The images created by this interpretation of North African history have been sufficiently long-lasting to ensure that the true significance of the invasions, beyond that of a devastating and regressive flux, has never been explored.

With regard to the direct impact of the Kabyle Myth on anthropology and ethnography, in pre-independence Algeria it was undeniable. Physical anthropologists continued to search for evidence of a specific Berber racial type. Ely Leblanc, dean of the Algiers Medical Faculty in the 1930s, explained that rather than trying to pin a haphazard label on to the Berbers as a whole, what mattered for physical anthropologists was to find a dominant type, as free as possible from miscegenation, with well-defined features and recognizable morphological characteristics. In this way it would be possible to have a representative specimen of the race or of a sizeable ethnic grouping within the race.[35] Furthermore, race continued to be put forward as grounds for assimilating the Kabyles to or associating them with the French.[36] In the years immediately after Algerian independence the disciplines of anthropology and ethnography gave colonial sources on the Kabyles and Arabs a wide berth. They were seen to be part of a vulgate encapsulating colonial assumptions.[37] Then too the pre-eminence of cultural anthropology, the advent of an acceptance of cultural pluralism, and, more recently, the emergence of interpretive anthropology first pushed physical anthropology to the sidelines and then discredited it. The Berbers needed to be studied afresh. The Kabyle Myth was denounced but it continued to intrigue, becoming a point of reference, if only as a footnote, in most works on the Berbers. Indeed, that the Myth continues to elicit interest in academic circles at all is in itself a type of legacy, a legacy which will only be laid to rest when the Myth sinks into oblivion.

The political legacy: Kabyles in twentieth-century Algeria

Paradoxically there was no political legacy as such in Algeria: no policy came into being that was preferential to the Berbers. On the contrary, the lack of such a policy drew criticism very much along the lines of that voiced by nineteenth-century *kabylophiles*. In 1926 an article appearing in the *Revue Africaine* declared that French policy in Algeria had not taken into account the essential difference in mentality and temperament between the Arabs and the Kabyles – so much so that it was possible to claim that Kabylia had been Arabized instead of Gallicized. Now was the time to alter this error and give Kabylia a special statue to accord with its secular traditions (which conformed, furthermore, with the French Republican ideal) and its degree of social and economic development.[38] Ten years later the author of the article still thought it necessary to elaborate on the Kabyle situation and to draw attention to their racial make-up as a prelude to exhorting his compatriots to change their policies towards the Kabyles. The Kabyles were part of the Mediterranean race and deserved to be granted 'the freedom of the French city', but in comparison with their intellectual development most still lacked a social education.[39] Rémond was an advocate of association but he none the less saw in the doctrine the possibility of drawing the Kabyles into the French fold, albeit selectively. He cautioned against trying to turn the average Kabyle into a mediocre Frenchman, suggesting that the better course would be to make a superior Kabyle French at heart.[40] While Rémond's views are an indication of the evolution of the Kabyle Myth within the framework of colonial theory, namely from assimilation, when the call was to assimilate all the Kabyles, to association, when selective integration was the accepted standard, such views are also evidence of the lack of a collective policy towards the Kabyles. If Kabyles acquired favoured status, as some may well have done, it was on an individual level rather than on a collective one.

What then of the allegation that the Kabyles had absorbed French education better than the Arabs? Did this at least signify some sort of preferential educational policy towards the Berbers? In fact education of the indigenous population proceeded very slowly. Only after the Second World War, when education in urban areas had dramatically increased, did the situation change, but even then the rate at which the indigenous population was being educated did not exceed 15 per cent.[41] Colonna points out that the first schools were built where the indigenous population was densest, which happened to be in Berber areas. Resistance to French education among all but the Kabyles was considerable at first, and only with the realization of the economic benefits that such an education could bring did the indigenous population start sending their children to school on a regular basis. If the Kabyles were less resistant it was due to the wretched economic straits they found themselves in, not the fact that the Berbers had been singled out. The Aurès, the second largest conglomeration of Berbers, showed just as much resistance to begin with and the M'zab, another Berber area, was one of the most recalcitrant of all. Nor was there a rush to the schools in Kabylia. Even in the colonial showpieces, Benni Yenni and Tizi Rached, the two Kabyle districts which produced the most diploma-holders, education got off to a poor start. That there was no educational policy in Kabylia after 1914 is demonstrated by the fact that classes in the area of Tizi Ouzou fell from 22.7 per cent (of the total available to the indigenous population throughout the country) in 1892 to 16.2 per cent in 1932. In Bougie there was a similar drop from 11.8 per cent to 8.8 per cent during the same time span.[42] It was the land sequestrations of the late nineteenth century in Kabylia, driving the Kabyles first towards the towns and then to France itself as migrant workers, which initially propelled the Kabyles into French schools. After the centenary celebrations in 1930 educational policy started to concentrate on urban areas. The exodus of the Kabyles from the land was accelerated in the late 1930s by acute poverty. (A series of articles by Albert Camus calling for reforms to alleviate the desperate situation of the Kabyles, now grouped together in *Actuelles III Chroniques Algériennes (1939–1958)*, testifies to the hardship they endured at that time.) It was in the towns and in France that the Kabyles gravitated to French schools, not because of a pro-Berber educational policy. Indeed, had there been such a Berber policy evidence of it would surely have been manifest among the Chaouia, the Mozabites and the Tuareg, but this was not the case. Although a political legacy was lacking in Algeria, the powerful popular legacy spread beyond the borders of the colony and, together with the more restricted academic legacy, maintained the necessary climate for Berber policies to be attempted elsewhere.

The political legacy: Berbers in
the protectorates

The inclusion of Tunisia (1881) and Morocco (1912) into the French colonial realm as protectorates extended the territory in which Arabs and Berbers coexisted under French rule. In Morocco Berbers predominated, in Tunisia their number was small. The experience of nineteenth-century Algeria with regard to indigenous population was a point of reference for developments in the two protectorates, especially in Morocco, where the Berber population was so large. Whatever the ramifications of colonial indigenous policy and however disparate the French differentiation between Arab and Berber was in the individual protectorates the fundamental legacy, common to both Morocco and Tunisia, was to view the population as Arabs *versus* Berbers rather than Arabs *and* Berbers. With this as a starting point the evolution of attitudes towards Arabs and Berbers followed an individual course coloured by local exigencies.

The socio-political image of Morocco that emerged under the French was a dichotomous one. In it the Moroccan domain was seen to encompass two areas in conflict: the *bled-el-makhzan* and the *bled-el-siba*. The former was presided over by a central government, where collection of taxes proceeded unhindered and governmental laws were satisfactorily implemented. The latter was an unruly area where the autocratic regime of the *bled-el-makhzan* could not be successfully imposed. In time the *makhzan/siba* dichotomy became equated with the Arab–Berber one, with the unruly Berber tendencies being attributed to the superficiality of their Islamic beliefs and their reliance on their own customary law rather than on the *sharia*.[43] Even before the protectorate was established the autocratic *makhzan* was seen as having destroyed the democratic assemblies of Berber notables.[44] With the establishment of the French protectorate of Morocco the potential for the emergence of the notion of the 'good' Berber was created; and emerge it did.[45]

There was a twofold relationship between Algeria and Morocco with regard to attitudes towards the Berbers. In the first place many of the leading figures in colonial Morocco, whether they were military experts or civilian scholars of the indigenous population, had begun their careers in Algeria.[46] Second, the copious literature that had emerged on the Arabs and Berbers as a result of military and civilian scholarship in Algeria served as a useful, and unavoidable, basis for similar studies in Morocco. That the focus would remain on the Berbers was confirmed as early as 1915 when an institute for Berber studies, the Ecole supérieure des Lettres et de la langue berbère, was set up in Rabat.[47] The Algerian experience provided the readymade stereotypes but allowed for a reappraisal of the situation with regard to indigenous policy. Whereas ethnological-cum-sociological studies on the Berbers would continue where studies in Algeria left off, with the literature on the Kabyles being considered relevant source material, in the political arena a conscious effort was made not to repeat what were seen to be the mistakes of indigenous policy in Algeria, in particular the excessive Islamization of the Kabyles. Policy discussion on this subject was by no means internal to the administration, but appearing in article of journals such as the *Revue des Deux Mondes*.[48] French efforts in Morocco would be geared not only to acquiring a better understanding of the Berbers, with the nerve centre of this effort being the Berber Institute, but also to developing, if necessary, a coherent Berber policy.

Lyautey and Berber policy in Morocco

Hubert Lyautey was appointed resident general of Morocco in 1912, the year in which the country was acquired by France in accordance with the Treaty of Fez. He was experienced in colonial North Africa, having served in Algeria, and was aware of the problems of Islam. He encouraged an understanding of Islam and Muslim values and believed it an error to try and eradicate Islamic culture, which he saw as rich in both tradition and achievement.[49] The administrative framework that Lyautey bequeathed to the colony was one of indirect rule. He was against excessive appropriation of land (although the land bills passed under his Residency were the basis of future land acquisition by the settlers) and tried his best to delay settler dominance in the country's administration. In 1917 he created the Direction des Affaires Indigènes, whose structure was based on Galliéni's system of *cercles* rather than the Bureaux Arabes of Algeria, although their task closely resembled that of the Algerian Bureaux. It was the officers of the Affaires Indigènes who were the main perpetrators of Lyautey's Berber policy.[50] This in itself was in the tradition of Algeria, where military men had been so instrumental in the formation of the Kabyle Myth. Lyautey was well aware of the curious bond which seemed to link the Berbers to the military and during his retirement he summed it up thus: 'the Berber element will only ever be understood by a soldier.'[51]

Berber Policy in Morocco rested on two assumptions, both elaborated within the Kabyle Myth, namely that the Berbers were of a different race from the Arabs and second, that they were only superficially Islamicized. The assessment of the Berber population of Morocco was undertaken in a manner reminiscent of Warnier's divisions of *Berber-berberisant* and *Berber-arabisant*. There were four types of Berber discernible, each residing in distinctive areas: those who had escaped all Arab influence save religion, those who had been subjected to some influence with the notables of the area speaking Arabic, those who had been subjected to considerable influence characterized by bilingualism among the men and the partial adoption of the *sharia*, and those who had fallen completely under the Arab spell, with intermarriage, a totally bilingual community and the seclusion of women.[52] There was no cohesion between these four groups of Berbers, a fact that encouraged attempts to prevent further encroachment of Arab mores and culture on Berber society.

It was under Lyautey that the *bled-el-siba* was pacified for the first time, and although he had no intention of creating autonomous Berber states he was reluctant to hand over control of Berber tribes from this area to the central government of the *makhzan*. One of Lyautey's officers, Colonel Frisch, prepared a handbook for the officers of the Affaires Indigènes during the Chaouia campaign, in which he encouraged the promotion of existing antagonisms between Berbers and Arab. It was, however, a policy Lyautey declined to adopt.[53] In true military tradition he was concerned with the maintenance of security, seeking to alleviate antagonism rather than encourage it. With such concerns in mind, like Randon before him in Algeria, in Berber areas he sought to mitigate resistance by allowing Berber customary law to remain intact. Looking back on his successes in Morocco, Lyautey was to say: 'my secret of conquest was to protect the Berber from intrusions into his personal life, into his clan customs and into his traditions. Had I not vanquished the Berber soul, I would never have been able to constitute a greater Morocco.'[54] In areas where Arab and Berber tribes coexisted they were placed under the jurisdiction of different bureaux of the Affaires Indigènes. By keeping the 'races' apart it was hoped that the Berbers, escaping further Arab influence, would be more amenable to French influence and eventual assimilation. To this same end attempts were made, through education, to encourage the Berbers to speak French, especially in non-Arabic speaking areas. In matters of governmental grants and similar benefits they were singled out in preference to the Arabs.[55] In 1928 the elite College of Azrou was established with the professed aim of penetrating Berber tribes through the education of the sons of Berber notables. Its graduates would be Berber leaders in tune with French rather than Islamic culture.

The linchpin of Berber policy was education, for it was considered to be the most powerful tool of assimilation. As in Algeria, however, two other potential channels existed through which to draw the Berbers into the French fold: Berber justice and the *djemâa*. With both it was a question of keeping Islam at bay. As early as 1914 a Dahir was passed decreeing that 'the tribes adhering to Berber custom would remain administered and ruled according to their own laws and traditions under the control of the authorities.'[56] The speed with which this decision was taken, in spite of an ignorance of Berber customary law in Morocco, is in itself indicative of the influence of Algeria. A year later the Comité des Etudes Berbères was set up to study the tribal code in detail. The intention was of course to extricate the Berbers, as far as possible and without creating too much fracas, from the clutch of *Sharia* law. The Berber Dahir of 1930 was the culmination of this idea.

One French institution which reacted to the Berbers as it had done to the Kabyles in Algeria was the Catholic Church. A concerted effort was made by Church missions to convert the Berbers, based on an assessment of their unorthodoxy as evidence of a feeble commitment to Islam. The Church's attempts at conversion were not approved by the French administration and Lyautey, in particular, did what he could to discourage them so as not to inflame Muslim resentment.

This did not stop the Church, however, and after Lyautey's departure, the force behind missionary zeal in Morocco emanated from the Bishop of Rabat, Mgr. Viel.[57] As was to be expected, the Church's efforts at converting the Berbers were a failure. The singling out of the Berbers by both the administration and the Church, for whatever the reasons, had a similar effect as it had had on the Kabyles in Algeria.

As time progressed the notion of Berber superiority, associated with the Kabyle Myth in Algeria, made itself felt in Morocco, and the idea emerged that the Berbers were worthy of nationhood in a way the Arab never could be. For all the desire of the French to eschew the Algerian tradition with regard to the Berbers, the basic French assumption that Moroccan Arabs and Berbers were of opposing cultures rather than different ones inexorably led to similar social conclusions and hence to an erroneous appreciation of local political realities. Just how misguided Moroccan Berber policy was became clear on 16 May 1930, when the Berber Dahir was promulgated. The Dahir transferred penal justice from the *caids* to French tribunals and endorsed the legal jurisdiction of Berber customary courts.[58] Any judicial power the *makhzan* may have had in Berber areas was thus eliminated. Muslims, both Berber and Arab, were enraged and a wave of protest swept the country. The coalescence of Moroccan nationalism is usually attributed to this event.[59] It took four years for the alarmed French to realize their mistake. The Berber Dahir was partially rescinded on 8 April 1934.

French attitudes towards Berbers in Morocco were more than an echo of the Kabyle Myth. Not only were the stereotypes similar but the effort to shield the Berbers from the 'noxious' effects of Islam led to actual policy decisions in their favour. The question thus arises of whether or not Berber policy in Morocco was one of divide and rule. Certainly divide and rule was a by-product of these policy decisions but the concept was neither the initiating nor the motivating force of Berber policy; that was the marginalization of Islamic culture (and hence the Arabs) seen to be incompatible with French civilization. Divide and rule was not an axiom of French colonial policy in Morocco. Divide-and-rule tactics, when they did occur, were a product of the French clash with Islam.

Tunisia: A legacy without practical application

Of the one million souls making up the indigenous population of Tunisia on the eve of French takeover, the number of Berbers was extremely small.[60] The few Berbers there mainly inhabited the mountains of the south. As a result, unlike Morocco where the Berbers were so numerous, the legacy of the Kabyle Myth was of little practical use, serving as a basis principally for socio-political analysis rather than for concrete policy application. In an article on the subject Gianni Albergoni and François Pouillon have indicated that there was no Berber policy as such in Tunisia, although there is evidence of pro-Berber measures being taken on a piecemeal basis which had the undesired effect of exacerbating Arab resentment.[61] In the socio-political analysis of the indigenous population, however, the Kabyle Myth served as a blueprint. As is to be expected, the linchpins of this analysis were the sedentary–nomad, mountain–plain, indigenous–usurper divides. The sedentary mountain Berber was contrasted to the nomadic Arab of the plains, with favourable conclusions being drawn with regard to the former. The mountains were the sanctuary into which the Berber race, as the first settlers of North Africa, had withdrawn and survived. Here they had resisted the pillaging nomads and maintained their independence from the long arm of the bureaucracies of former conquerors. (Albergoni and Pouillon indicate the extent of this mythology by referring to the nineteenth-century Beylic archives, from which it would appear that the Berbers were in fact more heavily taxed.[62]) Retreating into the mountains at the time of the Hillali invasion, the Berbers had shown their enterprise by converting the barren slopes into an arboricultural haven.[63] Such activity was imputed to a persistent Berber characteristic, thus one that was inherently racial, namely the will to cultivate. Put in terms of the Kabyle Myth, it indicated a predisposition of the race to a sedentary lifestyle. The sedentariness of Tunisia's mountain Berbers was acclaimed but, interestingly enough, their reclusive independence was not. The blame for this insufficiency was laid at the Arab door, for they had forced the Berbers into the mountains.[64] Thus, in Tunisia too, positive Berber attributes were contrasted to negative Arab ones giving rise to conclusions of a spurious nature. Because of the small number of Berbers, the legacy in Tunisia was less tangible and hence less disruptive than it was in Morocco but it was no less potent. No policy was needed as a preventive measure against Berber discontent but colonial mythology on the subject was as much in evidence in Tunisia as elsewhere.

The post-independence legacy: a question of historical memory

The long-term impact of the Kabyle Myth was directly related to the binary opposition on which it was based. On the one hand, as a result of positive stereotyping, the notion of Kabyle (hence Berber) superiority became part of France's received ideas on the peoples it had colonized. Nor has the image disappeared of the Berber as fair-haired, fair-skinned (even blue-eyed), essentially democratic, and religiously unorthodox. The more profound consequence, however, arose out of the negative stereotyping of the Arab. It was not so much the negative image of the Arab but the fact the Arab was equated with Islam. The image the myth created of Islam as incorrigible in terms of French civilization has never really been expunged. Within its national perimeters Islam was, and has remained, the French stumbling-block. Certainly the single-minded pursuit in the colony of secularization, in contrast to its more erratic progress in France, accompanied by the relentless denigration of Islamic society and mores had its roots in a desire to neutralize Islam and render it impotent. Although this aim was never accomplished, Islam was in effect shunted to the side throughout the colonial period with the result that the French remained both ignorant and fearful of Islam. It was considered to be a subversive religion given to fanatical, irrational outbursts of violence. During the colonial period, little attempt had been made to look beyond this conviction and analyse the reasons for these outbursts. Indigenous disturbances within the colony, whatever their origins, had inevitably been laid at the door of Islam. Indeed, blaming Islam became the easiest way of passing the buck for the political, economic and social shortcomings of the colonial administration in dealing with the indigenous population. The lack of any concerted effort to accommodate the religion within the framework of colonial society had made of it an outsider's religion, transforming it into a quintessential expression of the Other, a conviction which is still evident today in the anti-North African immigrant propaganda of the French Right. In the long run, in France, the negative expression of the Kabyle Myth was the more powerful: the Islamic cause was damaged more than the Kabyle one was enhanced.

This then was the legacy to the French, but what of the legacy to the Kabyles and the Arabs? It is an intriguing question, about which it is easy to speculate but difficult to pin down. The period between the two world wars, when the Algerian nationalist movement was dominated by the centralizing vision of Messali Hadj, saw the emergence of the Berberist movement (*mouvement berbériste*). Colonization had had an impact on existing notions of regionalism. The advent of colonial capitalism to Kabylia and the ensuing emigration of Kabyle workers to France and urban centres in Algeria had coalesced village and tribal allegiances into a wider regional loyalty.[65] During this period too, French replaced Arabic as the second language of the majority of

Kabyle males.[66] Messali made no allowances for regionalism, believing that cultural and linguistic differences had been encouraged by the colonizing power for their own ends.[67] Many Kabyles, on the other hand, resented the Arabization implied in Messalism. For them regionalism was the way of maintaining their cultural identity and safeguarding their linguistic rights. When a schism occurred in Messali's ranks between those, like Messali, who advocated parliamentary reform and those, like the Kabyle Amar Imache, who advocated a bid for independence, Imache found himself the head of an essentially Kabyle faction.[68] Messali's followers remained multi-regional, hence the schism was not an ethnic Kabyle–Arab divide but rather a cultural and linguistic one in which Arabizationist and Berberist tendencies clashed.

Immediately after the Second World War the Berberist movement gathered strength, fed by continuing fractiousness in Messali's ranks, growing nationalist sentiments in Kabylia and tactical errors in the leadership of the pro-independence PPA (*Parti du Peuple Algérien*).[69] It was not a separatist movement as such; rather it opposed the concept of Algerian nationalism as essentially Arabo-Muslim in cultural content. At the time its adherents were left-wing and secular.[70] Anti-Berberist sentiments were exacerbated by a feeling among the Kabyles that their politics were more advanced than elsewhere in Algeria. Rising resentment became apparent in the 1945 local elections when the PPA issued orders to the district of Kabylia to liquidate its candidates.[71] The region was thrown into disarray and numerous militants took to the *maquis*. Although the orders were never carried through for fear of French reprisals the Kabyle continent was decimated following the 1945 Sétif rebellion, when PPA candidates were rounded up in numbers out of all proportion to the events. It was suggested by some Kabyles that the PPA had denounced them to the French authorities.[72] Berberism had become a useful stick with which to beat dissenters. This was born out by Messali during a 1954 congress of the MTLD (*Mouvement pour le Triomphe des Libertés Démocratiques*) when speaking of the Central Committee purge. He admitted it had been possible to 'eliminate bothersome candidates indiscriminately by branding them as Berberist'.[73] What role can be imputed to the Kabyle Myth in these developments? That historical memory can be and is used randomly by interested parties to further their own ends is undeniable, but just how much can be laid at its door is impossible to assess.

Then too there was the Algerian War of Independence, whose tragedy did not rest solely on what happened between the French and the Algerians. The internal purges carried out by the FLN (*Front de*

Libération Nationale) were devastating and Kabylia was especially savagely hit. The most extensive and seemingly the most senseless occurred in Wilaya III, the wilaya encompassing Kabylia, when, under the leadership of Amirouche, himself a Kabyle, resentment at the *francisant* element of the Kabyle population erupted, resulting in the liquidation of hundreds of French-educated students, newly recruited to the *maquis*.[74] The purges continued throughout 1958 and 1959, spilling over into neighbouring wilayas. Their vindictive nature was remarked upon at the time by both members of the FLN and Algerian civilians, incredulous that so many traitors should exist.[75] On receipt of the list of victims from Wilaya III Belkacem Krim, also a Kabyle and one of the FLN leaders, is reported to have said, 'it is unthinkable that men whom I knew so well, whom I trained, who fought at my side and whose patriotism is above suspicion, should have become traitors.'[76] That Kabyle turned against Kabyle should not obscure the fact that such times provide the ideal opportunity to settle old scores and exorcise existing resentments. Did the historical memory of the Kabyle Myth contribute to the magnitude of the purges by giving Arab animosity free reign or did the purges merely confirm Pierre Vergniaud's observation that the revolution, like Saturn, devours its own children? (It is of interest to note that the only group who were purged in greater numbers were the *harkis*, Algerians who served in or were attached to the French armed forces. This lends weight to the argument that the magnitude of the purges bore a relation to the extent of involvement with the French.) Nor has Algeria been free of Arab-Kabyle clashes since independence. The most violent of these occurred in 1980 and was dubbed 'The Berber Spring' by the French press; an up-dated echo of past attitudes. In 1989 the Berber movement was transformed into a political party with a cultural unity base when the RCD (*Rassemblement pour la culture et la démocratie*) was created in Tizi Ouzou. Its main objective was to promote democracy and, as one spokesmen declared, in the name of progress to foster the idea of separating Islam and State.[77] Further disturbances connected to the political and cultural differences of the Kabyles occurred in 1990 and again in 1994, when an Algerian journalist called it a clash between the 'Berber Spring' and the 'Fundamentalist Winter'.[78]

Just how are such events relevant? To go beyond an exposition of the facts and link them causally to the Kabyle Myth is impossible. Nor is it possible to say what Kabyle–Arab relations would have been without the legacy of the Myth. None the less the very fact that these questions can be raised illustrates the power of racial myths, and suggests some general conclusions on the legacy of this type of myth-making. To be sure, regionalism and culture difference are strong forces in identity expression, forces that spontaneously emerge when circumstances necessitate them to do so. The existence of a well-defined racial or ethnic myth, on the other hand, provides a ready-made framework around which such an identity can coalesce or against which an opposing identity can react. For better or for worse such myths enter the historical consciousness of a people and then become difficult to dislodge, it being easier to rely on existing images than to be imaginative and re-create ones appropriate to the moment. The existence of such myths exacerbates existing ethnic tensions by creating a memory difficult to lay to rest. Yesterday's racial identity can easily become today's ethnic one. The power of racial and ethnic myths lies in the control they exercise over a given situation. On the one hand the myth can be manipulated consciously to incite or control the population; on the other by its very existence it spontaneously establishes perimeters beyond which action becomes difficult, in short it can limit the field of cooperation.

Conclusion

The legacy was thus a complex one. Its most enduring, but least definable, aspect was that of historical memory. In the post-independence era both the French and the Algerians felt the weight of its presence. While the substantive legacy was extensive in that evidence of its components was to be found in popular, academic and political circles, the focus and intensity of each was different. In the popular domain the legacy was essentially social, with both its practical and theoretical expression being dependent on the positive and negative stereotypes elaborated around the Berbers and the Arabs. Thus it found expression on a practical level in the discriminatory behaviour of the settlers and on a theoretical level in the portrait of Berbers and Arabs in novels and popular ethnography. These works, acclaimed for their realism, were in fact a compendium of stereotypes rather than an accurate depiction of ethnicity. Furthermore, the inadvertent presentation of the social realities of a racially hierarchical society from the vantage point of a 'detached' observer merely confirmed such tendencies as existed in the reader to view colonial society from a Eurocentric or even racist standpoint. Little room remained to redress the situation. This, coupled with the facility with which stereotypes are mentally absorbed by the public, ensured a wider dissemination and more tenacious legacy than in the academic or even political fields.

In academic circles, where overt stereotypes were consciously rejected, the legacy was a conceptual one characterized by a tendency to oppose two systems one to the other: sedentary/nomad, mountain/

plain, indigenous/invader. The Kabyle Myth was not the font out of which these concepts emerged, rather the indigenous population of Algeria provided the first and most convenient case study in which existing notions could be examined and 'proved' or 'disproved'. The contribution of the Kabyle Myth was to colour this process by imbuing the dual contrasts with positive and negative connotations. Hence the rigours of a mountain environment were seen to impinge on social development by stimulating the evolution of certain characteristics such as endurance, thrift, industriousness, innovation and, in some cases, frugality, all of which are Western middle-class virtues undoubtedly valued by the predominantly middle-class academics that were expounding them. In contrast stood the enervating plain. Similarly, sedentary populations with their settled habits, their varied economies and their easily defined institutions were identifiable in relation to Western civilization in a way nomadic populations were not and sedentary came to signify a step up the evolutionary ladder. Undoubtedly the most unfortunate legacy of the Myth was the implicit acceptance of an essentially negative vision of Islam (in relation to Western civilization).

The political legacy was straightforward in comparison. Attitudes to Berbers in the protectorates were an extension of those to the Kabyles in Algeria. In Tunisia, where the Berber population was small, no policy *per se* was elaborated; rather, piecemeal measures were adopted favourable to the Berbers. In Morocco, on the other hand, where the French army was a considerable presence and where the Berber population was large, a Berber policy did emerge conditioned by what had gone before in Algeria. Indigenous policy in the Protectorates was no longer a question of trial and error, instead policies were adopted with reference to the 'successes' and 'mistakes' of Algeria. Paradoxically, the basis of Berber policy in Morocco was not founded in the realities of the Algerian situation, as its perpetrators would liked to have believed, but in its mythology, namely that the Berbers were only superficially Islamized. This erroneous belief induced the French to try and shield the Moroccan Berbers from further encroachments by Islam through inducements to espouse French rather than Islamic culture. It was a cruel paradox, and an indication of the extent to which mythology can obscure reality, for instead of moving away from the errors committed in Algeria they merely compounded them.

PART V

I I

Conclusion

Category formation is a part of social definition. Intrinsic to this process is the development and maintenance of a mythical classification, that is to say the mental collages of stereotypes which align an individual or group of individuals in relation to a culturally accepted norm. Such a classifications arises out of an impulse to symbolize personal or collective convictions in order to formulate an easily recognizable identity. The Kabyle Myth was a colonial response to such an impulse. By creating a binary opposition of vertical contrasts (superior/inferior) it valorized one sector of the population while denigrating the other, thus centralizing one and marginalizing the other. The valorization of the Kabyles and their society was the symbolic endorsement of the values of French Republican society.

In the colonial situation, where two different but well-established societies confronted each other, the formation of the new collective identity could only be achieved by the domination of one of these societies by the other, initially through the use of force and then by negating the underlying beliefs and values of the dominated society, thus rendering it socially and politically impotent. The dialogue that developed between the two was value-laden, replete with its own cue-words and metaphors reflecting both the desires of the dominant partner and the grievances of the dominated one. Colonial myths and ethnic categorization were part of this dialogue. They were the metaphors of control and instruments of marginalization arising out of the need to maintain dominance without a perpetual recourse to force. Formulated by the dominant partner they changed or were redefined according to circumstance and need. In considering colonial metaphors, myths and categories, Algeria is noteworthy in that during the process of social category formation an image of a sub-group of the colonized society was co-opted by the colonizer to promote European values and beliefs. This situation arose out of the circumstances of the initial confrontation and because of the particular nature of the two societies involved.

The mythology evolved during category formation can be calculated, in which case it can be said to form part of a personal or collective propaganda elaborated for manipulative reasons. It can also evolve spontaneously, triggered by the need to formulate a symbolic identity yet conditioned by prevailing circumstances and conforming to current canons of thought. The Kabyle Myth was of the latter type. Common to both processes, however, is the transformation of relevant prejudices and values into easily assimilated stereotypical images which can then be transmitted as 'received wisdom'. The homogeneity of the stereotype makes it an inaccurate image: a generalization at best, a falsehood at worst. This elastic quality allows its user the comfort of imprecision; the underlying reason, no doubt, for the uncritical and often rapid acceptance of even the most inaccurate stereotypes. Once accepted as a valid image the stereotype can be used with impunity to marginalize or valorize at will.

In the case of the contrast between the *positive* Kabyle and the *negative* Arab, the inaccuracies immanent in stereotyping were magnified. It is impossible for one group to mirror negatively, across the board, the positive features of another. The diversity of any given group excludes such simplification. A social dichotomy of this type is spurious and is a myth in itself. None the less, binary contrasting of groups within societies, with its Manichean overtones of good and evil, is a persistent feature of human reasoning. In the nineteenth century, when the question of race first became a central issue, such dichotomies were inherent to racial conceptualizing. The insistence on the racial differences between the Kabyles and Arabs linked this dichotomy to the mainstream of nineteenth-century racial ideology, placing it in a similar category to the more familiar Aryan/Semitic or White/Black divisions.

The use of antithetical images are central to identity or category formation. They give rise to subliminal notions of Self and Other, emerging in common parlance as 'We' and 'They'. In Algeria French images were conditioned not only by uneasy perceptions of indigenous society, but also by a measure of uncertainty regarding their own. The French Revolution of 1789–99 had called into question the ideological, social and political bases of French society. Their re-definition was an essential process in the post-revolutionary era. Religion, or more precisely the influence of the clerics, non-meritocratic social hierarchies and feudal power structures, had been discredited and, theoretically, banished. But a consensus of what should replace them was lacking, beyond the conviction, among the Republican elements at least, that society should be secular, egalitarian and democratic. (The subsequent revolutions of 1830, 1848 and the Paris Commune of

1870–71 served as reminders of the lack of consensus.) Nonetheless, the strength of this conviction was such that the era of the French Revolution saw the emergence of an expansionist movement motivated by Republican sentiments, namely a desire to sweep away *ancien régimes* and install in their place societies in the image of the new French one. Philosophers in France concentrated on devising the ideal framework of such societies based on alternative power structures and religions to those of the *ancien régime*. The emphasis placed on breaking the stranglehold of absolute power and religion brought these two concepts to the centre of intellectual discourse and made them a yardstick against which progress could be measured and the key factors in any process of change. In Algeria, where French ideological supremacy was maintained by the negative comparison of indigenous society with that of the French, they assumed special importance.

In the first quarter of the nineteenth century the movement of Republican expansionism and the new philosophical currents came together under the aegis of one of France's leading educational institutions, the Ecole Polytechnique, France's primer scientific establishment of higher learning. Napoleon Bonaparte's militarization of the school had in effect institutionalized the two by linking science to the military. The process was endorsed by the association of utopian philosophers such as Saint-Simon, Enfantin and Fourier with the school. Its graduates, many of whom found their way to Algeria, were products of an education which drew its source from revolutionary modes of thought (both ideological and scientific). Over and above the influence exerted by the Ecole Polytechnique through its officer graduates in Algeria, the army as a whole, at this stage, was still revolutionary. The antithetical images they took with them to Algeria were those of the Republic and of the *ancien régime*. When they first occupied Algeria in 1830 they encountered a society which was organizationally, structurally and philosophically different from their own. Their perception of these differences gave concrete form to these quiescent images.

Binary stereotypes are used in identity formation or manipulative control to valorize the essential values of the individual or collective norm: the positive image being one to emulate; the negative image one to repudiate. If attached to extant identities and opposed one to the other the message becomes more forceful. In Algeria the existing identity which became the negative stereotype, or subliminal Other, was that of Islamic Arab Society. On arriving in Algeria the French had existing preconceptions about the Arabs and residual fears of Islam, as well as knowledge of the Berbers in the form of imprecise descriptions as to their singularity. French occupation of Algeria, however, forced a renewed assessment in the light of actual experience. First-hand contact brought value differences into the open, creating an atmosphere in which latent concepts could assume stereotypical form.

Manipulating value differences to create a polarity is an initial step in the formation of categories which are, in effect, composites of positive and negative values. Colonial society used such categories as the mainstay of a class-based logic which had race as its primary determinant. In a society where ethnic differences and conflicting interests were potentially explosive, racial categories incorporating positive or negative social values allowed, on the one hand, the maintenance of a consensus among the multi-ethnic settlers by providing them with a means of identifying their similarities and, on the other hand, for authority to be upheld by creating a seemingly insuperable boundary between the settlers and the indigenous population.

The most obvious value difference, and a potentially dangerous factor of Algerian society for the French from a security point of view, was religion. In a society characterized by sparsity of population, by fragmentation and by decentralization, as was the case in Algeria in 1830, religion was the only cohesive force. The indigenous population was clustered in towns, such as Algiers and Constantine, and in the tribal communities of the rural areas. The lack of any communication or transport networks and the prevalent inter-tribal tensions ensured that these clusters were autonomous. There was neither political centralization as represented by the overall executive and legislative institutions of France, nor the social centralization as represented by the hierarchy of the French class system.[1] Social and political interaction between population clusters was minimal, preventing the emergence of across-the-board divisions characteristic of European society.

The only common thread was Islam. Algerian society was above all a religious one, and by that it is not meant an excessively pious one, but one in which religion permeated all aspects of life: personal, social and judicial. Islamic law encompassed civil, criminal and constitutional law and regulated private and public life by means of its code of religious ethics.[2] Unlike Roman law it was immutable, being of divine inspiration. Deviation by Muslims from Islamic law brought sanctions, and renunciation was equated with apostasy. That the unifying bond of this segmented, decentralized society was religion contrasted markedly to France, where religion was a divisive force. The 1789–99 revolution had ended the idea of society as a spiritual hierarchy headed by a divinely appointed king. It had introduced anti-clericalism of the most virulent sort and, with it, the concept of a secular state. An alliance between Church and state was re-established in 1801, but ecclesiastical France never regained the strength it had under the *ancien régime*. In nationalizing Church lands, the revolution had effectively eradicated the Church's temporal power. Although nineteenth-century France was characterized by a debilitating and continued friction between Catholicism and anti-clerical elements, secularism as a force gathered strength throughout the century. Anti-clerics, unbelievers and many Republicans identified religion with reaction and unscientific attitudes; in short it was a barrier to progress. A society wedded to Islam, with no dissenting opinion, was the negation of all the Revolution had achieved by way of crippling the power of religious institutions. In their appraisal of the religious tendencies of Algerian society it was the Arabs who were deemed to be obscurantist, for they were unswervingly orthodox. Breaking the stranglehold of their religion appeared to be an insurmountable task. The Kabyles, on the other hand, offered more hope. With their *marabouts* and their non-religious customary law, were they not dissenters of sorts? It was even alleged that they had been converted from Christianity. The fact that for over two decades most of Kabylia remained outside French jurisdiction, and hence out of direct contact, helped to maintain the fiction that the Kabyle was a bad Muslim. As such there was a potential to secularize his society and encourage its development along French lines.

The second factor of concern to the French occupiers was property. That this was also ordered by Islam accentuated the need to undermine the force of religion in the colony. In general among Muslims, ownership was regarded as depending more on God's will than on any independent activity of man.[3] *Melk*, the approximation of private land-holding, was predominant in Kabylia. Property among the Arabs was largely communally held and indivisible, with a Koranic code of property regulation. Property, therefore, was not a defining feature of personal status; it was a means of livelihood. The collective nature of land tenure precluded the possibility of prestige accruing to the individual and prevented the inclusion of land ownership in the political stakes of the society. Individualism and individual enterprise, concepts closely connected to private ownership, were alien in a society which functioned in close-knit collective groups, where each group member reacted in relation to the unit as a whole and not on a personal basis. Satisfaction of immediate needs was the essence of both urban and rural economies; concern for productivity was non-existent, and competition limited.[4] In France, on the other hand, only individual property survived the Revolution. This allowed for a greater development of individual enterprise, in both industry and agriculture, speeding up the process by which the French economy was moving from subsistence to capitalistic modes of production. The underlying concepts of this economic renewal were productivity and modernity. France, in Sewell's words, had become a voluntary association of productive citizens.[5] By comparison, therefore, it was easy to categorize Arab society, with its collective land holdings, disparate subsistence economies and pre-industrial methods of production, as archaic. The nomadic lifestyle of the Arab tribes restricted the capacity to produce for gain by imposing transportable limits on any excess produce amassed, a fact that could only encourage the idea that the Arab was incapable of productivity. The Kabyles, on the other hand, had the potential to produce for gain as their sedentary lifestyle allowed for the possibility of storage. This placed them on a par with the small-holding French peasant; and also fostered the notion that the Kabyles were more industrious than the Arabs. Furthermore, the main commercial contacts with Kabyles prior to the conquest of Kabylia were with itinerant vendors who came down from Kabylia to sell their produce, enhancing any existing image of the Kabyle as a 'productive citizen'.

The third value difference between French and Arab society had to do with the ideology of power. Reduced to its most simple equation that of the French was political, that of the Arab judicial. In other words, the former was shaped by the ideology of political factions which arose out of the Revolution (initially the basic monarchist or republican factions and eventually the whole spectrum of right and left), while the latter were shaped by the tenets of Islamic law. There were no legislative or governing institutions comparable to those of the French; nor was there any separation of powers. These apparent shortcomings were highlighted by the fact that the governing structure the French found in place on their arrival was that set up by the Turks. The imposition of Turkish rule had restricted the development of Arab power structures in urban areas, where they most logically would have developed. The Kabyles, who had remained outside Turkish control, had been able to maintain their own governing institutions, in particular the *djemâa*, which was appraised by the French as a rudimentary democratic institution. If Algerian society was considered to be pre-political a distinction was made between the Arab and the Kabyle. The former, aligned with the Dark Ages, was medieval and hence labelled 'feudal', the word being used in the derogatory sense of obscurantist. The latter, less tangibly situated historically, was an incipient democracy, a notion based essentially on perceptions of its egalitarianism. It was a somewhat romanticized interpretation of the power structure of Kabyle society which allowed for a positive value assessment in relation to French society. Furthermore, by comparing Arab society to a Western past, at the time not yet rescued by historians from the opprobrium with which it had been viewed since the Renaissance, and Kabyle society to an idealized past, parameters were established with regard to progress. The image of the Arab became entrenched in an obscurantist past, suggesting that progress to the modern French present would be slow and arduous; the image of the Kabyle in a less benighted past, leaving the door open for more generous interpretations about their capacity for progress and the speed with which they could be be propelled into 'the present'.

The fourth value difference that set the French and Algerian societies apart was that of collective consciousness. The French defined themselves as a nation and the Algerians as a collection of tribes. Nationalism was, of course, a key feature in nineteenth-century European thought. Allegiance to the nation served to counteract internal political or regional schisms and unite the country behind a secular banner. In France the unifying concept of the nation was extensively used during the 1789–99 revolution when the revolutionary Deists sought to replace God with it as the bond of society, thus connecting it with concepts of progress and political evolution. Furthermore, the nationalism of the revolutionary era was linked to the expansionary movement. It was in the name of the values of the new French nation that the first engagements of the Republican Army took place. Republican nationalism persisted in the Army of the First Empire, becoming entwined with Napoleon Bonaparte's imperial designs. This enmeshing of republican nationalism and Napoleonic imperialism was the foundation of the *mission civilisatrice* of the colonial era.

The nation was equated with unity, and nation formation was therefore a sign of a progressive civilization. That there was no conception in Algeria of a nation, as the French conceived it, was interpreted as an indication of the backward state of its society. Personal allegiance was tribal and, in a wider context, religious. Both types of allegiance countered French values and represented a potential for indigenous instability under French occupation. Centuries of Ottoman occupation had blurred the political boundaries between the various North African states and prevented the formation of geographical entities that could be construed as nations. Beyond the geo-political definition, just what constituted a nation was a cause for debate. In Algeria the question arose in regard to the Kabyles, among whom, it was suggested, the idea of nationhood could be implanted. Their language, their cultural cohesion and their unorthodox religious practices were the basis on which this assessment was made, for these three factors were essential to the French notion of community.

Daumas defined the touchstone of nationality as language, and stated that linguistically the Kabyles could be considered to be a nation.[6] Four decades later Caix de Saint Aymour amplified these conclusions, adding that the nomadic Arabs could never be considered as such.[7]

The fifth value difference was one of morality. This encompassed the family, sexuality and social morals. The legal French family unit was monogamous; the legal Algerian family unit was polygamous. The Arabs, both urban and rural, practised polygamy; the Kabyles seldom did. The reasons for this are not clear, but they certainly had more to do with demography and economics than with morality. It was, however, on morality that the French focused. Arab polygamy was interpreted as the manifestation of their innate licentiousness and contempt for women; Kabyle monogamy as a sign of their superior morality to the Arabs. Both French and Algerian society were patriarchal, but it was the condition of women that served as the point of departure for comparison. Women's condition in French society was of course much more varied than in Algerian society. When it came to comparison, however, it was the French middle-class or peasant woman who served as the yardstick. The French middle-class woman was well educated, socially if not academically, had a secondary economic role in the family unit and was not confined to her home socially. The French peasant woman, on the other hand, did not always have the privilege of education, had a primary economic role in the family unit and was, as a result, confined more to her home than her middle-class counterpart. These two models were used selectively: the middle-class model was the 'civilized' ideal; the peasant model was the starting point for a progression towards this ideal. By any French yardstick, Arab and Kabyle women had shortcomings but the latter – unveiled, usually part of a monogamous unit, and involved in economic pursuits that were analogous to the French peasant woman – came out ahead of the Arab.

Finally mention needs to be made of what were felt to be modal differences, for want of a better term, between the two societies. These were not part of the essential panoply of value differences necessary for the creation of positive and negative categories; rather their perception was climatic, thus augmenting the disparity of values between the two. French society throughout the nineteenth century was, from all appearances, a society 'on the move'. The succession of revolutions and regimes from 1789 to 1871 brought political and social ferment. On each occasion society was, to some degree, realigned. There was more continuity than the pattern of shifts would suggest, but there was also much experimentation, however short-lived it proved to be. New ideas and ideologies, coupled with an overriding faith in the capability of civilization to engender change and further progress, characterized much of the century. Algerian society appeared static in comparison. It was internally stable, with no upheavals necessitating radical redefinitions of society, and such dislocation as it did undergo during this period was not self-generated but the result of practices and policies imposed by the French as an occupational force. Social feuding in the two societies was also seen to be different, for in Algeria it was supposed not to have assumed the abstract structure it had in France. Social clashes took the form of inter-tribal vendettas rather than political or class opposition. In tribal vendettas conflict resolution was achieved by physical aggression, and bloodshed was usually a prerequisite for success. In political and class opposition, where physical violence had been sublimated and verbal aggression was considered the norm, the recourse to bloodshed was an aberration and a sign of the failure of conventional modes of conflict resolution. The basic human reasons behind social feuding in the respective societies may have been the same, but each was regulated differently. These differences emphasized the perception of Algerian society as static and traditional, or even primitive, and French society as progressive and modern. Distinction was not made in this case between Arab and Kabyle, although by advocating the assimilation of the latter the underlying assumption was that Kabyle society had the potential to be made progressive whereas Arab society did not.

In a situation where two culturally dissimilar groups of people cohabit in social or political inequality, therefore, the composite negative and positive images that emerge have underlying precepts conditioned by value differences as perceived by the dominant group. The metaphors and cue-words vital to the formation of binary stereotypes, however, are usually circumstantial. In Algeria the underlying precepts had their ideological source in the Revolution, and were thus conditioned by republican goals. The metaphors and cue-words, on the other hand, spontaneously emerged from the circumstances of conquest and occupation within the colony. Warfare, reconnaissance and the need for security created points of reference by formalizing adjectival and nominal terms and fixing them as sociological categories. Mountain, plain, sedentary, nomad became metaphors for Berber (Kabyle) or Arab. In this way mountain came to be identified with resistance, intensive labour, individuality and an independent frame of mind; an environment in which the constrictive forces of religion and power were less likely to take hold and primitive forms of democracy were more likely to be present. In contrast the plain was identified with a collective society whose religion and power structures were coercive and feudal. 'Sedentary' and 'nomad' became similarly value-laden, representing stages of civilization with concomitant cultural, social, political and moral implications rather than definitions of economically determined lifestyles.

The creation of sociological categories is a necessary step in the process of racial discrimination. These categories, when they become racial cue-words, serve to evoke instantly the complete negative or positive gamut. Although they are often readily accepted in the field or on a popular level, it is their incorporation into polemical works and scholarly literature that constitutes a major step in the transformation from a limited, and hence more benign, racial differentiation to a dogma which uses race as an organizing principle of society. It must be said, however, that the initial incorporation of racial categories or cue-words into scholarly work is by no means an indication of racism, in the modern sense of the word. Certainly it was not in Algeria, where the scholarly predilections of the officers inclined them to contribute their opinions to scholarly journals or to participate in learned societies with the intention of fulfilling the desire for information on overseas territories and the fascination with exotica that was beginning to grip the metropolis. None the less by providing material on hitherto little-known peoples the officer-scholars did contribute, however inadvertently, to the emerging debate on race.

Algeria under military rule set the course for the emergence of racial patterns of thought in the colony. The decision, in 1848, to divide the colony into three departments established it as part of the metropolis and signalled the official sanction of the colonial enterprise. Shortly afterwards the boom began in the establishment of scholarly societies, both in France and in the colony. The statistics, monographs, descriptions and reports which emanated from the colony as of the mid-1840s created the need, on a practical level, for centres of classification and, on an intellectual level, for discussion and debate. Scholarly institutions centralized this material according to discipline and provided suitable venues for debate. Interest in the indigenous population thus became institutionalized in ethnological and anthropological societies. Once established, these institutions were in a position to dictate the form the continuing quest for material was to take. Hence the material that had initially served to stimulate interest in the metropolis became conditioned and eventually shaped by the same interest. This implied a change in perspective and a shift in the focal point of investigation from the pragmatic concerns of the colonial administration to the abstract concerns of metropolitan intellectuals and scholars. It was during this shift that material that was not overtly racial was drawn into and became part of the panoply of racial thought.

Conclusion

The intellectual exchange between Algeria and the metropolis under the military was dynamic in both directions. The military first awakened and then sustained an interest in the colonial enterprise. The conquest and occupation of Algeria placed it on the political agenda in France. This drew attention to the area, making it a centre of interest which was then maintained by the scholarly activities of military officers. Primary material, gathered under the intellectual aegis of and in accordance with the circumstantial needs of the military, went from the colony to France, where it was analysed in the light of current intellectual developments. The ensuing interpretations found their way back to the colony to be incorporated into further research on the indigenous population. The emergence of race as an accepted starting point for a certain type of intellectual analysis meant that abstract concepts allied with this way of thought were introduced into the colony and were used to substantiate the social, cultural and political incompatibilities within the colony's multi-ethnic population produced by the colonial situation. This was an essential part of the intellectual legacy military rule bequeathed to the civilians.

As a study in prejudice, stereotyping and the formation of racial images, Algeria is interesting because the span of colonial occupation encompassed two distinctive sorts of rule: military and civilian. In some ways they were similar. Both functioned within the same occupying state, necessitating the need to form an identity as an occupying force. Identity formation for both had its ideological parameters grounded in French republican values, but whereas under the military the positive and negative images involved in category formation were conditioned by the republican images *of France*, under the civilians they developed into the republican images *of Algeria*, that is to say the positive category became the image of the settler and the negative the image of the indigenous society as a whole. It was the intrinsic differences between military and civilian rule and society which dictated the extension of these images and the way in which they were used. The characteristics of the military epoch, relevant to image formation, were the custodial nature of its rule and its socially secure society: a self-contained society with a well-established hierarchy within the larger framework of French society. It was able, therefore, to envisage the inclusion of those members of indigenous society who could conform to its values. In contrast the civilian period was marked by proprietorial rule and the presence of a polyglot, multi-ethnic society, with no previously established hierarchy, made up of immigrants from the shores of the countries along the Northern Mediterranean, many of whose identity with France was purely idealistic. As a largely immigrant society it was socially and economically insecure, its non-

French members having to rely on their enterprise as a means of establishing their position, rather than on their education, their class or, as in the case of the military, their rank. Some were as unfamiliar with French culture as the Arabs and Kabyles, and yet to become part of the settler society they had to identify with French values rather than with indigenous ones. This forced an exclusively European image of the Self.

The evolution of positive and negative images and their simultaneous formation into categories was dependent on several factors and was gradual, for the paradigms of settler control emerged during the last three decades of the nineteenth century. To some extent there was an overlap in ideas between the custodial form of rule that had gone before and the emergence of a fully fledged proprietorial form of rule in which settler interests, political and economic, achieved the upper hand. That the Kabyles continued to be championed in certain situations was therefore natural enough. Demands for increased indigenous labour, for example, gave rise to a situation where Kabyles rather than Arabs could be solicited as workers. However, the transformation of the agricultural economy in the colony from a subsistence economy largely in the hands of the indigenous population to a market-oriented economy in the hands of the settlers meant a loss of status on the part of indigenous subsistence farmers, as they were driven off their land by sequestration and acquisitions and were obliged to join an itinerant labour force. (In this respect the Kabyles suffered more, during this period, than the Arabs, due, on the one hand, to punitive land seizure in Kabylia following the 1871 insurrection – the first large-scale appropriation in the area – and, on the other, to the fact that the pastoral Arabs had already lost most of their land.) This loss of status, although through no fault of their own, engendered a loss of respect and facilitated the process of marginalization. Superior to the Arab or not, the Kabyle was still an *indigène* and this placed him beneath the settler in any nascent social hierarchy.

Social hierarchy had, of course, much to do with the emergence of racial determinism as a mechanism of control and a means of maintaining the status quo. All societies spontaneously establish a hierarchy based on prevailing notions of elitism. The determinants of class can be inflexible (birth) or elastic (merit, education, financial success), depending on the nature of the society and the degree to which social mobility is a requisite for maintaining the dynamism of the existing elites. In colonial Algeria, to preserve the political and economic dominance of the settlers the elite classes had to remain European. The spontaneous mechanism to maintain such a status quo and yet allow for the social mobility so necessary to the formation of a new society, was a duality of inflexible and elastic determinants. Race became the inflexible determinant that indefinitely separated the indigenous and settler sectors of the population, while education, merit and financial success allowed for social mobility within the two sectors. In the same way as an absolute monarch elevated a worthy vassal from one class into another, thus enhancing his birthright, so individuals from the indigenous population could be and were assimilated into the settler population, but the *évolué* class remained small, with little autonomous power. Although the Kabyles found themselves on the wrong side of the divide with regard to the settlers, they could be, and on occasion indeed were, championed over the Arabs. The Kabyle Myth certainly persisted but it was no longer relevant to the practical evolution of colonial society.

The notion of race in Algeria under civilian rule was predominantly a cultural one. Physical anthropologists continued to accumulate statistical data on skeletal and body measurements in an endeavour to draw some sort of definitive conclusion on the population inhabiting the colony, but it was not such measurements that were considered the determinants in the evaluation of the 'new Mediterranean race'. Its physical attributes, a vital component of the racial panoply, were palpable not visible: virility and endurance rather than colouring or facial form. Indeed to have considered the latter two as paramount would have been embarrassing, there being little physically to distinguish Kabyles and Arabs from the settlers. Vigour and enterprise, measured in terms of economic and sexual prowess, and a healthy hedonism were the distinguishing traits of this 'new race', seen by *fin de siècle* pessimists preoccupied with French decadence and demographic decline as a potential force for the rejuvenation of the former and the reversal of the latter.[8] If this was to be the relationship between colony and mother country the indigenous population would not be called upon to play a role. A clear racial distinction had to be maintained between the settler and indigenous population, and if this could not be done physically it had to be done culturally. The choice of Rome and the ancient Christian Church in North Africa as the intellectual and cultural antecedents of the Mediterranean race effectively shut out Islam and excluded all members of the indigenous population who were not prepared to embrace French culture and its heritage. This enabled strict control of indigenous integration into mainstream settler society, the sort of control military society had been able to maintain due to its endogenous nature.

Tracing the emergence, evolution and decline of the Kabyle Myth has illustrated the components inherent to identity formation in a colonial situation and the way in which differing factors can change the focus of the process. Its ramifications were more complex than implied by the simple binary opposition of good Kabyle/bad Arab. It was not just a convenient political tool but part of the panoply of a colonial identity mythology that established ethnic and racial patterns of dominance in the colony. That it was part of an identity mythology endowed it with a staying power that enabled it to be transformed in the post-colonial era into a historical memory of significance. It is the historical memory, shorn of the origins of its existence, that has continued to stimulate interest. The positive aspect of the myth has undoubtedly made it central to that interest, but it is its negative aspect, namely the denigration of Islam and the Arab, that has made it relevant historically. The Kabyle Myth is an exceptionally well documented example of stereotyping and image-making and it is here, above all, that its importance lies.

Notes

Introduction

1. Lucette Valensi, *On the Eve of Colonialism. North Africa before the French Conquest*, N.Y., Africana, 1977 (translated by K.J. Perkins; first published in 1969), p. 7. Records contemporary to conquest put the figure at about 2 m.
2. Ibid.
3. Ismaël Urbain, 'Les Kabyles du Djurdjura', *Revue de Paris*, March 1857, Vol. 36, pp. 91–110, 100.
4. Jean Morizot, *l'Algérie kabylisée*, Paris, Peyronnet, 1962, p. 32.
5. Ibid. See also Hugh Roberts, *Algerian Socialism and the Kabyle Question*, Monographs in Development Studies no. 8, University of East Anglia, 1981, p. 28.
6. Morizot, 1962, p. 32.
7. Ibid., p. 34.
8. Emile Masqueray, 'Impressions de voyage. La Kabylie. Le pays berbère', *Revue politique et littéraire*, 1876, vol. XVII, pp. 177–83.
9. Charles Tailliart, *L'Algérie dans la littérature française. Essai de bibliographie méthodique et raisonnée jusqu'à 1924*, Paris, Champion, 1925.
10. The best general history of the period is *Histoire de l'Algérie contemporaine*, 2 Vols, Paris, P.U.F., 1979 (Vol. I, Charles-André Julien, *La Conquête et les débuts de la Colonisation 1827–1871*; Vol. II, Charles-Robert Ageron, *De l'Insurrection de 1871 au déclenchement de la guerre de libération (1954)*).
11. Annie Rey-Goldzeiguer, 'La France coloniale de 1830 à 1870' in *Histoire de La France Coloniale* (Jean Meyer et al.) 2 Vols, Paris, Armand Colin, 1991, Vol. I, pp. 547–8.
12. Assimilation and association in relation to the subject matter of this book are discussed in Chapter 8. For the evolution of the theory of Assimilation and Association in general see Raymond F. Betts, *Assimilation and Association in French Colonial Theory 1890–1914*, New York, Columbia University Press, 1961.
13. Annie Rey-Goldzeiguer, *Le Royaume Arabe, La Politique Algérienne de Napoleon III 1861–1870*, Alger, S.N.E.D., 1977, p. 427.
14. For details of these reforms and other assimilatory measures see Ageron, *Histoire de l'Algérie Contemporaine*, pp. 19–38. For their impact on Algerian Muslims see his *Les Algériens Musulmans et la France (1871–1919)*, 2 Vols, Paris, PUF, 1968.
15. Ibid., p. 38.
16. Ibid., pp. 33–8.
17. Ibid.
18. Saint-Simon and his disciples. See Frank E. Manuel, *Prophets of Paris*, Cambridge, Harvard University Press, 1962.

19. 'La France a-t-elle eu une politique Kabyle ?', *Revue Historique*, Vol. 223–4, 1960, pp. 311–2; 'La politique kabyle sous le Second Empire', *Revue française d'Histoire d'Outre Mer*, Vol. 52, no. 186, 1965, pp. 67–105; 'Du mythe kabyle aux politiques berbères', *Mal de Voir (Cahiers Jussieu 2)*, Paris, Union Générale d'Edition, 1976, pp. 331–48. See also chapters on Kabylia and Kabyle Policy in *Les Algériens musulmans et la France* and 'La politique Berbère 1871–1914' (Chapter 1, Book III) in *Histoire de l'Algérie contemporaine*.

20. 'Du mythe kabyle aux politiques berbères', pp. 333–47.

21. Discussed below.

22. Camille Lacoste, *Bibliographie Ethnologique de la Grande Kabylie*, Paris, Mouton, 1962; Camille Lacoste-Dujardin, 'Genèse et évolution d'une représentation géopolitique: L'imagerie kabyle à travers la production bibliographique de 1840 à 1891', in *Connaissances du Maghreb. Sciences sociales et Colonisation* (ed. Jean-Claude Vatin et al.), Paris, CNRS, 1984, pp. 257–77.

23. Fanny Colonna, *Instituteurs Algériens 1883–1939*, Travaux Recherches de Science Politique, no. 36, Paris, Chirat, 1975.

24. Edmund Burke III, 'The image of the Moroccan State in French ethnological literature: A new look at the origin of Lyautey's Berber policy', in *Arabs and Berbers, From Tribe to Nation in North Africa* (ed. E. Gellner and C. Micaud), Lexington, MA., Lexington Books, 1972, pp. 175–99; Gianni Albergoni et François Pouillon, 'Le fait berbère et la lecture coloniale: l'extrême sud tunisien', in *Mal de Voir*, pp. 349–96; William B. Quandt, 'The Berbers in the Algerian Political Elite', pp. 285–303; Jeanne Favret, 'Traditionalism through ultra-modernism', pp. 307–24, all in *Arabs and Berbers*.

25. Norman Daniel, *Islam and the West: The Making of an Image*, Edinburgh, University Press, 1962 (first published 1960); and *Islam, Europe and Empire*, Edinburgh, University Press, 1966; Christopher Harrison, *France and Islam in West Africa, 1860–1960*, Cambridge, Cambridge University Press, 1988; Lisa Lowe, *Critical Terrains. French and British Orientalisms*, Cornell, Ithaca, 1991; Edward Said, *Orientalism*, New York, Vintage Books, 1979; Edmund Burke III, 'The first crisis of Orientalism, 1890–1914', in *Connaissances du Maghreb*, pp. 213–26; J.W. Fück, 'Islam as an Historical Problem in European Historiography since 1800', in *Historians of the Middle East*, B. Lewis and P.M. Holt (eds), London, Oxford University Press, 1962, pp. 303–14.

26. A.S. Kanya-Forstner, *The Conquest of the Western Sudan. A Study in French Military Imperialism*, London, Cambridge University Press, 1969, p. 20.

1 The conquest: Kabyles and Arabs in warfare

1. Charles-André Julien, *Histoire de l'Algérie Contemporaine. Tome I. La conquête et les débuts de la colonisation (1827–1871)*, 2 Vols, Paris, P.U.F., 1986 (first published 1966. The second volume [1871–1954] is by Charles-Robert Ageron), Vol. I, p. 179–80. [There were four main brotherhoods in Algeria: the Qadiriya, the Derkawa, the Tidjania and the Rahmaniya. The Qadiriya was one of the leading urban orders of Islam. It was among the most tolerant and progressive of the Islamic orders, being distinguished by philanthropy, piety, humility and its aversion to fanaticism (H.A.R. Gibb, *Mohammedanism*, New York, Oxford, 1970, p. 106); an irony in view of the attitudes the French were to assume].

2. Julien, 1986, p. 270.

3. A.E.H. Carette, *Etudes sur la Kabilie proprement dite*, Paris, Imprimerie nationale, 1848, 2 Vols, p. 490, Vol. I. Carette estimated that there were 47 inhabitants per square kilometre in Kabylia.

4. Anon, *Journal d'un Officier de l'Armée d'Afrique*, Paris, Anselin, 1831, p. 11.

5. See Colonel F. Ribourt, *Le Gouvernement de l'Algérie de 1852 à 1858*, Paris, Panckoucke, 1859, p. 20.

6. Charles Tailliart, *L'Algérie dans la littérature française*, Paris, Librairie de la Société d'Histoire, 1925, p. 48.

7. *Journal d'un Officier de l'Armée d'Afrique*, p. 58.

8. Ibid., p. 51.

9. Ibid., p. 11.

10. Ibid., p. 38.

11. E. Lapène, *Vingt-Six Mois à Bougie*, Paris, Anselin, 1839, p. 197

12. Honoré Fisquet, *Histoire de l'Algérie depuis les temps anciens jusqu'à nos jours. Publiée d'après les Ecrits et les Documents les plus officiels*, Paris, Baudouin, 1842, pp. 7–8.

13. Roger Germain, *La Politique Indigène de Bugeaud*, Paris, Larose, 1955, p. 187.

14. p. 31 Général de Rumigny, 'De l'établissement de colonies militaires Kabaïles en Algérie', *Le Spectateur Militaire*, Vol. 49, 1850, pp. 31–53. (The February Days (22, 23 and 24), which culminated with the the abdication of Louis-Philippe, triggered the collapse of the July Monarchy.)

15. Pascal Duprat, 'Une Guerre Insensée. Expédition contre les Kabyles ou Berbers de l'Algérie', *Revue Indépendante*, pp. 242–56, Vol. 19, 1845, pp. 248–9.

16. Lapène, *Vingt-Six Mois à Bougie*, pp. 138–9.

17. *Spécimen Colonial de l'Algérie. Résumé, Réfutation ou Complément des systèmes de MM. Leblanc de Prébois, l'Abbé Landmann, de La Moricière, Bedeau et Bugeaud*, Paris, Moquet, 1847, pp. 40 and 12.

18. Edouard Lapène, 'Tableau Historique de l'Algérie depuis l'occupation Romaine jusqu'à la conquête par les Français en 1830', *Mémoires de l'Académie Royale de Metz*, XXVe année, 1843–44, pp. 158–244, p. 158.

19. Op. cit., p. 177; see also pp. 186–92.

20. Ibid., p. 123.

21. Mosse and Poliakov have already indicated the importance the *Germania* assumed as of the seventeenth century to link German virtues to those of the Aryan forefathers. George L. Mosse, *Toward the Final Solution. A History of European Racism*, Madison, University of Wisconsin Press, 1985 (first published 1978), p. 48; Léon Poliakov, *The Aryan Myth. A History of Racist and Nationalist Ideas in Europe* (translated by Edmund Howard), London, Sussex University Press, 1974 (first published 1971), p. 46.

22. Adolphe J.C.A. Dureau de la Malle, *L'Algérie* (Histoire des guerres des Romains, des Byzantins et des Vandales, accompagnée d'Examens sur les moyens employés anciennement pour la conquête et la soumission de la portion de l'Afrique septentrionale nommée aujourd'hui l'Algérie), Paris, Firmin Didot, 1852, p. 30.

23. Ibid., p. 38.

24. M. Rozet, *Voyage dans la Régence d'Alger ou Description du Pays occupé par l'armée française en Afrique*, Paris, Arthus Bertrand, 1833, pp. 9, 29, 32.

25. *Journal d'un Officier de l'Armée d'Afrique*, pp. 84–5 (1831).

26. *Vingt-Six Mois à Bougie*, p. 117.

27. Ibid., pp. 117–18.

28. p. 131, 'Première Lettre sur l'Algérie (23 Juin 1837)' in *Ecrits et Discours Politiques, Vol. III, Œuvres Complètes*, Paris, Gallimard, 1962. The two letters on Algeria were originally published in the journal *La Presse de Seine-et-Oise*. His sources for this information are uncertain. In preparation for his first trip to Algeria (May–June 1841) he read the published volumes of *Le Tableau de la situation des Etablissements français dans l'Algérie*. Publication did not commence until 1838 and continued until 1853. The ideas expressed in his letters would have been obtained elsewhere. Tocqueville was friendly with de La Moricière, who had had first-hand experience of the Kabyles, and an exchange of ideas between the two men on the subject may have taken place, but on this it is possible only to speculate. Relevant pre-conquest works which Tocqueville may have used included: Abbé Raynal, *L'Histoire philosophique et politique des établissements et du commerce des Européens dans l'Afrique septentrionale*, 2 Vols, published posthumously in 1826; William Shaler, *Esquisse de l'Etat d'Alger considéré sous les rapports politique, historique et civil*, Paris, Lavocat, 1830 (first published in Boston in 1826); Dr Thomas Shaw, *Voyage dans la Régence d'Alger*, Paris, Merlin, 1830 (Shaw's complete work, of which this was a section, was first published as *Travels and observations relating to several parts of Barbary and the Levant*, in 1738, and translated into French in 1743 as *Voyages en Barbarie*).

29. Ibid., pp. 132–3.

30. 'Seconde Lettre sur l'Algérie (22 Août 1837)', p. 146.

31. Tocqueville, 'Notes du Voyage en Algérie de 1841' (29 mai 1841) in *Œuvres Complètes*, Vol. V, Paris, Gallimard, 1958, p. 215. The entry for this date followed a meeting with Lieutenant-Colonel Picouleau, stationed at Djijelli.

32. Lapène, *Vingt-Six Mois à Bougie*, p. 93.

33. Lapène (ibid.) gives the number at 40,000.

34. Pelissier de Reynaud, *Annales Algériennes*, 3 Vols, Alger, Bastide, 1854, Vol. I, p. 305 (Livre XI).

35. '29 mai au soir' [1841], 'Notes du Voyage en Algérie', p. 215 [Constantine fell to the French in 1837].

36. Battalion leader of the *2e Chasseurs d'Afrique*, de Musis arrived in Bougie in April 1836. At the time of the assassination in August 1836 he was acting commanding officer of Bougie. Descriptions of the assassination are to be found in such varied works as: Pellisier de Reynaud, 1854; Lapène Op. cit.; Emile Carrey *Récits de Kabylie. Campagne de 1857*, Paris, Levy, 1858; Charles Farine *Kabyles et Kroumirs*, Paris, Ducrocq, 1882 (first published as *A Travers la Kabylie 1865*).

37. Pelissier de Reynaud, Vol. II, p. 110.

38. Lapène, *Vingt-Six Mois à Bougie*, pp. 124–5.

39. Pellissier de Reynaud, pp. 241–2.

40. Maréchal Comte Boniface de Castellane, *Journal du Maréchal de Castellane. 1804–1862*, 5 Vols, Paris, Plon, 1895–1897 [entry for 25 January 1838], Vol. 3 (1831–1847), pp. 153–4.

41. Germain, p. 18.

42. 1843 expedition to the Ouar-Senis-Chéliff valley; 1844 expedition to Dellys; 1844–45, 1846–47 marked the initial stages of penetration into Kabylia proper.

43. Comte Pierre de Castellane, *Souvenirs de la Vie militaire en Afrique*, Paris, Victor Lecou, 1852, p. 15 [Serialized in the *Revue des Deux Mondes* from July 1849 to July 1852 and translated into English in 1886].

44. Capitaine Leo Lamarque, 'La Kabylie', *Le Spectateur Militaire*, Vol. 39, 1845, pp. 314–27; 449–60. Lamarque (p. 317) estimates the required number at 15,000 [The original invading force was only 18,000 men rising to 108,000 men in 1846, on the eve of the first major campaign against Kabylia].

45. Tocqueville, in his 1847 report on Algeria, drew attention to the fact that the commissions set up to study Algerian affairs had all opposed such a scheme. He added that the majority of deputies felt likewise. *Œuvres complètes*, Vol. 3, p. 359. [Extra credits for Algeria had been under review since 1845, these being 14 million Francs destined to finance 22,000 extra men for the infantry and cavalry, to march against Kabylia.] Duprat, 1845, sets out the arguments against both granting the credits and the conquest of Kabylia in his article.

46. *La Kabylie. Recherches et Observations sur cette riche contrée de l'Algérie par un Colon établi à Bougie depuis les premiers jours d'octobre 1833*, Paris, Maistrasse & Wiart, 1846, p. 81. [The *colon* in question was M. Maffre; his was the first civilian account of Kabylia after the French landing. Nothing is known about Maffre beyond the fact that he lived in Bougie from 1833 onwards. Knowledge of his work, however, was more widespread.]

47. Pellissier de Reynaud, Vol. 3, p. 286.

48. Capitaine d'artillerie J. Brunet, 'Expéditions dans la Kabylie Centrale pendant l'automne de 1844', *Le Spectateur Militaire*, Vol. 39, 1845, pp. 44–89.

49. Ibid., pp. 87–8. See also 'Lettre n° 234 & Lettre n° 235, Expédition de 1847 en Kabylie', in *Campagnes d'Afrique 1835–1848. Lettres adressées au Maréchal de Castellane par les Maréchaux Bugeaud, Clauzel, Valée, et al.*, Paris, Plon, 1898, pp. 512, 516.

50. Maffre, p. 4.

51. *Du Ministère de la Guerre en 1850, et de l'Algérie en 1851*, Paris, Lib. Militaire de J. Dumaine, 1851, p. 100 (in late 1851, d'Hautpoul was a member of the *Assemblée Législative*, having held the posts of minister of war and governor of Algeria).

52. Ibid, p. 102.

53. General de Rumigny, p. 49.

54. In the early nineteenth-century French military tactical science was based on four formations: the marching column, the infantry square, the extended firing line and the assault column. While these were used early on in Algeria, the ability to switch from one tactical situation to another, in accordance with circumstances, required lengthy drilling and training. The disease that decimated troop numbers, necessitating a need for constant reinforcements, and the difficult climatic and topographical conditions rendered these tactics cumbersome. It was the introduction, by Bugeaud, of mobile strike columns based at a few large, well-stocked, strategically placed garrisons that turned the tide in favour of the French. No wagons were used, but columns were organized around pack mules and individual troop packs were reduced from 75 lbs to around 40–45 lbs. The columns, which carried enough provisions for seven to ten days, could inflict damage rapidly and withdraw as quickly. The *razzia*, based on Roman tactics of attacking the enemy's economic strength, was also adopted. This had the additional advantage for the French of providing them with victuals at no cost.

55. François Ducuing, 'La Guerre de Montagne', *Revue des Deux Mondes*, Part I: 'La Navarre et La Kabylie', Vol. 9, 1851, pp. 661–700 and Part II: 'La Kabylie', Vol. 10, 1851, pp. 225–74, p. 269.

56. Pierre de Castellane, p. 419 (campaign of 1843).
57. See for example p. 411.
58. The myths surrounding guerrillas and guerrilla warfare are complex and merit a study of their own. One need only contemplate the hagiography attached to Ernesto ('Che') Guervara (1928–67) in the 1960s and 1970s to realize their potency.
59. Brunet, p. 70. See also 'Lettre n° 156, Expédition en Kabylie' in *Campagnes d'Afrique*, p. 352.
60. *Vingt-Six Mois*, p. 237.
61. See Pierre de Castellane, pp. 419 and 430.
62. See Ducuing, Vol. 9, p. 662.
63. The metaphor of a nest is Duprat's: 'dans le nid même de leurs montagnes', p. 174.
64. Thomas R. Bugeaud de la Piconnerie, 'De la stratégie, de la tactique des retraites et du passage des défilés dans les montagnes des Kabyles', in *Par l'Epée et par la Charrue. Ecrits et Discours* (ed. P. Azan), Paris, PUF, 1948, pp. 110–11.
65. Ibid., pp. 117 and 112.
66. Brunet, pp. 52 and 81.
67. Ducuing, Vol. 9, p. 661.
68. Ibid., p. 663.
69. Ibid., (Vol. 10), pp. 233 and 255.
70. Ibid., pp. 227 and 232. The Kabyles, of course, never resigned themselves to defeat. The most consequential uprising of the nineteenth century was in 1871, resulting in extensive sequestration of Kabyle land. Sporadic revolts continued, however, as did passive resistance, especially in the form of forest fires. The latter often coincided with the imposition of colonial laws (e.g. the 1873 Land Law, or the 1881 law introducing the *Indigénat*). In the twentieth century, the 1945 Sétif (Petite Kabylie) uprising was the most significant before the war of independence, which started in the Berber region of the Aurès.
71. Ribourt, 1859, p. 20.
72. Ibid., p. 17.
73. A few examples of works in which comparisons to French peasantry occurred are: Jules Duval, 'Algérie. Population Indigène et Européenne', *Revue de l'Orient*, Vol 14, 1853, pp. 432–43. [It was Duval, a magistrate, who first compared them to the Auvergnats and the Savoyards.] Léo Lamarque, *De la Conquête et de la Colonisation de l'Algérie*, Paris, Ancelin, 1841 [Lamarque, who was an officer, compared them to Corsicans]. Henri Aucapitaine, *Les Kabyles et la Colonisation de l'Algérie*, Paris, Challamel, 1864. [Aucapitaine, who was also an officer, made no specific regional comparisons likening the Kabyles to the French peasant generally.]
74. Duprat, p. 247.
75. 'L'Algérie. Des moyens de conserver et d'utiliser cette conquête', in *Œuvres Militaires du Maréchal Bugeaud Duc d'Isly*, réunies et mises en ordre par Weil ancien capitaine de cavalerie, Paris, L. Baudoin, 1887 (the pamphlet first appeared in 1842).
76. 'Discours du Maréchal Bugeaud dans un banquet offert par la population d'Alger au comte de Salvandy, Ministère de l'instruction publique, le 16 juillet 1846', *Par l'Epée et par la Charrue*, p. 277.
77. 'Rapport sur l'Algérie 1847", *Œuvres completes*, Vol. III, p. 359.
78. Letter to Fourrichon, *Fonds Enfantin*, Vol. 7610, Document 50.

2 Security and reconnaissance part 1: The elaboration and confirmation of categories

1. Bugeaud, 'Du service des avant postes et des reconnaissances en Afrique', *Œuvres Militaires*, p. 85.
2. A.E.H. Carette, *Etudes sur la Kabilie Proprement dite*, 2 Vols, Paris, Imprimerie Nationale, 1848, p. 6 [4th and 5th volumes of *Exploration scientifique de l'Algérie pendant les années 1840, 1841, 1842*].
3. *Richesse minérale de l'Algérie*, Paris, Carilian-Gœury & Dalmont, 1850.
4. On this topic see: Robert A. Stafford, *Scientist of Empire: Sir Roderick Murchison, Scientific exploration and Victorian Imperialism*, Cambridge, Cambridge University Press, 1989; John M. Mackenzie, *Imperialism and the Natural World*, Manchester, Manchester University Press, 1990; Benedict Anderson, *Imagined Communities. Reflections on the Origin and Spread of Nationalism*, London, Verso, 1991.
5. Stafford, p. 207.
6. Mackenzie, p. 9.
7. Stafford, p. 1.
8. Ibid., p. 3.
9. Bugeaud, *Quelques réflexions sur trois questions fondamentales de notre établissement en Afrique*, Algiers, Besancenez, 1846, p. 25.
10. Bugeaud, 'L'Algérie. Des moyens ...', in *Œuvres militaires*, p. 272.
11. 'De l'établissement de légions de colons militaires dans les possessions françaises du Nord de l'Afrique', *Œuvres militaires*, p. 248.
12. Bugeaud to de Brossand, Tafna, 2 June 1837, Doc. 9, *Par l'Epée et par la Charrue*, p. 32.
13. J.J. Virey, *Histoire naturelle du genre humain*, 2 Vols, Paris, F. Dufait, 1800, Vol. I, p. 233.
14. Bugeaud 'Mémoire sur notre Etablissement dans la Province d'Oran par suite de la paix' (1837) *Œuvres militaires*, p. 199.
15. Bugeaud to Thiers, 5th August, 1836, Doc. 4, *Par l'Epée et par la Charrue*, p. 19.
16. 'Rapport sur la Colonisation. 12 Septembre 1850', p. 64.
17. Henri Aucapitaine, *Etudes sur le passé et l'avenir des Kabyles. Les Kabyles et la Colonisation de l'Algérie*, Paris, Challamel, 1864, p. 33 [emphasis added].
18. Dr. Eugène Bodichon, *Considérations sur l'Algérie*, Paris, Comptoir Central de la Librairie, 1845, pp. 103–4.
19. Annie Rey-Goldzeiguer, 'La France coloniale de 1830 à 1870' in Meyer et al., *L'Histoire de la France Coloniale*, Vol I, p. 762, footnote 84. [*Le National* was founded in 1830 as an Orleanist voice piece with the liberals Thiers and Mignet as editors. In 1832 Armand Carrel took over as editor and it became Republican. It was one of two leading newspapers during the February Revolution of 1848 to oppose the Bonapartist candidature, supporting that of Cavaignac.]
20. Annie Rey-Goldzeiguer, *Le Royaume Arabe. La Politique Algérienne de Napoleon III. (1861–1870)*, Alger, SNED, 1977, pp. 70.
21. In the early 1890s the indigenous question was once more publicly debated. Henri de Sarrauton, a civil servant serving in Algeria, summed up the debate as a choice between assimilation and elimination. *La Question Algérienne*, Oran, Perrier, 1891, pp. 3–4. Mme. Pierre Coeur, a pro-assimilationist, concluded her contribution

to the subject with the words 'assimiler ou détruire; être assimilé ou détruit'. *L'Assimilation des Indigènes musulmans*, Paris, Guédan, 1890.

22. Ibid., p. 102.

23. *Discours prononcé par M. de Lamartine, Deputé du Nord (Bergues) à la Chambre des Deputés sur Alger le 2 mai 1834*, Paris, Imprimerie de Petit, 1834.

24. *L'Algérie*, pp. 37–8.

25. 'Des Diverses Races qui peuplent l'Algérie' in *Revue de l'Orient*, Vol. 6, 1845, pp. 347–61, p. 357.

26. M. Canton, 'Algérie. Industrie des huiles', *Revue de l'Orient de l'Algérie et des Colonies*, pp. 139–45, Vol. 8, 1850, pp. 140–41.

27. e.g. Aucapitaine, p. 46.

28. Other members relevant to this thesis were Louis-Adrien Berbrugger (1801–69), Saint-Simonian; Charles-Henri E. Brosselard (1816–89); Captain (later Colonel) A. Ernest H. Carette (1808–90) *Polytechnicien* and Saint-Simonian; Prosper Enfantin (1796–1864), *Polytechnicien* and Saint-Simonian; Henri Fournel (1801–76), *Polytechnicien* and Saint-Simonian; Captain (later General) L.J. Adolphe C.C. Hanoteau (1814–97), *Polytechnicen;* Captain (later General) F. Edouard de Neveu (1809–71), Saint-Simonian; Captain Edmond Pellissier de Reynaud (1800–58); Baron W. M.-G. de Slane (1801–78); J.A.N. Perier (1809–80); Dr Auguste H. Warnier (1810–75), Saint-Simonian.

29. Marcel Emerit, *Les Saint-Simoniens en Algérie*, Paris, Les Belle Lettres, 1941, p. 175.

30. The Treaty of Tafna signed by Abd-el-Kader and the French in 1837 put a temporary end to combat but it was broken in 1838. War ensued in 1840, only coming to an end with Abd-el-Kader's surrender in 1847, to be followed soon thereafter by the conquest of Kabylia.

31. Bory de Saint-Vincent, 'Sans adresse, Alger 10 Août 1840', *Supplément à la Correspondance de Bory de Saint-Vincent*, publiée et annotée par Philippe Lauzun, Agen, Imp. Moderne, 1912, p. 65. [The letter was addressed to his life-long friend, Dr Léon Dufour at Saint-Sever (Landes).]

32. The works produced in its context fell under five headings: I. *Sciences historiques et géographiques*, II. *Sciences médicales*, III. *Physique générale*, IV. *Sciences physiques. Zoologie, Botanique, Géologie*, V. *Archéologie et beaux-arts*.

33. J. Alazard, E. Albertini, F. Braudel, et al., *Histoire et Historiens de l'Algérie. Collection du Centenaire de l'Algérie. Vol IV*, Paris, Alcan, 1931, pp. 7–8.

34. Johann Gottfried Herder, *Über den Ursprung der Sprache* (1772); Georges de Cuvier, 'Variétés de l'espèce humaine', *Le règne animal* (1817); James Cowles Prichard, *Researches into the Physical History of Mankind* (1818) and *The Natural History of Man* (1843, translated into French the same year). Frédéric-Gustave Eichhoff, *Parallèle des langues de l'Europe et de l'Inde*, Paris, 1836; Jacob Grimm, *Histoire de la Langue allemande*, (translated) Paris, 1848; Ernest Renan, *Histoire des langues sémitiques*, Paris, 1855; Franz Bopp, *Grammaire comparée des langues indo-européennes*, (translated) Paris 1866–74, 5 Vols.

35. Anderson, p. 71.

36. Dr Walter Oudney, *Berber Alphabet* (1822); W.B. Hodgson, 'Memoire on the Berber Language' in the *Transactions of the American Philosophical Society* (1834); J. H. Delaporte, 'Vocabulaire Berbère' in the *Journal Asiatique* (1836); Warden, 'Esquisse du système grammatical de la langue bérbère' in the *Bulletin de la Société de Géographie de Paris* (1836).

37. Kenneth J. Perkins, *Quaids, Captains and Colons*, NY, Africana, 1981, p. 61.

38. *Dictionnaire Français-Berbère*. (Dialecte écrit et parlé par les Kabaïles de la Guerre), Paris, Imprimerie Royale, 1844; *Grammaire et Dictionnaire abrégé de la langue berbère*, Paris, Imprimerie Royale, 1844. (The members of the commission were Amédée Jaubert (President), J.D. Delaporte (interpreter), E. de Nully (from the Ministry of War), Charles Brosselard (former civil servant at the commissariats of Bougie and Blidah), and Sidi Ahmed ben el Hadj Ali (Imam of Bougie).)

39. H. Aucapitaine, 'Etudes recéntes. Les Dialectes Berbères de l'Algérie', *Nouvelles Annales des Voyages de la Géographie, de l'Histoire, et de l'Archéologie*, Vol. 2, 6th series, 1859, pp. 170–92, p. 171.

40. Carette, pp. 60–61.

41. Ibid., p. 62.

42. Ibid., pp. 69–70.

43. Ibid., p. 3.

44. J. Berque, in 'Cent Vingt-Cinq Ans de Sociologie Maghrébine', *Annales E.S.C.*, Vol. 11, 1956, pp. 296–324, claims that many of the acquired historical assumptions on the Maghreb can be traced to Carette's works (p. 304).

45. Carette, p. 217. (There were six books in the first volume. The second volume is divided into 16 sections, and is discussed below.)

46. Ibid., pp. 341–51.

47. Julien, pp. 158.

48. Louis de Baudicour, *La Colonisation de l'Algérie*, Paris, Lecoffre, 1856, p. 191.

49. Suggestions for the mass importation of labour were diverse and included Maronites from Lebanon, Annamites from the Indochinese peninsula, and Jews from Russia. More fanciful was the proposition to use poor orphans as a possible alternative: Edouard de Tocqueville (Conseiller-général de l'Oise), *Des enfants trouvés et des orphelins pauvres comme moyen de colonisation de l'Algérie*, Paris, Amyot, 1850; L'abbé Landmann, *Colonisation de l'Algérie par les enfants trouvés*, Paris, 1853.

50. Carette, p. 491.

51. Ibid., pp. 142–4.

52. Ibid., p. 83.

53. Ibid., p. 172.

54. An indication of Carette's debt to prevailing military thought for his own ideas can be obtained by a close reading of the government publication *Exposé de l'Etat actual de la Société arabe, du gouvernement et de la législation qui la régit*, Alger, Imprimerie du Gouvernement, 1844 (drawn up by the Director of Arab Affairs under orders from Bugeaud) and of General F.F. Duvivier's *Solution de la Question de l'Algérie*, Paris, Gaultier, Lagouonie, 1841.

55. The three works on Kabylia that preceded Carette's were Capitain Lapène's (*Vingt-Six Mois*, 1839); le colon Maffre's (*La Kabylie*, 1846); and General Daumas and Capitain Faber, *La Grande Kabylie. Etudes historiques*, Paris, Hachette, 1847.

56. President du Conseil, Ministre Secrétaire d'Etat de la Guerre, à M. Enfantin, Paris, le 22 Novembre 1842, *Fonds Enfantin*, Vol. 7610, Doc. 11.

57. An early positive review written by Cavaignac appeared in a two-part article appearing in *La Revue Indépendante*, Vols 7 and 8, 1843, pp. 193–227 and 321–30 respectively. For the impact of Enfantin's work see Marcel Emerit, *Les Saint-Simoniens en Algérie*, Paris, Les Belles Lettres, 1941, p. 123.

58. *La Colonisation d'Algérie*, Paris, Bertrand, 1843, p. 145.

59. Ibid., p. 174.

60. 'Introduction' *Revue Africaine*, Vol. I, 1856, p. 8. [Berbrugger was a member of the Scientific Commission, as were de Slane and de Neveu, also members of the Société Historique Algérienne.]

3 Security and reconaissance part 2:
Islam and society

1. 'Travail sur l'Algérie (Octobre 1841)', *O.C.*, Vol. III, p. 220.
2. See p. vii. (Extracts were also published under the title: 'Des Diverses races qui peuplent l'Algérie' in the *Revue de l'Orient*, Vol. 6, 1845, pp. 347–61.)
3. Ibid., pp. v and vii.
4. Quoted by Jardin, Introduction to *O.C.*, Vol. III, p. 25.
5. Between 1830 and 1890 anti-clericalism in the French army was pronounced and in personal beliefs religious indifference prevailed until the end of the nineteenth century. See William Serman, *Les Officiers Français dans la Nation 1848–1914*, Paris, Aubier Montaigne, 1982, Chapters 5 and 6.
6. *Exposé de l'état actuel de la société arabe*, p. 49.
7. Ibid., pp. 45–6.
8. Ibid., p. 15.
9. The second edition appeared in 1846 and the third in 1913.
10. *Les Khouans. Ordres Religieux chez les Musulmans de l'Algérie*, Paris, A. Guyot, 1845, p. 15.
11. Ibid., p. 78.
12. Norman A. Daniel, *Islam, Europe and Empire*, Edinburgh, Edinburgh University Press, 1966, p. 157.
13. For the progression of this idea see F.F. Manuel, *The Prophets of Paris*, Cambridge, Harvard University Press, 1962, p. 277 and M.A.P. d'Avezac-Macaya, *Esquisse générale de l'Afrique et Afrique Ancienne* in *l'Univers, Histoire et Description de tous le peuples, de leurs Religions, Mœurs, Industrie, Coutumes, etc.*, Paris, Firmin Didot, 1844, p. 23.
14. de Neveu, p. 64.
15. Ibid., p. 105.
16. Ibid., pp. 109–10.
17. Commandant Louis Marie Rinn, *Marabouts et Khouans, Etude sur l'Islam en Algérie*, Alger, Jourdan, 1884. Charles Brosselard, *préfet* of Oran, published a 36-page pamphlet entitled *Les Khouans. De la constitution des ordres religieux musulmans en Algérie*, Alger, Bourget, 1859. It was along the lines of de Neveu's work, underlining the danger of the brotherhoods and the need to oppose them.
18. A. Cochut, 'Les Khouans. Mœurs religieuses de l'Algérie. *Revue des Deux Mondes* (Belgian edition), Vol. 10, 15 mai 1846, pp. 328–45.
19. *Etudes sur la Kabilie*, Vol. I, p. 477–9.
20. Colonel Trumelet, *Les Saints de l'Islam, légendes hagiologiques et croyances musulmanes algériennes. Les saints du Tell.* Paris, Didier, 1881.
21. H. Aucapitaine, 'Origine arabe des fractions de Marabouts dans les confédérations kabyles', *Nouvelles Annales des Voyages de la Géographie de l'Histoire et de l'Archéologie*, Vol. I, 6th series, 1859, pp. 170–73, (also published under the title 'Origine des fractions de marabouts dans les populations K'baïles' in the *Revue de L'Orient, de l'Algérie et des Colonies*, Vol X, 1859, pp. 471–3); M. Gueymard, 'Le

marabout de la Zaouïa de Chellata', *Revue de L'Orient et de l'Algérie*, Vol. XII, 1852, pp. 5–7.

22. Dr Baudens, *Relation de l'Expédition de Constantine*, Paris, L.B. Baillière, 1838, p. 56.

23. E.M.J. Daumas and Capitain Fabar, *La Grande Kabylie. Etudes historiques*, Paris, Hachette, 1847, p. 55.

24. *Vingt-Six Mois*, p. 139 (The 'Tableau Historique, Moral et Politique sur Les Kabyles' from which this is a quotation, formed the second part of Lapène's volume and was reprinted separately in the *Mémoires de l'Académie Royale de Metz*, 1845, pp. 225–87).

25. *Etudes sur la Kabilie*, Vol. I, p. 474.

26. Aucapitaine, p. 171.

27. Similar conclusions were drawn in West Africa. See Christopher Harrison, *France and Islam in West Africa, 1860–1960*, Cambridge, Cambridge University Press, 1988, p. 42.

28. Serman, pp. 68–9; 95.

29. Ibid., p. 70.

30. *The Passionate Nomad. The Diary of Isabelle Eberhardt*, (translated by Nina de Voogd. Edited and introduced by Rana Kabbani), London, Virago, 1987, p. viii. See also Annette Kobak, *Isabelle, The Life of Isabelle Eberhardt*, NY, Vintage, 1990, pp. 213–14 and Julia Clancy-Smith, 'The "Passionate Nomad" reconsidered. A European Woman in *L'Algérie Française* (Isabelle Eberhardt, 1877–1904)' in *Western Women and Imperialism. Complicity and Resistance*, Napur Chaudhuri and Margaret Strobel (eds), Bloomington, Indiana University Press, 1992, pp. 61–78, pp. 70–72.

31. Ernest Gellner, 'The unknown Apollo of Biskra: The social base of Algerian puritanism', in *Muslim Society*, Cambridge, Cambridge University Press, 1985 (first published 1981), p. 158.

32. See for example Henri Verne, *La France en Algérie*, Paris, C. Douniol and Challamel Ainé, 1869, p. 31.

33. Daumas (with Fabar) *La Grande Kabylie*, p. 77.

34. Auguste Warnier, *L'Algérie devant l'Empereur*, Paris, Challamel Ainé, 1865, p. 15.

35. L'Abbé Charmetant, *Les peuplades kabyles et les tribus nomades du Sahara*, Montréal, La Minerve, 1875.

36. As will be remembered, the opening paragraph (p. vii) of the *Exposé de l'état actuel de la société arabe* concerned itself with this.

37. In addition to his major work on Kabylia produced with Faber (1847), Daumas's works include: *Exposé de l'état acuel de la société arabe*, Alger, 1844; *Mœurs et Coutumes de l'Algérie: Tell, Kabylie, Sahara*, Paris, Hachette, 1853; *La Vie arabe et la Société musulmane*, Paris, Levy, 1869; published posthumously: *La femme arabe*, Alger, Jourdan, 1912. In addition to his works on Kabylia Daumas also produced books on the Algerian Sahara, the Arab horse, the desert, and numerous articles on allied subjects.

38. Richard's works on Algeria include: *Etude sur l'insurrection du Dhara*, Alger, Besancenez, 1846; *Scènes et mœurs arabes*, Paris, Challamel, 1848; *Du gouvernement arabe et de l'institution qui doit l'excercer*, Alger, Bastide, 1848; *De l'esprit de la législation musulmane*, Alger, 1849; *De la civilisation du peuple arabe*; Alger, Dubois, 1850; *Les mystères du peuple arabe*, Paris, Challamel ainé, 1860. He also wrote poetry and numerous sociological and philosophical works on subjects unrelated to Algeria.

39. *La Vie Arabe et la Société musulmane*, p. 52.

40. *Les mystères du peuple arabe*, p. viii.

41. *Etude sur l'insurrection du Dhara* (1846), p. 146; *Les mystères du peuple arabe* (1860), p. xiii.

42. Daumas, *La vie arabe*, p. 50; Richard, *Les mystères du peuple arabe*, p. ix

43. Lamouroux, 'De la polygamie en Algérie', *Revue de l'Orient, de l'Algérie et des Colonies*, 1851, Vol. 10, pp. 41–4; Adrien Berbrugger, 'La polygamie musulmane; ses causes fatales et le moyen de la détruire', *Revue Africaine*, 1858–59, Vol 3, pp. 254–8.

44. Lamouroux, p. 41.

45. Ibid., p. 44.

46. Richard, pp. 7–8.

47. Richard, *Du gouvernement arabe*, p. 54.

48. *La Kabylie*, p. 6.

49. *Vingt-six mois à Bougie*, p. 132.

50. Maffre, p. 7.

51. *La Grande Kabylie. Etudes historiques*, pp. 40–43. See also C. Devaux, *Les Kabaïles de Djerdjera*, Paris, Challamel, 1859. Chapter VI is devoted to the Kabyle woman. Devaux, captain in the first regiment of the Zouaves and officer of the Bureaux Arabes, relied heavily on Daumas for his sources.

52. *Les Kabyles et la Colonisation de l'Algérie*, Paris, Challamel Ainé, 1864, p. 36.

53. *La vie arabe*, p. 309.

54. *Du gouvernement arabe*, p. 55.

55. Richard, in *De la civilisation du peuple arabe*, was particularly derogatory (p.8). A less condemnatory opinion was expressed by Prince Nicolas Bibesco in 'Les Kabyles du Djurjura', *Revue des Deux Mondes*, 1865, Vol 56, pp. 562–601, 951–76 and 1866, Vol. 57, pp. 862–97. Bibesco compared and contrasted the condition of Arab and Kabyle women. These images continued to appear, little changed, throughout the nineteenth century as can be seen from the work of Vicomte Amédée Caix de Saint-Aymour, *Questions Algériennes: Arabes et Kabyles*, Paris, Ollendorff, 1891. It was not until the end of the century that an attempt was made to situate the condition of women in the context of Islamic doctrine: Ernest Mercier, *La condition de la femme musulmane dans l'Afrique septentrionale*, Alger, Jourdan, 1895. Mercier's work, which was about Muslim women generally, was the first of several studies in this genre. Only in 1919 was an attempt made to redress the generally gloomy portrayal of the Arab woman in Algeria: Marie Bugjea, 'A travers l'Algérie. Impression de la femme musulmane', *Bulletin de la Société de Géographie de'Alger*, 1919, pp. 70–86, followed by *Nos sœurs musulmanes*, Paris, La revue des études littéraires, 1921, also by Bugjea.

56. Bibesco, Vol. 56, pp. 578–81.

57. Thomas Williams and James Calvert, *Fiji and the Fijians*, New York, G.S. Rowe, 1859.

58. G.W. Stocking, *Victorian Anthropology*, pp. 204–5.

59. Most notable among these were those by: Lt.-Gen. Bedeau, Gen. Bugeaud, Gen. Duvivier, Prosper Enfantin, L'abbé Landmann, Gen. de Lamoricière, Capt. Lapasset, Capt. Leblanc de Prébois, and Capt. Richard. In 1847 a discussion of some of these works appeared under the title: *Spécimen colonial de l'Algérie. Résumé, réfutation ou complément des systèmes de MM. Leblanc de Prébois, L'Abbé Landmann, de Lamoricière, Bedeau, et Bugeaud*, Paris, Moquet, 1847. [De Prébois' military

career came to an end with the publication in 1840 of his pamphlet 'Nécessité de substituer le gouvernement civil au gouvernement militaire'; a fervent advocate of assimilation, he was elected republican deputy for Algeria in 1848.]

60. *Annales Algériennes*, Vol. I, p. 303. (Publication of Pellissier's *Annales Algériennes* commenced in 1836. It was originally intended as a bi-annual review with a historical section and a section dealing with documents related to current events in Algeria, but it did not work out this way and publication was irregular. A corrected and revised collection of the material published between 1836 and the fall of Abd-el-Kader (1847) appeared in 1854.)

61. Ibid., footnote p. 304.

62. 'Des diverses races qui peuplent l'Algérie', *Revue de l'Orient*, 1845, Vol. 6, pp. 347–61, pp. 347, 350 and 354.

63. Ibid., pp. 357 and 360.

64. *Etudes sur la Kabilie*, Vol. I, p. 470.

65. Ibid., p. 479.

66. *La Kabylie*, Paris, Hachette, 1857, p. 11.

67. *Mœurs et coutumes de l'Algérie*, p. 15.

68. Daumas (with Fabar), *La Grande Kabylie*, p. 76.

69. Ibid., p. 75.

70. *Etudes sur le passé et l'avenir des Kabyles*, p. 11.

71. Ibid., footnote 1, and pp. 11–12.

72. For an amplification of Guizot's contribution and the ramifications of the debate see Chapter 2 of Léon Poliakov, *The Aryan Myth. A History of Racist and Nationalist Ideas in Europe* (trans. Edmund Howard), London, Sussex University Press, 1974 (first published 1971).

73. Vol. 56, pp. 570–71.

74. For a recent evaluation of Arab and Berber societies in the early nineteenth century see Lucette Valensi, *On the Eve of Colonialism*, trans. K.J. Perkins, NY, Africana, 1977 (first pub. 1969). Valensi shows that both were equally democratic. See especially pp. 16–20. See too Ernest Gellner, 'Flux and reflux in the faith of men' in *Muslim Society*, In his explanation of tribal societies in the Maghreb and Near East Gellner points out that labour-intensive societies tend to be hierarchical, defence-intensive ones egalitarian (p. 20).

75. *Du gouvernement arabe*, pp. 5–6.

76. Ibid., pp. 13–14.

77. *De la civilisation du peuple arabe*, p. 28. Richard counted seven stages in the progression from 'chaotic barbarism' to 'democratic civilization', namely 1. *barbarie confuse (point de départ); 2. féodalité indigène instable; 3. féodalité indigène stable; 4. féodalité française; 5. commune aristocratique; 6. commune démocratique; 7. civilisation démocratique.* (p. 31).

78. Stephen H. Roberts, *The History of French Colonial Policy*, London, Frank Cass, 1963, pp. 204–5.

79. A. Hanoteau and A. Letourneux, *La Kabylie et les Coutumes Kabyles*, 3 Vols, Paris, Imprimerie Nationale, 1871, Vol II, p. 136.

80. Daumas (with Fabar) *La Grande Kabylie*, p. 50.

81. *La Kabylie*, pp. 51–2.

82. 'Kanoun du village de Thaourirt Amokran chez les Aith Iraten (Kabïlie)', *Revue Africaine*, Vol. 7, 1863, pp. 279–85. [The article appeared in amended form in *Etudes sur le passé et l'avenir des Kabyles*, pp. 69–78].

83. Bibesco, pp. 584 and 581.
84. Warnier, p. 68.
85. Bibesco, p. 569.
86. Paul Leroy-Beaulieu, *Algérie et Tunisie*, Paris, Guillaumin, 1897 (first pub. 1887). pp. 244 and 247.
87. For a discussion on French Orientalism see Edmund Burke, 'The First Crisis of Orientalism 1890–1914' in *Connaissances du Maghreb*, Paris, CNRS, 1984, pp. 213–26. According to Burke, French Orientalism, which flowered at the end of the nineteenth century and owed much to colonial Algeria, had by the early decades of the twentieth century acquired unrivalled intellectual weight.

4 The 'Royaume Arabe' (1860–1870)

1. *Lettre sur la Politique de la France en Algérie adressée par l'Empereur au Maréchal de MacMahon 1865*, Paris, Imp. Royale, 1865, pp. 8–11.
2. The most comprehensive analysis of this era is Annie Rey-Goldzeiguer, *Le Royaume Arabe. La Politique Algérienne de Napoleon III 1861–1870*, Alger, SNED, 1977. See also relevant chapters in Charles-André Julien, *Histoire de l'Algérie Contemporaine*, Vol. I, Paris, PUF, 1979 and Byron Cannon 'Perceptions of the Algerian *Douar-Commune* and reactions to *arch* land law 1863–1881', in *Connaissances du Maghreb*, (ed. Vatin and Fremeaux) Paris, Ed. du CNRS, 1984, pp. 369–85.
3. The two most comprehensive studies of the Bureaux Arabes to date are: Xavier Yacono, *Les Bureaux Arabes et l'évolution des genres de vie indigènes dans l'ouest du Tell algérois*, Paris, Larose, 1953 and Kenneth J. Perkins, *Quaids, Captains, and Colons. French Military Administration in the Colonial Maghrib 1844–1934*, New York, Africana, 1981.
4. Perkins, p. 15.
5. Ibid., p. 86.
6. Sixty-three per cent of Bureaux Arabes officers serving in Algeria between 1830 and 1870 were graduates of these four schools. In contrast a normal infantry regiment in France would have about 30 per cent such graduates. Even the engineer regiments, where such graduates predominated in France, seldom topped the 60 per cent mark. Perkins, p. 42.
7. G.G. Iggers, *The Doctrine of Saint-Simon*, New York, Schocken, 1972, p. xiv.
8. *L'Algérie Assimiliée. Etude sur la Constitution et la Réorganisation de l'Algérie par un Chef de Bureau Arabe*, Paris, Challamel, 1871, p. v. [The work is by Louis Rinn although it was published anonymously to comply with regulations concerning works written by military personnel while on active service and does not ressemble his usual style.]
9. *Lettres à Monsieur le Président de la République*, Oran, 1848. Quoted by Yacono, p. 213.
10. Richard, *Du Gouvernement arabe et de l'institution qui doit l'excercer*, Alger, Bastide, 1848, p. 17.
11. Ferdinand Hugonnet, *Souvenirs d'un Chef de Bureau Arabe*, Paris, Michel Levy, 1858, p. 5.
12. Yacono is most thorough in his discussion of the social mission of the Bureaux Arabes and in providing the details of their doctrine, programme and accomplishments.

13. The insurrection of 1864–66 started in the outermost fringes of military territory as an isolated disturbance. This triggered a chain reaction of similar disturbances, but although it had the makings of a generalized revolt there was no real unity between the individual uprisings. For an analysis of the 1864–66 insurrection see Rey-Goldzeiguer, pp. 275–313.
14. Richard, pp. 7–8.
15. Yacono, pp. 373–90; Perkins, p. 141.
16. Hugonnet, p. 62. Hugonnet, whose *Souvenirs* is one of the better works in this genre, was at pains to point out the contribution of the officers of the Bureaux Arabes to the creation of negative ideas regarding the indigenous population.
17. ANOM 43KK 70, *Registre des Rapports mensuels et trimestriels du cercle de Bougie, N°14 du 6 février 1850.*
18. Yacono, p. 46.
19. ANOM 42, I 6 *Cercle de Drâ-el-Mizan. Rapports Trimestriel. 2ème trimestre 1858*; ANOM 44 I 1 *Cercle de Tizi Ouzou. Rapport retrospectif sur l'année 1861.*
20. *Solution de la Question de l'Algérie*, pp. 153–4.
21. ANOM 44 I 1, *Cercle de Tizi Ouzou. Rapport Annuel 1867*; ANOM 40 I 1 *Sub-Division de Dellys. Rapport d'Inspection générale 1868.*; ANOM 31 Mi 9 *Lettre n° 7 de de Neveu à Urbain, Souk-el-Arba le 3 juin 1857* [de Neveu entered the Bureaux Arabes in 1845, was posted to Dellys (Kabylia) in 1859 where he remained until 1870. At the time of the letter he was head of the political bureau, a post which he held from 1853 to 1858.]
22. ANOM 44 I 1.
23. ANOM 42 I 1, *Cercle de Drâ-el-Mizan, Rapport faisant suite à l'inspection générale de 1858.* (This *cercle* was established in 1857.)
24. ANOM 91 I 2, *Cercle de Cherchell. Rapport Annuel de 1862.*
25. ANOM 41 I 7, *Cercle de Dellys. Rapport Annuel de 1865*; ANOM 40 I 1, *Sub-Division de Dellys, Rapport d'Inspection Générale 1868.* (The *caïd* was in control of security, collected taxes, administered the Arab tribe and was accountable to the French commanding officer. The *cadi* was the Muslim judge. The *amin el oumena* was the elected leader of the Kabyle *arch* or tribe which comprised several *douar* (group of tents), each headed by an *amin. Douar* was the term adopted by the French as an administrative unit.]
26. ANOM 44 I 1, *Cercle de Tizi Ouzou, Rapport annuel 1861.*
27. Perkins, p. 107.
28. ANOM 44 I 1, *Sub-Division de Dellys, Cercle de Tizi Ouzou, Inspection Général. Rapport retrospectif sur l'année 1857.*
29. ANOM 44 I 1, *Cercle de Tizi Ouzou. Rapport Annuel 1864*; ANOM 42 I 1, *Cercle de Drâ-el-Mizan. Rapport annuel 1867.*
30. ANOM 41 I 1, *Cercle de Dra-el-Mizan. Rapport annuel 1868.* (The *djemâa* were abolished by decree on 10 March 1873 and replaced by French tribunals.)
31. ANOM 42 I 1, *Cercle de Drâ-el-Mizan, Rapport annuel 1866*, also *Rapport annuel 1867.*
32. *L'Algérie Assimilée*, pp. 53–4.
33. A notable exception was the Cherchell *cercle* after 1865 (ANOM 91 I 2, *Rapports d'ensemble 1861–67*). The 1865 Annual Report is particularly harsh. From the reports of this period it is of interest and relevance to note that [a] in the early 1860s there is little evidence of this harshness, and [b] the troubles marking the beginning of the 1864–66 revolt gave rise to considerable unrest among the Kabyle

tribes of the Cherchell *cercle*, negatively effecting Kabyle attitudes and creating an unusually tense atmosphere according to the 1864 Report. This change in Kabyle attitudes within the *cercle* seems to have been reciprocated by a change in French attitudes towards the Kabyles.

34. ANOM 44 I 1, *Cercle de Tizi Ouzou. Rapport Annuel de 1867.*

35. *L'Algérie Assimilée*, pp. 40 and 52.

36. ANOM 91 I 2, *Cercle de Cherchell. Rapport annuel 1862.*

37. ANOM 44 I 1, *Cercle de Tizi Ouzou. Rapport annuel 1863*; ANOM 42 I 6, *Cercle de Drâ-el-Mizan, Rapports Trimestriels. Première trimestre 1868.*

38. ANOM 44 I 1, *Cercle de Tizi Ouzou, Rapport annuel 1867.*

39. ANOM 42 I 6, *Cercle de Drâ-el-Mizan, Rapports Trimestriels. Première trimestre 1861.*; ANOM 40 I 1 *Sub-division de Dellys. Rapport d'ensemble pour l'année 1866.*

40. Hollins M. Steele Jnr., *European Settlement vs. Muslim Property: The Foundation of Colonial Algeria 1830–1880*, Unpublished PhD thesis, NY, Columbia University, 1965, p. 91.

41. For discussions of the land question see: Cannon, 1984; André Nouchi, *Enquête sur le niveau de vie des populations rurales constantinoises de la conquête jusqu'en 1919*, Paris, PUF, 1961; Steele, 1965; Rachid Tlemcani, *State and Revolution in Algeria*, London, Zed, 1986. For the later period see: Charles-Robert Ageron, *Les Algériens musulmans et la France 1871–1919*, 2 Vols, Paris, PUF, 1968; Stephen Roberts, *History of French Colonial Policy 1870–1925*, London, P.S. King, 1929.

42. Before the introduction of French policies collective land tenure was made up of five groups: *beylick* (state lands); *habous* (religious lands); *ârch* (tribal lands) on which the occupant had the right of usufruct in return for payments of a special levy; *makhzen* lands which were given by the State to individuals or groups in return for military service; and *axel* which were granted by Turkish rulers to members of their families. The only designated private property was *melk*.

43. Tlemcani, pp. 23–4.

44. Henri Verne, *La France en Algérie*, Paris, Challamel, 1869, p. 30.

45. Dr Auguste Warnier, *L'Algérie devant l'Empereur*, Paris, Challamel, 1865, pp.24–5.

46. Ibid., pp. 25–6.

47. Julien, *Histoire de l'Algérie Contemporaine*, p. 426.

48. The exceptions were those tribes whose lands were not *melk*, such as the Ameraoua in the *cercle* of Tizi Ouzou. ANOM 44 I 1 *Rapport Annuel 1867.*

49. Pierre Bourdieu, *The Algerians*, (trans. A.C.M. Ross) Boston, Beacon Press, 1962, p. 82.

50. Steele, p. 207.

51. ANOM 91 I 2, *Cercle de Chercell. Rapport Annuel 1867.*

52. ANOM 42 I 1, *Cercle de Drâ-el-Mizan. Rapport Annuel 1867.*

53. Forest lands were the first to be interfered with on a large scale in Kabylia It was decreed that all forest lands belonged to the State unless individual claimants could produce title deeds proving otherwise. As this applied even in areas of melk designation, the ruling deprived Kabyles tribes of their forest holdings. The first seizures took place in 1867. See Steele, p. 241.

54. Rey-Goldzeiguer, p. 471.

55. A. Hanoteau and A. Letourneux, *La Kabylie et les Coutumes kabyles*, 2 Vols, Paris, Imp. Nationale, 1871, Vol. 2, footnote pp. 57–8.

56. 'Reconcilier les colons et les Arabes ... telle est la marche à suivre ...' Napoleon III, *Lettre sur la politique de la France en Algérie (1865)*, p.8.

57. Rey-Goldzeiguer, p. 508.

58. ANOM 30813, *L'Avenir Algérien*, 23.3.1868, 'Les Vols en Algérie' p. 1.

59. ANOM 30810, *Courrier de l'Algérie*, 10.1.1869, 'Faits algériens' (extract from *Courrier de Mostaganem*), p. 3.

60. *Journal des Debats* and *Le Figaro*, both of March 1868; Rey-Goldzeiguer, p. 509.

61. ANOM 42 I 6, *Cercle de Drâ-el-Mizan. Rapports Trimestriels. Première trimestre 1868.*

62. *Lettres sur la race noire et blanche*, Paris, Paulin, 1839.

63. A. Nouschi, Introduction to *Correspondance du Dr. A. Vital avec I. Urbain. 1845–1874*, Paris, Larose, 1959, p. 9.

64. The 31 Mi (formerly 1X) series of the Archives Nationales d'Outre Mer, which contains his letters to and from members of the Algerian colonial hierarchy, includes over 40 correspondents.

65. 'Algérie. Du Gouvernement des Tribus de l'Algérie', *Revue de L'Orient et de l'Algérie*, Vol. II, 1847, pp. 241–59; 'Chrétiens et Musulmans. Français et Algériens', *Revue de L'Orient et de l'Algérie*, Vol. II, 1847, pp. 351–59.

66. 'Chrétiens et Musulmans ...', pp. 351 and 358. [The article to which he was responding, signed A.T. and dated 28th July 1847, was 'Orient. Etude sur la lutte engagée entre le christianisme et l'Islamisme.', *Revue de L'Orient et de l'Algérie*, Vol. II, 1847, pp. 17–21.]

67. 'Du gouvernement des tribus', p. 245.

68. 'Les Kabyles du Djurdjura', *Revue de Paris*, 1 March 1857, Vol. 36, pp. 91–110.

69. Ibid., p. 98–9.

70. Ibid., p, 106.

71. Ibid., p. 100.

72. ANOM 31 Mi 2, *Lettre No 104, Urbain à Lacroix, Constantine, le 10 juin 1862*.

73. ANOM 31 Mi 2, *Lettre n° 144, Urbain à Lacroix, le 11 novembre 1862*.

74. ANOM 31 Mi 2, *Lettre n° 172 Urbain à Lacroix, le 7 février 1863*. [Hanoteau, who was a definite Kabylophile, eschewed vulgar comparisons between Kabyle and Arab. His contribution to the imagery was more nuanced. See Chapter 7 below.]

75. Urbain alludes to these reactions in his correspondence with Lacroix. ANOM 31 Mi 2, *Lettre n° 167 du 17.1.1863 and n° 168 du 20.1.1863*. See also Rey-Goldzeiguer, p. 229.

76. *L'Algérie pour les Algériens*, pp. 73; 90; 142; 154–5.

77. Julien, *Histoire de l'Algérie contemporaine*, p. 422.

78. 'Lettre de Vital à Urbain, Constantine le 17 Mai 1861' *Correspondance*, p. 52.

79. Rey-Goldzeiguer, *Le Royaume Arabe*, p. 313.

80. *De l'Algérie au Point de Vue de la Crise actuelle*, Paris, Challamel, 1868, p. 24.

81. Ibid, pp. 44–45; 49; 55–52; 75.

82. Victor Courtet de L'Isle, a disciple of Saint-Simon and, according to Boissel, the font of Gobineau's ideas, expressed the view that there were naturally stupid races, childlike races and adult races. *Tableau éthnographique du genre humain*, Paris, Bertrand, 1849, p. 28. The Saint-Simonian Gustave d'Eichthal, who was a friend

of Urbain's and had close links with the colony, believed that there were feminine and masculine races, suggesting that the black race belonged to the former category and the white race to the latter. 'Eichthal to Urbain, 19.3.1838', *Lettres sur la race noire et blanche*, p. 22. The variation is interesting: while maintaining an accepted superior/inferior hierarchy both men, who believed in feminine emancipation (albeit limited by modern standards), were indirectly advocating a similar emancipation for blacks.

83. *De l'Algérie au Point de Vue de la Crise actuelle*, p. 101.

84. Edward Said, *Orientalism*, New York, Vintage, 1979.

85. Said, 1979; Sophie Monneret, *L'Orient des Peintres*, Paris, Nathan, 1989.

86. Quoted by Said, p. 51.

87. Gérard de Nerval, *Voyage en Orient*, 2 Vols, Paris, Michel Levy, 1867, Vol. II, p. 215 (first published 1851).

88. It is interesting that no other renowned novel had Algeria as its setting. Flaubert's *Salammbô* was set in ancient Carthage. France's involvement in Algeria, grounded in disturbing political reality, no doubt made it too topical a subject to serve as the drawing board for literary creativity with the universality of the human condition as its object.

89. Charles Tailliart, *L'Algérie dans la littérature française*, Paris, Librairie de la Société de l'Histoire de France, 1925, p. 520.

90. In particular about women and the harem. A whole section was devoted to Cairene women in his *Voyage en Orient*; this was first published as 'Les Femmes du Caire. Scènes de la Vie Egyptienne', *Revue des Deux Mondes*, Vol. 14, 1846, pp. 404–35.

91. *Voyage en Orient*, 'Appendice sur les Mœurs des Egyptiens modernes', Vol. II, p. 216.

92. Ibid, Vol. I, p. 246

93. Gustave Flaubert, 'Voyage à Carthage', *Œuvres Complètes*, 2 Vols, Paris, Ed. du Seuil, 1964, Vol. II, p. 707.

94. Ibid., p. 720.

95. *Voyage en Orient*, Vol. I, p. 35.

96. Ibid., p. 38.

97. '19 novembre, 1849, Voyage en Orient: Egypte', *Œuvres complètes*, Vol. II, p. 559.

98. de Nerval, *Voyage en Orient*, Vol. I, p. 192.

99. Said, p. 187.

100. *Aziyadé*, Paris, Calmann-Levy, 1987, p. 37.

101. Ibid., p. 45.

102. Friedrich Max Müller (1823–1900) was among the first to define the Aryan race.

103. 'La Société Berbère' *Œuvres complètes*, Vol. II, Paris, Calmann-Levy, 1948, p. 558 (this essay first appeared in the *Revue des Deux Mondes*, Vol. 10, 1873, pp. 138–57).

5 The Ecole Polytechnique, Saint-Simonianism and the army

1. In the British Army, for example, in 1821 the price for a Captain's commission, fixed by the Royal Warrant of the same year, was £3,500 in the Royal

Horse Guards, £3,225 in the Dragoon Guards, and £1,800 in a Marching Regiment of Foot Guards. For a Lieutenant-Colonel in the same regiments it was £7,250, £6,175 and £4,500 respectively. These were the official prices but elite regiments, such as the seven regiments of the Royal Household, had a higher 'unofficial' price.

2. *Ecole Polytechnique. Livre du Centenaire 1794–1894*, 3 Vols, Paris, Gauthier-Villars, 1895, Vol. I, p. 88.

3. F.B. Artz, *The Development of Technical Education in France 1500–1850*, Cambridge, MIT Press, 1966, p. 118.

4. T.N. Clark, *Prophets and Patrons: The French University and the Emergence of the Social Sciences*, Cambridge, Harvard University Press, 1973, p. 34.

5. *Livre du Centenaire*, Vol. I, pp. 454–5. (A high point was reached during the years 1867–71, when 40 per cent of the Academy members were *Polytechniciens*.)

6. L. Pearce Williams, 'Science, Education and Napoleon I', pp. 80–91 in *The Rise of Science in Relation to Society* (ed. L. Marsak), NY, Macmillan, 1964, p. 81.

7. Ibid., p. 84.

8. Under the Restoration (1816–30) the Ecole Polytechnique was transferred to the jurisdiction of the Ministry of the Interior, reverting to the Ministry of War for the 1830–50 period.

9. Raoul Girardet *La Société Militaire dans la France Contemporaine. 1815–1939*, Paris, Plon, 1953, p. 152.

10. See for example: Louis Lyautey, 'Du rôle social de l'officier', *Revue des Deux Mondes*, Vol. 105, March 1891, pp. 443–59.

11. *Livre du Centenaire*, Vol. I, p. 12.

12. For example: Gaspard Monge (1746–1818), mathematician and one of the founders of the Ecole Polytechnique; Claude Berthollet (1748–1822) chemist and co-founder; Eugène Chevreul (1786–1889), chemist; Pierre Louis Dulong (1785–1838), physicist; Pierre Simon, Marquis de Laplace (1749–1827), astonomer, mathematician and physicist; Denis Poisson (1781–1840), mathematician; and Jacques Thénard (1777–1857), chemist.

13. 'Histoire de l'Algèbre. Sur l'Algèbre des Indiens', *Correspondance sur l'Ecole Polytechnique*, Vol. III, Paris, Courcier, 1816, p. 3.

14. Egyptian mathematical texts would only have been available in Greek or Latin transcriptions at the time, the key to hieroglyphics having only been discovered in 1821 when Jean-François Champollion (1790–1832) started to decipher the Rosetta Stone. Indian, Chinese and Arabs texts would have been consulted in translation by most students, whereas Greek texts would have been read in the original.

15. Ian Hacking, *The Taming of Chance*, Cambridge, Cambridge University Press, 1990, p. 160. (Hacking has produced a trilogy on the impact on society of the mathematical discipline of probability, of which this is the second volume.)

16. Ibid., pp. 103–7.

17. In fact socially the Ecole Polytechnique was equally elitist, with about 60 per cent of its places going to the sons of the *haute bourgeoise* during 1830–48 (Roger Magraw, *France 1815–1914. The Bourgeois Century*, London, Fontana, 1987 [1st edition 1983], p. 68). The myth, however, was otherwise and its image was more egalitarian.

18. J.W. Fück, 'Islam as an Historical Problem in European Historiography since 1800', (pp. 303–14) in *Historians of the Middle East*, B. Lewis and P.M. Holt (eds), London, Oxford University Press, 1962, p. 304.

19. Edward Said, *Orientalism*, NY, Vintage, 1979, p. 76.
20. *Livre du Centenaire*, Vol. III, p. 3.
21. See the glowing description of the expedition in the *Livre du Centenaire*, Vol. II, pp. 6–8; Vol. III, pp. 3–4.
22. 'Description de l'Egypte', *Correspondance sur l'Ecole Royale Polytechnique. Janvier 1814–1816*, Vol. III, Paris, Courcier, 1816, p. 85.
23. Published under the full title of *Description de l'Egypte ou Recueil des Observations et des Recherches qui ont été faites en Egypte pendant l'expédition de l'Armée française publié par les ordres de sa Majesté l'Empereur Napoléon le Grand*, Paris, Imprimerie Impériale, 1809–28, the study comprised nine volumes of Descriptions and *Mémoires* divided into three sections: *Antiquités; Etat Moderne* and *Histoire Naturelle* and 14 volumes of plates, maps, etc.
24. Said, p. 84.
25. Namely: *Tableau de la situation des Etablissements français dans l'Algérie*, 19 Vols, Paris, 1838–53; *Exploration scientifique de l'Algérie pendant les années 1840, 1841, 1842, publiée par ordre du gouvernement*, 39 Vols, 2 Atlases, Paris, Imp. Royale, 1844–1867.
26. M. de Chabrol, 'Essai sur les mœurs des habitants modernes de l'Egypte', pp. 361–526, in *Description de L'Egypte*, Vol. 7, p. 361.
27. *Livre du Centenaire*, Vol. II, p. 6.
28. Respectively: Plate 4, 'Thèbes – Louqsor. L'Entrée du Palais. Vue Particulière du Palais. Prise du Sud', Vol. 13, *Description de l'Egypte*, 1812; Ibid., Plate 17, 'Thèbes-Karnak. Vue générale des Ruines du Palais. Prise du Nord-Ouest'; Ibid., Plate 19, 'Thèbes-Karnak. Vue du Palais. Prise de l'Interieur de la Cour.'
29. E. Jomard, 'Description d'Antinoë, in *Description de l'Egypte*, Vol. II, p. 1. (As a point of interest, E. Jomard was one of the *Polytechniciens* on the expedition.)
30. For example, de Chabrol, *Essai sur les mœurs*; E. Jomard 'Observations sur les Arabes de l'Egypte moyenne'; and le Baron Larrey, 'Notice sur le Conformation physique des Egyptiens et des différentes races qui habitent en Egypte'.
31. Norman Daniel, *Islam, Europe and Empire*, Edinburgh, University Press, 1962, p. 96.
32. M. Savary, *Letters on Egypt*, (anonymous translated version), 2 Vols, London, Robinson, 1799 (3rd edition); C.F. Volney, *Voyage en Syrie et en Egypte pendant les années 1783, 1784 & 1785*, 2 Vols, Paris, Durand, An VII (3rd edition; 1st published 1786).
33. Savary, Vol. I, pp. 25–9.
34. Volney, Vol. I, p. 87.
35. Ibid., p. 366.
36. Ibid., Vol. II, pp. 318–20.
37. *Journal d'un Officier*, p. 34.
38. Cohen, *The French Encounter with Africans*, pp. 224–5 and George L. Mosse, *Towards the Final Solution. A History of European Racism*, Madison, University of Wisconsin Press, 1985, p. 27.
39. Cohen, p. 225.
40. Dr Thomas Shaw, *Voyage dans la Régence d'Alger*, Paris, Merlin, 1830 (first published as part of *Travels and observations relating to several parts of Barbary and the Levant*, Oxford, 1738 and translated into French in 1743 as *Voyages en Barbarie*); Abbé Guillaume Thomas François Raynal, *Histoire philosophique et politique des établissements et du commerce des Européens dans l'Afrique septentrionale*, (ouvrage

posthume, augmenté d'un aperçu sur l'état actuel de ces établissements et du commerce qu'y font les Européens, notamment avec les puissances barbaresques et la Grèce moderne, par M. Peuchet) 2 Vols, Paris, Maumus, 1826.

41. Cohen, pp. 71 and 85.

42. Slane translated Book III in 1852 as *Histoire des Berbères* (Algiers). The full translation by Slane was published in 1862–68 (Paris). The first fully annotated translation in English, by Dr Franz Rosenthal, only appeared in 1958.

43. Discussions of Ibn Khaldun's work in relation to the colonial Maghreb appear in: Ernest Gellner, 'Cohesion and identity: the Maghreb from Ibn Khaldun to Emile Durkheim' in *Muslim Society*, Cambridge, Cambridge University Press, 1985; Yves Lacoste, *Ibn Khaldoun. Naissance de l'Histoire Passé du tiers monde*, Paris, Editions La Découverte, 1985; N.J. Dawood (ed.) 'Introduction' and 'Preface' to Ibn Khaldûn. *The Muqaddimah. An Introduction to History* (trans. Franz Rosenthal), Princeton, Princeton University Press, 1967; and, more generally, in Jacques Berque, *Maghreb, Histoire et Sociétés*, Alger, SNED, 1974.

44. Emile Gautier, 'Le Cadre Géographique de l'Histoire en Algérie' in *Histoire et Historiens de l'Algérie*, Paris, Alcan, 1931, p. 19.

45. *The Doctrine of Saint-Simon. An Exposition*, trans. and introduced by G.G. Iggers, NY, Schocken, 1972 (first published 1958), p. xxiii.

46. Ibid., p. xxiv.

47. Gaston Pinet, *Ecrivains et Penseurs polytechniciens*, Paris, Ollendorff, 1898, p. 143.

48. Letter written on 27 December 1831 from Capitaine Lefranc in Algiers to M. Chevalier, editor-in-chief of *Le Globe*, 'Correspondance du Globe 1831–1832', Document 74, Volume 7609, *Fonds Enfantin*.

49. Michel Collinet, 'Le Saint-Simonisme et l'Armée', *Revue Française de Sociologie*, 1961, II, pp. 38–47, p. 38–9.

50. Quoted by Pinet, p. 144.

51. Gaston Pinet, 'L'Ecole Polytechnique et les Saint-Simoniens', *La Revue de Paris*, Vol. 3, May–June 1894, pp. 73–96, p. 80.

52. Iggers, p. xxxviii.

53. Ibid., pp. xxiv and xxv.

54. For the role of the Saint-Simonians in Algeria see Marcel Emerit, *Les Saint-Simoniens en Algérie*, Paris, Les Belles Lettres, 1941.

55. *De la civilisation du people arabe.*

56. Of the *Polytechniciens* in the artillery corps mentioned in the biographical notices in the *Livre du Centenaire* nearly all had gone to Metz.

57. Pinet, *Ecrivains et Penseurs*, p. 183.

58. Frank E. Manuel, *Prophets of Paris*, Cambridge, Harvard University Press, 1962, p. 211.

59. Pinet, *Ecrivains et Penseurs*, pp. 224–8.

60. Ibid., p. 209.

61. William Coleman, *Death is a Social Disease*, Madison, University of Wisconsin Press, 1982, pp. 14 and 17.

62. Ibid., pp. 21 and 23.

63. Ibid., pp. 124, 274 and 304.

64. Ibid., p. xvii.

65. Ibid., p. 16.

66. *Livre du Centenaire*, Vol. III, p. 52.

67. Ibid., Vol. II, p. 292.

68. Ibid., p. 30

69. Fournel, who had been a member of the Saint-Simonian 1833–36 expediton to Egypt, drew up and presented a plan to Mehemet Ali for the construction of a canal at Suez. It was rejected. See Rouchdi Fakkar, 'Le Saint-Simonisme en Egypte' in *Les Saint-Simoniens et l'Orient* (ed. Magali Morsy), Paris, Edisud, 1989, p. 13.

70. Pouyanne's chief collaborator was the palaeontologist and geographer, Nicolas Pomel, who later wrote *Des Races Indigènes de l'Algérie.*

71. A.E.H. Carette, *Etudes sur la Kabilie Proprement dite* (1848); A. Hanoteau, *La Kabylie et les Coutumes Kabyles* (1872–73), compiled with the assistance of A. Letourneux. (Carette and Hanoteau were *Polytechniciens*); H. Aucapitaine, *La Kabylie et les Kabyles* (1857) and E.M.J. Daumas, *La Grande Kabylie. Etudes Historiques* (1847), produced in collaboration with Captain Fabar, who was a *Polytechnicien.* All four authors were army officers.

72. Two examples of his ethnological research are: 'Les Berbères et les Arabes des Bords du Sénégal', *Bulletin de la Société de Géographie de Paris*, 1854, pp. 89–112; 'Les Berbères et les Arabes', *Bulletin de la Société de Géographie de Paris*, 1855.

73. 'Instructions sur l'anthropologie de l'Algérie', *Bulletin de la Société d'Anthropologie*, Vol. 8 (2nd series), 1873, pp. 603–59 (published separately under the same title: Paris, A. Hennuyer, 1874).

74. Faidherbe's and other works on this matter are discussed in a series of articles by Commandant Louis Rinn entitled 'Essai d'études linguistiques et ethnologiques sur les Origines Berbères', appearing in the *Revue Africaine*, Vol. 25, 1881 through Vol. 33, 1889.

75. *Projets de Colonisation pour les provinces d'Oran et de Constantine*, Paris, Ancelin, 1841 (written in collaboration with Lieutenant-General Bedeau).

76. Such was the case of artillery captain, Leo Lamarque, whose contribution to the ideas on colonization were published in: *De la Conquête et de la Civilisation de l'Algérie*, Paris, Ancelin, 1841. Lamarque eventually went to Algeria and took part in the 1844 campaign against the Kabyles.

77. Bugeaud's animosity, particularly towards de La Moricière, was probably tinged with resentment. De La Moricière was one of the most notable examples of a *carrière rapide* enjoyed by so many officers in Africa, particularly *Polytechniciens.* Arriving in Algeria as a capitain he had attained the rank of general within 11 years (1841), at the age of 35. (It took Bugeaud 16 years to progress from colonel to *maréchal de camp.*)

78. K.J. Perkins, *Qaids, Captains, and Colons*, New York, Africana, 1981, p. 44.

79. Ibid., p. 14.

6 Race and scholarship in Algeria: the impact of the military

1. F. Manuel, *Prophets of Paris*, p. 117.

2. A. de Quatrefages de Bréau, *Recueil des Rapports sur les Progès des Lettres et des Sciences en France. Rapport sur les progrès de l'anthropologie*, Paris, Imp. Impériale, 1867, pp. 25–6.

3. For an introduction to new approaches to the problem see David Arnold (ed.), *Imperial Medicine and Indigenous Societies*, Manchester, Manchester University

Press, 1988; Roy MacLeod and Milton Lewis (eds), *Disease, Medicine and Empire*, London, Routledge, 1988.

4. Arnold, p. 3.

5. Yvonne Turin, *Affrontements Culturels dans l'Algérie coloniale. Ecoles, Médecine, Religion, 1830–1880*, Paris, Maspero, 1971.

6. Arnold, p. 4.

7. Ibid., p. 7.

8. Ibid., p. 19.

9. Gabriel Esquier, *La Prise d'Alger 1830*, Paris, Larose, 1929, pp. 502–3.

10. Turin, p. 13.

11. Perkins, *Quaids, Captains and Colons*, pp. 132–3.

12. Ribourt, *Le Gouvernement de l'Algérie de 1852 à 1858*, pp. 31–2.

13. Docteur Trolliet (also spelt Trollier), *Mémoire sur la nécessité et les avantages de la colonisation d'Alger*, Lyon, Barret, 1835; Trolliet, *Extrait d'un voyage fait à Alger au commencement du mois de juillet 1836*, lu en séance publique de la Société royale d'agriculture, histoire naturelle et arts utiles de Lyon le 12 sept 1836, Lyon, Barret, 1836. See also: Dr Lucien Baudens, *Relation de l'expédition de Constantine*, Paris, Baillière, 1838, originally published in the the *Revue de Paris*, 1 and 8 April 1838; Dr J.A.N. Périer, *De l'hygiène en Algérie*, 1847 (Part of the 39 volumes produced by the Scientific Commission); Dr F. Jacquot and Dr Topin, *De la Colonisation et de l'Acclimatement en Algérie*, Paris, 1849.

14. Tocqueville, *Notes sur l'Algérie*, p. 205.

15. Baudens, pp. 57–8.

16. *Considérations sur l'Algérie*, Paris, Comptoir Central de la Librairie, 1845, p. 64.

17. Ibid., p. 79.

18. Ibid., p. 86.

19. Ibid., p. 87–9.

20. Ibid., p. 80.

21. Ibid., p. 103.

22. Jean Boissel, *Victor Courtet (1813–1867): Premier théoricien de la hiérarchie des races*, Paris, PUF, 1968, p. 58.

23. Virey was also influenced by the German art historian Johann J. Winckelmann. (For information on the impact of Lavater and Winckelmann see Mosse, *The Final Solution* and Cohen, *The French Encounter with Africans*.)

24. *Histoire naturelle du genre humain*, Paris, Dufait, 1800, Vol. I, p. 148.

25. Ibid., pp. 293–4.

26. *Science politique fondé sur la Science de l'homme ou étude des races humaines pour le rapport philosophique, historique et social*, Paris, A. Bertrand, 1837, p. 26.

27. *Tableau Ethnographique du Genre Humain*, Paris, A. Bertrand, 1849, pp. 2–3.

28. Virey, Vol. I, pp. 117, 312, 233 and Vol. II, p. 274.

29. 'Séance du 20 novembre 1862': M. Armand 'Aperçu sur les variétés de races humaines observées de 1842 à 1862, dans les diverses campagnes de l'armée française', *Bulletin de la Société d'Anthropologie*, Vol. 3, 1862, p. 553 (Armand held the rank of Medical Officer first class and his report, in spite of the somewhat misleading title, was about Algeria).

30. *Hygiène à suivre en Algérie. Acclimatement des Européens*, Algiers, Delavigne, 1851; *Hygiène à suivre en Algérie. Hygiène Morale*, Algiers, Delavigne, 1851.

31. *Hygiène Morale*, p. 5.

32. Ibid., pp. 15, 25 and 28.

33. See Dave Kennedy, 'The perils of the midday sun: climatic anxieties in the colonial tropics', in *Imperialism and the Natural World* (ed. John Mackenzie), Manchester, Manchester University Press, 1990, pp. 118–40.

34. *De l'Humanité*, (Part I) Algiers, n.p., 1852; Part II, Geneva, n.p., 1853, p. 7.

35. Ibid, pp. 7, 24, 37 and 39 (North America, France, Great Britain, Germany and Russia).

36. Ibid., pp. 15 and 21.

37. J. Assézat, 'L'Acclimatement', *Revue d'Anthropologie*, Vol. 4, 1875, pp. 294–305 (this was a review article of four works on the subject by doctors and specialists).

38. 'Séance du 23 août 1860', *Bulletin de la Société d'Anthropologie de Paris*, Vol. I, 1869, p. 166.

39. 'Du non-cosmopolitanisme des Races humaines', *Mémoires de la Société d'Anthropologie de Paris*, Vol. I, 1860–63, pp. 93–123.

40. Broca, Séance du 20 mai 1880", *Bulletin de la Société d'Anthropologie*, Vol. III (3rd series), p. 402. See Poliakov, *The Aryan Myth*, p. 280, for Boudin's contribution to Jewish racial mythology.

41. *De l'hygiène en Algérie* (1847) published as part of the 39 volumes of the *Exploration scientifique de l'Algérie.*

42. First presented to the *Société d'Anthropologie de Paris* in 1870 and later published in *Mémoires de la Société d'Anthropologie de Paris*, Vol. I, 2nd series, 1873, pp. 1–54.

43. 'Discours prononcé sur la tombe de M. Périer le 15 mai 1880', Séance du 20 mai 1880, *Bulletin de la Société d'Anthropologie*, Vol. III (3rd series), p. 402.

44. Among these mentioned above are: Aucapitaine, Berbrugger, Bibesco, Bodichon, Bory de Saint-Vincent, Carette, Daumas, Devaux, Duprat, Dureau de la Malle, Duveyrier, Faidherbe, Féraud, Hanoteau, Hodgson, Ibn-Khaldun, Pellissier, Peysonnel, Sallust, Shaw, de Slane, Topinard, Urbain, Warnier.

45. Alphonse Esquiros, 'Des Etudes Contemporaines sur l'Histoire des Races', *Revue des Deux Mondes*, Vol. 21 n.s., 1848, pp. 992–1002, p. 992.

46. Jean Finot, *Le Préjugé des Races*, Paris, Alcan, 1905, p. 107.

47. 'Daumas à Auvray, Mascara, le 7 janvier 1838', *Collections de Documents inédits sur l'Histoire de l'Algérie après 1830. Correspondance du Capitaine Daumas, Consul à Mascara,. 1837–1839*, (ed. Georges Yver) Algiers, Jordan, 1912 p. 61.

48. 'Daumas à Rapatel, Mascara, le 11 février 1838', ibid., p. 105 (Lieutenant-General Baron Rapatel replaced Auvray in February. The warm feelings of Daumas for Warnier were not reciprocated, nor indeed was Warnier as sanguine concerning French success among the local population. See footnote pp. 231–3).

49. ANOM 31 Mi 9, Lettre N° 53, de Neveu à Urbain, 7 février 1861 (de Neveu was serving in Dellys at the time).

50. H. Verne, *La France en Algérie*, p. 8. (This is but one example. Warnier was frequently referred to in works on Algeria)

51. *L'Algérie devant l'Empereur*, p. 44.

52. Ibid., pp. 5, 16 and 51.

53. Ibid., pp. 4, 18 and 49.

54. George W. Stocking, Jnr., *Victorian Anthropology*, London, Macmillan, 1987, pp. 250–52.

55. Ibid, p. 251. Two-thirds of the 'ethnologicals' were Liberal and one-third Tory; the ratio was reversed among the 'anthropologicals'.

56. For the reception of Darwin's ideas and the impact of social Darwinism in France see Linda L. Clark, *Social Darwinism in France*, Alabama, University of Alabama Press, 1984.

57. Gillebert d'Hercourt, 'Etudes Anthropologiques sur Soixainte-Seize Indigènes de l'Algérie, *Mémoires de la Société d'Anthropologie de Paris*, Vol. 3, 1868, pp. 1–25; Paul Topinard, 'Les types indigènes de l'Algérie', *Bulletin de la Société d'Anthropologie de Paris*, Vol. 4, 3rd series, 1881, pp. 438–46; L. Bertholon and E. Chantre, *Recherches anthropologiques dans la Berbérie orientale*, 2 vols, Lyon, Rey, 1912 and 1913.

58. *Etudes sur la Kabilie Proprement dite*, p. 3.

59. Louis Faidherbe and Paul Topinard, 'Instructions sur l'Anthropologie de l'Algérie', *Bulletin de la Société d'Anthropologie de Paris*, Vol. 8. (2nd series), 1873, pp. 603–58.

60. Ibid., p. 647.

61. Ibid., p. 614–15.

62. *Œuvres de Saint-Simon*, Vol. I, Paris, Dentu, 1868, p. 204.

63. Ibid., p. 205.

64. Pierre Bourdieu, *Sociologie de l'Algérie*, Paris, PUF, 1958, pp. 27 ff., quoted by Ernest Gellner, *Saints of the Atlas*, Chicago, University of Chicago Press, 1969, p. 28.

65. Courtet de l'Isle, 'Mémoire sur les races humaines. De l'influence des races humaines sur la forme et le développement des sociétés', *Journal de l'Institut historique*, February–July 1835, pp. 225–37, p. 228.

66. *Histoire générale et système comparé des Langues Semitiques*, in *Œuvres Complètes de Ernest Renan*, Vol. 8, Paris, Clamann-Levy, 1958, pp. 145–6. (first published 1855).

67. Daumas, *La Vie Arabe* (1869) p. 586.

68. Hanoteau, *Essai de Grammaire Kabyle*, Algiers, Bastide, 1858, p. xix.

69. Ibid., p. xi.

70. Ibid., p. viii–ix.

71. Ibid., p. viii.

72. 'L'Exploration scientifique de l'Algérie. La Société Berbère', *Revue des Deux Mondes*, Vol. 107, 1873, pp. 138–57, p. 141.

73. Ibid, p. 139.

74. Hanoteau and Letourneux, *La Kabylie et les Coutumes Kabyles*, 3 Vols., Paris, Imprimerie Nationale, 1871, Vol I, p. 305.

75. In 1956 J. Berque assessed the work as follows: 'Cette étude monumentale a représenté jusqu'à nos jours, c'est-à-dire pendant plus de 80 ans, le seul travail valable sur la fervente et tortueuse Kabylie', in 'Cent ving-cinq ans de sociologie maghrébine', *Annales E.S.C.*, Vol. II, 1956, pp. 296–324.

76. 'La Société berbère', p. 143.

77. *La Kabylie et les Coutumes Kabyles*, Vol. II, pp. 8–9 (similar assertions abound).

78. Ibid., p. 7.

79. Ibid., pp. 2–3.

80. Ibid., pp. 3–4.

81. 'La Société berbère', p. 155.

82. Ibid., p. 140.
83. *La Kabylie et les Coutumes Kabyles*, Vol. III, p. 56.
84. Ibid., Vol. II, p. 136.
85. 'La Société berbère', p. 154.
86. *Revue Africaine*, Vol. I, 1856, p. 6.
87. Two other societies of note, *L'Académie d'Hippone* and the *Société de Géographie et d'Archéologie de la Province d'Oran* were founded in 1863 and 1878 respectively. Although these two societies have not been cited in the examples above, a similar case could be made for both.
88. *Les époques militaires de la Grande Kabylie*, Paris, Challamel, 1857 (simultaneously published in Algiers by Bastide).
89. The Société archéologique also published the *Recueil des Notices et Mémoires de la Société archéologique de Constantine.*
90. *Revue Africaine*, Vol. I, 1856, p. 10.
91. Ibid., p. 497.
92. *Esquisse générale de l'Afrique* from *L'Univers, ou Histoire et description de tous les peuples, de leurs religions, mœurs, industrie, coutumes, etc.*, Paris, Firmin Didot, 1844. D'Avezac classified African races into ten groups and African languages into two, the *cohesive* and the *diacritique*, placing the Berber language in the former. He also suggested that the white race was the basic human type (*type fondamental*); the yellow race the sub-type (*sous-type*) and the black race an aberration (*groupe aberrant*). Gobineau was greatly influenced by d'Avezac.
93. Editor's note at the end of an article by Alphonse Meyer, 'Origine des Habitants de la Kabilie d'après la tradition locale', *Revue Africaine*, Vol. II, 1858–59, pp. 357–67.
94. Dureau de la Malle, *Algérie*, p. 30, for example. See Chapter I above.
95. This hypothesis was refuted in H. Tauxier, 'Lettre sur les origines libyennes', *Revue Africaine*, Vol. 29, 1885, pp. 232–40.
96. Louis Rinn, 'Essai d'études linguistiques et ethnologiques sur les origines bèrberes', *Revue Africaine*, Vol. 33, 1889, p. 121. (Rinn's 'Essai' was published in the journal over a period of eight years, commencing in Vol. 25, 1881 and ending with Vol. 33.)
97. Ibid., Vol. 32, 1888, p. 86.
98. This was in fact an ancient classification. In the Middle Ages it was applied to a social order: the serfs were descendants of Ham, the clerks of Shem and the nobles of Japheth. In nineteenth-century Germany, Japheth had sired the Germans, Shem the Semites. In a more general rendering, the nomads of the world were believed to be descended from Shem. See Léon Poliakov, *The Aryan Myth*, trans. E. Howard, London, Heinemann, 1974, for the evolution of these ideas.
99. E. Mercier, 'Ethnographie de l'Afrique Septentrionale', *Revue Africaine*, Vol. 15, 1871, pp. 420–33.
100. 'Lettre à M. Renan', *Revue Africaine*, Vol. 14, 1870, pp. 79–87.
101. *Revue Africaine*, Vol. I, 1856, p. 510 (Discussion of Hanoteau's *Littérature orale des Touareg*).
102. *Les Epoques militaires de la Grande Kabilie*, p. 280.
103. This thesis is developed by James Malarkey, 'The Dramatic Structure of Scientific Discovery in Colonial Algeria: A Critique of the Journal of the 'Société Archéologique de Constantine' (1853–1876)' in *Connaissances du Maghreb*, Paris, CNRS, 1984, pp. 137–59.

104. *Revue Africaine*, Vol. 8, 1864, p. 160.
105. Buffon, Cuvier, Lamarck, Etienne Geoffroy Saint-Hilaire and his son, Isidore, for example.

7 Scholarly societies in France: the Kabyle Myth as a racial paradigm

1. J. Halévy, 'Etudes Berbères', *Journal Asiatique*, Vol. 3 (7th series), 1874, pp. 73–203, (The scholars in question included Reboud, Duveyrier, Letourneux and Judas, all of whom were involved in Berber or Kabyle studies.)
2. 'La Société Berbère', *Revue des Deux Mondes*, Vol. 107, 1873, pp. 138–57. The others were literature, history, religion and legislation.
3. *De L'origine du langage*, Paris, Calmann-Levy, 1983 (first published 1848), p. 69.
4. *Psychologie de la colonisation française dans ses rapports avec les sociétés indigènes*, Paris, Alcan, 1899, p. 165 (first published 1890).
5. Edmund Burke III, 'The First Crisis of Orientalism 1890–1914', *Connaissances du Maghreb*, Paris, CNRS, 1984, p. 217.
6. See Donald McKay, 'Colonialism in the French Geographical Movement 1871–1881', *Geographical Review*, Vol. 33, 1943, pp. 214–33; William H. Schneider, *An Empire for the Masses. The French Popular Image of Africa 1870–1900*, Conn., Greenwood Press, 1982, and 'Geographical reform and municipal imperialism in France 1870–1880' in *Imperialism and the Natural World* (ed. John M. Mackenzie), Manchester, Manchester University Press, 1990, pp. 90–117.
7. Schneider, *An Empire for the Masses*, p. 21.
8. Preamble to the first volume of the society's journal and Article 1 of the regulations, the *Bulletin de la Société de Géographie*.
9. Schneider, 'Geographical reform and municipal imperialism', p. 94.
10. Other, non-military journals, used by the officers were the *Journal Asiatique* (journal of the Société Asiatique founded in 1822), the *Revue des Deux Mondes* (1829), the *Revue de Paris* (1829), the *Revue indépendante* (1841), and the *Revue de l'Orient* (journal of the Société Orientale, founded in 1841, which later became the *Revue de l'Orient, de l'Algérie et des Colonies*).
11. Schneider, 'Geographical reform and municipal imperialism', pp. 90–117.
12. *Bulletin de la Société Ethnologique*, Vol. I, 1841, p. ii.
13. William Cohen, *The French Encounter with Africans. White response to Blacks. 1530–1880*, Bloomington, Indiana University Press, 1980, p. 219.
14. 'Des caractères physiologiques des Races humaines', *Mémoires de la Société Ethnologique*, Vol. I, 1841, p. 30. (Thierry, like his brother Augustin, envisaged history as one of racial conflict.)
15. Ibid, pp. 37–8.
16. 'Procès-verbal de la séance du 27 mars 1840', *Bulletin de la Société d'Ethnologie*, Vol. I, 1841, p. xxx.
17. 'Procès-verbaux des Séances (Année 1840 à 1841)', ibid., pp. xliv–xlv.
18. The *Revue Indépendante* was founded in 1841 by Pierre Leroux, George Sand and Louis Viardot and inclined to severe criticism of governmental policies. Philosophy, literature and economics were treated with equal consideration, placing it among the most widely circulated journals of the time.

19. Augustin Thierry conceived the idea that race exerted an influence on the history of nations in his *Historie de la conquête de l'Angleterre par les Normands,* published in 1825. He presented the history of England in terms of race and class, equating the conquering Normans with the aristocracy and the Saxons with the lower classes. Differentiating characteristics were inherited and only lost over great periods of time. Amédée Thierry's *Histoire des Gaulois,* published in 1828, also saw history in racial terms but was less preoccupied with antagonistic relationships between races than with the definition of race. By examining the history and linguistics of a nation he attempted to determine the races from which it was formed. Moral characteristics, he believed, were passed down through the generations.

20. *Essai historique sur les races anciennes et modernes de l'Afrique septentrionale, leurs origines, leurs mouvements et leurs transformations, depuis l'antiquité la plus reculée jusqu'à nos jours,* Paris, Jules Labitte, 1845, p. 165. [The concept of the 'soul' of a people reached its pinnacle of elaboration in Hitlerian Germany when the German *volk* was contrasted to the soulless Semitic Jew.]

21. Ibid., p. 255.

22. Ibid., pp. 264–5; 257–8; 293.

23. Ibid., pp. 259 and 261.

24. Mosse, *Toward the Final Solution,* p. 97.

25. 'Histoire des Langues Semitiques', *Œuvres Complètes,* Vol. 8, p. 147 (first published 1855).

26. Duprat, pp. 296–302. (His argument against the proposed credits for a major expedition against Kabylia in 1845 appeared in 'Une Guerre Insensée', *Revue Indépendante,* Vol. 19, 1845, pp. 242–56).

27. Mosse, p. 11.

28. Duprat, p. 192.

29. Mosse, p. 18.

30. Bory de Saint Vincent, *L'Homme,* 2 Vols, Paris, Gravier, 1827 (first published as part of the *Dictionnaire classique d'histoire naturelle* in 1817). His *espèce Japétique,* for example, was sub-divided into four races: *Caucasique, Pelage, Celtique* and *Germanique,* the latter being further divided into two *variétés: Teutones* and *Sclavones,* Vol I, pp. 82–3.

31. The *espèce Neptunienne,* which he describes thus: '*essentiellement riveraine, cette espèce ne peuple que des îles.*' Ibid., Vol. I, p. 19.

32. 'Le Transformisme', *Mémoires de la Société d'Anthropologie de Paris,* Paris, Reinwald, 1871–1878, Vol. 3, pp. 165.

33. Jules Harmand, *Domination et Colonisation,* Paris, Flammarion, 1910, p. 55.

34. 'Personnel de la Société', *Mémoires de la Société d'Anthropologie de Paris,* Vol. I. (introductory pages, no pagination).

35. Thierry, p. 4 (Thierry's *Galls,* which he differentiated from the *Gaulois,* were sometimes referred to as the Celts by nineteenth-century scholars; Thierry denied this link; p. xiv).

36. 'Recherches sur l'ethnologie de la France' Séance du 21 juillet 1859, *Bulletin de la Société d'Anthropologie,* Vol I, pp. 6–15, p. 6. (Knox was British; Nott and Gliddon, American; only de Gobineau was French.)

37. 'Discussion sur la mémoire de M. Broca. Séance du 4 août 1859', ibid., pp. 16–30, p. 20.

38. Ibid., p. 22.

39. 'Sur les Kabyles de l'Auress (*sic*)', 13e séance, 2 février 1860, ibid., pp. 163–6.

40. *Bulletin de la Société d'Anthropologie de Paris*, Vol. I, p. 166.

41. 'Séance du 23 août 1860', ibid., p. 497.

42. 'Séance du 15 mai 1862', *Bulletin de la Société d'Anthropologie de Paris*, Vol. III, 1862, pp. 237–8.

43. Ibid., p. 239.

44. 'Etudes anthropologiques sur soixante-seize indigènes de l'Algérie', *Mémoires de la Société d'Anthropologie*, Vol. 3, pp. 1–24. (The two cephalic types were dolichocephalic and brachycephalic. Cephalic indices below 77.77 were the former; above were the latter. Europeans were in the latter category. Brachycephaly signified highly developed faculties of intellect.)

45. L. Bertholon and E. Chantre, *Recherches anthropologiques dans la Berbèrie orientale. Tome I. Anthropometrie, craniométrie, ethnographie. Tome II. Album de 174 portraits ethniques.*, Lyon, Rey, 1912 and 1913.

46. See: Stephen Jay Gould, *The Mismeasure of Man*, New York, Norton, 1981; Nancy Leys Stepan, 'Race and Gender: The Role of Analogy in Science', *Isis*, Vol. 77, n° 287, June 1986, pp. 261–77.

47. Stepan, p. 272.

48. 'Séance du 16 avril 1868', *Bulletin de la Société d'Anthropologie de Paris*, Vol. III (2nd series), pp. 265–9. Duhousset's paper was later published in the *Mémoires de la Société*.

49. The members of the Commission were: the geographer d'Avezac, Duhousset, Dureau de la Malle, Gillebert d'Hercourt, Lagneau, Faidherbe and Topinard.

50. 'Instructions sur l'Anthropologie de l'Algérie', *Bulletin de la Société d'Anthropologie*, Vol. 8 (2nd series), 1873, pp. 603–59.

51. *Elements d'Anthropologie Générale*, Paris, Delahaye and Lecrosnier, 1885, p. 184.

52. Ibid., p. 190.

53. 'Séance du 19 mai 1881', *Bulletin de la Société d'Anthropologie de Paris*, Vol. 4 (3rd series) 1881, p. 438.

54. 'Les types indigènes de l'Algérie', ibid., p. 440.

55. Renan, *Histoire des langues sémitiques*, p. 587.

56. Broca, 'Anthropologie', *Mémoires d'Anthropologie*, Vol. I, p. 32.

57. J.J. Virey, *Histoire naturelle du genre humain*, 2 Vols, Paris, Dufait, 1800, Vol. II, p. 121.

58. 'Les types indigènes de l'Algérie', pp. 450–51.

59. '431e séance–2 juin 1881. A propos du procès verbal. Les Kabyles du Fort-National', *Bulletin de la Société d'Anthropologie*, Vol. 4, 3rd series, 1881, pp. 471–6.

60. Gabriel de Mortillet along with C.A. Coudereau, André Lefèvre, and Charles Letourneau broke away from Broca and Topinard, and used anthropology to promote radical republicanism. (See Michael Hammond, 'Anthropology as a weapon of social combat in late nineteenth-century France', *Journal of the History of the Behavioural Sciences*, Vol 16, 1980, pp. 118–32 and Linda L. Clark, *Social Darwinism in France*, Alabama, University of Alabama Press, 1984.)

61. 'Colonization de l'Algérie', *L'Homme*, Vol. I, 1884, pp. 395–7, Cited by Hammond, p. 132.

62. On governmental interference in the early days of the Société d'Anthropologie see Linda Clark, p. 20 and Terry N. Clark, pp. 117–18.

63. 'Séance du 16 juin 1881,' *Bulletin de la Société d'Anthropologie de Paris*, Vol. 4 (3rd series) 1881, p. 521.

64. 'Etude sur la femme Kabyle', *Revue d'Anthropologie*, Vol. 6, 2nd series, 1883, pp. 56–69, p. 69.

65. Gabriel de Mortillet, *Bulletin de la Société d'Anthropologie*, Vol. 9, 1886, p. 703; Ely Leblanc, 'Le Problème des Berbères. Etudes d'ethnographie physique' in *Histoire et Historiens de l'Algérie*, Paris, Alcan, 1931 p. 75.

66. 'Sur les diverses appellations employées par les anciens pour désigner les populations de l'Afrique', *Bulletin de la Société d'Anthropologie*, Vol. 4 (3e série), 1881, pp. 606–13, pp. 607–608.

67. 'Essai de détermination anthropologique des deux types ou races confondus sous le nom moderne de Kabyles', *Bulletin de la Société d'Anthropologie*, Vol. 5 (3rd series), 1882, pp. 888–96.

68. 'Essai sur l'origine, l'évolution et les conditions actuelles des Berbers sédentaires', *Revue d'Anthropologie*, Vol. 5, (2nd series), 1882, pp. 412–442, pp. 420–21.

69. Ibid., pp. 416; 423; 429–30.

70. Mosse, p. 42.

71. 'Discours d'ouverture du cours de langues hébraïques, chaldaïque et syriaque au Collège de France prononcé le 21 février 1862", *De la part des peuples sémitiques dans l'histoire de la civilisation*. Oeuvres complètes, Vol. II, p. 324.

72. Mosse, p. 49.

73. 'Histoire des langues sémitiques', p. 137.

74. 'La Société Berbère', *Revue des Deux Mondes*, p. 144.

75. 'Discours', p. 333.

76. Mosse, p. 35.

77. Lapène had included a section on Kabyle origins in his *Vingt-Six Mois*: 'Comparaison des Kabaïles modernes avec les anciens peuples d'ou ils sont présumés tirer leur origine', pp. 177–92. Carette had adopted this angle in the work he produced for the Scientific Commission. Others included: H. Aucapitaine, 'Etudes sur l'origine et l'histoire des tribus berbères de la Haute Kabylie', *Journal Asiatique*, Vol. 14 (5th series), 1859, pp. 273–86; Alphonse Meyer, 'Origines des habitants de la Kabylie d'après la tradition locale', *Revue Africaine*, Vol. 3, 1859, pp. 357–67; Ernest Mercier, 'Ethnographie de l'Afrique septentrionale. Notes sur l'origine des peuples berbères', *Revue Africaine*, Vol. 15, 1871, pp. 420–33; David Kaltbrunner, *Recherches sur l'origine des Kabyles*, Geneva, Georg, 1871; J.A.N. Perier, 'Des Races dites berbères et de leur ethnogénie', *Mémoires de la Société d'Anthropologie de Paris*, Vol. I, 2nd series, 1873, pp. 1–54; Louis Rinn, 'Essais d'études linguistiques et ethnologiques sur les origines berbères', *Revue africaine*, serialized in vols 25–33, 1881–89. Such studies, of which these are only a sample, continued well into the twentieth century.

78. *La Science Politique fondée sur la Science de l'Homme ou Etude des races humaines sur le rapport philosophique, historique et sociale*, Paris, Bertrand, 1838, p. 374.

79. Jean Boissel, *Victor Courtet (1813–1867): Premier théoricien de la hierarchie des races*, Paris, PUF, 1968. (Although Boissel sees Courtet as the forerunner to de Gobineau, he emphasizes the radical differences in approach, namely that Courtet believed in progress, thus looking to the future and contemplating new forms of society, albeit hierarchical while de Gobineau was a pessimist who believed in degeneration, looked to the past and was anti-democratic.)

80. 'La Société Berbère', p. 140.

81. 'Essai', p. 442.

82. 'Etude sur la femme kabyle', p. 67.

83. M. Dally, Séance du 19 mai 1881, 'Discussion sur *Les Types Indigènes de l'Algérie* [by Topinard]' *Bulletin de la Société d'Anthropologie*, Vol. 4 (3rd series), 1881, p. 465.

84. Dally, 'Séance du 2 décembre 1886. Discussion sur les Couleurs chez les Arabes' *Bulletin de la Société d'Anthropologie*, Vol. 9,(3rd series), 1886, p. 702.

85. Kaltbrunner, p. 6.

86. Gabriel de Mortillet, 'Séance du 2 décembre 1886', p. 703.

87. 'La Société Berbère', p. 140.

88. 'Au capitaine Hanoteau, attaché au Bureau politique des Affaires arabes à Alger, Paris, 2 juin, 1858', *Correspondance*, 2 Vols, Paris, Calmann-Levy, 1926, p. 142.

89. 'La Société Berbère', p. 140

90. Jules Mohl, 'Rapport de l'année 1840–1841", *Vingt-sept ans d'histoire des Etudes orientales. Rapports faits à la Société Asiatique de Paris de 1840 à 1867*, 2 Vols, Paris, Reinwald, 1879, Vol. 1, pp. 14–15.

91. *Histoire Générale de la Presse française*, 5 vols, Paris, PUF, 1972, Vol. 3, pp. 390–91.

92. Schneider, *Empire for the Masses*, p. 9.

93. *Kabyles et Kroumirs*, Paris, Ducrocq, 1882 (an enlarged edition of a work first published as *A Travers la Kabylie* in 1865), pp. 318–22.

94. Emile Violard, *Le Banditisme en Kabylie*, Paris, Savine, 1895, p. ix.

95. Charles Géniaux, *Sous les Figuiers de Kabylie. Scènes de la vie berbère (1914–1917)*, Paris, Flammarion, 1917.

8 Civilian rule

1. Ageron, *Histoire de l'Algérie Contemporaine*, pp. 119 and 121. Of these, in the first instance, 121,600 were French and 115,000 of other European nationality and in the second instance 384,000 were French and 237,000 of other European nationality.

2. The Declaration of Rights appeared in the constitution of the Fourth and Fifth Republics, but not of the Third. None the less it was fundamental to the values of the constitution.

3. It is difficult to pigeonhole assimilationists and associationists socially or ideologically. Among intellectuals and theorists it might be conceivable to try but to generalize about the European population as a whole would be as hazardous as claiming that French collaborators in the Second World War were all from the right. Few settlers in Algeria, and many were ideologically from the left, believed in full integration of the indigenous to the European population as the theory of assimilation implied. On the other hand many were for the integration of the colony to France. In France, where contact with the colonial peoples was limited, the concept of assimilation in its complete sense was more readily accepted. The relationship between the settlers and the indigenous population was the crux of the failure of assimilation and this had little to do with the political tendencies of the settlers but much to do with economic and social pressures, personal convictions and experiences and received assumptions of national heritage.

4. The application of 1874 French Municipal Law in the colony greatly reduced the eligibility of Muslim voters. In Constantine, for example, the number of eligible Muslim voters was reduced from 2,000 (out of a population of 23,000) before the law to 500 after. Indigenous administrative power was further eroded by the increase (from 96 in 1868 to 249 in 1891) of the *communes de plein exercice*, in which the mayor was appointed and the councillors elected, to the detriment of the *communes mixtes* in which members of the indigenous population held non-elective posts as assistants to the *cercle* commander and as members of the five-man council. See Ageron, *Histoire de l'Algérie Contemporaine*, Vol. II, pp. 19–38.

5. For a discussion of the reasons for, and events leading to, the Crémieux Laws see Annie Rey-Goldzeiguer, 'La France Coloniale de 1830–1870' in *Histoire de la France Coloniale*, (ed. Jean Meyer, Jean Tarrade, Annie Rey-Goldzeiguer, Jacques Thobie), 2 Vols, Paris, Colin, 1991, Vol. I, pp. 538–42.

6. Louis Rinn, *Histoire de l'Insurrection de 1871 en Algérie*, Alger, Adolphe Jordan, 1891, pp. 646–7. (Preliminary disturbances occurred as of January 1871; the first major revolt occurred in March 1871).

7. Louis Bertrand, *Africa*, Paris, Michel, 1933 (originally published 1904), p. 33.

8. The Crémieux Laws were passed in October 1870. It was claimed that Arab/Kabyle anger at this move was a factor in provoking the insurrection. This theory was sufficiently widespread to elicit various written repudiations including Rinn's (1891) study of the insurrection, and Louis Forest, *La naturalisation des Juifs Algériens et l'Insurrection de 1871*, Paris, SFIL, no date. (A second edition of the book was published in 1900.)

9. 'Vital à Urbain, Constantine, le 21 Février 1871', *Correspondance du Docteur A. Vital avec I. Urbain (1845–1874)*, (ed. André Nouschi), Paris, Larose, 1959, p. 318.

10. See 'Vital à Urbain, Constantine, le 2 Mai 1871; Constantine, le 31 Mars 1873; Constantine le 14 Avril 1873', pp. 323, 389, 390.

11. Rey-Goldzeiguer, 'La France Coloniale de 1830–1870' in *Histoire de la France Coloniale*, p. 542.

12. 'Vital à Urbain, Constantine, le 26 Février 1872', p. 349.

13. Hollins Steele Jnr., *European Settlement vs. Muslim Property: The Foundation of Colonial Algeria 1830–1880*, Unpublished PhD Thesis, Columbia University, 1965, p. 249.

14. Charles-André Julien, 'L'Insurrection de Kabylie (1870–1871)', *Preuves*, December 1963, pp. 60–66, p. 65 (a more detailed treatment of the insurrection appears in Vol. I of *Histoire de l'Algérie contemporaine*, pp. 453–500).

15. Steele, p. 255.

16. Julien, 'L'insurrection de Kabylie', p. 65.

17. See for example J.D. Luciani, 'Chansons Kabyles', *Revue Africaine*, Vol. 43, 1899, pp. 17–33 and 142–71.

18. Charles-Robert Ageron, *Les Algériens Musulmans de la France 1871–1919*, 2 Vols, Paris, PUF, 1968, Vol. I, p. 281.

19. Stephen H. Roberts, *The History of French Colonial Policy 1870–1925*, London, Frank Cass, 1963 (first published 1929), p. 205.

20. Ageron, *Les Algériens Musulmans de la France* Vol. I, p. 281. [Gueydon was the second governor-general of the civilian administration, but the first to take up a post in Algeria. His predecessor and first appointee, Henri-Gabriel Didier, never assumed his post.]

21. Rinn, pp. 1–2.

22. Nicolas Auguste Pomel, *Des Races Indigènes de l'Algérie et du rôle que leur réservent leurs aptitudes*, Oran, Veuve Dagorn, 1871, pp. 59–60.

23. Ibid., pp. 18–19.

24. Guy de Maupassant, *Lettres d'Afrique*, (introduction and editing by Michèle Salinas) Paris, La Boîte à Documents, 1990, p. 264.

25. Ageron, *Histoire de l'Algérie contemporaine*, Vol. II, p. 208.

26. de Maupassant, 'Les Incendies en Algérie' (written on 23 August 1881 and published in *Le Gaulois* on 29 August 1881), pp. 115–16.

27. Ibid., 'Le Feu en Kabylie' (published in *Le Gaulois*, 3 September 1881), p. 125.

28. Ibid., p. 128.

29. 'Lettre d'Afrique' (published in *Le Gaulois*, 7th September 1881), p. 134–5.

30. Especially Charles-André Julien, 1963, Charles-Robert Ageron, *Les Algériens Musulmans*, André Nouchi, *Enquête sur le niveau de vie des populations rurales constantinoises de la conquête jusqu'en 1919*, Paris, 1961. In Julien's words it marked the advent of 'la colonisation triomphante'.

31. First used in 1901 *(Petit Robert*, p. 1433).

32. Quotation cited by Xavier de Montclos, *Le Cardinal Lavigerie. La Mission universelle de l'Eglise*, Paris, Ed. du Cerf, 1968, p. 36.

33. C. Lavigerie, 'Lettre pastorale pour la prise de possession du diocèse d'Alger, 5 mai, 1867", *Recueil de Lettres publiées par Mgr. L'Archevêque d'Alger sur les Œuvres et Missions Africaines*, Paris, Plon, 1869, p. 11.

34. 'Lettre pastorale de son Eminence le Cardinal Lavigerie, administrateur apostolique de Carthage et de la Tunisie, sur la dernière page connue de l'histoire de l'ancienne Eglise d'Afrique et mandement pour le carême de l'an de Grace 1883", *Ecrits d'Afrique* (ed. A. Hamman), Paris, Ed. Grasset, 1966.

35. Julien, *Histoire de l'Algérie Contemporaine*, Vol. I., p. 440.

36. Lavigerie refused to return 'his' orphans to their tribesmen who were reclaiming them. This prompted the intervention of Mac-Mahon. See Rey-Goldzeiguer, *Le Royaume Arabe*, pp. 498–99 and Julien, *Histoire de l'Algérie Contemporaine*, pp. 440–42 for the details and ramifications of this dispute.

37. The Père Blancs made relatively few conversions in Kabylia but there is still evidence of their cultural impact today. Ali Habib, 'Les Kabyles, algériens d'abord', *L'Express*, 17 February 1994, pp. 30–31, p. 30.

38. Augustine was one of the 'great Latin fathers of the Church'. The others were Lactantius (d.c. 325), Ambrose (340–97), and Jerome (340–420).

39. 'Lettre pastorale pour la prise de possession du diocèse d'Alger', *Recueil*, pp. 8–14.

40. 'De la formation d'auxiliaires indigènes (prêtres et médecins) pour assurer l'avenir de la mission' (1874), from *Ecrits d'Afrique*, p. 129.

41. 'La Kabylie', *Missions des Pères Blancs. Haute-Congo Belge, Grands Lacs, Sahara, Soudan, Kabylie,* (no place name), Joseph Servais, (no date), p. 33.

42. 'Lettre à M. le Directeur de l'œuvre des Ecoles d'Orient sur l'Emploi des offrandes pour les pauvres Arabes du diocèse d'Alger', *Recueil*, p. 41 (the emphasis is Lavigerie's).

43. *Lettre de son éminence la Cardinal Lavigerie faisant hommage à sa majesté le Roi Léopold II des documents sur la fondation de l'œuvre anti-esclavagiste publiés à l'occasion de la conférence de Bruxelles*, Alger, Adolphe Jordan, 1889, p. xxi.

44. N. Daniel, *Islam, Europe and Empire*, p. 306.

45. 'Lettre pastorale ... sur la dernière page connue de l'Histoire de l'ancienne Eglise d'Afrique ...', *Ecrits d'Afrique*, p. 219.

46. 'Rapport confidentiel du Procureur Général près de la Cour d'Appel d'Alger en 1883', from *La Mission universelle de l'Eglise*, p. 164.

47. Paul Bert, *Lettres de Kabylie. La politique Algérienne*, Paris, Lemerre, 1885, pp. 11–12.

48. Paul Leroy-Beaulieu, *L'Algérie et la Tunisie*, Paris, Guillaumin, 1897 (first published 1887), p. vi.

49. The only naturalization bill to receive serious consideration was proposed in the 1930s by Maurice Viollette. The Blum–Viollette Bill, as it came to be known, would have granted citizenship to a small number of the Algerian elite (25,000 out of a population of 6 million) without renunciation of the *statut personnel*, but it was never passed.

50. Ageron, *Histoire de l'Algérie contemporaine*, Vol. II, p. 33.

51. Pomel, pp. 65–6.

52. Cited by Ageron, *Histoire de l'Algérie contemporaine*, p. 33.

53. *A Travers la Kabylie et les Questions Kabyles*, Paris, Plon, 1889 (the work was re-issued in 1899), pp. 121–2.

54. Ibid., pp. 112 and 124.

55. See Pierre Cœur (pseudonym for Mrs Anne C.J. de Voisin d'Ambre), *L'Assimilation des indigènes musulmans*, Paris, Imprimerie coloniale, 1890.

56. *Ecole Polytechnique. Livre du Centenaire 1794–1894*, Vol. II, p. 253.

57. Bertholon and Chantre, *Recherches Anthropologiques dans la Berberie Orientale*, Lyon, Rey, 1913, p. ii.

58. Pomel, p. 57.

59. Ibid., pp. 47–8.

60. Ibid., pp. 49 and 60.

61. In 1830 an estimated 50 per cent of the indigenous population comprised Berbers from the M'zab, Aurès and Kabylia.Valensi, *On the eve of colonialism*, p. 11. At its conquest by the French Kabylia, had an estimated 100 inhabitants per square kilometre. Jean Morizot, *L'Algérie kabylisée*, Paris, Peyronnet, 1962, p. 48.

62. Pushing the Arabs into the Sahara would liberate lands for colonization. Ibid., p. 44.

63. Ibid., p. 35.

64. Ibid., pp. 67–8.

65. Ibid., pp. 73–4.

66. For an analysis of anti-Jewish sentiment in the colony at the time see Ageron, *Histoire de l'Algérie contemporaine*, Vol. II, pp. 60–67.

67. Amédée Caix de Saint-Aymour, *Questions algériennes, Arabes et Kabyles*, Paris, Ollendorf, 1891, pp. 99–100 [Algerian is used in its nineteenth-century sense of European Algerian].

68. Ageron, *Histoire de l'Algérie contemporaine*, Vol. II, p. 120.

69. Gide on the Mediterranean race cited by Marc Baroli, *La Vie Quotidienne des Français en Algérie 1830–1914*, Paris, Hachette, 1967, p. 214.

70. Caix de Saint-Aymour, pp. 11–12.

71. Ibid., p. 37.

72. Ibid., pp. 75 and 117.

73. Ibid., pp. 85 and 155.

74. *Les Kabyles et la colonisation française*, p. 60
75. Caix de Saint-Aymour, pp. 33 and 169–70.
76. Ageron has devoted most time to the question of Kabyle policy. With regard to educational policy, Fanny Colonna has contributed an excellent analysis on what the French termed the *'miracle kabyle'* in her *Instituteurs Algériens*, Paris, Presses de la Fondation nationale des sciences politiques, 1975. Masqueray's influence on Jules Ferry is dealt with briefly in 'Du Bon Usage de la Science coloniale', *Mal de Voir*, pp. 221–41 published in collaboration with Claude Haïm Brahimi.
77. *Races Berbères. Kabylie du Jurjura*, Paris, Ernest Leroux, 1893, p. xiv. (Liorel also wrote a book on the M'zab).
78. Hanoteau and Letourneux's work on the Kabyles was published in 1871 but it was researched and written under the military regime and falls within the intellectual framework of military scholarship.
79. *Formation des Cités chez les populations sédentaires de l'Algérie (Kabyles du Djurjura, Chaouia de l'Aurès, Beni M'zab)*, Paris, Leroux, 1886, pp. 13–14.
80. Ibid., pp. 221–2 and 261.
81. Ibid., pp. 30 and 86 (this comparison was frequent by now).
82. Ibid., pp. 15–16 and 88.
83. See Colonna and Brahimi, p. 234.
84. Caix de Saint-Aymour, p. 240. As would be expected Caix de Saint-Aymour negatively contrasted the Arab experience. In fact there was little evidence of the Kabyle Miracle, as it is called, until the twentieth century.
85. *La Civilisation des Arabes*, Paris, Firmin-Didot, 1884, pp. 34–6.
86. Ibid., pp. 54, 254 and 257.
87. Robert Nye, *The Origins of Crowd Psychology: Gustave Le Bon and the Crisis of Mass Democracy in the Third Republic*, Beverly Hills, Sage Publications, 1975.
88. Raymond F. Betts, *Assimilation and Association*, p. 65.
89. Warnier, p. 44. For Warnier's figures and views see Chapter 6 above. [Most *kabylophiles* argued their case in favour of the 1 million pure Berbers.]
90. Augustin Bernard, Obitury of Emile Masqueray in *Revue Africaine*, Vol. 38, 1894, pp. 350–75, p. 328.
91. du Maupassant, p. 103.
92. Notably: Léopold de Saussure, *Psychologie de la Colonisation Française dans ses rapports avec les société indigènes*, (1890); Jules Harmand, *La Domination et colonisation* (1910); Albert Sarraut, *La Mise en Valeur des Colonies françaises* (1923).
93. The first of these, *bicot*, made its appearance in 1891. *Bougnoul*, from the Ouolof meaning black, was first attached to the blacks of Senegal by the *Pères Blancs*. It was assimilated into the Algerian repertoire of racial slurs in the twentieth century along with *melon* and *raton*. *Le Petit Robert* Paris, Société du Nouveau Littré, 1977, pp. 181, 205, 1178 and 1612.

9 Algeria, the melting pot of the Mediterranean: the impact of Louis Bertrand

1. Faidherbe et Topinard, 'Instructions sur l'Anthropologie de l'Algérie', *Bulletin de la Société d'Anthropologie de Paris*, Vol. 8 (2nd series), 1873, pp. 603–65, p. 654.
2. Bert, 'Première Lettre. Philippeville, le 18 avril 1885', *Lettres de Kabylie*, p. 6.

3. Octave Houdas, *Ethnographie de l'Algérie*, Paris, Leclerc, 1886, pp. v–vi.

4. Jules Ferry, 'De la Responsabilité du Gouverneur-Général' in *Le Gouvernement de l'Algérie*, Paris, Colin, 1892, p. 78.

5. Ibid., pp. 80–81.

6. Quoted by Odile Husson, *Lorraine et Afrique dans l'œuvre de Louis Bertrand*, Nancy, Sté. d'Impressions Typographiques, 1966, p. 161.

7. L. Bertrand, *Les Villes D'Or. Algérie et Tunisie Romaines*, Paris, Fayard, 1921, pp. 5–10.

8. The short-lived literary movement *decadentisme*, is best remembered by its poets, especially Baudelaire, Verlaine and Mallarmé. For discussions of *fin de siécle* decadence see: Eugen Weber, *France. Fin de Siècle*, Cambridge, Harvard University Press, 1986; Eric C. Hansen, *Disaffection and Decadence. A Crisis in French Intellectual Thought 1848–1898*, Washington, University Press of America, 1982.

9. Quoted by Zeev Sternhell, *Maurice Barrès et la Nationalisme Français*, Paris, Editions Complexe, 1985 (first published 1972), pp. 41–2.

10. Husson, pp. 114–15.

11. Quoted by Sternhell, p. 52.

12. Roger Macgraw, *France 1815–1914. The Bourgeois Century*, London, Fontana, 1987, p. 269.

13. L. Bertrand, *Sur les Routes du Sud*, Paris, Fayard, 1936 (9th ed), pp. 217 and 219. [Foreigners, especially Christians, were known as *Roumi* by the Arabs and Berbers. The word originates from the arabic *roum*, meaning land subjugated by Rome.] See also p. 204.

14. Ibid., pp. 60–61 and 216–17.

15. Bertrand, *Le Sang des Races*, Paris, Albin Michel, 1926 (first published 1899), p. 6,

16. Bertrand, 'Le Centenaire du cardinal Lavigerie', in *Devant l'Islam*, Paris, Plon, 1926, p. 83.

17. Ibid., p. 96.

18. The principal works developing the subject were: *Le Livre de la Méditerranée* (1911), *Les plus belles pages de Saint Augustin* (1916), *Les Villes d'Or* (1921), *Carthage* (1931, *L'Eglise d'Afrique* (1931), *Africa* (1933, first published as *Le Jardin de la Mort*, 1905), *Vers Cyrène, terre d'Appolon* (1935) and the novel *Sanguis martyrum* (1918).

19. *Les Villes d'Or*, pp. 8–9.

20. *Sur les Routes du Sud*, p. 60.

21. *Les Villes d'Or*, p. 36.

22. Ibid., p. 33.

23. 'Notre Afrique' in *Devant l'Islam*, p. 143.

24. *Le Sens de l'Ennemi*, Paris, Fayard, 1917, pp. 185–6.

25. Bertrand's African cycle contained five novels of which *Le Sang des Races* (1899), *La Cina* (1901) and *Pepète le Bien Aimé* (1904) (subsequent editions were entitled *Pepète et Balthazar*) were the most renowned.

26. *Sur les Route du Sud*, p. 61.

27. Ibid., p. 72.

28. *Les Villes d'Or*, pp. 7 and 23.

29. *Sur les Routes du Sud*, p. 217.

30. Ibid., p. 218.

31. Ibid., p. 52.

32. *Les Villes d'Or*, p. 243.
33. *Le Sens de l'Ennemi*, p. 151.
34. Ibid., p. 169.
35. *Les Villes d'Or*, p. 19.
36. Ibid., p. 10.
37. 'Notre Afrique' in *Devant l'Islam*, p. 141.
38. Preface to *Sang des Races*, p. 9.
39. *Les Villes d'Or*, p. 10.
40. *Le Sens de l'Ennemi*, p. 22.
41. 'Notre Afrique' in *Devant l'Islam*, p. 141.
42. *Le Sens de l'Ennemi*, p. 11.
43. *Les Villes d'Or*, p. 157.
44. *Le Sens de l'Ennemi*, pp. 31–2 and 221–2.
45. See for example *Les Villes d'Or*, pp. 30–31, in which he compares the architecture of the two traditions.
46. 'Retour d'Egypte' in *Devant l'Islam*, p. 43.
47. 'Le Centenaire du Cardinal Lavigerie', ibid., p. 92.
48. Ibid., pp. 70 and 86–7.
49. 'Sur un livre de Paul Adam', ibid., p. 198.
50. Quoted by Charles Tailliart, *L'Algérie dans la Littérature française*, Paris, Champion, 1925, pp. 569–70 from Bertrand's 'La résurrection de l'Afrique latine', *Revue l'Afrique Latine*, March 1922.
51. 'Notre Afrique' in *Devant l'Islam*, pp. 127–8.
52. Ibid., p. 146. Robert Randau (pseudonym for Robert Arnaud), Charles Hagel and Louis Lecoq (who collaborated for the best known of their novels) and Musette (pseudonym for V.M. Auguste Robinet) were the most popular among the settler novelists of the late nineteenth and early twentieth century.
53. David Clark Cabeen, *The African Novels of Louis Bertrand: A Phase of the Renascence of National Energy in France* (Ph.D. Thesis presented at the University of Philadelphia), Philadelphia, Westbrook, 1922, p. 98.
54. Pierre Martino, 'La Littérature Algérienne', in *Histoire et Historiens de l'Algérie*, pp. 331–48, p. 341.
55. Maurice Ricord was one of his most extensive commentators. His book *Louis Bertrand, l'Africain*, Paris, Fayard, 1947 contains the best bibliography available of Bertrand's work.
56. 'Les amours de Cagayous', the first of a series of stories, appeared in 1896. The series was published in pamphlet form in weekly instalments and was still running in 1920 with 'Cagayous poilu'. Musette died prematurely in 1930. Martino, writing in the year of Musette's death, claimed his work to be the most remarkable to have emerged from the colony since the turn of the century (Martino, p. 346).
57. These included Hughes Le Roux, Magali Boisnard, Raymond Marival, Ferdinand Duchêne, Elissa Rhaïs, Charles Hagel, Louis Lecoq and Robert Randau. For bibliographies of these and other authors see Jean Dejeux, *Bibliographie de la littérature 'algérienne' des français*, Paris, CNRS, 1978.
58. Charles Hagel and Louis Lecoq, 'Broumitche et le Kabyle', *Mercure de France*, Vol. 143, 1920, pp. 316–66. The book, published by Fayard, came out in the same year.
59. *Les Algérienistes. Roman de la patrie algérienne*, Paris, Sansot, 1911 (3rd edn), p. 5.

The two other major novels are: *Les Colons. Roman de la patrie algérienne* (Preface by M.-A. Leblond), Paris, Sansot, 1907; *Cassard le Berbère*, Paris, Belles-Lettres, n.d. (published after the Second World War).

60. *Les Colons*, p. iv.

61. Ibid., p. 32.

62. Ibid., p. 309.

63. Quoted by Albert Sadouillet, 'Le Temoignage de Robert Randau Ecrivain et Homme d'action', *Algéria*, January–February 1951, pp. 10–13, p. 13.

64. G. Sergi, *The Mediterranean Race: A Study of the Origin of European Peoples*, Oosterhout N.B., Anthropological Publications, 1967.

65. Ibid., pp. 118–19.

66. L. Bertholon and E. Chantre, *Recherches Anthropologiques dans la Berberie Orientale*, 2 Vols, Lyon, Rey, 1913, Vol. I, p. 72.

67. Dr Laupts, 'Lettre à M. Zaborowski sur l'état et l'avenir des populations de l'Algérie et de la Tunisie', *Bulletin de la Société d'Anthropologie*, Vol. 9, 4th series, 1898, pp. 388–406, pp. 392–3.

68. *Domination et Colonisation*, Paris, Flammarion, 1910, p. 156.

69. Ibid., p. 53.

70. *L'Œuvre française aux colonies*, Paris, Larose, 1913, p. 218.

71. Karl Mannheim, *Ideology and Utopia. An introduction to the Sociology of Knowledge* (trans. Louis Wirth and Edward Shils), New York, Harcourt Brace Janovich, 1936 (first published 1929).

72. *De la part des Peuples Sémitiques* from *Œuvres complètes*, Vol. II, p. 333.

73. *Les races et les langues*, Paris, Alcan, 1893, p. 50.

74. Ibid., p. 150.

10 Persistent stereotypes and resultant policies

1. *Le Choc des Races*, Paris, Fayard, 1911.

2. P. Martino, 'La Littérature algérienne', in *Histoire et Historiens*, p. 315.

3. 'Kamir. Roman d'une femme arabe' in *La Petite Illustration*, 27 March, 3 and 10 April 1926, pp. 3–64.

4. Ibid., p. 62.

5. *Orientale 1930*, Paris, 'Les Ecrits' Grasset, 1930, p. 96.

6. *Un Dimanche dans la Casbah*, Paris, Fayard, 1936, p. 20.

7. *Mille et un Jours, Mourad*, Brussels, Ed. de la Toison d'Or, 1943, pp. 11, 14, 16, and 333.

8. Christine Achour and Simone Rezzoug, 'Brisure dans une cohérence discursive: l'autochtone dans les textes coloniaux de 1930 en Algérie', in *Les Années Trente*, (ed. Anne Roche and Christian Tarting), Paris, CNRS, 1985 pp. 75–94.

9. Charles Géniaux, *Sous les Figuiers de Kabylie, Scènes de la vie berbère (1914–1917)*, Paris, Flammarion, 1917. Géniaux also contributed a series of articles to the *Revue des Deux Mondes* on Kabylia and the Kabyles during the period 1916–17.

10. *Ceux d'Algérie*, Paris, Horizons de France, 1929, p. 96.

11. Ibid., p. 93.

12. Ibid., p. 99.

13. Ibid., p. 127.

14. Mouloud Feraoun, *Les Poèmes de Si Mohand*, Paris, Les Editions de Minuit, 1960, p. 10.

15. Eugène Guernier, *La Berberie, l'Islam et la France*, 2 Vols, Paris, Ed. de l'Union française, 1950, Vol. II. p. 173.

16. Ibid., pp. 175–6.

17. Pierre Bourdieu, *The Algerians* (trans. Alan C.M. Ross from *Sociologie de l'Algérie*, Paris, 1958) Boston, Beacon, 1962, p. 24.

18. Emile-Félix Gautier, 'Le Cadre Géographique de l'Histoire en Algérie', in *Histoire et Historiens*, p. 34.

19. Guernier, Vol. I, p. 240.

20. Gautier, p. 22.

21. Ibid., p. 31.

22. Fernand Braudel, *The Mediterranean and the Mediterranean World in the Age of Philip II*, (trans. Siân Reynolds), 2 Vols, New York, Harper, 1972 (first published 1949), Vol. I, p. 88.

23. Gautier, p. 20.

24. Ibid., p. 17.

25. Braudel, Chapter 1, Vol. 1.

26. By way of introduction see R.K. Burns, 'The Circum-Alpine Area: A Preliminary View', *Anthropological Quarterly*, Vol. 36, n° 3, 1963, pp. 130–55.

27. See Dale Eickelman, 'New Directions in Interpreting North African Society', in *Connaissances du Maghreb*, pp. 279–89.

28. Gautier, p. 32.

29. Ely Leblanc, 'Le Problème des Berbères', in *Histoire et Historiens*, p. 74.

30. Eugène Albertini, 'L'Algérie Antique' in *Histoire et Historiens*, p. 89.

31. Marçais and Julien quoted by Yves Lacoste in *Ibn Khaldoun. Naissance de l'Histoire Passé du tiers monde*, Paris, Ed. La Découverte, 1985, p. 91.

32. Guernier, Vol. II, pp. 176–7.

33. Ibid., p. 181.

34. Jacques Berque, 'Cent vingt-cinq ans de sociologie maghrébine', *Annales E.S.C.*, Vol. II, 1956, pp. 296–324.

35. Leblanc, pp. 78–9.

36. Martial Rémond, 'La Kabylie', *Revue Africaine*, Vol. 80, 1937, pp. 108–16.

37. Eickelman, p. 280.

38. Martial Rémond, 'L'Elargissement des Droits Politiques des Indigènes. Ses conséquences en Kabylie', *Revue Africaine*, Vol. 67, 1926, pp. 153–213, 253.

39. Martial Rémond, 'La Kabylie', p. 114. [The article was the last chapter of a book later published under the same title.]

40. Ibid., p. 116.

41. From the time the schools were first set up in the 1880s the situation evolved as follows: 2 per cent of the indigenous population in 1889; 8.9 per cent in 1930 and 15 per cent in 1954. The indigenous population represented approximately 85 per cent of the total population of Algeria. In contrast in 1901, 81 per cent of the Europeans had received some form of education. Fanny Colonna, *Instituteurs Algériens. 1883–1939*, Paris, Presses de la Fondation nationale des Sciences politiques, 1975, p. 50.

42. Ibid., pp. 26–8 and 46.

43. Henri Terrace, *Histoire du Maroc*, Casablanca, 1950, pp. 307, 410 and 433. Quoted by Edmund Burke III, 'The Image of the Moroccan State in French Ethnological Literature: a New Look at the Origin of Lyautey's Berber Policy', in *Arabs and Berbers*, (ed. E. Gellner and C. Micaud), London, Heath, 1972, pp. 175–99, p. 177.

44. Marquis de Segonzac, *Au Cœur de l'Atlas, Mission au Maroc*, (Paris, 1910), quoted by Burke, p. 184.

45. Burke, p. 187.

46. Ibid., p. 193.

47. In 1921 the institute was renamed the Institut des Hautes Etudes marocaines and produced its own journal, the *Archives Berbères*.

48. e.g. Robert de Caix, 'Le Maroc français et la question indigène', *Revue des Deux Mondes*, Vol. 349 (Belgian ed.), 1914, pp. 806–41, pp. 820–21.

49. Alan Scham, *Lyautey in Morocco. Protectorate Administration 1912–1925*, Berkeley, University of California Press, 1970, p. 41.

50. Robin Bidwell, *Morocco under Colonial Rule: French Administration of Tribal Areas 1912–1956*, Cass, London, 1973, p. 48. For further discussions on Berber Policy in Morocco see: C-R. Ageron, 'Du Mythe Kabyle aux Politiques Berbères', in *Le Mal de Voir. Cahiers Jussieu 2*, Paris, UGE, 1976, pp. 331–48; S.H.R. Roberts, *The History of French Colonial Policy 1870–1925*, London, Frank Cass, 1963 (first published 1929); A. Scham, 1970.

51. Quoted by Bidwell, p. 51.

52. Bidwell, p.49.

53. Ibid., p. 50.

54. Quoted by Bidwell, p. 51.

55. Bidwell, p. 53.

56. Quoted by Bidwell, p. 273.

57. Bidwell, p. 54.

58. Ibid., p. 275.

59. See especially J. Berque, *French North Africa: The Maghrib between the Two World Wars*, (trans. Jean Stewart), London, Faber & Faber, 1967. Berque considers 1930 to have been a critical year throughout the Maghreb, with crucial events in all three countries stimulating the emergence of nationalism.

60. Lucette Valensi, *On the Eve of Colonialism. North Africa before French Conquest*, N.Y., Africana, 1977 (trans. K.J. Perkins), p. 11.

61. Gianni Albergoni and François Pouillon, in 'Le fait berbère et sa lecture coloniale: l'extrême Sud Tunisien', in *Mal de Voir*, pp. 349–96, p. 386.

62. Ibid., p. 359

63. Pervinquière, Le Sud Tunisien', *Revue de géographie annuelle*, 1909, pp. 447–50, quoted by Albergoni and Pouillon, p. 357.

64. Ibid., p. 371.

65. Mohammed Harbi, *Le F.L.N. Mirage et Réalité des origines à la prise du pouvoir (1945–1962)*, Paris, Editions J.A., 1980, pp. 59–60.

66. Hugh Roberts, *Algerian Socialism and the Kabyle Question*, Monographs in Development Studies n° 8, School of Development Studies, University of East Anglia, 1981, p. 189.

67. Harbi, p. 59.

68. Ibid., p. 61.

69. Ibid.

70. H. Roberts, pp. 221–3.

71. Harbi, p. 61.

72. Ibid., p. 62.

73. Quoted by H. Roberts, p. 221–2.

74. During the War of Independence Algeria was divided up into six wilayas,

each under the leadership of an F.L.N. commander. Harbi, op. cit, p. 235 gives a figure of 2,000 for the number of men and women killed in Wilaya III. Alistair Horne, *A Savage War of Peace, Algeria 1954–1962*, London, Penguin, 1979, gives a figure of 3,000. (p. 323), as does Ferhat Abbas, *Autopsie d'une guerre*, Paris, Editions Garnier, 1980, p. 221. On the purges, see also Roberts, pp. 261–2 and Yves Courrière, *L'Heure des Colonels*, Paris, Fayard, 1970, pp. 132–3.

75. See in particular Mouloud Feraoun, *Journal 1955–1962*, Paris, Seuil, 1962 (Feraoun's diary is an eloquent testimony to the human tragedy of this war).

76. Abbas, p. 221.

77. Quoted by Jean de la Guérivière, 'Des berbéristes ont formé un embryon de parti légal', *Le Monde*, 15 February 1989.

78. Meziane Ourad, 'Lettre de Kabylie', *L'Evenement de Jeudi*, 21–27 April 1994. (Ourad is a journalist for the weekly *Algérie-Actualité*.)

11 Conclusion

1. The question of whether Islamic society is a classless one is the subject of debate. The point is that in 1830 there was no overarching social hierarchy. Any extant social divisions were within tribal/urban units.

2. Ignaz Goldziher, *Introduction to Islamic Theology and Law* (trans. Andras and Ruth Hamori), Princeton, Princeton University Press, 1981 (first published 1910), p. 3.

3. Maxime Rodinson, *Islam and Capitalism* (trans. Brian Pearce), Austin, University of Texas Press, 1981, p. 15.

4. Pierre Bourdieu, *The Algerians* (trans. A.C.M. Ross), Boston, Beacon, 1962, p. 61.

5. William H. Sewell, Jr., *Work and Revolution in France*, London, Cambridge University Press, 1982 (first published 1980), p. 145.

6. *Mœurs et Coutumes*, p. 152.

7. *Arabes et Kabyles*, p. 38.

8. That sexuality was so intricately involved in the settler image is interesting, in view of the castigation of Arab sexuality, but not surprising. Racial ideology, like other ideologies seeking to maintain a hierarchical status quo, is full of paradoxes and double standards of this sort.

APPENDIX

Biographical sketches

Lieutenant le Baron Henri Aucapitaine (1833–67) of the 1st regiment of the *tirailleurs indigènes* served as an officer in the Bureaux Arabes. He was a member of the Société Historique Algérienne and a regular contributor to the *Revue Africaine*.

Marie Armand Pascal d'Avezac de Castera-Macaya (1800–75), a geographer of renown, was secretary of the Société géographique de Paris and a member of the Geographical Societies of London and Frankfurt and the Société historique algérienne. He was also a member of the Institut de France. He was editor, with Eichthal and the orientalist Kasimirski, among others, of the journal, *Pittoresque*. D'Avezac classified African races into ten groups and African languages into two, the *cohesive* and the *diacritique*, placing the Berber language in the former. He also suggested that the white race was the basic human type (*type fondamental*), the yellow race the sub-type (*sous-type*), and the black race an aberration (*groupe aberrant*). Gobineau was greatly influenced by d'Avezac.

Dr Baudens was the principal surgeon and medical professor of the army and a member of the medical academies of Marseille, Lyon and Montpellier.

Dr Louis-Adrien* Berbrugger (1801–69) arrived in Algeria in 1834. He was a Saint-Simonian and a *kabylophile* who interested himself in every aspect of scholarship in Algeria. A member of the Scientific Commission, he helped found the Bibliothèque Nationale d'Alger, later becoming its chief librarian. As well as being president of the Société historique algérienne, he was editor-in-chief of the *Moniteur Algérien*. He wrote regularly for the *Revue Africaine*, the journal of the Société historique, and published various works of which *Les époques militaires de la Grande Kabylie* (1857) is the best known. He married a Muslim and was an Arabist.

---

* The asterisk indicates the name commonly used, in this case Adrien.

Biographical sketches

Paul Bert (1833–86) was a physiologist who held posts as minister of education and governor-general of Indo-China. He was a militant anti-cleric who advocated secular education and, during his assignment as governor-general, encouraged the spread of secular schools throughout the colony of Indo-China. He was also the honorary president of the Société protectrice des colons, founded in 1882, and a member of the Institut de France. He was closely associated with Jules Ferry and Emile Masqueray, appointing the latter to his position as director of the Faculty of Letters in Algiers.

Louis Marie Emile Bertrand (1866–1941) was born in Lorraine. He was an author who found his true voice in Algeria. In 1925 he was elected to the Académie Française to hold the seat vacated by the death of Barrès. Although he saw himself as distinct from Barrès he shared many of his preoccupations, which he transposed and adapted to the Algerian scene.

Johann-Friedrich Blumenbach (1752–1840), a German physiologist and anthropologist, studied medicine at Jena and held the post of professor of medicine at Göttingen. He classified human beings into five racial groups and coined the word Caucasian. He emphasized the importance of comparative anatomy in man's history and was a pioneer of craniology. He is considered to be the 'father of physical anthropology'.

Dr Eugène Bodichon (1810–85), who had a medical practice in Algiers, was an occasional contributor on Algeria to the *Bulletin de la Société de Géographie de Paris* and to the *Revue de l'Orient*. He was a moderate republican who, at one time, was placed on the list of candidates for the legislative elections of the radical newspaper, *Le National*.

Baron Laurent-Estève Boissonnet (1811–1901), who had Saint-Simonian tendencies, graduated from the Polytechnique in 1830. He was promoted to the rank of captain in 1840. In 1844 he was appointed director of the Affaires Indigènes in Constantine. A Berber-speaker, he was a friend of Abd-el-Kader and Urbain and an adviser to Louis-Napoleon. He arranged the publication of the Arabic text of Abd-el-Kader's poems and regulations for his army.

Baron Jean-Baptiste Georges Marie Bory de Saint-Vincent (1778–1846) was a naturalist who joined Captain Nicholas Baudin's expedition to Australia in 1798. Leaving the vessel at Mauritius, he spent two years exploring Réunion and other islands. He then joined Napoleon's army, taking part in some of the major campaigns. In 1829 he was nominated to lead a scientific expedition to Morea and ten years latter was placed at the head of the Scientific Commission of Algeria. He was the author of *L'Homme. Essai zoologique sur le genre humain*, (1827), in which he classified man into 15 different species. He was one of the most popular ethnologists-cum-anthropologists of his day.

Dr Jean-Christian Boudin (1806–67), senior physician at the Vincennes asylum, member of the Anthropological Society and its president in 1862, pioneered the science of medical statistics in his *Traité de géographie et de statistiques médicales* (1856). He spent four years as a military doctor in Algeria, first in Constantine (1837) and then in Algiers (1838–40) and seven years as a senior physician at the military hospital of Marseilles, which dealt with all severe cases from Algeria.

Paul Broca (1824–80), *Polytechnicien*, surgeon and anthropologist, was a professor at the Faculty of Medicine in Paris and a member of the Académie de Médecine. He founded the Société de Libres Penseurs in 1848 and the Société d'Anthropologie de Paris in 1859, remaining the society's secretary for the rest of his life. As a young man he was a polygenist, having been greatly influenced by the lectures of Professor Bérard on the subject, but later he distanced himself, preferring to remain uncommitted to any particular school of thought on racial origins. He inclined to the view that the Berbers were of Celtic origin.

Charles-Henri Emmanuel Brosselard (1816–89) was an interpreter and civil servant who spent his whole career in Algeria. He served at the commissariats of Bougie and Blidah, was appointed *sous-préfet* of Tlemcen in 1859 and *préfet* of Oran in 1864. In 1873 he was made director-general of Algerian Affairs at the ministry. He spoke both Arab and Berber and was considered to be an expert in Arabic epigraphy. He was a member of both the Scientific Commission and the Commission involved in the compilation of a French–Berber dictionary. He was a member of the Société Asiatique.

Georges-Louis Leclerc, Comte de Buffon (1707–88) was a French author and naturalist, whose best-known work, *Histoire Naturelle de l'Homme*, ran into several editions and was translated into a number of languages. Buffon was a member of the French Academy, treasurer of the Academy of Science, fellow of the Royal Society of London, and a member of numerous learned societies throughout Europe. He divided human beings into six races, distinguishing them by their skin colour, stature and bodily form and psychic traits.

Thomas Robert Bugeaud de la Piconnerie (Field Marshal, Marquis of Piconnerie and Duc of l'Isly) (1784–1849) was governor of Algeria from 1840 to 1847, during which time he introduced innovative if brutal tactics which led to the defeat of Abd-el-Kader. He believed in the colonization of Algeria by the military and elaborated a theory to this end.

Pierre Jean George* Cabanis (1757–1808) was a physiologist who obtained an appointment as administrator of hospitals in Paris on the publication in 1789 of his *Observations sur les hôpitaux*. In 1795 he was appointed professor of hygiene at the Paris medical school and four years later he obtained the chair of legal medicine and the history of medicine. He was physician to Mirabeau and was involved in national politics until the advent of Napoleon.

Amédée Vicomte de Caix de Saint-Aymour (1843–1921), was a *colon*, self-professed *kabylophile* and author of a number of historical works. He was also a contributor to the Société d'Anthropologie de Paris .

Antoine Ernest* Hippolyte Carette (1808–90) was a graduate of the Ecole Polytechnique and one of the colony's leading Saint-Simonians. A captain in the Engineers, he had attained the rank of colonel by 1863. He was secretary to the Scientific Commission of 1840–42, and became a member of the Société Historique Algérienne in 1859, contributing regularly to its journal, the *Revue Africaine*.

François Charvériat (1855–89) was professor of Roman and maritime law at the Algiers School of Law, where he had taken up his post in 1884 on receiving his *Agrégation*.

Victor Courtet de L'Isle (1813–67) was a Saint-Simonian with an active interest in race. He was a member of the Société Géographique de Paris and the Société Ethnologique de Paris, holding the post of assistant secretary of the latter in 1846. He elaborated a theory on the hierarchical nature of human races, using physical beauty and the degree of social development as criteria for classification.

Géorges Léopold Chrétien Frédéric Dagobert Cuvier (Baron) (1769–1832), a naturalist and professor of natural history at the Collège de France, established the disciplines of comparative anatomy and palaeontology in France. His *magnum opus*, *Règne animal distribué d'après son organisation*, appeared in four volumes in 1817 (a revised five-volume edition was published in 1829–30). He was raised to the peerage by Louis-Philippe.

Melchior Joseph Eugène* Daumas (1803–71), officer, senator and writer, graduated from Saumur in 1827. (His father was a military doctor and Daumas had himself started medical studies but his father was not satisfied with his progress and pressured him to take up a military career.) He arrived in Algeria with Clauzel and served as consul in Mascara and as an officer in the Bureaux Arabes, rising to the rank of general. He was director of Arab Affairs in Algeria and later director of Algerian Affairs at the

Ministry of War. He was president of the Société de Géographie de Paris in 1858–59 and contributed a wide range of articles on Algeria to numerous scholarly journals. Daumas was a relative of de Slane, translator of Ibn Khaldoun.

Ferdinand Victor Eugène* Delacroix (1798–1863) was a leader of the French Romantic movement and is best remembered for his large historical pictures, many of which were inspired by the poetry of Byron. Thanks to Thiers, in 1835 he received a commission to decorate the interior of the Chamber of Deputies. He also painted the centre of the ceiling of the Apollo Gallery in the Louvre, parts of the interior of the library of Luxembourg, and murals in the church of Saint Sulpice and the Salon de la Paix in the Hotel de Ville. He visited Algeria in 1832, painting and drawing while he was there. His sojourn in Algeria had a profound effect on his work.

Jacques Denis Delaporte (1777–1861) was a member of Bonaparte's expedition to Egypt. He was chief interpreter in Algiers and re-organized the whole service of interpreters. In 1836 he was appointed director of Arab Affairs, a post he held only briefly. He was a member of the five-man commission designated by the minister of war to draw up a French–Berber dictionary and served as French consul at Mogador

Jean-Honorat Delaporte (?–1871) was an interpreter at the bureau of civil administration in Algiers and eldest son of Jacques.

Général Nicolas Gilles Toussaint Desvaux (1810–84) graduated from Saumur, first of the year. He was commander of the Constantine Division from 1858–1864. He took a 15-year old indigenous woman as his common-law wife.

Jean-Charles Devaux, (1824–?) was a captain in the first regiment of the Zouaves and an officer of the Bureaux Arabes, serving as commanding officer at Beni-Mançour and Drâ-el-Mizan.

Diophantus of Alexandria (circa third century AD), a Greek Algebraist and author of a celebrated book, *Arithmetica*, is best remembered for the Diophantine equations.

Pierre Pascal Duprat (1815–85) was editor-in-chief of the *Revue Indépendante*. The journal was founded in 1841 by Pierre Leroux, George Sand and Louis Viardot, and inclined to severe criticism of governmental policies. Philosophy, literature and economics were treated with equal consideration, placing it among the most widely circulated journals of the time. Duprat later held public office and was a professor at the Lausanne Academy.

Franciade Fleurus Duvivier (1794–1848), was a graduate of the Ecole Polytechnique and the Ecole d'Application de Metz who spent much of his career in Algeria. He was promoted to the rank of lieutenant-colonel in 1834 as a result of his action at Bougie, to colonel in 1837 as a result of Guelma, and to general in 1840 when he took the Tenia pass. He was in charge of one of three columns in the battalion that made an assault on Médéah and Milianah (Kabylia) in 1840. Although he has taken second place to Bugeaud, his role in the conquest of Algeria was an important one. He was erudite, cultured and an untiring worker who wrote a book and several pamphlets on Algeria, in addition to numerous works on other subjects.

William Frederick Edwards (1777–1843) was a medical doctor born in Jamaica and naturalized as a Frenchman in 1828. He founded the Société Ethnologique de Paris in 1839 and was a member of the Académie des sciences morales et politiques and the Académie de médecine.

Isabelle Eberhardt (1877–1904) arrived in Algeria in 1897. She assumed the name of Si Mahmoud, donned male attire and penetrated one of the North African brotherhoods, the Qadiriya. She had numerous Muslim lovers, eventually marrying one of them, Slimène Ehni. Eberhardt was well versed in Islam and was considered to be a 'man of letters'. Her belief in French rule led to close ties with Lyautey (then in Algeria) and direct work for the Deuxième Bureau. She drowned in a flash-flood in Aïn Sefra.

Prosper Enfintin (1786–1864) was student at the Ecole Polytechnique, although he never graduated. He was a disciple of Saint-Simon, becoming the movement's leader after Saint-Simon's death. He went to Algeria in 1839 and was a member of the Scientific Commission. He founded the journal *L'Algérie*.

Louis Léon César Faidherbe (1818–89) was a graduate of the Ecole Polytechnique and the Ecole d'Application de Metz. He spent three years in Kabylia from 1849 to 1852 before being sent to Senegal, where he made his name, rising to the rank of general and eventually becoming governor-general. He had a passion for ethnology and anthropology and was elected vice-president of the Anthropological Society of Paris in 1873. In 1871 he was elected as deputy, but he resigned shortly afterwards.

Honoré Jean-Pierre Fisquet (1818–83) was a man of letters from Montpellier and claimed to be a member of 'plusieurs sociétés savantes'. He wrote a multi-volume work on the archbishops and bishops of France by diocese and several books on ecclesiastical history, and compiled a dictionary of Parisian celebrities.

Henri Fournel (1801–76) was a Polytechnicien and Saint-Simonian who served as head (Inspecteur Général) of the Service des Mines from 1842 to 1848. During this time he organized the geological and mineralogical exploration of Algeria. His work in this field resulted in a celebrated two-volume work, *Richesse minérale de l'Algérie*. He was a member of the Scientific Commission.

Franz Joseph Gall (1758–1828) was a German physician who developed the 'science of phrenology'. He believed that the back of the head served as a measure of the brain and hence as an indicator of human accomplishment. His ideas were adopted by the Société Ethnologique de Paris and were deemed by some physical anthropologists to be a confirmation of Lavater's ideas on physiognomy. Gall's ideas permeated literary and political circles : Balzac, Taine and Proudhon, for example, all made use of phrenology.

Emile Félix Gautier (1864–?) was professor at the University of Algiers. He was a geographer, renowned in his day, and an expert on the Sahara. He served as Directeur de l'Enseignement in Madagascar and lectured frequently in the United States.

Louis Josephe Adolphe Charles Constance Hanoteau (1814–97) was a graduate of the Ecole Polytechnique. He was an officer of the Bureaux Arabes, serving for 13 years in Algiers and eight in Kabylia, where he commanded the *cercles* of Dra-el-Mizan (1859–60), Fort Napoleon (1870) and the sub-division of of Dellys (1871–72). He eventually rose to the rank of brigadier-general in 1870. In 1860 he received the Prix Volney from the Académie des Inscriptions for his work on Berber and Tuareg languages, a distinction he shared with Ernest Renan, who received the prize in 1847. His work on Kabylia, published in 1871, was the prime reference book on the area for three-quarters of a century. He was a regular contributor to the *Revue Africaine*. He was an accomplished linguist, speaking German, English, Arabic, Berber and Italian.

Dr François Jules* Harmand (1845–1921), a naval doctor and diplomat, believed assimilation to be a profound error in view of the irreducible mental differences between races and ethnic groups. He was an advocate of the policy of Association, publishing his *Domination et Colonisation* in 1910.

Johann Gottfriend Herder (1744–1803), German philosopher, critic and clergyman, was a leader of the *Sturm und Drang* movement. He was appointed court preacher at Weimar, where he became a theorist of the German Romantic movement. His *On the Origin of Language* and *Outlines of the Philosophy of Man* made a considerable impact both in Germany and abroad.

Octave Houdas, (1840–1916) professor at the Ecole spéciale des Langues orientales and member of the Société d'Ethnographie, was a much-respected Orientalist. He was married to the daughter of Maurice Delfosse.

Captain Ferdinand Victor Hugonnet, (1822–?) was a graduate of St Cyr and an officer of the Bureaux Arabes at Bône (1843), La Calle (1848) and Constantine (1853).

Frédéric Lacroix was born in Mauritius but registered in France only in 1811; he died in 1863. He was nominated director-general of civil affairs in Algeria in 1848. In addition to his active role in Algerian public life he wrote numerous geographical and historical studies on the Mediterranean basin, Patagonia, Peru and North America. He was at one time editor-in-chief of the *Le Monde*.

Jean-Baptiste de Monet de Lamarck (1744–1829) was a naturalist and the chief protagonist of the doctrine of *transformisme*, which was in opposition to Georges Cuvier's doctrine of the *fixité des espèces*. It was not Lamarck, however, but his colleague and admirer, Etienne Geoffroy Saint-Hilaire, who actually clashed with Cuvier over his doctrine of immutability.

Christophe-Louis-Léon Juchault de La Moricière (1806–65) was a graduate of the Ecole Polytechnique and, on arrival in the colony, a Saint-Simonian. Considered by his *alma mater* to be one of its most brilliant students, he arrived in Algeria in 1830, quickly rising to the rank of general. An Arabist, he was an officer of the Bureaux Arabes and headed the first Bureau in 1832. He believed in civilian colonization and in this he clashed with Bugeaud, but his influence on the colony, in particular the officers of the Bureaux Arabes, was profound. During the July Monarchy, which tolerated legal opposition among officers, he was a deputy of the dynastic left.

Général Ferdinand Lapasset (1817–75) graduated from St Cyr and was a member of the Bureaux Arabes, an Arabist, and one of the leaders of the *arabophile* camp. He was promoted to the rank of general in 1865, having crushed the Flitta tribe in the 1864–66 revolt and prevented an uprising among the Dahra.

Edouard Lapène had attained the rank of lieutenant-colonel in 1839. He was in active service during the conquest and served as commanding officer in Bougie. Little is known of Lapène beyond the works he produced as a result of his military service both in France and in Algeria. He contributed articles to the *Mémoires de l'Académie Royale de Metz* on Algeria, but more significant was his *Vingt-Six Mois à Bougie*, a work referred to, either implicitly or explicitly, in all subsequent works on Kabylia and the Kabyles.

Johann Kaspar Lavater (1741–1801) was renowned in his day as a poet, mystic, theologian and physiognomist. He took orders in 1769 in Zürich, the town in which he was born, and remained in the area as a pastor or deacon for the rest of his life. His work on physiognomy, *Physiognomische Fragmente auf Beförderung der Menschen-*

kenntnis und Menschenliebe, published in 1775–78, was well received in Germany, Britain and France, where it was published in 1781 as *Essai sur la Physiognomie*.

Charles Martial Allemand Lavigerie (1825–92) was appointed Bishop of Algiers in 1867 and Cardinal and Primate of all Africa in 1882. He was influential in colonial politics, advising and guiding Gambetta and Ferry in colonial matters, especially with regard to the establishment of the Tunisian Protectorate. His greatest religious legacy to Africa was the creation of the Société des Pères Blancs, whose members fanned out across the continent and are still present there today.

Ely Leblanc was dean of the Faculty of Medicine at the University of Algiers and a member of the International Institute of Anthropology.

André Lefevre (1834–1904), a professor at the Ecole anthropologique de Paris, believed that there was an intelligence-linked hierarchy of language.

Paul Leroy-Beaulieu, who was a professor of political economy at the Collège de France and director of *l'Economiste francais*, is best known for *De la Colonisation chez les peuples modernes*, his doctoral thesis published in 1874. By 1908 it had run into five editions. In it Leroy-Beaulieu maintained colonization was paramount if France was to retain its position as a world power. Leroy-Beaulieu was none the less a 'liberal' and condemned the excesses towards the indigenous population of the civilian regime in Algeria. He was president of the Société française pour la protection des indigènes.

Louis Hubert Lyautey (1854–1934), born in Nancy, served in Tonkin, Madagascar under Gallieni, who proved a seminal influence, and in Algeria [for two years (1880–82) as a lieutenant and for seven years under the governorship of Jonnart, from 1903 to 1906 in the Sud Oranais and from 1906 to 1910 in Oranie and on the Algero-Moroccan border]. He was responsible for the organization of the Moroccan protectorate (1912–25). He attained the rank of general in 1906 while serving in Algeria, and field-marshal in 1921. He was minister of war in 1916–17 and was elected to the Académie française in 1920.

Mr Maffre: nothing is known about Maffre other than the fact that he was a settler who lived in Bougie from 1833 onwards.

Konrad Malte-brun (1775–1826) was a Danish geographer who lived in France and was a founder of the Société de Géographie de Paris in 1821. His best-known work was *Précis de la Géographie Universelle*, six vols, 1810–29 (completed posthumously).

Général Jean Auguste Margueritte (1823–70) was born in Lorraine but brought up in Algeria, speaking better Arabic than French. He was a member of the Bureaux Arabes and supporter of Field Marshal Randon. He was killed in action during the Franco-Prussian war.

Emile Masqueray (1843–94) was a graduate of the Ecole Normale Supérieure, where he was awarded his *agrégation* in history and geography. He was at one time secretary to Victor Cousin. He went to Algeria for the first time in 1872 to take up a post at the Lycée of Algiers, although he was eventually appointed director of the Faculty of Letters in Algiers by Paul Bert. He spent many years in Kabylia, the Aurès and the M'zab researching his seminal work on the three Berber societies of Algeria. He was adviser to Jules Ferry.

Alphonse Meyer was an interpreter with the Army.

Michel Auguste Martin Agénor Azéma de Montgravier (1805–?) entered the Affaires Arabes in 1846 as the assistant officer in the Oran bureau. He became chief officer in 1849, moving to the advisory committee on Algeria at the Ministry of War in 1850. While in Oran he carried out archaeological and historical studies which earned him a reputation as an able 'scientist'.

Gabriel de Mortillet (1821–98), along with C.A. Coudereau, André Lefèvre and Charles Letourneau, broke away from Broca and Topinard, and used anthropology to promote radical republicanism.

Friedrich Maximilian Müller (1823–1900), an Orientalist and comparative philologist, studied Sanskrit at the University of Leipzig. He was appointed Taylorian professor of modern languages at Oxford in 1850 and became an honorary fellow of Christ Church, a fellow of All Souls and curator of the Bodleian Library. He failed to obtain the chair of Sanskrit because of his foreign birth but eventually had a chair of comparative philology created for him. Müller did much to popularize the subject of philology.

René François Edouard* de Neveu (1809–71), was a student at La Flèche, and at St Cyr, from where he graduated in 1829, going on to the Ecole d'Etat-Major in 1832. He was an officer of the Bureaux Arabes, a member of the Scientific Commission and head of the topographical service in Algeria (Service géodesique). He entered the Bureaux in 1845 and was posted to Dellys in Kabylia in 1859, serving there for eleven years. During this time he attained the rank of brigadier-general (1864). He was a Saint-Simonian and was married to an indigenous woman, although it is not clear whether she was an Arab or a Kabyle.

Jules Henri François Edmond* de Pellissier de Reynaud (1798–1858) arrived in Algeria with the expeditionary force of 1830 and remained until 1842, returning regularly thereafter. He served as an officer of the Bureaux Arabes, being first posted to Algiers in 1834, and headed the Directorate of Arab Affairs from 1837 to 1839, the year in which it was disbanded. He was a member of the Scientific Commission of 1840–42. He was later consul in Malta and Baghdad. He shared the paternalism of his age but, unusually for the time, his work was a critical assessment of the colonial regime. In common with many of his fellow officers he harboured feelings of anti-clericalism but, without denying Christian superiority, he offered one of the few balanced views of Islam and attempted to dispel some of the negative preconceptions of his compatriots. This elicited criticism, from some quarters, that he was too pro-Arab.

Joanny-Napoléon Périer (1809–80), senior physician at the Hôtel des Invalides, was the member of the Scientific Commission to Algeria in charge of hygiene. His contribution to the volumes produced within its framework was *De l'hygiène en Algérie* (1847). Périer was one of a minority of Frenchmen sharing many of the opinions of de Gobineau on race. His paper on the Berbers, *Des Races dites Berbères et de leur ethnogénie*, was presented to the Société d'Anthropologie de Paris in 1873. He was a member of the Society from its inception and its president in 1866.

Nicolas Auguste Pomel (1821–98) was senator for Oran. He was considered a scholar and wrote numerous works on geological, zoological and palaeontological subjects. He was joint director with the *Polytechnicien* Chief-Engineer Pouyanne, of the service established to compile a geological map of Algeria which produced the *Carte géologique provisoire de l'Algérie* in 1881. In 1880 he was appointed Director of the Ecole des Sciences in Algiers.

James Cowles Prichard (1786–1848), an anthropologist who believed in monogenesis, began to study race in 1800. He was president of the Ethnographical Society and a member of numerous learned societies and institutions, including the Royal Academy of Medicine, the National Institute, both of London, and the Statistical Society of Paris. His two-volume *Researches into the Physical History of Man* was first published in 1818 and had run into four editions by 1841. Equally successful was *The Natural History of Man*.

Dr Pruner-Bey was physician to the Viceroy of Egypt and produced several papers on Egyptian ethnography. He was greatly interested in craniometry.

A. de Quatrefages de Bréau (1810–92) was a leading member and president of the Anthropological Society (1863) as well as being a member of the Academy of Sciences. He was a monogenist and one of the first anthropologists to declare that new races were formed by cross-breeding.

Lambert Adolphe* Jacques Quetelet (1796–1874) was a Belgian statistician, popular in France, whose major work on social statistics, *Sur L'Homme et le développement de ses facultés, ou essai de physique sociale*, was first published in 1835 and revised in 1869. Using statistics he created the concept of the 'average man', the nearest one could hope to get to perfection. He was a leading international propagandist for the value of statistics.

Charles Richard (1815–188?), a graduate of the Ecole Polytechnique greatly influenced by the ideas of Saint-Simon, Considerant and Fourier, was a captain in the Engineers. He arrived in Algeria in 1840 as a lieutenant and served as commanding officer of the Bureau Arabe at Bougie and later at Orléanville, where he remained until his departure from Algeria in 1850. He was an Arabist and an acknowledged 'expert' on the Arabs. In spite of his lack of promotion, he was deemed to be a good administrator and was considered to be one of the best officers of the Bureaux Arabes. In recompense, perhaps, for his lack of promotion, he was awarded the Légion d'Honneur, an unusual distinction for someone of his rank.

Louis Marie Rinn (1838–1905) graduated from St Cyr in 1855 and joined the 83 infantry, which took him to Algeria in 1864. He served in the Bureaux Arabes from 1865 to 1885 and was appointed director of the Service Central des Affaires Indigènes in 1880. In 1885 he was appointed adviser to the government on Algerian affairs. He was also governor-general, vice-president of the Société Historique Algérienne, and president of the Société Géographique d'Alger. Of all the officer-scholars of the Bureaux Arabes Rinn was the most prolific, being matched in output only by Daumas, and was among the most esteemed.

Pierre Germain Damaze Jean Camille* Sabatier was born in Tlemcen in 1851 and trained as a lawyer. He held posts in Kabylia: at Fort National as administrator of the *commune mixte* and at Tizi Ouzou, as judge. He was later deputy for Oran.

Etienne Geoffroy Saint-Hilaire (1722–144) was a zoologist and professor at the museum of natural history in Paris and a member of the scientific expedition accompanying Napoleon's campaign to Egypt.

Guiseppe Sergi (1841–1936) was a psychologist by training and the first professor of anthropology at the University of Bologna. He was a founder of the Instituto di Antropologia at Rome, the Società Romana di Anthropologie and the review *Revista di Anthropologia*. His contribution to anthropology in Italy was prodigious.

William Shaler was American representative in Algiers from 1815 to
1827. His *Sketches of Algiers, Political, Historical and Civil* (Boston
1826), a work acknowledged as full of interest by his contemporaries, stressed the importance of Sidi Ferruch as an embarkation
point along the coast; this was the site finally chosen by the French.

Baron Willian Mac-Guchin de Slane (1801–78) who was born in
Belfast, was principal interpreter of the Army of Africa and a member of the Scientific Commission. In 1862 he was elected to the
Académie des Inscriptions et belles lettres. He is best known for
his translation of Ibn Khaldoun.

Paul Topinard (1830–1911), a former student of Broca's, was trained
as a doctor and became France's pre-eminent anthropologist after
Broca's death. He was editor for the *Revue d'anthropologie* until it
ceased publication in 1889. His *L'Anthropologie*, first published in
1876, had run to five editions by the end of the century.

Dr Trolliet, who was head physician of the civilian hospital in Algiers,
was in favour of colonization. He was acquainted with Tocqueville,
with whom he discussed the problem.

Ismaël Urbain (alias Georges Voisin) (1812–84) was a Saint-Simonian
and *arabophile*. He was a first-class interpreter who became deeply
involved in the administration of Algeria. His knowledge of the
Arabs and Islam brought him to the notice of Napoleon II, whom
he was to influence.

Julien-Joseph Virey (1775–1846), who had a doctorate in medicine,
wrote his *Histoire naturelle* while serving in the army. On his release
from the army, with the assistance of a group of naturalists, he
produced the *Nouveau Dictionnaire d'histoire naturelle* (1819). His
main contribution to science was to vulgarize scientific ideas. His
Histoire naturelle was translated into English and published in 1837.
Virey initially classified the human races according to colour. In
the amended edition of his *Histoire naturelle* he introduced facial
angles as an important criterion in the determination of race. He
was also deputy for the Haute Marne and a member of the Academy of Medicine.

Dr Auguste Edmond Vital (1810–74) was a student in surgery at the
Val-de-Grace hospital in 1830 and went on to become a military
doctor, serving for much of his career in Constantine. A close
friend of Urbain's and an influential person in the colony, he was
considered by his contemporaries to be a man of moderation,
honesty and great culture.

Constantin François Chasseboeuf, Comte de Volney (1757–1820),
philosopher and travel-writer, was professor of history at the newly
founded Ecole Normale. During the revolutionary era he was a

member of both the States-General and the Constituent Assembly and although he was imprisoned by the Jacobins, he escaped the guillotine. He was raised to the peerage during the Restoration and became a member of the Institute. Although he is best remembered for his *Voyage en Egypte et en Syrie* (1786), he wrote philosophical essays and others works on his travels in various parts of the world.

Dr Auguste Hubert Warnier (1810–75) was a Saint-Simonian and a member of the Scientific Commission. Arriving in Algeria in 1834, he joined the Service des Affaires Arabes in 1837 and spent two years (1837–39) with Daumas in Mascara, when the latter was consul there, combating cholera among the local tribes. In 1839 he was appointed assistant surgeon to the military. He was appointed directeur des affaires civiles to the province of Oran in 1848 and préfet of Algiers in 1870. He was elected deputy in 1871. He wrote numerous works on Algeria.

Général Yusuf (circa 1808–66) was commander of the Algiers Division in 1864.

Bibliography

Archives National, Section Outre-Mer (ANSOM), Aix-en-Provence.
Série H. Affaires Indigènes.
Série I. Bureaux arabes de l'Algérois.
Série K. Bureaux arabes du Constantinois.
Série X. Dons et Acquisitions.
Bibliothèque de l'Arsenal, Paris.
Fonds d'Eichthal.
Fonds Enfantin.

Abd al-Aziz Bakri, A. *Description de l'Afrique septentrionale.* Translated by W. McG. Slane. Alger, 1857–58. Translation of *Kitab Al-Matnalik wa Al-Masalik.*

Aboudaou, Said. *I Was an Algerian Preacher.* Translated by W. N. Heggoy. New York: Vantage, 1971.

Accardo, F. *Répertoire alphabétique des Tribus et Douars de l'Algérie.* Dressé d'après les documents officiels sous la direction de Le Myre de Vilers. Alger: Adolphe Jourdan, 1879.

Acte Consultatif de la Société du Jardin Zoologique d'Acclimatation du Bois du Boulogne. Paris: Imprimerie Martinet, 1859.

Amrouche, Jean. *Chants Berbères de Kabylie.* Paris: Éd. Charlot, 1947.

Amrouche, Marguerite-Taos. *Le grain magique: Contes, poèmes et proverbes berbères de Kabylie.* Paris: Maspero, 1966.

Anonymous [F. A. Desprez]. *Journal d'un officier de L'Armée d'Afrique.* Paris: Anselin, 1831.

Anselin, Dr. Jules-René. *Essai sur la topographie médicale de Bougie et le pays limitrophe.* Paris: Rignoux, 1855.

Assezat, J. "L'acclimatement." *Revue d'Anthropologie* 4 (1875): 294–305.

A. T. "Étude sur la lutte engagée entre le Christianisme et l'Islamisme." *Revue de l'Orient et de l'Algérie* 2 (1847): 17–21.

Aucapitaine, Henri. "Colonies noires en Kabylie." *Revue Africaine* 4 (1860): 73–77.

Bibliography

————. *Contes militaires de la Grande Kabylie.* Paris, 1857.

————. "Djemâa Sahridj et Beni-Raten." *Revue Africaine* 3 (1859): 233–36.

————. *Ethnographie: Nouvelles observations sur l'origine des Berbères-Thamou à propos des Lettres sur le Sahara adressées par M. le Prof E. Desor à. M. E. Liebig.* Paris: Châllamel aîné, 1867.

————. "Etudes récentes sur les dialectes berbères de l'Algérie." *Nouvelles Annales de Voyages de la Géographie, de l'Histoire et de l'Archéologie,* 6e série, 2 (1859): 170–92.

————. "Étude sur la domination romaine dans la Haute-Kabylie." *Bulletin de la Société de Géographie de Paris* (1860, 2e trimestre): 233–46.

————. *Etude sur le passé et l'avenir des Kabyles: Les Kabyles et la Colonisation de l'Algérie.* Paris: Châllamel aîné, 1864. First ed. 1860.

————. *Etude sur l'Histoire et l'Origine des tribus berbères de la Haute-Kabylie.* Paris, 1860. First published 1859 in *Journal Asiatique.*

————. "Etudes sur l'origine et l'histoire des tribus berbères de la Haute Kabylie." *Journal Asiatique* (octobre–novembre 1859): 273–86.

————. "Kanoun du Village de Thaourirt-Amokran chez les Ait Iraten." *Revue Africaine* 7 (1863): 279–85.

————. *La Zaouïa de Chellala: Excursion chez les Zouaoua de la Haute Kabylie.* Paris: Châllamel aîné, 1860.

————. *Le Pays et la Société Kabyle.* Paris: Arthus Bertrand, 1857. Extrait des *Nouvelles Annales de Voyage.*

————. *Les Beni Mzab: Sahara Algérien.* Paris: Châllamel aîné, 1867.

————. *Les confins militaires de la Grande Kabylie sous la domination turque.* Paris: Moquet, 1857.

————. "L'insurrection de le Grande Kabylie 1850–51: Le Chérif Bou-Barla." *Revue de l'Orient et de l'Algérie et des Colonies,* n.s., 12 (1860): 395–407; 13: 37–53.

————. "Notice sur la Tribu des Ait Fraoucen." *Revue Africaine* 4 (1860): 446–58.

————. "Nouvelles d'Algérie Voyage de Mr. Bou-Der'ba à R'at (Ghat): Lettre de M. le Baron Aucapitaine au Rédacteur." *Nouvelles Annales de Voyages de la Géographie, de l'histoire et de l'Archéologie,* 6e série, 2 (1859): 339–40.

————. "Origine arabe des fractions de Marabouts dans les confédérations kabyles." *Nouvelles Annales des Voyages de la Géographie de l'Histoire et de l'Archéologie,* 6e série, 1 (1859): 170–73.

————. "Origine des fractions de marabouts dans les populations kabyles." *Revue de l'Orient et de l'Algérie et des Colonies* 10 (1859): 471–73.

Audisio, Gabriel. *Héliotrope.* Paris: Gallimard, 1928.

————. *Trois hommes et un minaret.* Paris: Rieder, 1926.

Avezac-Macaya, M. A. P. d'. *Esquisse générale de l'Afrique et Afrique Ancienne,* in *L'Univers, Histoire et Description de tous les peuples, de leurs Religions, Mœurs, Industrie, Coutumes, etc.* Paris: Firmin Didot, 1844.

311

Bibliography

————. *Etudes de géographie critique sur une partie de l'Afrique septentrionale.* Paris, 1836.

————. "Les Berbères." In *Encyclopédie nouvelle.* Paris, 1836.

Azan, Paul (Général). *L'Armée d'Afrique 1830 à 1858.* Paris, 1930.

————. *L'Empire Français.* Paris: Flammarion, 1943.

Basset, Henri. *Essai sur la littérature des Berbères.* Alger: Carbonnel, 1920.

Basset, René. "L'Algérie arabe." In *Histoire de l'Algérie par ses monuments.* Paris: L. Baschet, 1900.

————. *L'Insurrection algérienne de 1871 dans les chansons populaires kabyles.* Louvain: Istas, 1892.

Battandier, Jules-Aimé, and Louis Trabut. *L'Algérie.* Paris: Baillière, 1898.

Baudens, Dr. *Relation de l'Expedition de Constantine.* Paris: Baillière, 1838. First published 1838 in *Revue de Paris,* April.

Baudicour, Louis de. *Des indigènes de l'Algérie.* Paris: Ch. Doumiol, 1852.

————. *La Colonisation de l'Algérie: Ses éléments.* Paris: Lecoffre, 1856.

Berbrugger, Louis-Adrien. *Algérie: Historique, pittoresque et monumentale.* Paris: Delahaye, 1843.

————. *Les époques militaires de la Grande Kabylie.* Paris: Châllamel aîné, 1857; Alger: Bastide, 1857.

Bernard, A., and Louis Millot. "Les qanouns Kabyles dans l'ouvrage de Hanoteau-Letourneux." *Revue des Études Islamiques* 7 (1933): 1–44.

Bernard, Dr. "Etudes sur la Petite Kabylie: Donnés climatologiques et médicales sur le cercle d'El-Melia (Kabylie Orientale)." *Recueil des Mémoires de Médecine, de Chirurgie et de Pharmacie militaires* 28 (1872): 417–75, 529–88.

Bert, Paul. *Lettres de Kabylie: La politique algérienne.* Paris: Lemerre, 1882.

Berteuil, Arsène. *L'Algérie française: Histoire, mœurs, costumes, industrie, agriculture.* Paris: Dentu, 1856.

Berthezène, le Général. *18 mois à Alger.* Montpellier, 1834.

Bertholon, Dr. Lucien. *Quel doit être le rôle de la France dans l'Afrique du Nord? Coloniser ou Assimiler?* Beaugency: Imprimerie Laffray, 1898. Extraits des *Bulletins de la Société d'Anthropologie.*

————. "Quel est le role de la France dans l'Afrique du Nord-Coloniser ou assimiler?" *Bulletin de la Société d'Anthropologie de Paris,* 4e série, 8 (1897): 509–36.

Bertholon, Dr. Lucien, and E. Chantre. *Recherches anthropologiques dans la Berbèrie orientale.* Tome 1, *Anthropométrie, craniométrie, ethnographie.* Tome 2, *Album de 174 portraits ethniques.* Lyon: Rey, 1912 and 1913.

Bertrand, Louis-Marie-Emile. *Africa.* Paris: A. Michel, 1933. First ed. 1904 as *Le Jardin de la Mort.*

————. "Africa." *Revue des Deux Mondes* (mars 1922): 114–35.

————. *Autour de Saint Augustin.* Paris: Fayard, 1921.

————. *Devant L'Islam.* Paris: Plon, 1926.

————. *La Cina.* Paris: Ollendorf, 1901.

————. *La Fin du Classicisme et le Retour à l'Antique dans le second moité du XVIIIe siècle et les premières années du XIXe en France*. Paris: Hachette, 1897.

————. *Le Jardin de la Mort*. Paris: Ollendorf, 1921. First ed. 1904.

————. *Le Livre de la Méditerranée*. Paris: Plon, 1923.

————. *Le mirage orientale*. Paris: Plon, 1924.

————. *Le Sang des Races*. Paris: A. Michel, 1930. First published in serial form 1898–99.

————. *Le Sens de l'Ennemi*. Paris: Fayard, 1917.

————. *Les Villes d'Or: Algérie et Tunisie Romaines*. Paris: Fayard, 1921.

————. *Pépète et Balthazar*. Paris: Ollendorf, 1920. First ed. 1909 as *Pépète le Bien Aimé*.

————. *Saint Augustin*. Paris: Georges Crés, 1920.

————. *Sanguis Martyrum*. Paris: Fayard, 1918.

————. *Sur les Routes du Sud*. Paris: Fayard, 1936.

————. *Terre et Résurrection*. Paris: Ed. NF, 1947.

Beynet, Léon. *Les Colons Algériens*. Paris: Châllamel aîné, 1863.

Bibesco, (Prince) Nicolas. "Les Kabyles du Djurdjura." *Revue des Deux Mondes* 56 (mars–avril 1865): 562–601, 951–77.

Billiard, Auguste. "Études sur les Colonies et particulièrement des Moyens de rattacher l'Algérie à la France." *La Revue Indépendante* 21 (1845): 266–93.

Blumenbach, J. F. *The Anthropological Treatise of Johann Friedrich Blumenbach*. London, 1865.

Bocher, Charles. "Le Siège de Zaatcha." *Revue des Deux Mondes* (avril–juin 1851): 70–100.

Bodichon, Barbara L. Smith. *Guide Book: Algeria Considered as a Winter Residence for the English*. London: Odell & Ives, 1858.

Bodichon, Dr. Eugène. *Considérations sur l'Algérie*. Paris: Comptoir Central de la Librairie, 1845.

————. *De l'humanité*. Alger, 1852.

————. "Disparition des Musulmans soumis au pouvoir et au contact des Chétiens." *Revue de L'Orient, de l'Algérie et de Colonies* 10 (1851): 35–40.

————. *Études sur l'Algérie et l'Afrique*. Alger: Chez l'Auteur, 1847. Collection of his articles published in Algerian newspapers 1838–44.

————. *Hygiène à Suivre en Algérie: Acclimatement des Européens*. Alger: Delavigne, 1851.

Boissier, Gaston. *Roman Africa: Archeological Walks in Algeria and Tunis*. Translated by Arabella Ward. New York: G. P. Putnam & Sons, 1899.

Boissière, Gustave. *L'Algérie romaine*. 2 vols. Paris: Hachette, 1883.

Bonaparte, Louis-Napoléon. *Lettre sur la Politique de la France en Algérie*. Paris: Imp. Impériale, 1865.

Bonaparte, Pierre-Napoléon. *Un mois en Afrique*. Paris: Pagnerre, 1850.

Bonnafont, Dr. J. P. *Douze ans en Algérie 1830 à 1842*. Paris: E. Dentu, 1880.

——. *Pérégrination en Algérie 1830 à 1842: Histoire, ethnographie, anecdotes.* Paris: Châllamel aîné, 1884.

Bory de Saint-Vincent, J. B. *Correspondance de Bory de Saint-Vincent.* Edited by Philippe Lauzan. Agen: Imprimerie moderne, 1908; supplement, Agen: Imprimerie moderne, 1912.

——. *L'Homme, Essai zoologique sur le genre humain.* Paris: Rey & Gravier, 1827.

——. "Sur les hommes blancs des mont de l'Aurès." *Compt. rend. hebd. de l'Académie des Sciences* 21 (1845): 1412.

——. *Voyage to and Travels through the Four Principal Islands of the African Seas.* In vol. 2 of *A Collection of Modern and Contemporary Voyages and Travels.* London: R. Phillips, 1806. Translation of *Voyage dans les quatre principales îles des mers d'Afrique.*

Bourde, Paul. *A travers l'Algérie: Souvenirs de l'excursion parlementaire de Sept.–Oct. 1879.* Paris: Charpentier, 1880.

Broca, Paul. "Documents relatifs au croisement des races très différentes." *Bulletin de la Société d'Anthropologie de Paris* (1860): 255–68.

——. "Les peuples Blonds et les monuments Mégalithiques dans l'Afrique septentrionale: Les Vandales en Afrique." *Revue d'Anthropologie* 5 (1876): 393.

——. *Les races humaines.* Paris: Taillard, 1836.

——. *Mémoires.* 5 vols. Paris: C. Reinwald & Cie, 1871–88.

Brosselard, Ch. H. E. *Dictionnaire berbère.* Paris, 1862.

——. *Les Khouan.* Alger: Bouyet, 1859.

Brunet, J. "Expeditions dans la Kabilie centrale pendant l'automne de 1844." *Le Spectateur Militaire* 39 (1845): 44–89.

Bugeaud de la Piconnerie, Thomas Robert. "De diverses races qui peuplent l'Algérie: Les Arabes et les Kabyles." *Revue de l'Orient* 6 (1845): 345–61.

——. *De la colonisation de l'Algérie.* Paris: Imp. A. Guyot, 1847.

——. *L'Algérie: Des moyens de conserver et utiliser cette conquête.* Paris: Dentu, 1842.

——. *Le Maréchal Bugeaud d'après sa correspondence intimate et des documents inédits, 1784–1849, par Le Comte Henry d'Ideville.* Paris: Firmin-Didot, 1881.

——. *Le peuplement français de l'Algérie.* Paris: Société d'éditions géographiques, maritimes et coloniales, 1920.

——. *Observations de M. le Maréchal gouverneur-général sur le projet de colonisation présenté pour le province d'Oran par M. le lieutenant-général de Lamorcière.* Alger: Imprimerie du Gouvernement, 1847.

——. *Œuvres Militaires du Maréchal Bugeaud Duc d'Isly réunies et mises en ordres par Weil ancien Capitaine de Cavalerie.* Paris: L. Baudoin, 1883.

——. *Par l'épée et par la charrue: Ecrits et discours.* Edited and introduced by P. Azan. Preface by C. Julien. Paris: PUF, 1948.

Bibliography

————. *Quelques réflexions sur trois questions fondamentales de notre établissement en Afrique*. Alger: Imp. Besancenez, 1846.

————. *Une lettre de M. le maréchal Bugeaud au sujet du rapport de M. Ch. Dupin du 15 février 1850 sur l'Algérie*. Douai: Imp. A. d'Aubers, 1850.

————. "Une lettre du maréchal Bugeaud sur l'Algérie." *Carnet de la Sabretache* (1907): 753–60. Revue militaire rétrospective publié par la Société "la Sabretache."

————. *Veillées d'une chaumière de la Vendée*. Lyon: Guyot frères, 1849.

Cagnat, R., R. Basset, et al. *Histoire de l'Algérie par ses monuments*. Paris: L. Baschet, 1900.

Caix, Robert de. "Le Maroc Français et la Question Indigène." *Revue des Deux Mondes* 349 (1914): 806–41.

Caix de Saint-Aymour, A. *Questions Algériennes: Arabes et Kabyles*. Paris: Ollendorff, 1891.

Campagnes d'Afrique 1835–1848. Lettres adressées au Maréchal de Castellane par les Maréchaux, Bugeaud, Clauzel, et al. . . . séptembre 1897. Paris: Plon Nourrit & Cie, 1898.

Camus, Albert. *Actuelles III: Chroniques algériennes, 1939–1958*. Paris: Gallimard, 1958.

Carette, A. E. H. *Du commerce de l'Algérie avec l'Afrique Centrale et les États barbaresques*. Paris: Guyot, 1844.

————. *Étude des routes suivies par les Arabes dans la partie méridionale de l'Algérie*. Vol. 1 of *Exploration scientifique de l'Algérie*. Paris: Imprimerie royale, 1844.

————. *Études sur la Kabilie Proprement dite*. 2 vols. Vols. 4 and 5 of *Exploration scientifique de l'Algérie*. Paris: Nationale, 1848.

————. *Rapprochement d'une inscription trouvée à Constantine et d'un passage des Actes des martyrs fournissant une nouvelle preuve de l'identité de Constantin et Cirta*. In *Académie des inscriptions et belles-lettres, Paris*. Mémoire présentée par divers savants. Paris, 1843.

————. *Recherches sur la géographie et le commerce de l'Algérie méridionale*. Vol. 2 of *Exploration scientifique de l'Algérie*. Paris: Imprimerie royale, 1844.

————. *Recherches sur l'origine et les migrations des principales tribus de l'Afrique septentrionale et particulièrement de l'Algérie*. Vol. 3 of *Exploration scientifique de l'Algérie*. Paris: Imprimerie impériale, 1853.

Carette, A. E. H., and A. Warnier. *Description et division de l'Algérie*. Paris: Hachette, 1847.

Carette, A. E. H., and Capt. Rozet. *Algérie*. Paris: Firmin Didot, 1850.

Carrey, Emile. *Récits de Kabylie-Campagne de 1857*. Paris: M. Levy Frères, 1858.

Castellane, Comte Pierre de. "La dernière expedition de Kabylie." *Revue des Deux Mondes* 10 (1851): 154–75.

————. *Souvenirs de la Vie militaire en Afrique*. Paris: Lecon, 1852.

Bibliography

Castellane, Maréchal Comte Boniface de. *Journal du Maréchal de Castellane 1804–1862*. 5 vols. Paris: Plon, 1895–97.

Cat, Édouard. *Biographie algériennes: Colons, fonctionnaires, savants, commerçants, industriels*. Alger: Imprimerie de l'Algérie nouvelle, n.d.

———. "Les Kabyles." *Nouvelle Revue* 11 (1881).

Cauvet, G. (Cmdt.). "Les origines caucasiennes des Touareg." *Bulletin de la Société de Géographie d'Alger* 25 (1924): 419–44; 26 (1925): 1–38.

Cavaignac, G. "Colonisation de l'Algérie." *La Revue Indépendante* 7 (1843): 193–227.

———. "Colonisation de l'Algérie." *La Revue Indépendante* 8 (1843): 321–60.

Chaix, Paul G. G. *Étude sur l'ethnographie de l'Afrique*. Génève: Fick, 1860.

Charles-Roux, Jules. *Nos Colonies et l'Exposition de 1900*. Paris, 1901.

Charmetant, L'Abbé P. "Kabylie." *Annales de la Propagation de la foi* 46, no. 277 (1874): 420–36.

———. *Les peuplades Kabyles et les tribus nomades du Sahara*. Montréal: La Minerve, 1875.

Chartrieux, Emilien. *Études Algériennes: Contribution à l'enquête sénatoriale de 1892*. Paris: Châllamel aîné, 1892.

Charvériat, François. *A travers la Kabylie et les questions Kabyles*. Paris: Plon, 1889.

Clamageran, Jean-Jules. *L'Algérie: Impressions de voyage*. Paris: Germer, 1874.

Clerc, Eugène Timoléon (Capt.). *Campagne de Kabylie en 1857*. Lille: Imprimerie de Lefebvre-Ducrocq, 1859.

Clonard, Général Sutton Cte. de. *Système mixte de colonisation algérienne*. 4 mai 1865, s 1.

Cochut, André. "De la colonisation de l'Algérie: Les essais et les systèmes." *Revue des Deux Mondes* 17 (1847): 498–537.

———. "L'Algérie et le budget: Les indigènes; Les Européens." *Revue des Deux Mondes* 1 (1849): 787–812, 926–55.

———. "Les Khouan: Mœurs religieuses de l'Algérie." *Revue des Deux Mondes* (Belgian ed.) 10 (May 1846): 328–45; (French ed.): 589–611.

Code Algérien: Recueil des Actes du Gouvernement d'Algérie. Paris, 1830.

Coeur, Mme. Pierre (pseudonym for Anne Caroline Josephine de Voisins d'Ambre). *L'Assimilation des indigènes musulmans*. Paris: Guédan, 1890.

Coinze, d'Altroff (Meurthe). *Introduction à un plan général d'Administration civile et de colonisation agricole en Algérie*. Paris: Frey, 1847.

Condorcet, marquis de. *Esquisse d'un Tableiu historique des Progrès de l'Esprit humain*. Presented by O. H. Prior. Rev. ed. by Y. Belavel. Paris: J. Vrin, 1970.

Corrieras, J. "L'Assimilation des Arabes, est-elle possible?" *Bulletin de la Société de Géographie et d'Archéologie de la province d'Oran* (1904): 140–70.

Courtet de l'Isle, Victor. *La science politique fondée sur la science de l'homme, ou Étude des races humaines, sous le rapport philosophique, historique et social*. Paris: Arthus Bertrand, 1837.

————. "Mémoire sur les races humaines: De l'influence des races humaines sur la forme et le développement des sociétés." *Journal de l'Institut historique* (février–juillet 1835): 225–37.

————. "Origines Indo-européenes: Étude historique sur les peuples de race blonde." *Revue Indépendante* (1847): 436–67.

————. *Tableau ethnographique du genre humain.* Paris: Bertrand, 1849.

Cuvier, G. *Éloges historiques des membres de l'Académie Royale des Sciences 1811–1818.* 3 vols. Strasbourg: Leverault, 1819.

————. *Le Règne Animal distribué d'après son organisation.* Paris: Deterville, 1829.

Daumas, E. M. J. *Correspondance du Capt. Daumas, Consul à Mascara (1837–39).* Edited by George Yver. Vol. 1 of *Collection de documents inédits sur l'histoire de l'Algérie.* Paris: Geuthner, 1912.

————. *Exposé de l'état actuel de la société arabe.* Alger, 1844.

————. "La chasse en Afrique." *Revue des Deux Mondes* (mars 1853): 1001–11.

————. "La civilité puerile et honnête chez les Arabes." *Revue de Paris* (octobre 1853); *Revue Africaine* (1857): 157–76.

————. *La Kabylie.* Paris: Hachette, 1857.

————. "La panthère." *Revue de Paris* (juillet 1853).

————. "La société kabyle." *Revue de l'Orient, de l'Algérie et des Colonies,* n.s., 7 (1858): 1–31, 305–21.

————. *La Vie Arabe et la Société musulmane.* Paris: Levy, 1869.

————. "Le lévrier du Sahara." *Revue de l'Orient* 13 (1853): 158–63.

————. *Le Sahara Algérien, études géographiques, statistiques, et historiques sur ls region du Sud des établissements français en Algérie.* Paris: Langlois, 1845.

————. *Moeurs et Coutumes de l'Algérie, Tell, Kabylie, Sahara.* Paris: Hachette, 1853.

————. "Scènes de la vie arabe: La noblesse du désert." *Revue des Deux Mondes* (août 1854): 492–511.

————. "Voyage de l'Emir Abd-el-Kader dans l'Est de l'Algérie en 1839." *Bulletin de la Société de Géographie de Paris,* série 3, 2 (1844): 31–55.

Daumas, E. M. J., and Capt. Fabar. *La Grande Kabylie, Études historiques.* Paris: Hachette, 1847.

d'Eichthal, Gustave. "Histoire et Origine des Foulahs ou Fellans." *Mémoires de la Société Ethnologique* 1, part 2 (1841): 1–285.

————. "Types des races humaines." *Bulletin de la Société Géographique de Paris,* 4e série, 7 (1854): 91–94.

De l'Algérie du point de vue de la crise actuelle. Paris: Châllamel aîné, 1868.

Delaporte, Jacques. *Dictionnaire Français-Berbère (Dialecte écrit et parlé par les Kabaïles de la Division d'Alger).* Ouvrage composé par ordre du ministre de la guerre. Paris: Imprimerie royale, 1844.

————. *Specimen de la langue berbère.* Paris, 1844.

Bibliography

Delporte, Jean-Honorat fils. *Guide de la conversation française-arabe, ou Dialogues avec le mot-à-mot et la prononciation.* 3rd ed. Alger: Bastide, 1845.

———. *Principes de l'idiome Arabe en usage à Alger.* Alger: J. B. Philippe (Imprimerie du Gouvernement), 1836.

Depont, Octave. *Les Berbères en France: D'une meilleure utilisation de la main d'œuvre des Nords-Africains.* Paris: Publication du Comité de l'Afrique Française, 1925.

Depont, Octave, and X. Coppolani. *Les Confréries religieuses musulmanes, publié sous le patronage de M. Jules Cambon, gouverneur général de l'Algérie.* Alger: Adolphe Jourdan, 1897.

Description de l'Égypte ou Recueil des Observations et des Recherches qui ont été faites en Égypte pendant l'expédition de l'armée française, publié par les ordres de Sa Majesté l'empereur Napoléon le Grand. 23 vols. Paris: Imprimerie impériale, 1809–28.

Desjobert, A. *L'Algérie.* Paris: Guillaumin, 1847.

Desmoulins, A. *Histoire naturelle des races humaines du nord-est de l'Europe, de l'Asie boréale et orientale et de l'Afrique astrale.* Paris: Méquequin-Marvis, 1826.

Desparmet, J. "L'Entrée des Français à Alger par le Cheikh Abdelkader." *Revue Africaine* 71 (1930): 225–56.

Dessoliers, Felix. *De la fusion des races européennes en Algérie par les mariages croisés et de ses consequences politiques.* Alger: Imprimerie P. Fontana, 1899.

Devaux, C. (Capitaine). *Les Kebaïles du Djerjera: Études nouvelles sur le pays vulgairement appelés la grande Kabylie.* Paris: Châllamel aîné, 1859.

Dib, Mohamed. *La grande maison.* Paris: Seuil, 1952.

———. *Qui se souvient de la Mer.* Paris, 1962.

Dictionnaire des sciences médicales. Paris: C. L. F. Panckouche, 1819. See esp. article by Virey, 398–403.

The Doctrine of Saint-Simon: An Exposition; First Year, 1828–1829. Translated with notes and an introduction by G. G. Iggers. New York: Schocken Books, 1972. First ed. 1831, Paris.

Dournon, Robert. *Autour du tombeau de la chrétienne: Documents pour servir à l'histoire de l'Afrique du nord.* Alger: Charlot, 1946. Includes biographical details of Berbrugger.

Doutté, E. "Une mission d'Études." *Renseignements Coloniaux* (1901).

Duchêne, Ferdinand. *Au pas lent des caravanes.* Paris: L'Illustration, 1910. Reissued 1922 as *Les Barbaresques: Au pas lent des caravanes,* Paris: A. Michel.

———. *Ceux d'Algérie.* Paris: Horizons de France, 1929.

———. *France nouvelle: Moeurs algériennes.* Paris: C. Levy, 1903.

———. *Kamir, Roman d'une femme arabe.* Paris: La Petite Illustration, 1926.

———. *Thamil'la.* Paris: L'illustration, 1907. Reissued 1921 as *Les Barbaresques: Thamil'la,* Paris: A. Michel.

Ducrot, Le général A. *La vérité sur l'Algérie.* Paris: Dentu, 1871.

Ducuing, François. "La Guerre de Montagne: La Kabylie." *Revue des Deux Mondes* (avril–juin 1851): 225–74.

———. "La Guerre de Montagne: La Navarre et La Kabylie." *Revue des Deux Mondes* (janvier–mars 1851): 661–700.

Dugas, le Père Joseph. *La Kabylie et le peuple Kabyle*. Paris: Lecoffre, 1877.

Duhousset, Commandant. "Les races algériennes: Les Kabyles du Djurjura." Mémoire presenté à l'Académie des sciences. *Revue des cours scientifiques* (avril 1868).

Duprat, Pascal. *Essai historique sur les races anciennes et modernes de l'Afrique septentrionale*. Paris: J. Labitte, 1845.

———. "Une guerre insensée: Expédition contre les Kabyles ou Berbères d'Algérie." *La Revue Indépendante* 19 (1845): 242–56.

———. "Une Révolution dans l'Afrique du Nord, ou Abd-el-Kader et l'émigration arabe." *La Revue Indépendante* 23 (1845): 251–61.

Dureau de la Malle, A. "La colonisation de l'Algérie." *Journal des Débats* (janvier 1843).

———. *L'Algérie*. Paris: Firmin Didot, 1852.

———. *Province de Constantine*. Paris: Gide, 1837.

Durkheim, Emile. *The Rules of the Sociological Method*. Translated by Sarah A. Solovay and John H. Mueller. Edited by George E. G. Catlin. New York: Free Press, 1938. First ed. 1895.

Duval, Jules. "Algérie: Population Indigène et Européenne." *Revue de L'Orient, de l'Algérie et des Colonies*, n.s., 14 (1853): 432–43.

———. *Concessions et Ventes des Terres de Colonisation*. Paris: Guillaumin, 1857.

Duval, Jules, and Dr. Warnier. *Bureaux arabes et colons*. Paris: Châllamel aîné, 1869.

———. *Programme de politique algérienne*. Paris: Châllamel aîné, 1868.

Duvernois, Alexandre. *Sous Chef de Bureaux Arabes: La question Algérienne au point de vue des Musulmans*. Milana, 1863.

Duvernois, Clément. *L'Algérie, ce qu'elle est, ce qu'elle doit être*. Paris: Rouvier, 1858.

Duvivier, Général F. F. *Solution sur la Question de l'Algérie*. Paris: Gaultier, 1841.

Eberhardt, Isabelle. *Oblivion Seekers and Other Writings*. Translated by P. Bowles. San Francisco: City Light Books, 1975.

———. *The Passionate Nomad: The Diary of Isabelle Eberhardt*. Translated by Nina de Voogd. Edited and introduced by Rana Kabbani. London: Virago, 1987.

Edwards, W. F. "Des caractères physiologiques des races humaines dans leurs rapports avec l'histoire." *Mémoires de la Société Ethnologique* 1 (1841): 1–108. First ed. 1829, Paris.

———. "Esquisse de l'état actuel de l'anthropologie ou de l'histoire naturelle de l'homme." *Mémoires de la Société d'Ethnologie* 1 (1841): 109–29.

Bibliography

Ellis, Havelock. *Studies in the Psychology of Sex*. London, 1905.

Enfantin, Prosper. *Colonisation de l'Algérie*. Paris: Bertrand, 1843.

Erckmann-Chatrian (Emile Erckmann and Alexandre Chatrian). *Une campagne en Kabylie, récit d'un chasseur d'Afrique, et autres récits*. Paris: Hertzel, 1873.

Esquieros, Alphonse. "Des études contemporaines sur l'histoire des Races." *Revue des Deux Mondes*, n.s., 21 (mars 1848): 982–1002.

Etienne, Eugène. *Son œuvre coloniale algérienne et politique 1881–1906*. Discours et écrits divers réunis et édités par la Dépêche coloniale. Paris: Flammarion, 1907.

Exploration scientifique de l'Algérie pendant les années 1840, 1841, 1842 publiée par ordre du gouvernement. 39 vols. Paris: Imprimerie royale, 1844–67.

Exposé de l'état actuel de la société arabe, du gouvernement et de la legislation qui la régit Alger: Imprimerie du gouvernement, 1844.

Fabar, Paul-Dieudonné (Capt.). "L'Algérie et l'opinion." *Journal des Sciences Militaires* 1 (1847): 15–69, 161–225. Also published in book form 1845, Paris: Imp. Rigoux.

Fabre, Césaire-Antoine. *Grande Kabylie: Légendes et souvenirs . . .* Paris: L. Vanier, 1901.

Faidherbe, Louis (Général). *Collection complète des inscriptions numidiques (libiques) avec des aperçus ethnographiques sur les numides*. Paris: A. Franck, 1870.

———. "Considération sur les populations de l'Afrique septentrionale." *Nouvelles Annales des Voyages de a Géographie, de l'Histoire et de l'Archéologie*, 6e série, 3 (1859): 290–306.

———. *Essai sur la langue peul*. Paris: Maisonneuve & Cie., 1875.

———. "Les Berbères et les Arabes." *Bulletin de la Société de Géographie de Paris*, 4e série, 9 (janvier–février 1855).

———. "Les Berbères et les Arabes des Bords du Sénégal." *Bulletin de la Société de Géographie de Paris*, 4e série, 7–8 (1854): 89–112.

———. *Les dolmens d'Afrique*. Paris: Leroux, 1873.

———. *Recherches anthropologiques sur les tombeaux mégalithiques de Roknia*. Bône: Imprimerie de Dagand, 1868.

———. "Quelques mots sur l'ethnographie du nord de l'Afrique et sur les tombeaux mégalithiques de cette contrée." *Bulletin de la Société des Sciences Physiques, Naturelles, Climatiques d'Alger*, no. 1 (1869): 4–19.

Faidherbe, Louis (Général), and Dr. Paul Topinard. *Instructions sur l'anthropologie de l'Algérie*. Paris: Typographie A. Hennuyer, 1874.

Fallot, Ernest. *Par delà la Mediterrannée, Kabylie, Aurès, Kroumerie . . .* Paris: Plon, 1887.

Farine, Charles. *Kabyles et Kroumirs*. Paris: Ducrocq, 1882. First ed. 1865 as *A Travers La Kabylie*.

Favre, Lucienne. *Bab el Oued*. Paris: Crès, 1927.

———. *L'homme derrière le mur*. Paris: Crès, 1926.

————. *Mille et un jours: Mourad*. Brussels: Éditions de la Toison d'Or, 1943.

————. *Orientale 1930*. Paris: "Les Ecrits" chez B. Grasset, 1930.

————. *Un dimanche dans la Casbah*. Paris: "Les œuvres libres" Fayard, 1936.

Feraoun, Mouloud. "Destins de femmes." *Algérie* (1955): 9–13.

————. *Journal (1955–1962)*. Paris: Seuil, 1962.

————. *Jours de Kabylie*. Paris: Seuil, 1968.

————. "La légende de Si Mohand." *Algérie* (septembre 1958): 16–20.

————. *Le fils du pauvre: Menrad, instituteur Kabyle*. Paris: Seuil, 1954.

————. *Les poèmes de Si Mohand*. Paris: Éditions de Minuit, 1960.

————. *Le terre et le sang*. Paris: Seuil, 1955.

Ferry, Jules. *Le Gouvernement de l'Algérie*. Paris: Colin, 1892.

Finot, J. *Le préjugé des races*. Paris: Alcan, 1908.

Fisquet, Honoré. *Histoire de l'Algérie*. Paris: Baudouin, 1842.

Flaubert, Gustave. *Œuvres Complètes*. 2 vols. Paris: Seuil, 1964.

Flourens, P. *Analyse Raisonné des Travaux de Georges Cuvier, précedée de son éloge historique*. Paris: Paulin, 1841.

Forest, Louis. *La Naturalisation des juifs algériens et l'insurrection de 1871*. Paris: Société Française d'imprimerie et de librairie, 1897.

Fortin, d'Ivry T. "L'Algérie, son importance, sa colonisation, son avenir." *Revue de l'Orient, de l'Algérie et des Colonies* 6 (1845): 55–71, 108–32.

Fourcy, A. *Histoire de l'École Polytechnique*. Paris: Imp. Belin, 1828.

Fournel, Marie Jérôme Henri. *La Richesse minérale de l'Algérie*. 2 vols. Paris, 1850–54.

————. *Les Berbères: Études sur la conquête de l'Afrique par les Arabes, d'après les textes arabes imprimés*. 2 vols. Paris: Imprimerie nationale, 1875.

Fries, Jean. *Onze années d'esclavage chez les Kabyles, ou récit des aventures de Jean Fries, né à Deux-Ponts, Bavière*. Alger: Imp. Bastide, 1876.

Fromentin, Eugène. *Voyage en Egypte (1869)*. Paris: Fernand Aubier, 1935.

Gaffarel. Paul. *L'Algérie*. Paris: Firmin-Didot, 1883.

Gastu, F.-J. *Le Peuple Algérien*. Paris: Châllamel aîné, 1884.

Geniaux, Charles. *Sous les Figuiers de Kabylie: Scènes de la vie berbère (1914–17)*. Paris: Flammarion, 1917.

Geoffroy, Auguste. "Le Bordier Berbère de la Grande Kabylie." Extrait de *Les Ouvriers des Deux Mondes*, 2e série, 2, no. 57 (1890): 53–92.

Geoffroy Saint-Hilaire, I. "Philosophie des Sciences Naturelles." *La Revue Indépendante*, 2e série, 8 (1847): 207–26.

Gide, André. *Amyntas*. Paris: Nouv. Rev. Franç., 1905.

Gillebert D'Hercourt, Dr. "Études Anthropologiques sur Soixainte-Seize Indigènes de l'Algérie." *Mémoires de la Société d'Anthropologie de Paris* 3 (1868): 1–25.

Girardin, Emile de. *Civilisation de l'Algérie*. Paris: Michel Levy, 1860.

Gobineau, A. de. *L'Essai sur l'Inégalité des Races humaines*. Paris, 1967. First ed. 1853.

———. *Selected Political Writings*. Edited and introduced by M. Biddiss. New York: Harper & Row, 1970.

Grasset de Saint Sauver, Jacques. *Tableaux des principaux peuples de l'Europe, de l'Asie, de l'Afrique et de l'Amérique*. Paris, 1797.

Guizot, François P.-G. *Discours prononcés . . . dans la discussion du projet de loi relatif aux crédits extraordinaires pour le service de l'Algérie en 1847*. Paris: Imp. Panckoucke, 1847.

Hachette, M., ed. *Correspondance sur l'école royale polytechnique: Janvier 1804–1816*. 3 vols. Paris: Courcier, 1816.

Hagel, Charles. *Drames africains*. Alger: Soubiron, 1930.

Hagel, Charles, and Louis Lecoq. *Broumitche et le Kabyle*. Paris: Fayard, 1921. Serialized 1920 in *Mercure de France*.

Halevy, J. "Etudes Berbères." *Journal Asiatique*, 7e série, 3 (1874): 73–203.

Hanoteau, A. "Archéologie du Territoire des Beni Raten." *Revue Africaine* 5 (1861): 174–83.

———. *Essai de grammaire Kabyle*. Alger: Bastide, 1859.

———. "Littérature orale des Touareg: Fables dans la langue Touareg." *Revue Africaine* 1, no. 4 (1856): 510.

———. *Poésies populaires de la Kabylie du Djurdjura*. Paris: Imprimerie impériale, 1867.

———. "Travaux sur la langue kabyle." *Revue Africaine* 1 (1856): 71.

Hanoteau, A., and A. Letourneux. *La Kabylie et les Coutumes Kabyles*. 3 vols. Paris: Imprimerie nationale, 1871.

Hanoteau, Maurice. "Quelques souvenirs sur les collaborateurs de 'La Kabylie et les coutumes kabyles.'" *Revue africaine* 64 (1923): 134–49.

Harmand, Jules. *Domination et colonisation*. Paris: Flammarion, 1910.

Hatin, E. *Histoire pittoresque de l'Algérie*. Paris: Bureau centrale de publication, 1840.

Hérisson, Maurice d'Irrison Comte d'. *La chasse à l'homme*. Paris: P. Ollendorf, 1891.

Hodgson, W. B. "Memoire on Berber Language." *Transactions of the American Philosophical Society* (1834).

Houdas, L. *Ethnographie de l'Algérie*. Paris: Maison neuve frères et Ch. Leclerc, 1886.

Hugonnet, Ferdinand (Capt.). *Français et Arabes en Algérie*. Paris: Sartorius, 1860.

———. *Souvenirs d'un Chef de Bureau Arabe*. Paris: Michel Levy, 1858.

Humbert, Charles. *L'œuvre française aux colonies*. Paris: E. Larose, 1913.

Hun, Felix. *Excursion dans la Haute Kabylie et Ascension au Tamgoutt de Lella Khedidja par un Juge d'Alger en vacances*. Alger: Bastide, 1859.

Ibn Khaldun. *The Muqaddimah: An Introduction to History*. Translated by Franz Rosenthal. Edited and abridged by N. J. Dawood. Princeton: Princeton University Press, 1969.

Janon, René. "Une nuit de noël en Kabylie." *Algérie* (Noël 1954): 53–59.

Bibliography

Jaubert, Amédée, ed. *Grammaire et Dictionnaire: Abr. de la langue berbère.* Composés par feuVenture de Paradis, revus par A. Jaubert. Paris: Imprimerie impériale, 1844.

Jomard, E. *Observations sur les Arabes de l'Égypte moyenne.* Paris: Panckoucke, 1821. *Mémoire* published following Bonaparte's expedition to Egypt and deposited at the École Polytechnique. Later published in *Description de l'Égypte*, vol. 12.

Jouffroy, Th. "De la politique de la France en Afrique." *Revue des Deux Mondes*, 4e série, 14 (avril 1838): 581–622.

Kaltbrunner, D. *Recherches sur l'origine des Kabyles.* Génève: Georg, 1871.

Kiva, P. (pseudonym for Lt. Col. Paul Wache). "Les troubles en Algérie." *Le Spectateur Militaire* (1882–84). A series of articles.

Knox, Robert. *The Races of Man.* London, 1862.

La Fausse direction donnée aux affaires d'Alger par le système d'expedition. Paris: Delaunay, 1836.

Lagneau, G. "Berbers." Ext. du *Dictionnaire encyclopédique des sciences médicales.* Paris: Masson, 1869.

L'Algérie assimilié: Étude sur la constitution et la réorganisation de l'Algérie. Par un chef de bureau arabe. Constantine: L. Marle, 1871.

Lamarck, J. B. *Philosophie zoologique.* 2 vols. Paris, 1809. Reprinted 1960, New York.

Lamarque, Léo (Capt.). *De la Conquête et de la Colonisation de l'Algérie.* Paris: Ancelin, 1841.

————. "La Kabylie (Alger, le 10 avril 1845)." *Le Spectateur Militaire* 39 (1845): 314–27, 449–60.

Lamartine, Alphonse de. *Discours prononcé par M. de Lamartine, Député du Nord (Bergues) à la Chambre des Députés sur Alger.* Paris: Imprimerie de Petit, 1834.

Lamoricière, Christophe Louis Léon Juchault, de et Marie Alphonse Bedeau (lt. generaux). *Projets de Colonisation pour les provinces d'Oran et de Constantine.* Paris: Ancelin, 1841.

Lancelot, F. *L'Algérie au Point de Vue Belge.* Part 1, Paris: Librairie Centrale, 1867; Part 2, Alger: Imp. Duclaux, 1867.

Langlès, Louis, trans. *Voyage de Hornemann dans l'Afrique septentrionale.* Paris, 1802.

Lanoaille de Lachèse, Dr. *Les races latines dans la Bérbérie septentrionale.* Limoges: Barbou, 1878.

Lapasset, Ferdinand. *Aperçu sur l'organisation des indigènes dans les territoires militaires et dans les territoires civils.* Alger: Dubos frères, 1850.

Lapène, Edouard (Lt. Col.). *Tableau historique, moral et politique sur les Kabyles.* Metz: Lemort, 1846.

————. "Tableau historique de l'Algérie depuis l'occupation romaine." *Mémoires de l'Académie de Metz* 25 (1843–44): 158–244; 26 (1844–45): 107–315.

————. "Tableau historique de la province d'Oran." *Mémoires de l'Académie de Metz* 23 (1841–42): 43–92.

————. *Vingt-six mois à Bougie ou Collection de mémoires sur sa conquête, son occupation et son avenir: Notice historique, morale, politique et militaire sur les Kabyles.* Paris: Anselin, 1838.

Lapouge, G. de. "Questions Aryennes." *Revue d'Anthropologie*, 3e série, 4 (1899): 180–93.

Larrey, M. le baron. *Notice sur la conformation des différentes races qui habitent en Égypte, suivie de quelques réflexions sur l'embaumement des momies. Mémoire* published following Bonaparte's expedition to Egypt and deposited at the École Polytechnique.

Lavater, Gaspard. *L'Art de Connaître les Hommes par la Physionomie.* Edited by M. Moreau. Paris, 1820.

Lavigerie, Le Cardinal. *Documents sur la Fondation de l'Œuvre anti-esclavagiste.* Saint-Cloud: Belin, 1889.

————. *Écrits d'Afrique.* Edited by A. Hamman. Paris: Ed. Grasset, 1966.

————. *La Mission universelle de l'Église.* Introduction and commentary by X. de Montclos. Paris: Éditions du Cerf, 1968.

————. *L'esclavage Africain, Conférence sur l'esclavage dans le Haut Congo faite à Saint-Gedule de Bruxelles.* Bruxelles: Société anti-esclavagiste, 1888.

————. *Lettre de son éminence le Cardinal Lavigerie faisant hommage à Sa Majesté le Roi Léopold II des documents sur la fondation de l'œuvre anti-esclavagiste publiés à l'occasion de la conférence de Bruxelles.* Alger: Adolphe Jordan, 1889.

————. *Missionnaires d'Afrique.* Paris: Éditions SOS, 1980.

————. *Recueil de lettres publiées par Mgr. L'Archevêque d'Alger sur les œuvres et missions africaines.* Paris: Plon, 1869.

Lavollée, C. "Algérie: Les Kabyles." *Revue de l'Orient de l'Algérie et des Colonies*, n.s., 8 (1850): 13–21.

————. "Algérie: Production des Céréales (1852); Bureaux Arabes Militaires." *Revue de l'Orient, de l'Algérie et des Colonies*, n.s., 14 (1853): 168–74.

Lawrence, Sir William. *Lectures on the Physiology, Zoology and Natural History of Man.* 3rd ed. London: J. Smith, 1823.

Le Bon, Gustave. "Application de la Psychologie à la classification des Races." *Revue Philosophique* 22 (juillet 1886): 593–619.

————. "Ethnographie: L'Algérie et les idées régnantes en France en matière de colonisation." *Revue scientifique* (Revue Rose) (octobre 1887): 449–57.

————. *La Civilisation des Arabes.* Paris: Firmin-Didot, 1884.

————. "L'Anthropologie Actuelle et l'Étude des Races." *Revue Scientifique* 11, no. 17 (décembre 1881): 772–82.

Leclerc, Dr. L. *Une mission médicale en Kabylie.* Paris: J. B. Baillière, 1864.

Lecoq, Louis. *Cinq dans ton œil.* Paris: Rieder, 1925.

————. *Pascualette l'Algérien.* Paris: A. Michel, 1934.

Lecoq, Louis, and Charles Hagel. "Broumitche et le Kabyle." *Mercure de France* 143 (1920): 316–66.

Lecoq, Louis, with Charles Hagel. *Broumitche et le Kabyle.* Paris, 1921. First serialized 1920 in *Mercure de France.*

Lefevre, André. "Cours d'Ethnologie et Linguistiques: Races, peuples, langues de l'Afrique." *Revue Mensuelle de l'École d'Anthropologie,* 2e année (1892): 65–79.

———. *Les races et les langues.* Paris: Alcan, 1893.

Leglay, Maurice. "Les populations berbères." *Afrique française* (1914).

Le Roy, Jean. *Un peuple de Barbares en territoire français: Deux ans de séjour en Petit Kabylie.* Paris: Châllamel aîné, 1911.

Leroy-Beaulieu, Paul. *De la colonisation chez les peuples modernes.* Preface by E. Masqueray. Paris, 1882.

———. "La colonisation de l'Algérie: Européens et Indigènes." *Revue des Deux Mondes* 15 (octobre 1882): 758–92.

———. "La France dans l'Afrique du Nord (Indigènes et colons)." *Revue des Deux Mondes* (mai 1906): 45–83; (janvier 1908): 5–39; (juin 1912): 815–58.

———. *L'Algérie et la Tunisie.* Paris: Guillaumin, 1897. First ed. 1887.

Les Kabyles en France, rapport de la commission chargée d'étudier les conditions de travail des algériens dans la metropole. Beaugency: Imprimerie de R. Barrelier, 1914.

L'Estoille, Vicomte A. de. *En Kabylie, le commandant.* Paris: Librairie des bibliophiles, 1888.

Leynadier, Camille, and M. Clausel. *Histoire de l'Algérie française précédée d'une introduction sur les dominations carthaginoise, romaine, arabe et turque suivi d'un précis historique sur l'empire du Maroc.* Paris: Morel, 1846.

Liorel, Jules. *Races Berbères: Kabylie du Jurjura.* Preface by E. Masqueray. Paris: Leroux, 1893.

Lorin, Henri. *L'Afrique à l'entrée du XXe siècle: Le pays et les indigènes.* Paris: Châllamel aîné, 1901.

Loti, Pierre. *Aziyadé.* Paris: Calmann-Levy, 1987. First ed. 1879.

Louandre, Charles. "La Statistique et l'Archéologie en Afrique." *Revue des Deux Mondes* (juillet–séptembre 1852): 1179–99.

Luciani, J. D. "Chansons Kabyles de Smail Azzekiou." *Revue Africaine* 43 (1899): 17–33, 142–71. Reproduced in Urbain, *Correspondance du Dr. A. Vital avec I. Urbain,* 330–32.

Lyautey, Louis Hubert. "Du role de l'officier." *Revue des Deux Mondes* 105 (mars 1914).

———. *L'Africain: Textes et Lettres 1912–1918.* 3 vols. Paris: Plon, 1953.

———. *Les Plus Belles Lettres de Lyautey.* Présentée par Pierre Lyautey. Paris: Calmann-Lévy, 1962.

———. *Vers le Maroc, Lettres du Sud-oranais 1903–1906.* Paris: Armand Colin, 1937.

MacCarthy, O. "La Kabylie et Les Kabyles." *Revue de L'Orient et de l'Algérie*, n.s. (1847): 29–68, 137–47.

———."La Press Arabe." *Revue de l'Orient et de l'Algérie*, n.s., 2 (1847): 297–304.

Maffre (attributed to). *La Kabylie: Recherches et observations sur cette riche contrée de l'Algérie*. Par un colon établi à Bougie depuis 1833. Paris: Maistrasse et Wiart, 1846.

Mammeri, Mouloud. *La colline oubliée*. Paris: Plon, 1952.

———. *Les Iséfra: Poèmes de Si Mohand-ou-M'hand*. Paris: Maspero, 1969.

———. *Poèmes Kabyles anciens*. Paris: Maspero, 1980.

Marcus, M. L., and F. Duesberg. *Géographie ancienne des États barbaresques d'après l'allemand de Mannert*. Paris: Librairie Encyclopédique de Roret, 1842.

Marival, Raymond. "La Rekba: Mœurs Kabyles." *Mercure de France* 42 (1902): 685–740; 43: 116–76, 414–66.

Martin, Ch. "De la guerre en Afrique et de la soumission des Kabyles." *Le Spectateur militaire*, 2e série, 18 (1857).

Masqueray, Emile. "Documents historiques recueillis dans l'Aurès." *Revue Africaine* 21 (1877): 97–123.

———. "Impressions de voyage: La Kabylie et le pays berbère." *Revue politique et littéraire* 10 (1876): 177–83, 203–7.

———. *La formation des cités chez les populations de l'Algérie (Kabyles du Djurdjura, Chaouïa de l'Aurès, Beni-Mezâb)*. Paris: Leroux, 1886.

———. "Observations sur la Kabylie et ses habitants." *Bulletin de la Société de Géographie d'Alger* (1876).

———. *Souvenirs et Visions d'Afrique*. Paris: Dentu, 1894.

Mathieu, Auguste. *Études algériennes: Les races et les religions en Algérie*. Lyon: Imprimerie X, Jevain, 1894.

Maunier, René. *La construction collective de la maison en Kabylie: Etude de coopération économique chez les Berbers du Djurdjura*. Paris: Travaux et Mémoires de l'Institute d'Ethnologie, III, 1926.

Maupassant, Guy de. *Lettres d'Afrique*. Edited by Michèle Salinas. Paris: La Boîte à Documents, 1990.

Mauroy, P. *Précis de l'histoire et du commerce de l'Afrique septentrionale*. Paris: Ledoyen, 1852.

Mercier, Ernest. "Ethnographie de l'Afrique septentrionale: Notes sur l'origine des peuples berbères." *Revue Africaine* 15 (1871): 420–33.

Meyer, Alphonse. "Origine des habitants de la Kabylie d'après la tradition locale." *Revue Africaine* 3 (1859): 357–67.

Missions des Pères Blancs: Haut-Congo Belge, Grands Lacs, Sahara, Soudan, Kabylie. N.p.: Joseph Servais, n.d.

Mohl, Jules. *Vingt-Sept ans d'Histoire des Études orientales: Rapports faits à la Société Asiatique de Paris de 1840 à 1867*. 2 vols. Paris: Reinwald, 1879.

Bibliography

Montaudon, Jean-Baptiste. *Étude sur l'Algérie pour la fusion des races.* 2 manuscript notebooks. F 80–1681.

Montesquieu, Charles Secondant, Baron de La Brède et de. *Lettres persanes.* Paris: Garnier-Flammarion, 1964.

Montvéran, M. de. "Sur la population du royaume d'Alger." *Le Spectateur Militaire* 23 (1837): 178–79.

Mortillet, Gabriel de. "Colonisation de l'Algérie." *L'Homme* 1 (1884): 395–97.

Ned-Noll (pseudonym for Capt. Édouard-Constant Olivier). *Étude général sur le mouvement géographique africain.* Paris: Charles-Lavarizelle, 1893.

Nerval, Gérard de. "Les Femmes du Caire: Scènes de la vie Égyptienne." *Revue des Deux Mondes* 14 (1846): 404–35.

———. *Voyage en Orient.* 2 vols. Paris: Michel Levy, 1867.

Neveu, E. de. *Les Khouans, ordre religieux chez les musulmans de l'Algérie.* Paris, 1845. Reprinted 1846, Paris; 1913, Alger: Jourdan.

Nott, Josiah, and George Gliddon. *Indigenous Races on the Earth.* London: Trübner & Co, 1857.

———. *Types of Mankind.* London: Trübner & Co, 1854.

Novicow, J. *L'Avenir de la Race Blanche: Critique du Pessimisme Contemporain.* Felix: Alcan, 1897.

Palgrave, William Gifford. *Narrative of a Year's Journey through Central and Eastern Arabia 1862–63.* London: Macmillan, 1865.

Pellissier de Reynaud, E. *Annales Algériennes.* 3 vols. Alger: Bastide, 1854. First ed. 1836–39, Paris.

———. *Mémoires historique et géographiques sur l'Algérie.* Vol. 6 of *Exploration Scientifique de l'Algérie.* Paris: Imp. Royale, 1844.

Penchenat, aîné. *La guerre de la Kabylie ou description historique et militaire de cette confédération.* Paris: Ledoyen, 1854.

Périer, J. A. N. "De l'influence des milieux sur la Constitution des Races Humaines et particulièrement sur les mœurs." *Mémoires de la Société d'Anthropologie de Paris,* 2e série, 1 (1873): 153–200.

———. "Des races dites berbères et leur ethnologie." *Mémoires de la Société d'Anthropologie de Paris,* 2e série, 1 (1873): 1–5.

Peysonnel, Jean-André, et L. René Desfontaines. *Voyage dans les Regénces d'Alger et de Tunis.* Paris: Gide, 1838.

Picard, Alfred. *Exposition universelle internationale de 1900 à Paris: Rapport général administratif et technique.* Paris: Imp. Nationale, 1902–3.

Piquet, Victor. *Les civilisations de l'Afrique du Nord.* Paris: Colin, 1909.

Pomel, A. *Races indigènes de l'Algérie: Et du rôle que leur réservent leurs aptitudes.* Oran: Veuve Dagorn, 1871.

Prébois, F. Leblanc de. *Bilan du Régime Civil de l'Algérie à la Fin de 1871.* Paris: Dentu, 1872.

Prichard, James Cowles. *The Eastern Origin of the Celtic Nations.* London: Houlston & Wright, 1857.

———. *The Natural History of Man.* 2 vols. 4th ed. Enlarged and edited by E. Norris. London: H. Baillière, 1855. First ed. 1843.

———. *Researches into the Physical History of Mankind.* 2 vols. 2nd ed. London: J. & A. Arch, 1826. Also 5 vols. 4th ed. London: Sherwood & London, Houlston, 1841–51. See in particular vol. 2, *Researches into the Physical Ethnography of the African Races.*

Quatrefages de Bréau, A. de. *Histoire de l'Homme.* Paris: Hachette, 1867–68.

———. *Histoire Générale des Races Humaines: Introduction à l'étude des races humaines.* 2 vols. Paris: Hennuyer, 1887.

———. *Rapport sur les Progrès de l'Anthropologie.* Paris: L'Imprimerie Impériale, 1867.

———. *Unité de l'Espèce humaine.* Paris: Hachette, 1861.

Quatrefages de Bréau, A. de, with Ernest T. Hamy. *Les Cranes des Races Humaines.* 2 vols. Paris: J. B. Baillière, 1882.

Quérouil Archinard, Louis. *L'autre France (Tunisie, Algérie, Maroc).* Bordeaux: Féret & fils, 1914.

Randau, Robert (pseudonym for R. Arnaud). *Cassard, le berbère.* Paris: Les Belles Lettres, 1921.

———. *Diko frère de la côte.* Paris. A. Michel, 1929.

———. *Les Algérianistes.* Paris: Sansot, 1919.

———. *Les colons.* Paris: Sansot, 1907.

Rasteil, Maxime. *Les Scandales Algériens: Un Centre de Colonisation en Algérie.* Bone: Rombi & Rasteil, 1895.

Raynal, Abbé Guillaume Thomas François. *Histoire philosophique et politique des établissements et du commerce des Européens dans l'Afrique septentrionale.* Paris: Maumus, 1826.

Renan, Ernest. *Correspondance.* 2 vols. Paris: Calmann-Levy, 1926.

———. *De la part des peuples sémitiques dans l'histoire de la civilisation.* Paris: Levy, 1875.

———. *De l'origine du langage.* Paris: Calmann Lévy, 1883. First ed. 1848.

———. "Exploration scientifique de l'Algérie: La société berbère." *Revue des Deux Mondes* 107 (1873): 138–57.

———. *Histoire générale et système comparé des langues sémitiques.* Vol. 8 of *Œuvres Complètes.* Paris: Calmann-Levy, 1958. First ed. 1855.

———. *La reforme intellectuelle et morale de la France.* Introduction by J-F. Revel. Paris: Union général d'edition, 1967.

———. *Les sciences de la nature et les sciences historiques: L'Avenir de la science; Pensées de 1848.* Paris: Calman-Lévy, 1890.

———. *Œuvres Complètes.* 11 vols. Paris: Calmann-Lévy, 1948.

———. *The Poetry of the Celtic Races and Other Studies.* Translated by W. G. Hutchison. New York: Kennikat Press, 1970.

———. "Qu'est-ce qu'une nation?" In *Renan et L'Allemagne,* edited by Emile Buré. New York: Brentanos, 1945.

———. "Services rendus aux sciences par la philology." *Bulletin de l'Association scientifique de France*, no. 540 (mars 1878): 353–59.

Ribourt, Colonel. *Le Gouvernement de l'Algérie de 1852 à 1858*. Paris: Panckoucke, 1859.

Richard, Charles. *De la Civilisation Arabe*. Alger: Dubois, 1850.

———. *De l'esprit de la l'égislation musulmane*. Alger, 1849.

———. *Du gouvernement arabe et de l'institution qui doit l'exercer*. Alger: Bastide, 1848.

———. *Étude sur l'insurrection du Dhara*. Alger: Besancenez, 1846.

———. *Les mystères du peuple arabe*. Paris: Châllamel aîné, 1860.

———. *Scènes de moeurs arabes*. Paris: Châllamel aîné, 1848.

Rinn, Louis. "Deux chansons Kabyles sur l'insurrection de 1871." *Revue Africaine* 31 (1887): 55–71.

———. "Essai d'études linguistiques et ethnologiques sur les origines berbères." *Revue Africaine* 25 (1881): 161–76, 241–56, 353–70; 26 (1882): 139–60, 257; 27 (1883): 89–96, 245–59, 405–15; 28 (1884): 5–14, 81–89, 161–71, 241–52; 29 (1885): 28–40, 132–40, 351–58; 30 (1886): 64–78, 121–29, 275–93, 392–98, 440–51; 31 (1887): 44–54, 132–57, 231–39, 266–76, 401–15; 32 (1888): 28–51, 81–116, 384–96; 33 (1889): 97–121.

———. *Histoire de l'insurrection de 1871 en Algérie*. Alger: Adolphe Jourdan, 1891.

———. "Les grands tournants de l'histoire de l'Algérie." *Bulletin de la Société de Géographie d'Alger et de l'Afrique du Nord* 8 (1903): 1–24.

———. *L'Insurrection de la Grande Kabylie en 1871*. Paris: Ch. Lavauzelle, 1901.

———. *Marabouts et Khouans: Études sur l'Islam en Algérie*. Alger: Jourdan, 1884.

Robin, N. "Notes et documents concernant l'insurrection de la Kabylie en 1856 et 1857." *Revue Africaine* 42 (1898): 310–21; 43 (1899): 41–77, 204–29, 321–38.

———. "Notes historiques sur la grande Kabylie de 1830 à 1838." *Revue Africaine* 19 (1875): 41–56, 81–96, 193.

———. "Notes historiques sur la grande Kabylie de 1838 à 1852." *Revue Africaine* (1902, 1903): 190.

———. "Soumission des Beni-Yala." *Revue Africaine* 42 (1898): 22–57, 140–64; 44 (1900): 79–96, 135–64, 193–227; 45 (1901): 155–95, 322–66.

Rolland de Denus, André. *Dictionnaire des Appellations ethniques de la France et des Colonies*. Paris: Emile Lechevalier, 1889.

Roussel, Charles. "La Justice en Algérie." *Revue des Deux Mondes* 16 (1876): 678–97.

Rozet, Claude Antoine (Capt.). *Relation de la guerre d'Afrique pendant les années 1830 & 1831*. 2 vols. Paris: Firmin Didot & Arthus Bertrand, 1832.

———. *Voyage dans la Régence d'Alger ou Description du Pays occupé par l'armée française en Afrique*. Paris: Arthus Bertrand, 1833.

Rumigny, de (Général). "De l'établissement de colonies militaires Kabaïles en Algérie." *Le Spectateur Militaire* 49 (1850): 31–53. Also published in book form 1850, Paris: Imp. L. Martinet.

Sabatier, Camille. "Essai de détermination anthropologique des deux types ou races confondus sous le nom moderne de Kabyles." *Bulletins de la Société d'Anthropologie*, 3e série, 5 (1882): 888–97.

————. "Essai sur l'ethnologie de l'Afrique du Nord." *Revue d'Anthropologie*, 2e série, 7 (1884): 404–59.

————. "Essai sur l'origine, l'évolution et les conditions actuelles des Berbères sédentaires." *Revue d'Anthropologie*, 2e série, 5 (1882): 413–42.

————. "Études sociologique sur les Kabyles." *Compte Rendu de l'Association française pour l'Avancement des sciences* 10 (1881): 1050–52.

————. "Étude sur la femme Kabyle." *Revue d'Anthropologie*, 2e série, 6 (1883): 56–69.

————. "La crise franco-kabyle." *Revue Politique parlementaire* 57 (1908): 552–66.

————. "Sur les diverses appellations employés par les anciens pour désigner les populations de l'Afrique." *Bulletin de la Société d'Anthropologie de Paris*, 3e série, 4 (1881): 606–14.

Saint-Arnaud, General. "Expedition dans la Grande Kabylie du 6 mai au 30 juin 1847." *La Sentinelle de l'Armée* (1847): 260, 367, 301, etc.; (1848): 19, 29, 52, 61.

Saint-Simon, H. de. *Œuvres Complètes de Saint-Simon et d'Enfantin*. Paris: Dentu, 1865–74.

Sallust. *The Jurgurthine War*. Translated by S. A. Handford. Middlesex, England: Penquin Books, 1983.

Sarraut, Albert. *La mise en Valeur des Colonies françaises*. Paris: Payot, 1923.

Sarrauton, Henri de. *La Question Algérienne*. Oran: Perrier, 1891.

Saussure, L. D. *Psychologie de la colonisation*. Paris: Alcan, 1899. First ed. 1890.

Savary, M. *Letters on Egypt*. 2 vols. London: J. Robinson, 1799. Translation from the French.

Savignac, Pierre. *Poésie populaire des Kabyles*. Paris: Maspero, 1964.

Sedira, Bel Qacem Ben. *Une mission en Kabylie et l'Assimilation des indigenes*. Alger: Jourdan, 1887.

Sergi, G. *The Meditarranean Race*. Oosterhout N.B., Netherlands: Anthropological Publications, 1967. First published 1895. Translation of *Origine e diffusione della stirpe mediterranea*.

Shaler, William. *Sketches of Algiers, Political, Historical and Civil*. Boston: Cummings, Hilliard & Co., 1826.

Shaw, Dr. Thomas. *Voyage dans la Régence d'Alger . . .* Paris: Merlin, 1830. First published 1738 as part of *Travels and Observations Relating to Several Parts of Barbary and the Levant*, Oxford. First translated into French 1743 as *Voyages en Barbarie*.

Simon, H. "Les études berbères au Maroc et leurs applications en matière de politique et de l'administration." *Archives Berbères* 1 (1915).

Slane, Le Baron de, trans. *Histoire des Berbères.* Paris, 1852. Translation of vol. 2, pt. 4 and vol. 3 of *Kitab al-'ibar.*

Spécimen Colonial de l'Algérie: Résumé, Réfutation ou Complément des systèmes de MM. Leblanc de Prébois, l'Abbé Landmann, de Lamoricière, Bedeau, et Bugeaud. Paris: Moquet, 1847.

Tableau de la Situation des Etablissements français dans l'Algérie. 19 vols. N.p., 1838–53.

Tacitus. *The Germania.* Translated by H. Mattingly. Translation revised by S. A. Handford. Middlesex, England: Penquin Books, 1983.

Tarrit, André. *La direction générale des Affaires indigènes du Maroc.* Conference faite aux officiers du cours préparatoires aux Affaires indigènes. Rabat, 1928.

Tauxier, H. "Ethnographie de l'Afrique septentrionale au temps de Mohamet." *Revue Africaine* 7 (1863): 453–72; 8 (1864): 54–71; 9 (1865): 458–75; 11 (1867): 146–57, 220–32, 257–73, 327–56, 435–46.

———. "Etudes sur les migrations des tribus berbères avant l'islamisme." *Revue Africaine* 7, no. 1 (1863): 24–35.

———. "Examen des Traditions grecques, latines et musulmanes relatives à l'origine du peuple berbère." *Revue Africaine* 6 (1862): 353–63.

———. "Lettre sur les origines libyennes." *Revue Africaine* 29 (1885): 232–40.

Thierry, Amédée. *Histoire des Gaulois.* Paris: Didier & Co., 1863. First ed. 1828.

Thierry, Augustin. *Histoire de la Conquête de l'Angleterre par les Normands.* Paris: Jouvet & Cie., 1867. First ed. 1825.

Thierry, (Colonel). "L'Armée Indigène." *Revue des troupes coloniales* (1923): 506–33.

Thomas, M. V. *De l'Emploi des Arabes et de leur réforme considérés comme moyens de Domination en Algérie.* Alger: Bastide, 1847.

Tocqueville, A. de. *Écrits et discours politiques.* Edited by André Jardin. Vol. 3 of *Œuvres Complètes.* Paris: Gallimard, 1962.

———. *The European Revolution and Correspondence with Gobineau.* Edited and translated by J. Lukacs. Gloucester MA: Peter Smith, 1968.

———. *Notes du Voyage en Algérie de 1841.* Vol. 5 of *Œuvres Complètes.* Paris: Gallimard, 1958.

Topinard, Paul. "De la race indigène ou race berbère de l'Algérie." *Revue d'Anthropologie* 3 (1874): 491–98.

———. *Éléments d'Anthropologie générale.* Paris: Delahaye & Lecrosnier, 1885.

———. "Les types indigènes de l'Algérie." *Bulletin de la Société d'Anthropologie de Paris,* 3e série, 4 (1881): 438–46.

———. "Rapport sur le concours du prix Broca." *Bulletin de la Société d'Anthropologie de Paris,* 3e série, 11 (1888): 696–714.

————. "Un mot sur l'histoire de l'anthropologie en 1788." *Revue d'anthropologie* (mars 1888): 197–201.

Trenga, Dr. *L'âme Arabo-berbère: Étude sociologique sur la société musulmane nord-africaines.* Alger: Homar, 1913.

Urbain, Ismaïl. "Chrétiens et musulman: Français et Indigènes." *Revue de l'Orient et de l'Algérie,* n.s., 2 (1847): 351–59.

————. "Du gouvernement des tribus en Algérie." *Revue de l'Orient et de l'Algérie,* n.s., 2 (1847): 241–59.

————. "La tolérance dans l'Islamisme." *Revue de Paris* (avril 1851): 63–81.

————. "Les Kabyles du Djurdjura." *Revue de Paris* 36 (mars 1857): 91–110.

————. "Les Ziban (Oasis du Sahara Algérien)." *Revue de l'Orient (Bulletin de la Société Orientale)* 5 (1844): 316–19.

Urbain, Ismaïl (alias G. Voisin). *Correspondance du Dr. A. Vital avec I. Urbain (1845–1874).* Edited by A. Nouschi. Vol. 5 of *Collection de documents inédits et d'études sur l'histoire de l'Algérie.* Paris: Ed. Larose, 1959.

————. *L'Algérie française: Indigènes et immigrants.* Paris, 1862.

————. *L'Algérie pour les Algériens.* Paris: Lévy, 1861.

Urbain, Ismaïl, with G. de Eichthal. *Lettres sur la race noire et blanche.* Paris: Paulin, 1839.

Valée, Maréchal. *Correspondance: Septembre 1840–mars 1841.* Edited by George Yver. Vol. 5 of *Collection de documents inédits et d'études sur l'histoire de l'Algérie.* Paris: Éd. Larose, 1957.

Védrenne, Dr. "Climatologie générale de la Grande Kabylie et topographie physique et medicale de Tizi-Ouzou." *Recueil de Mémoires de Medecine, de Chirurgie et de Pharmacie militaire* 2 (1859): 213–78.

Verne, Henri. *La France en Algérie.* Paris: Châllamel aîné, 1869.

Vilbort, J. "Yasmina: Récit de Mœurs Kabyles." *Revue des Deux Mondes* (Belgian ed.) 34 (1879): 834–63.

Villot, Capitaine Constantine, Arnolet. *Mœurs, coutumes et institutions des indigènes de l'Algérie.* N.p., 1871. First published 1870 in *Recueil des Notices et Mémoires de la Société archéologique de Constantine.*

Violard, Emile. *Le Banditisme en Kabylie.* Paris: Savine, 1895.

Viré, Armand. "La Kabylie du Djurdjura." *Bulletin de la Société d'Anthropologie de Paris,* 4e série, 4 (1893): 66–93.

Virey, J. J. *Histoire naturelle du genre humain.* 2 vols. Paris: F. Dufait, 1800.

Vivien de Saint Martin, Louis. *Le Nord de l'Afrique dans l'Antiquité in Nouvelles Annales des Voyages,* 5e série, 40 vols. Paris, 1845–54.

————. "Recherches sur l'histoire de l'anthropologie." *Mémoires de la Société ethnologique* 2 (1845): 77–149.

————. "Richesses Naturelles de l'Algérie: Forêts et Mines." *La Revue Indépendante,* 2ème série, 10 (1847): 369–80.

Volney, C. F. *Voyage en Syrie et en Égypte.* 2 vols. 3rd ed. Paris: Durand, 1798. First ed. 1786.

Bibliography

Warnier, Auguste H. *Cahiers algériens.* Alger: Duclaux, 1870.

———. "Campagne du Maroc 1844." *Nouvelle Revue rétrospective* 9 (1898): 361–408.

———. *Des Moyens d'Assurer la Domination Française en Algérie par M. le lieutenant-général Baron de Létang: Examen par M. le docteur Warnier.* Paris: Guyot, 1846.

———. "Journal d'Auguste-Hubert, Chirugien-major, attaché à l'état major du prince de Joinville." *Nouvelle Revue rétrospective* 10 (1899): 1–48, 97–192, 217–34.

———. *L'Algérie devant l'Empereur.* Paris: Châllamel aîné, 1865.

———. *L'Algérie devant le Sénat.* Paris: Dubuisson, 1863.

———. *L'Algérie devant l'opinion publique.* Paris: Châllamel aîné, 1864.

———. *L'Algérie et les victimes de la guerre.* Alger: Duclaux, 1871.

Wolf, Alexis (intendant général de l'Armée). *Mes souvenirs militaires: École polytechnique, École de Metz, au regiment en Algérie, les deux expéditions de Constantine, expédition du Mexique.* Paris: A la direction du Spectateur Militaire, 1886.

Worms, Monsieur le docteur. *Recherches sur la constitution de la propriété territoriale dans le pays musulmanes: De la propriété rurale et urbaine en Algérie.* Paris: Au bureau de la Revue, 1844.

Yabès, B. *Récits et légendes de la Grande Kabylie.* Alger, 1894.

Zabrowski, M. "Choses d'Algérie." *Bulletins de la Société d'Anthropolgie de Paris,* 4e série, 8 (1897): 135–42.

Zehar, Aissa. *Hind à l'âme pure ou histoire d'une mère.* Alger: Imprimerie de Baconnier, 1948.

SECONDARY SOURCES

Abbas, Ferhat. *Autopsie d'une Guerre: L'aurore.* Paris: Éditions Garnier, 1980.

Abi-Mershed, Osama. *Apostles of Modernity: Saint-Simonians and the Civilizing Mission in Algeria.* Stanford CA: Stanford University Press, 2010.

Abu-Lughod, I., and B. Abu-Laban, eds. *Settler Regimes in Africa and the Arab World: The Illusion of Endurance.* Wilmette IL: Medina University Press International, 1974.

Ageron, Ch.-R. "Du mythe Kabyle aux politiques berbères." In *Le Mal de Voir,* 331–48. Cahiers Jussieu 2. Paris: Union Générale d'Édition, 1976.

———. *Histoire de l'Algérie Contemporaine.* Vol. 2, *De l'Insurrection de 1871 au déclenchment de la guerre de liberation (1954).* Paris: PUF, 1979.

———. "La France a-t-elle eu une politique Kabyle?" *Revue Historique,* no. 223 (1960): 311–52.

———. "*L'Algérie algérienne" de Napoléon III à de Gaulle.* Paris: Sinbad, 1980.

———. "La politique Kabyle sous le Second Empire." *Revue française d'Histoire d'Outre-mer* 53 (1966): 67–105.

333

———. *Les Algériens musulmans et la France 1871–1919*. 2 vols. Paris: PUF, 1968.

———. "Les Juifs d'Algérie: De l'abrogation du décret Crémieux à son rétablissement." *YOD*, nos. 15–16 (1982): 145–61.

———. *Modern Algeria: A History from 1830 to the Present*. N.p.: Africa World, 1992.

———. *Politiques Coloniales au Maghreb*. Paris: PUF, 1972.

Alazard, J., F. Braudel, et al. *Histoire et Historiens de l'Algérie*. Paris: Alcan, 1931.

Albergoni, G., and F. Pouillon. "Le fait berbère et sa lecture coloniale: L'extreme sud tunisien." In *Le Mal de Voir*, 349–96. Cahiers Jussieu 2. Paris: Union Générale d'Édition, 1976.

"Algeria: Bouteflika Promises." In *Africa News*. N.p.: All Africa, 2001.

Alleg, Henri. *La Question*. Paris: Éditions de Minuit, 1958.

Allport, Gordon W. *The Nature of Prejudice*. 1954. Reprint, Boston: Addison-Wesley Inc., 1986.

Amestoy, Georges. "Les universités françaises." Special issue, *Education et gestion* (1968).

Amrouche, Jean. "L'Eternel Jugurtha, Proposition sur le génie africain." *Arche* (February 1946): 58–70.

Anderson, Benedict. *Imagined Communities*. 1983. Reprint, London: Verso, 1991.

Arnold, David, ed. *Imperial Medicine and Indigenous Societies*. Manchester: Manchester University Press, 1988.

Artz, Frederick B. *The Development of Technical Education in France 1500–1850*. Cambridge: MIT Press, 1966.

Asad, Talal, ed. *Anthropology and the Colonial Encounter*. 1973. Reprint, London: Ithaca, 1975.

Astier Loufti, Martine. *Littérature et Colonialisme: L'Expansion Coloniale vue dans la littérature romanesque française 1871–1914*. Paris: Mouton, 1971.

Aussaresses, Paul. *Services Spéciaux: Algérie, 1955–1957*. Paris: Perrin, 2001.

Baker, Keith M. *Condorcet, Selected Writings*. Indiannapolis: Bobbs-Merrill, 1976.

Balandier, G. *Political Anthropology*. London: Penguin, 1970.

Baroli, Marc. *La vie quotidienne des Français en Algérie 1830–1914*. Paris: Hachette, 1967.

Barthélemy-Madaule, M. *Lamarck, the Mythical Precursor: A Study of the Relations between Science and Ideology*. Translated by M. H. Shank. 1979. Reprint, Cambridge MA: MIT Press, 1982.

Basset, René. *Moorish Literature*. London: Colonial Press, 1901.

Bathily, Abdoulaye. "Aux origines de l'Africanisme: Le rôle de l'œuvre ethnohistorique de Faidherbe dans la conquête française du Senegal." In *Mal de Voir*, 77–107. Cahiers Jussieu 2. Paris: Union Générale d'Édition, 1976.

Bedarida, François. "L'Armée de la Republique." *Revue historique* (September 1964).

Bellanger, Claude, Jacques Godechot, Pierre Guiral, and Fernand Terrou. *Histoire générale de la presse française.* 4 vols. Paris: PUF, 1969–75.

Benachnhou, Abdelatif. "Accumulation du Capital et évolution du materiel de la paysannerie en Algérie de 1880 à 1962." *Revue Algérienne* 13 (1976): 261–86.

Bender, Donald. "The Development of French Anthropology." *Journal of the History of the Behavioural Sciences* 1 (1965): 139–52.

Benichou, Paul. *Le Temps des Prophètes Doctrines de l'Age romantique.* Paris: Gallimard, 1977.

Benoune, Mahfoud. *The Making of Contemporary Algeria 1830–1987: Colonial Upheavals and Post Independence Development.* Cambridge: Cambridge University Press, 1988.

Ben-Ze'ev, Efrat, Ruth Ginio, and J. M. Winter, eds. *Shadows of War: A Social History of Silence in the Twentieth Century.* Cambridge: Cambridge University Press, 2010.

Berque, A. "Esquisse d'une histoire de la seigneurie algérienne II." *Revue de la Meditérrannée* (1949): 168–80.

Berque, Jacques. "Cent vingt-cinq ans de sociologie maghrébine." *Annales E. S. C.* 2 (1956): 96–324.

———. *Dépossession du Monde.* Paris: Seuil, 1964.

———. *French North Africa: The Maghrib between Two World Wars.* Translated by Jean Stewart. London: Faber & Faber, 1967.

———. *Maghreb: Histoire et Societés.* 1953. Reprint, Alger: SNED, 1974.

———. "Quelques problèmes de l'Islam maghrébin." *Archives de Sociologie des Religions* (1957).

———. "Vers une étude des comportements en Afrique du Nord." *Cahiers de Sociologie* 25 (1958).

Betts, Raymond F. *Assimilation and Association in French Colonial Theory 1890–1914.* New York: Columbia University Press, 1961.

———. *Tricouleur: The French Overseas Empire.* New York: Gordon & Cremonesi, 1978.

Biddiss, Michael D. *Father of Racist Ideology: The Social and Political Thought of Count Gobineau.* New York: Weybright & Talley, 1970.

———, ed. *Images of Race.* Surrey: Leicester University Press, 1979.

Bidwell, Robin. *Morocco under Colonial Rule: French Administration of Tribal Areas 1912–1956.* London: Cass, 1973.

Bohannan, P., and M. Glazer, eds. *High Points in Anthropology.* New York: A. A. Knopf, 1973.

Boissel, Jean. *Victor Courtet (1813–1867): Premier théoricien de la hiérarchie des races.* Paris: PUF, 1968.

Bolt, Christine. *Victorian Attitudes to Race.* London: Routledge & Kegan Paul, 1971.

Bouayed, M. "La participation de la famille al-Haddad à la révolte de 1871 vue par le Bashaga Benali Sherif." *Revue Hist. Magreb*, nos. 7–8 (1977): 57–64.

Boucherie, M. (Général). "Les Bureaux Arabes." *Revue de la Defense Nationale* 25 (julliet 1957): 1052–66.

Boulifa, Si Saïd. *Le Djurdjura à travers l'histoire*. Alger: J. J. Bringau, 1925.

Bourdieu, Pierre. *The Algerians, Sociologie de l'Algérie*. Translated by Alan C. M. Ross. 1958. Reprint, Boston: Beacon, 1962.

————. *Esquisse d'une théorie de la pratique précédée de trois études d'ethnologie de kabylie*. Genève: Droz, 1972.

Bousquet, G. H. *Justice française et coutumes kabyles*. Alger: Imprimerie Nord Africaine, 1950.

Bouteiller, M. "La Société des Observateurs de l'Homme, ancêtre de la Société Anthropologique de Paris." *Bulletin et Mémoires, S. A. P.*, 10e série, 7 (1956): 22–24.

Boyer, P. "L'Administration française et la réglementation du pèlerinage à la Mecque (1830–1894)." *Revue hist. Magreb*, no. 9 (1977): 275–93.

Branche, Raphälle. "Des Viols Pendant la Guerre d'Algérie." *Vingtième Siècle: Revue d'historie* 75 (2002–3): 123–32.

————. "FLN et OAS: Deux Terrorismes en Guerre d'Algérie." *European Review of History / Revue europénne d'Histoire* 14, no. 3 (September 2007): 325–42.

————. *La Guerre d'Algérie: Une Histoire Apaisée?* L'histoire en débats H351. Paris: Seuil, 2005.

————. *La Torture et L'armée Pendant la Guerre d'Algérie: 1954–1962*. Paris: Gallimard, 2001.

Brenier, Henri, and Leon Baiety. *La politique coloniale de la France*. Paris: F. Alcan, 1924.

Brett, Michael. "The Colonial Period in the Maghrib and Its Aftermath: The Present State of Historical Writing." *Journal of African History* 17 (1976): 291–305.

————, ed. *North Africa: Islam and modernisation*: London: Cass, 1973.

Brochier, André, and Jeanne Brochier. *Livre d'Or de l'Algérie: Dictionnaire des personnalités passés et contemporaines*. Alger, 1937.

Brower, Benjamin Claude. *A Desert Named Peace: The Violence of France's Empire in the Algerian Sahara, 1844–1902*. New York: Columbia University Press, 2009.

Brunschwig, Henri. *La colonisation française du pacte colonial à l'Union française*. Paris: Calmann-Lévy, 1949.

————. *Mythes et Réalités de l'Impérialisme colonial français 1871–1914*. Paris: Armand Colin, 1960.

Brunt, P. A. "Reflections on British and Roman Imperialism." *Comparative Studies in Society and History* 7 (1964–65): 267–88.

Buenzod, Janine. *La formation de la pensée de Gobineau et l'Essai sur l'inégalité des races humaines*. Paris, 1967.

Bibliography

Burns, Robert K., Jr. "The Circum-Alpine Culture Area: A Preliminary View." *Anthropological Quaterly* 36, no. 3 (July 1963): 130–55.

Cabeen, David Clark. "The African Novels of Louis Bertrand: A Phase of the Renascene of National Energy in France." PhD diss., University of Pennsylvania, 1922.

Camus, Albert. *Actuelles, III: Chroniques Algériennes, 1939–1958.* Paris: Gallimard, 1967.

———. *Algerian Chronicles.* Cambridge MA: Harvard University Press, 2013.

Cantier, Jacques. *L'Algérie Sous le Régime de Vichy.* Paris: Jacob, 2002.

Cassilly, Thomas A. "The Anticolonial Tradition in France: The Eighteenth Century to the Fifth Republic." PhD diss., Columbia University, 1975.

Chadbourne, Richard M. *Ernest Renan.* New York: Twayne, 1968.

Chadwick, Owen. *The Secularization of the European Mind in the Nineteenth Century.* 1975. Reprint, Cambridge: Cambridge University Press, 1990.

Chaker, R. "Journal des évènements de Kabylie." *Les Temps Modernes,* no. 432 (1982): 383–458.

Chaker, S. "La revendication culturelle berbère." *Les Temps Modernes,* no. 433 (1982): 439–47.

Chapman, Herrick, and Laura Levine Frader. *Race in France: Interdisciplinary Perspectives on the Politics of Difference.* New York: Berghahn Books, 2004.

Charléty, Sébastien. *Histoire du Saint-Simonisme 1824–1864.* 1896. Reprint, Paris: Paul Hartmann, 1931. See also 1965 ed.

Charlton, D. G. *Positivist Thought in France 1852–1870.* 1959. Reprint, Westport CT: Greenwood Press, 1976.

Charnay, Jean-Paul. *La vie musulmane en Algérie.* Paris: PUF, 1965.

Charnay, Jean-Paul, with J. Berque. *L'Ambivalence de la culture arabe.* Paris: Anthropos ed., 1967.

Chenntouf, Tayeb. "L'Evolution du travail en Algérie au XIXe siècle: La formation du salariat." *Revue Occident Musulman,* no. 31 (1981): 85–103.

Cherpin, Jean. "Les Arabes Chrétiens en Algérie." *Arts et Livres de Provence* 111 (1983): 56–59.

Christelow, Allan. *Muslim Law Courts and the French Colonial State in Algeria.* N.p., 1985.

Clancy-Smith, Julia. "Islam, Gender, and Identities in the Making of French Algeria, 1830–1962." In *Domesticating the Empire: Race, Gender, and Family Life in French and Dutch Colonialism,* edited by Julia Clancy-Smith and Frances Gouda. Charlottesville VA: University Press of Virginia, 1998.

———. *Muslim Notables, Populist Protest: Colonial Encounters (Algeria and Tunisia, 1800–1904).* Berkeley: University of California Press, 1994.

Clark, Linda. *Social Darwinism in France.* Tuscaloosa: University of Alabama Press, 1984.

Clark, Terry Nichols. *Prophets and Patrons: The French University and the Emergence of the Social Sciences.* Cambridge MA: Harvard University Press, 1973.

Bibliography

Cohen, A. "Political Anthropology: The Analysis of the Symbolism of Power Relations." *Man*, n.s., 4, no. 2 (1969): 215–35.

Cohen, William B. *The French Encounter with Africains: White Response to Blacks 1530–1880.* Bloomington: Indiana University Press, 1980.

———. *Rulers of Empire: The French Colonial Service in Africa.* Stanford CA: Hoover Institution Press, 1971.

Coleman, William. *Death is a Social Disease.* Madison: University of Wisconsin Press, 1982.

Collinet, Michel. "Le Saint-Simonisme et l'Armée." *Revue Française de Sociologie* (April 1961): 2, 38–47.

Colombe, Marcel. "Islam et nationalisme arabe à la veille de la première guerre mondiale." *Revue historique*, nos. 223–24 (1960): 85–98.

Colonna, Fanny. "Culture Resistance and Religious Legitimacy in Colonial Algeria." *Economy and Society* 3, no. 3 (1974): 233–52.

———. *Instituteurs Algériens 1883–1939.* Paris: PFNSP, 1975.

———. "La ville au village: Transfère de savoir et de modèles entre villes et campagnes en Algérie." *Revue française sociale* 19 (1978): 407–26.

———. "Les débuts de l'Islam dans l'Aurès 1936–1938." *Revue Algérienne* 14 (1977): 277–87.

———. "Production scientifique et position dans le champ intellectuel et politique: Deux cas; Augustin Berque et Joseph Desparmet." In *Le Mal de Voir*, 397–415. Cahiers Jussieu 2. Paris: Union Générale d'Édition, 1976.

———. "Saints furieux et saints studieux ou, dans l'Aurès, comment la religion vient aux tribus." *Annales ESC* 35 (1978): 642–62.

Colonna, Fanny, with Claude Haïm Brahimi. "Du bon usage de la science coloniale." In *Le Mal de Voir*, 221–41. Cahiers Jussieu 2. Paris: Union Générale d'Edition, 1976.

Colson, Elizabeth. *Tradition and Contract: The Problem of Order.* Chicago: Aldine Publishing Co., 1974.

Confer, Vincent. *France and Algeria: The Problem of Civil and Political Reform 1870–1920.* Syracuse NY: Syracuse University Press, 1966.

Connelly, Matthew James. *A Diplomatic Revolution: Algeria's Fight for Independence and the Origins of the Post-Cold War Era.* Oxford: New York, 2002.

Cooke, J. "The Army Archives at Vincennes: Archives for the Study of North African History in the Colonial Period." *Muslim World* (January 1971): 35–38.

———. "Eugène Etienne and the Emergence of Colon Dominance in Algeria 1884–1905." *Muslim World* 65 (1965): 39–53.

Coon, C. S. *The Tribes of the Rif.* Cambridge MA: Harvard, 1931.

Cossu D'Scamard, P. "L'insurrezione del 1871 in Cabilia e la confraternita Rahmaniyya." *Att. Lincei, Mem, Cl. Sci, mor. stor. et filol. ser.* 8, no. 20 (1977).

Count, E. *This is Race.* New York: Schuman, 1950.

Bibliography

Crapanzano, Vincent. *The Harkis: The Wound That Never Heals*. Chicago: University of Chicago Press, 2011.

Crowder, Michael. "Indirect Rule-French and British Style." *Africa* 34 (1964): 197–205.

———. *West Africa under Colonial Rule*. 1968. Reprint, London: Hutchinson, 1981.

Cudsi, A. S., and A. E. Dessouki. *Islam and Power*. London: Croom Helm, 1981.

Curtin, P. *The Image of Africa: British Ideas and Actions 1780–1850*. Madison: University of Wisconsin Press, 1964.

Daniel, Norman. *Islam and the West: The Making of an Image*. 1960. Reprint, Edinburgh: University Press, 1962.

———. *Islam, Europe and Empire*. Edinburgh: University Press, 1966.

Darbois, Dominique, and Philippe Vigneau. *Les Algériens en Guerre*. Milano: Feltrinelli, 1961.

Davis, David Brion. *The Problem of Slavery in Western Culture*. Ithaca NY, 1966.

Davis, Diana K. *Resurrecting the Granary of Rome: Environmental History and French Colonial Expansion in North Africa*. Athens: Ohio University Press, 2007.

Déjeux, Jean. *Bibliographie de la littérature "algérienne" des français (1896–1975)*. Paris: Ed. CNRS, 1978.

———. "Robert Randau et son *peuple franco-berbère*." *Littérature coloniale: Cahiers de Littérature générale et comparée*, no. 5 (1981): 91–99.

Delon, Michel, Robert Mauzi, and Sylvain Menant. *Littérature française*. Vol. 6, *De L'encyclopédie aux Méditations*. Paris: Arthaud, 1984.

Demontès, Victor. *La colonisation militaire sous Bugeaud*. Paris: E. Larose, 1916.

———. "Les instructions données par le maréchal Soult, Ministre de la Guerre à Bugeaud, gouverneur général de l'Algérie, au sujet de la colonisation." *Revue de l'histoire des Colonies françaises* (1917): 439–70.

———. "Lettre de Bugeaud à Soult (26 Nov. 1841): Réponse aux instructions ministerielle du 13 août." *Bulletin de la Société de Géographie d'Alger et de l'Afrique du Nord* (1919).

Dermenghem, Emile. "Le mythe de Psyché dans le folklore nord-africain." *Revue Africaine* 89 (1945): 41–81.

Deschamps, H. "Et maintenant Lord Lugard." *Africa* 33 (1963): 293–306.

Desparmet, J. "Elégies et satires politiques de 1830 à 1914." *Bulletin de la Société de Géographie d'Alger* (1933): 35–54.

———. "La chanson de geste de 1830 à 1914 dans la Mitidja." *Revue Africaine* (1939): 192–226.

———. "La conquête racontée par les Indigènes." *Bulletin de la Société de Géographie d'Alger* (1932): 437–56.

———. "L'Entrée des Français à Alger par le Cheikh Abd el Kader." *Revue Africaine* (1930): 225–56.

————. "L'œuvre de la France en Algérie jugée par les indigènes." *Bulletin de la Société de Géographie d'Alger* (1910).

————. "Naissance d'une histoire *nationale* de l'Algérie." *Afrique française* (1933).

Dine, Philip. *Images of the Algeria War: French Fiction and Film, 1954–1992.* Oxford: Clarendon Press, 1994.

d'Ocagne, Mortimer. *Les Grandes Écoles de France.* Paris: J. Hetzel, 1879.

Duchet, Michèle. *Anthropologie et histoire au siècles des lumières.* Paris: Maspero, 1971.

Dumézil, Georges. *L'ideologie tripartite des Indo-Européens.* Brussels, 1958.

Dussaud, René. *L'œuvre scientifique d'Ernest Renan.* Paris: Geuthner, 1951.

E. C. "Marriages mixtes des Kabyles en France." *La France Meditérranéenne et Africaine* 1 (1938): 110–17.

École Polytechnique: Livre du Centenaire 1794–1894. 3 vols. Paris: Gauthier-Villars, 1894.

Ehrard, Jean, and René Pomeau. *Littérature française.* Vol. 5, *De Fénélon à Voltaire, 1680–1750.* Paris: Arthaud, 1984.

Emerit, Marcel. "La conversion des musulmans d'Algérie." *Revue Historique,* nos. 223–24 (1960): 63–83.

————. *L'Algérie à l'époque d'Abd-el-Kader.* Vol. 4 of *Collection de documents inédits sur l'histoire de l'Algérie.* Paris: Ed. Larose, 1951.

————. "La lutte entre les généraux et les prêtres au début de l'Algérie française." *Revue Africaine* (1953): 66–97.

————. "Les mémoires d'Ahmed, dernier bey de Constantine." *Revue Africaine* (1949): 65–125.

————. "Les méthodes coloniales de la France sous le Seconde Empire." *Revue Africaine* (1943): 184–218.

————. *Les Saint-Simoniens en Algérie.* Paris: Sté. d'Éd. Belles Lettres, 1941.

————. "L'état d'esprit des Musulmans d'Algérie de 1847 à 1870." *Revue d'Histoire Moderne* (avril–juin 1961): 103–20.

————. "L'état intellectuel et moral de l'Algérie en 1830." *Revue d'Histoire moderne et contemporaine* (juillet–septembre 1954): 201–12.

————. "Toustain du Manoir au pays d'Abd-el-Kader." *Revue Africaine* (1954): 113–52.

————. "Un problème de distance morale: La résistance algérienne à l'époque d'Abd-el-Kader." *Informations Historiques* (1951): 129–31.

Enjelvin, Geraldine. "The Harki Identity: A Product of Marginalisation and Resistance to Symbolic Violence." *National Identities* 8 (2006): 113–27.

Esquer, Gabriel. *Les Commencements d'un Empire: La Prise d'Alger 1830.* 1923. Reprint, Paris: Larose, 1929.

Evans, Martin. *Mémoires de la Guerre d'Algérie.* Paris: L'Harmattan, 2007.

————. *The Memory of Resistance: French Opposition to the Algerian War, 1954–1962.* Oxford: Berg, 1997.

Bibliography

Evans, Martin, and Kenneth Lunn. *War and Memory in the Twentieth Century.* Oxford: Berg, 1997.

Fairchild, Hoxie Neale. *The Noble Savage: A Study in Romantic Naturalism.* New York: Columbia University Press, 1928.

Faucon, Narcisse. *Le livre d'or de l'Algérie: Histoire politique, militaire, administrative, événement et faits principaux biographie des hommes ayant marqué dans l'armée, les sciences, les lettres, de 1830 à 1889.* Paris: Châllamel aîné, 1889.

Favret, Jeanne. "Le traditionalisme par excès de modernité." *Archives européenes de Sociologie* (1967): 71–93.

Ferrand, Gaston. *La colonisation militaire du maréchal Bugeaud 1841–47.* Paris: E. Larose, 1909.

Fidus, L. Bertrand. "Silhouettes Contemporaines." *Revue des Deux Mondes* 63 (1924): 793–819.

Forde, Daryll. "Applied Anthropology in Government: British Africa." In *Anthropology Today*, edited by A. L. Kroeber. Chicago: University of Chicago Press, 1953.

Fortes, M., and E. E. Evans-Pritchard. *African Political Systems.* 1940. Reprint, London: Oxford University Press, 1961.

Foster, G. M. *Applied Anthropology.* Boston: Little Brown & Co., 1969.

Fourrier, Henri. *La colonisation officielle et les concessions de Terres dominales en Algérie.* Paris: Graid & Brière, 1915.

Franc, Julien. *La colonisation de la Mitidja.* Paris: Librairie Champion, 1928.

Fück, J. W. "Islam as an Historical Problem in European Historiography since 1800." In *Historians of the Middle East*, edited by B. Lewis and P. M. Holt. London: Oxford University Press, 1962.

Gallissot, R. "Abdel Kader et la nationalité algérienne: Interpretation de la chute de la Régence d'Alger et des premières resistances à la conquête française (1830–39)." *Revue Historique* (1965, 2ème trimestre): 339–68.

———. "La guerre d'Abdel Kader ou la ruine de la nationalité algérienne (1839–47)." *Hespéris Tamuda* (1964): 119–41.

Gallois, William. *A History of Violence in the Early Algerian Colony.* Basingstoke: Palgrave, 2013.

Gallup, Dorothea M. "The French Image of Algeria: Its Origin, Its Place in Colonial Ideology, Its Effect on Algerian Acculturation." PhD diss., University of California–Los Angeles, 1973.

Ganiage, Jean. *L'expansion coloniale de la France sous la 3ème République (1871–1914).* Paris: Payot, 1968.

Gann, L. H., and P. Duignan. *Colonialism in Africa 1870–1961.* 1969. Reprint, Cambridge: Cambridge University Press, 1981.

Gauthier, Robert. "Naissance et Mort du *Mythe Kabyle* de1830 à 1914." *Le Monde*, 9 octobre 1963.

Gay, Peter. *The Party of Humanity: Essays in the French Enlightenment.* New York: Norton, 1971.

Geertz, Clifford. "In Search of North Africa." *New York Review of Books* 16, no. 7 (April 1971).

Geiger, Roger L. "The Institutionalization of Sociological Paradigms: Three Examples from Early French Sociology." *Journal of the History of the Behavioural Sciences* 11 (1975): 235–45.

Gellner, Ernest. *Muslim Society*. London: Cambridge University Press, 1981.

———. *Saints of the Atlas*. Chicago: University of Chicago Press, 1969.

———. "The Struggle for Morocco's Past." *The Middle East Journal* (Winter 1961): 79–90.

Gellner, Ernest, and Ch. Micaud, eds. *Arabs and Berbers*. London: Heath, 1972.

Gellner, Ernest, and J.-C. Vatin, eds. *Islam et Politique au Maghreb*. Paris: Ed. CNRS, 1981.

Germain, Roger. *La politique indigène de Bugeaud*. Vol. 3 of *Collection de documents inédits et d'études sur l'histoire de l'Algérie*. Paris: Éd. Larose, 1955.

Gibb, H. A. R. *Mohammedanism*. 1949. Reprint, New York: Oxford University Press, 1970.

Gifford, P., and W. R. Louis. *France and Britain in Africa*. 1971. Reprint, New Haven CT: Yale University Press, 1978.

Gilman, Sander L. *Difference and Pathology: Stereotypes of Sexuality, Race and Madness*. Ithaca: Cornell University Press, 1985.

Girardet, Raoul. *La société militaire dans la France contemporaine 1815–1939*. Paris: Plon, 1953.

———. *L'idée coloniale en France 1871–1862*. Paris: La Table Ronde, 1972.

Goodman, Jane E. *Berber Culture on the World Stage: From Village to Video*. Bloomington: Indiana University Press, 2006.

Gordon, D. C. *The Passing of French Algeria*. London, 1966.

———. *Self-determination and History in the Third World*. Princeton: Princeton University Press, 1971.

Gosnell, Jonathan K. *The Politics of Frenchness in Colonial Algeria, 1930–1954*. Rochester NY: University of Rochester Press, 2002.

Gough, Kathleen. "Anthropologie et Impérialisme." *Les Temps Modernes*, nos. 293–94 (décembre 1970–janvier 1971): 1123–39. Followed by "Un Débat," 1140–53 and Gough's "Reponse," 1154–66.

———. "Anthropology: Child of Imperialism." *Monthly Review* 19, no. 11 (1968).

Gouhier, Henri. *Études d'histoire de la philosophie française*. Hildesheim: G. Olms, 1976.

———. *Études sur l'histoire des Idées en France depuis le XVIIe siècle*. Paris: Lib. Philo., 1980.

Gould, Stephen Jay. *The Mismeasure of Man*. New York: Norton, 1981.

Gourdan, Hubert, Jean-Robert Henry, and Françoise Henry-Lorcerie. "Roman colonial et idéologie coloniale en Algérie." *Revue algérienne des sciences juridiques, économiques et politiques* 11, no. 1 (mars 1974): 7–252.

Bibliography

Guerin, Adam. "Racial Myth, Colonial Reform and the Invention of Customary Law in Morocco, 1912–1930." *Journal of North African Studies* 16, no. 3 (2011): 361–80.

Guernier, Eugène. *La Bérbérie, l'Islam et la France*. 2 vols. Paris: Ed. de l'Union Française, 1950.

Guiral, P., and E. Temin, eds. *L'idée de race dans la pensé française contemporaine*. Paris: Éd. CNRS, 1977.

Guyot, Yver. *L'inventeur*. Paris: Armand le Chevalier, 1867.

Hacking, Ian. *The Taming of Chance*. Cambridge: Cambridge University Press, 1990.

Hale, Dana S. *Races on Display: French Representation of Colonized Peoples, 1886–1940*. Bloomington: Indiana University Press, 2008.

Halvorsen, Kj. H. "Colonial Transformation of Agrarian Society in Algeria." *Journal of Peace Research* 15 (1978): 323–43.

Hammond, Michael. "Anthropology as a Weapon of Social Combat in Late Nineteenth Century France." *Journal of the History of the Behavioural Sciences* 16 (1980): 118–32.

Hannoum, Abdelmajid. *Violent Modernity: France in Algeria*. Cambridge MA: Harvard University Press, 2010.

Hansen, Eric C. *Disaffection and Decadence: A Crisis in French Intellectual Thought 1848–1898*. Washington DC: University Press of America, 1982.

Harbi, Mohammed. *Le F.L.N. Mirage et Réalité des origines à la prise du pouvoir (1945–1962)*. Paris: Éditions Jeune Afrique, 1980.

———. "Nationalisme Algérien et Identité Berbère." *Peuples méditerranéens* 11 (1980): 31–37.

Hardy, Georges. *Faidherbe*. Paris: Edition de l'Encyclopédie de l'Empire français, 1947.

Harris, M. *The Rise of Anthropological Theory*. London: Routledge & Kegan Paul, 1968.

Harrison, Christopher. *France and Islam in West Africa, 1860–1960*. Cambridge: Cambridge University Press, 1988.

Hart, David M. "The Berber Dahir of 1930 in Colonial Morocco: Then and Now (1930–1996)." *Journal of North African Studies* 2, no. 2 (2007): 11–33.

Hayek, F. A. *The Counter-Revolution of Science: Studies in the Abuse of Reason*. Glencoe IL: Free Press, 1952.

Hayes, Carlton J. *France: A Nation of Patriots*. New York: Columbia University Press, 1930.

Headrick, Daniel R. *The Tentacles of Progress: Technology Transfer in the Age of Imperialism 1850–1940*. Oxford: Oxford University Press, 1988.

Heggoy, Alf A. *The French Conquest of Algiers 1830: An Oral Tradition*. Athens: Ohio University Press, 1986.

———. *Insurgency and Counterinsurgency in Algeria*. Bloomington: Indiana University Press, 1972.

————. "Some Useful French Depositories for the Study of the Algerian Revolution." *Muslim World* 58, no. 4 (October 1968): 345–47.

————. "Sources for Nineteenth Century Algerian History." *Muslim World* 54 (1964): 292–99.

Heizer, Robert F. "Long-Range Dating in Archeology." In *Anthropology Today*, edited by A. L. Kroeber. Chicago: University of Chicago Press, 1953.

Hemmings, F. W. J. *Culture and Society in France 1848–1898: Dissidents and Philistines.* New York: Charles Scribner's Sons, 1971.

Hervé, George. "Le Premier programme de l'anthropologie." *Revue scientifique* 30 (1909): 523.

Hobsbawm, Eric, and Terence Ranger, eds. *The Invention of Tradition.* Cambridge: Cambridge University Press, 1983.

Horne, Alistair. *A Savage War of Peace: Algeria 1954–1962.* London: Penguin Books, 1979.

Husson, Odile. *Lorraine et Afrique dans l'œuvre de Louis Bertrand.* Nancy: Société d'Impressions typographiques, 1966.

Iggers, G. G. *The Cult of Authority: The Political Philosophy of the Saint-Simonians.* The Hague, 1970.

Isnard, Hildebert. *Algeria.* Translated by O. S. Winder. London: N. Kaye, 1955.

————. *La réorganisation de la propriété rurale dans la Mitidja.* Alger: Impr. Joyeux, 1950.

Joly, Danièle. *The French Communist Party and the Algerian War.* New York: St. Martins Press, 1991.

Julien, Ch.-André. *Histoire de l'Algérie Contemporaine.* Vol. 1, *La Conquête et les debuts de la Colonisation 1827–1871.* 1962. Reprint, Paris: PUF, 1979.

————. "L'insurrection de Kabylie (1870–71)." *Preuves* (décembre 1963): 60–66.

"Kabylie: La Revue de Press." *Le Nouvel Observateur,* 2 May 2001.

Kanya-Forstner, A. S. *The Conquest of the Western Sudan: A Study in French Military Imperialism.* London: Cambridge University Press, 1969.

Keaton, Trica Danielle. *Muslim Girls and the Other France: Race, Identity Politics, and Social Exclusion.* Bloomington: Indiana University Press, 2006.

Kern, Stephen. *Anatomy and Destiny: A Cultural History of the Human Body.* Indiannapolis: Bobbs Merril, 1975.

Kiernan, V. G. *Lords of Human Kind.* 1969. Reprint, New York: Columbia University Press, 1986.

Kobak, Annette. *Isabelle: The Life of Isabelle Eberhardt.* New York: Vintage, 1990.

Lacheraf, Mostefa. *L'Algérie: Nation et société.* Paris: Maspero, 1965.

Lacoste, Camille. *Bibliographie ethnologique de la Grande Kabylie.* Paris: Mouton, 1962.

Lacoste, Yves. *Ibn Khaldun, Naissance de l'Histoire passé du tiers monde.* Paris: Maspero, 1966.

Bibliography

Lacoste, Yves, A. Nouschi, and A. Prenant. *L'Algérie passé et present: Le cadre et les étapes de la constitution de l'Algérie actuelle.* Paris: Éditions sociales, 1960.

Lacoste-Dujardin, Camille. *Le conte Kabyle: Étude ethnologique.* Paris: Maspero, 1970.

Lacouture, Jean. "Les français sont-ils racistes?" *Le Monde,* 20–22 mars 1970.

L'Afrique Française du Nord: Bibliographie Militaire des ouvrages français ou traduits en français et des articles des principales revues françaises relatifs à l'Algérie à la Tunisie et au Maroc de 1830 à 1926. Paris: Imprimerie nationale, 1975.

Lagarde, André, and Michard Laurent. *Les Grandes Auteurs Français du Programme.* Vol. 3 (XVIIe siècle); vol. 4 (XVIIIe siècle); vol. 5 (XIXe siècle). Paris: Bordas, 1967.

Laroui, Abdallah. *The History of the Maghrib: An Interpretive Essay.* Princeton: Princeton University Press, 1977.

Lasteyrie du Saillant, Robert C. *Bibliographie générale des travaux historiques et archéologiques publiés par les société savantes de la France.* Paris: Imprimerie nationale, 1888–1918.

Lawless, R. I. *Algeria.* World Bibliographical Series 9. London: Oxford University Press, 1980.

———. *Algerian Bibliography 1830–1973, English Language Publications.* New York: Bowher, 1976.

———. "The Kabyles." *The Family of Man,* no. 33 (1975): 1457–60.

Lazreg, Marina. *The Emergence of Classes in Algeria: A Study in Colonialism and Sociopolitical Change.* Boulder CO: Westian, 1976.

———. *Torture and the Twilight of Empire: From Algiers to Baghdad.* Human Rights and Crimes against Humanity. Princeton: Princeton University Press, 2008.

Le Centenaire de Saint-Cyr 1808–1908. Paris: Berger-Levrault & Cie, 1908.

Leclerc, Gerard. *Anthropologie et Colonialisme: Essai sur l'histoire de l'africanisme.* Paris: Fayard, 1972.

Le Sueur, James D. "France's Arabic Educational Reforms in Algeria during the Colonial Era: Language Instruction in Colonial and Anti-Colonial Minds before and after Algerian Independence." In *The French Colonial Mind, Volume 1: Mental Maps of Empire and Colonial Encounters,* edited by Martin Thomas, 194–218. Lincoln: University of Nebraska Press, 2012.

———. *Uncivil War: Intellectuals and Identity Politics during the Decolonization of Algeria.* Philadelphia: University of Pennsylvania Press, 2001.

Levallois, Michel, and Sarga Moussa. *L'orientalisme des Saint-Simoniens.* Paris: Maisonneuve & Larose, 2006.

Levin, Jack. *The Functions of Prejudice.* New York: Harper Row, 1975.

Lewis, William Hubert, ed. *French-speaking Africa: The Search for Identity.* New York: Walker, 1965.

Linderski, Jerzy. "Si Vis Pacem, Para Bellum: Concepts of Defensive Imperialism." *Papers and Monographs of the American Academy in Rome* 29 (November 1984): 133–64.

Lorcin, Patricia M. E., ed. *Algeria and France, 1800–2000: Identity, Memory, Nostalgia.* Syracuse NY: Syracuse University Press, 2006.

———. *Historicizing Colonial Nostalgia: European Women's Narratives of Colonial Algeria and Kenya 1900–Present.* New York: Palgrave, 2012.

———. "Imperialism, Cultural Identity and Race in Colonial Algeria: The Role of the Medical Corps, 1830–1870." *ISIS* 90, no. 4 (1999): 653–79.

———. "Rome and France in Africa: Recovering Algeria's Latin Past." *French Historical Studies* 25, no. 2 (2002): 295–329.

Lorimer, Douglas A. *Colour, Class and the Victorians.* Leicester: Leicester University Press, 1978.

Lounsbury, F. G. "Field Methods and Techniques in Linguistics." In *Anthropology Today*, edited by A. L. Kroeber. Chicago: University of Chicago Press, 1953.

Lucas, P., and J.-C. Vatin. *L'Algérie des Anthropologues.* Paris: Maspero, 1975.

Lyons, Amelia H. *The Civilizing Mission in the Metropole: Algerian Families and the French Welfare State during Decolonization.* Stanford CA: Stanford University Press, 2013.

Mackenzie, John H., ed. *Imperialism and the Natural World.* Manchester: Manchester University Press, 1990.

Macleod, Roy, and Milton Lewis. *Disease, Medicine, and Empire.* London: Routledge, 1988.

MacMaster, Neil. *Burning the Veil: Military Propaganda and the Emancipation of Women during the Algeria War 1954–1962.* Manchester: Manchester University Press, 2009.

Mafeje, A. "The Ideology of Tribalism." *Journal of Modern African Studies* 9 (1971): 253–61.

Magraw, Roger. *France 1815–1914: The Bourgeois Century.* 1983. Reprint, London: Fontana, 1987.

Magubane, B. "A Critical Look at Indices Used in the Study of Social Change in Colonial Africa." *Current Anthropology* 12 (1971): 419–30.

Malley, Robert. *The Call from Algeria: Third Worldism, Revolution and the Turn to Islam.* Berkeley: University of California Press, 1996.

Mammeri, Mouloud. "Evolution de la poésie Kabyle." *Revue Africaine* 94 (1950): 125–48.

Mannheim, Karl. *Ideology and Utopia: An Introduction to the Sociology of Knowledge.* Translated by Louis Wirth and Edward Shils. 1929. Reprint, New York: Harcourt Brace Janovich, 1936.

Mannoni, Otare Dominique. *Psychology de la Colonisation.* Paris: Seuil, 1950.

Manouvrier, L. "La Société d'Anthropologie de Paris." *Revue International de l'enseignement* 60 (1910): 234–51.

Bibliography

Manuel, F. E. *The New World of Henri Saint-Simon.* Cambridge MA: Harvard University Press, 1956.

———. *The Prophets of Paris.* Cambridge MA: Harvard University Press, 1962.

Marquet, J. "Objectivity in Anthropology." *Current Anthropology* 5, no. 1 (1964): 47–48.

Martel, A. "Note sur l'historiographie de l'insurrection algérienne de 1871." *Cahiers de Tunisie*, nos. 93–94 (1976): 69–84.

Martin, B. G. *Muslim Brotherhoods in Nineteenth Century Africa.* Cambridge: Cambridge University Press, 1976.

Martin, Claude. *La Commune d'Alger (1870–71).* Paris: Éditions Héraklès, 1936.

Mason, Philip. *Patterns of Dominance.* London: Oxford University Press, 1970.

———. *Prospero's Magic.* London: Oxford University Press, 1962.

Maunier, René. "Le culte domestique en Kabylie." *Revue d'Ethnographie et des Traditions populaires*, nos. 23–24 (1925): 248–65.

Maynial, Édouard. *Anthologie des Romanciers du XIXe siècle.* Paris: Hachette, 1945.

Mazouni, Abdullah. *Culture et enseignement en Algérie et au Maghreb.* Paris: Maspero, 1969.

McDougall, James. "Myth and Counter-Myth: 'The Berber' as National Signifier in Algerian Historiographies." *Radical History Review* 86 (2003): 66–88.

McKay, Donald. "Colonialism in the French Geographical Movement 1871–1881." *Geographical Review* 33 (1943): 214–33.

McLaren, Angus. "Prehistory of the Social Sciences: Phrenology in France." *Comparatives Studies in Society and History*, no. 23 (1981): 3–22.

Méliani, Abd-El-Aziz. *Le Drame des Harkis.* Reissue. Paris: Perrin, 2001.

Merad, Ali. *Le Réformisme musulmane en Algérie: 1920–1940.* Paris: Mouton, 1967.

Mercier, Gustave. *La découverte de l'Algérie: Initiation à l'Algérie.* Paris: Maison-Neuve, 1954.

Meuleman, J. H. *Le Constantinois entre les deux guerres mondiales: L'évolution économique et sociale de la population rurale.* Assen, Netherlands: Van Sorcum, 1985.

Meyer, Jean, Jean Tarrade, Annie Rey-Goldzeiguer, and Jacques Thobie, eds. *Histoire de la France Coloniale.* 2 vols. Paris: Colin, 1991.

Miller, Arthur G. *In the Eye of the Beholder: Contemporary Issues in Stereotyping.* New York: Praeger, 1982.

Ministère de la Guerre: Manuel à l'usage des troupes employés outre-mer. Parts 1 and 2. Paris: Imprimerie nationale, 1926.

Monneret, Sophie. *L'Orient des Peintres.* Paris: Nathan, 1989.

Monod, G. J. J. *Le maître de l'histoire: Renan, Taine, Michelet.* Paris: Calman-Lévy, 1894.

Montagne, Robert. *The Berbers: Their Social and Political Organisation.* Translated by D. Seddon. 1931. Reprint, London: Cass, 1973.

———. "L'émigration des musulmans d'Algérie en France." *L'Afrique et l'Asie,* no. 21 (1951): 5–19.

———. "L'évolution de la Kabylie, conclusion d'une conférence de 1951." *L'Afrique et l'Asie,* no. 32 (1955): 88–89.

Montagnon, Pierre. *La Conquête de l'Algérie.* Paris: Pygmalion, 1986.

Monteil, Vincent. "Les Bureaux Arabes au Maghreb (1833–1961)." *Esprit* 29 (1961): 575–608.

Morizot, Jean. *L'Algérie Kabylisée.* Paris: Peyronnet, 1962.

Mornet, Daniel. *Les Sciences de la Nature en France au XVIIe siècle.* Paris: Armand Colin, 1911.

———. *Le Sentiment de la Nature en France de J.-J. Rousseau à Bernadin de Saint-Pierre: Essai sur les rapports de la littérature et des mœurs.* Paris: Hachette, 1907.

Morsy, Magali. *Les Saint-Simoniens et l'Orient: Vers la modernité.* Paris: Edisud, 1989.

Mosse, Geroge L. *Toward the Final Solution: A History of European Racism.* New York: H. Fertig, 1978.

Moulis, Robert F. *Le Ministère de l'Algérie: 24 juin 1858–24 novembre 1860.* Alger: Carboul, 1926.

Nadir, Ahmed. "Les ordres religieux et la conquête française 1830–51." *Revue algérienne des sciences juridiques, économiques et politiques* (1972–74): 819–72.

Neuville, H. "L'Espèce, la race et le métissage en anthropologie." In vol. 2 of *Archives de l'Institut de paléontologie humaine, Mémoires.* Paris: Masson, 1933.

Nisbet, Robert. *Social Change and History.* London: Oxford, 1969.

———. *The Social Philosophers.* New York: Crowell, 1973.

Nora, Pierre. *Les Français d'Algérie.* Paris: Julliard, 1961.

Nouschi, A. "La crise économique de 1866 à 1869 dans le Constantinois: Aspect démographique." *Hespéris* (1959, 1–2 trimestre): 105–23.

———. "Les Archives de l'ex gouvernement général de l'Algérie." *Cahiers de Tunisie* 36 (1961): 1–80.

Nye, Robert A. *The Origins of Crowd Psychology: Gustave LeBon and the Crisis of Mass Democracy in the Third Republic.* Beverly Hills CA: Sage Publications, 1975.

Olender, Maurice, ed. *La Science face au Racisme.* Bruxelles: Editions Complexe, 1986.

Onians, R. O. *The Origins of European Thought.* Cambridge: Cambridge University Press, 1954.

Ortony, Andrew, ed. *Metaphor and Thought.* Cambridge: Cambridge University Press, 1979.

Bibliography

Ouerdane, Amar. *La Question Berbère Dans le Mouvement National Algérien: 1926–1980*. Sillery, Québec: Septentrion, 1990.

———. *Les Berbères et L'Arabo-Islamisme en Algérie*. Montréal: KMSA, 2003.

Ougrour, Jean. "Le fait berbère: Essai de démystification." In "L'Homme au Maghreb après l'Indépendance," special issue, *Confluent*, nos. 23–24 (October 1962): 17–634.

Paret, Roger. "Quand l'Algérie ne savait pas qu'elle était algérienne . . ." *Preuves* (octobre 1966): 68–79.

Parson, Talcott. *The Structure of Social Action*. New York: McGraw Hill, 1937.

Patte, Etienne. "Georges Vacher de Lapouge 1854–1936." *Revue générale du centre-ouest de la France* 12 (1937): 775.

Péan, Pierre. *Main Basse Sur Alger: Enquête Sur Un Pillage, Juillet 1830*. Paris: Plon, 2004.

Pearce Williams, L. "Science, Education and Napoleon I." In *The Rise of Science in Relation to Society*, edited by Leonard Mendes Marsak, 80–91. New York: Collier-Macmillan, 1964.

Penniman, T. K. *A Hundred Years of Anthropology*. London, 1935.

Perkins, K. J. *Qaids, Captains, and Colons*. New York: Africana, 1981.

Persell, Stuart M. *The French Colonial Lobby 1889–1938*. Stanford CA: Hoover Institution Press, 1983.

Perville, Guy. "Le role des intellectuels musulmans algériens de formation française dans l'évolution politique de l'Algérie (1908–1962)." *Soc. Hist. Moderne* 19 (1983): 18–24.

Petitbon, P. H. *Taine, Renan, Barrès, étude d'influence*. Paris: Société d'Éditions Belles Lettres, 1935.

Peyre, Henri. *Renan et la Grèce*. Paris: A. G. Nizet, 1973.

Peyronnet, Raymond. *Le Problem Nord Africain: I. Introduction générale aux études Nord Africain; II. Histoire générale du Nord Africain; III. Berbers*. Paris: Peyronnet & cie, 1924.

———. *Livre d'Or des Affaires Indigènes 1830–1930*. 2 vols. Alger, 1930.

Pinet, Gaston. *Ecrivains et penseurs polytechniciens*. Paris: Paul Ollendorff, 1898.

———. "L'École Polytechinque et les Saint-Simoniens." *Revue de Paris* (mai 1894): 73–96.

Pinon, Réné. "Les colonies françaises à Marseille." *Revue des Deux Mondes* 197 (octobre 1906): 823–85.

Piobetta, J. B. *Les Institutions Universitaires*. Paris: PUF, 1951.

Pogard, G. "Les Derniers travaux sur l'histoire militaire de l'Algérie." *Revue Internationale d'Histoire Militaire* 4 (1954): 65–68.

Poliakov, Léon. *The Aryan Myth: A History of Racist and Nationalist Ideas in Europe*. Translated by E. Howard. 1971. Reprint, London: Heinemann for Sussex University Press, 1974.

———, ed. *Hommes et bêtes: Entretiens sur le racisme*. Paris, 1975.

Bibliography

Prochaska, David. *Making Algeria French: Colonialism in Bône, 1870–1920*. Cambridge: Cambridge University Press, 1990.

Quandt, William B. *Revolution and Political Leadership: Algeria (1954–1968)*. Cambridge: MIT Press, 1969.

Radcliffe-Brown, A. R. "The Methods of Ethnology and Social Anthropology." *South African Journal of Science* 20 (October 1923). Reprinted in Graburn, Nelson. *Readings in Kinship and Social Structure*. New York: Harper Row, 1971.

Ratcliffe, Barrie M. "Saint-Simon and Messianism: The Case of Gustave d'Eichtal." *French Historical Studies* 9, no. 3 (1976): 484–502.

Reudy, John. *Modern Algeria: The Origins and Development of a Nation*. Bloomington: Indiana University Press, 1992.

Rey-Goldzeiguer, Annie. *Le Royaume Arabe: La Politique Algérienne de Napoleon III, 1861–1870*. Alger: SNED, 1977.

Richter, Melvin. "Tocqueville on Algeria." *Review of Politics* 25, no. 3 (July 1963): 362–98.

Rimbault, Paul. "Un bilan de généraux africains: Bugeaud, Lamorcière, Yusuf." *Bulletin de la Société de Géographie d'Alger* (1925): 105–25.

Rivlin, Benjamin. "A Selective Survey of Literature in the Social Sciences and Related Fields in Modern North Africa." *American Political Science Review* 48 (1954): 826–48.

Roberts, Hugh. "Algerian Socialism and the Kabyle Question." PhD diss., University of East Anglia, 1981.

———. "Algeria: Unrest and Impasse in Kabylia." N.p.: International Crisis Group, 2003.

———. *The Battlefield: Algeria, 1988–2002; Studies in a Broken Polity*. London and New York: Verso, 2002.

———. "Co-Opting Identity: The Manipulation of Berberism, the Frustration of Democratisation and the Generation of Violence in Algeria." In *Working Paper no. 7*. London: Destin, LSE; Crisis States Programme; Development Research Centre, 2001.

———. "Kabylia in Transition." *Maghreb Review* 3 (1978): 16–21.

———. "Towards an Understanding of the Kabyle Question in Contemporary Algeria." *Maghreb Review* 5, nos. 5–6 (1980).

Roberts, Stephen. *History of French Colonial Policy (1870–1925)*. London: P. S. King, 1929.

Robin, Marie-Monique. *Escadrons de la Mort, L'École française*. Paris: Découverte, 2004.

Roblès, Emmanuel. "Un grand écrivain berbère de langue française: Mouloud Feraoun." *Algeria* (février 1953): 17–18.

Roche, Anne, and Christian Tartig, eds. *Des Années Trente: Groupes et Ruptures*. Paris: Éditions du CNRS, 1985.

Bibliography

Rodinson, Maxime. *Islam and Capitalism.* Translated by B. Pearce. 1969. Reprint, Austin: University of Texas Press, 1981.

Rogers, Rebecca. *A Frenchwoman's Imperial Story: Madame Luce in Nineteenth-Century Algeria.* Stanford CA: Stanford University Press, 2013.

————. "Telling Stories about the Colonies: British and French Women in Algeria in the Nineteenth Century." *Gender & History* 21, no. 1 (2009): 39–59.

Rudorff, Raymond. *Belle Epoque: Paris in the Nineties.* Wiltshire: Redwood Press Ltd., 1973.

Ruthven, Malise. *Islam in the World.* New York: Oxford University Press, 1984.

Ryan, Alan. *The Philosophy of the Social Sciences.* London: Macmillan, 1970.

Said, Edward. *Orientalism.* New York: Vintage, 1979.

Sari, Djilali. *L'Insurrection de 1881–1882.* Alger: SNED, 1981.

Scham, Alan. *Lyautey in Morocco: Protectorate Administration, 1912–1925.* Berkeley: University of California Press, 1970.

Scheele, Judith. *Village Matters: Knowledge, Politics and Community in Kabylia, Algeria.* African Anthropology. Woodbridge, Suffolk: James Currey, 2009.

Schneider, W. H. *An Empire for the Masses: The French Popular Image of Africa 1870–1900.* Westport CT: Greenwood Press, 1982.

————. "Race and Empire: The Rise of Popular Ethnography in the Late Nineteenth Century." *Journal of Popular Culture* 11 (1977): 98–109.

Schoen, P. "Les institutions administratives, politiques et sociales et juridiques dans le groups Imazuen." *Renseignements Coloniaux* 38 (1928): 737.

Scott, David. *Conscripts of Modernity: The Tragedy of Colonial Enlightenment.* Durham: Duke University Press, 2004.

Scott, Joan Wallach. *The Politics of the Veil.* Princeton: Princeton University Press, 2007.

Selnet, Frédéric P. V. *Colonisation officielle: Crédit agricole en Algérie.* Alger: Imp. Minerva, 1930.

Serman, Willian. *Les Officiers français dans la Nation 1848–1914.* Paris: Aubier Montaigne, 1982.

Sessions, Jennifer E. *By Sword and Plow: France and the Conquest of Algeria.* Ithaca NY: Cornell University Press, 2011.

Shepard, Todd. *The Invention of Decolonization: The Algerian War and the Remaking of France.* Ithaca NY: Cornell University Press, 2006.

Silverstein, Paul A. *Algeria in France: Transpolitics, Race, and Nation.* Bloomington: Indiana University Press, 2004.

————. "The Kabyle Myth: Colonization and the Production of Ethnicity." In *From the Margins: Historical Anthropology and Its Futures,* edited by B. K. Axel, 122–55. Durham: Duke University Press, 2002.

Bibliography

Simon, Pierre-Henri. *Contre la Torture.* Paris: Éditions du Seuil, 1957.

Sivan, Emmanuel. "The Kabyles: An Oppressed Minority in North Africa." In *Case Studies on Human Rights and Fundamental Freedom: A World Survey,* vol. 1, edited by W. A. Vienhoven, 261–79. The Hague, 1975.

Slimani-Direche, Karina. *Histoire de L'émigration Kabyle en France au XXe Siècle: Réalités Culturelles et Politiques et Réappropriations identitaires.* Paris: Harmattan, 1997.

Stafford, Robert A. *Scientist of Empire: Sir Roderick Murchison, Scientific Exploration and Victorian Imperialism.* Cambridge: Cambridge University Press, 1989.

Stanley, John L., ed. *From Georges Sorel Essays in Socialism and Philosophy.* New York: Oxford University Press, 1976.

Stauder, J. "The Function of Functionalism: The Adaptation of British Social Anthropology to British Colonialism in Africa." Paper presented to the meetings of the American Anthropological Association, November 1971.

Staum, Martin S. *Labeling People: French Scholars on Society, Race and Empire, 1815–1848.* Montreal: McGill-Queen's University Press, 2003.

Steele, Hollins M., Jr. "European Settlement vs. Muslim Property: The Foundation of Colonial Algeria 1830–1880." PhD diss., Columbia University, 1965.

Stepan, Nancy. *The Idea of Race in Science: Great Britain, 1800–1960.* London: Macmillan, 1982.

Stepan, Nancy Leys. "Race and Gender: The Role of Analogy in Science." *ISIS* 77 (1986): 261–77.

Sternhell, Zeev. *Maurice Barrès et le Nationalisme Français.* 1972. Reprint, Paris: Éditions Complexe, 1985.

Stocking, George W., Jr. *Race, Culture and Evolution.* New York: Free Press, 1968.

———. *Victorian Anthropology.* London: Macmillan, 1987.

Stora, Benjamin. "The Algerian War in French Memory: Vengeful Memory's Violence." In *Memory and Violence in the Middle East and North Africa,* edited by Ussama Samir Makdisi and Paul A. Silverstein. Bloomington: Indiana University Press, 2006.

———. *La Gangrène et L'oubli: La Mémoire de la Guerre d'Algérie.* Paris: La Découverte, 1991.

———. *La Guerre des Mémoires: La France Face à Son Passé Colonial.* Paris: Éditions de l'Aube, 2007.

———. *Les Immigrés Algériens en France: Une Histoire Politique, 1912–1962.* Paris: Hachette, 2009.

Stora, Benjamin, and Linda Amiri. *Algériens en France: 1954–1962, la Guerre, L'exil, la Vie* Paris: Éd. Autrement; Cité nationale de l'histoire de l'immigration, 2012.

Stora, Benjamin, and Mohammed Harbi. *La Guerre d'Algérie: 1954–2004, la Fin de L'amnésie.* Paris: R. Laffont, 2004.

Strome, R. P. Marcel. *Rapports du Père Planque, de Mg. Lavigerie et de Mgr. Comboui sur l'Association Internationale Africaine.* Brussels: Édition J. Duculot, 1957.

Suret-Canale, J., *French Colonialism in Tropical Africa (1900–1945).* Translated by Till Gottheiner. New York: Pica Press, 1971. First ed. 1964.

Szajkowski, Zosa. "The Jewish Saint-Simonians and Socialist Anti-Semites in France." In *Jews and the French Revolutions of 1789, 1830 and 1848,* 1091–18. New York: Ktav, 1970.

Tailliart, Charles. *L'Algérie dans la littérature française.* Paris: Lib. de la Société d'histoire, 1925.

————. *L'Algérie dans la littérature française, Essai de Bibliographie méthodique et raisonnée jusqu'à l'année 1924.* Paris: Edouard Champion, 1925.

Talbi, Mohammed. "Ibn Haldūn et le sens de l'Histoire." *Studia Islamica* 26 (1967): 73–148.

Taylor, Maxime F. "Nascent Expansionism in the Geographical Society of Paris 1821–1848." *Proceedings of the Western Society for French History* 6 (1979): 229–38.

Temimi, A. "Lettres inédites de l'Emir Abdel Kader." *Revue Hist. Maghreb,* nos. 10–12 (1978): 159–202.

Thomas, Karen. "Berber Protests Shake Algeria's Military Elite: President Stalls as Riots Spread Throughout Country." *The Guardian,* 20 June 2001.

Thornton, A. P. *The Habit of Authority.* London: Allen & Unwin, 1966.

Tlemcani, Rachid. *State and Revolution in Algeria.* London: Zed, 1986.

Trumbull, George R., IV. *An Empire of Facts: Colonial Power, Cultural Knowledge, and Islam in Algeria, 1870–1914.* Cambridge: Cambridge University Press, 2009.

Turbet-Delof, Guy. *L'Afrique barbaresque dans la littérature française aux XVIe et XVIIe siècle.* Genève: Droz, 1973.

Turin, Yvonne. *Affrontements culturels dans l'Algérie coloniale, écoles, médecine, religion 1830–1880.* Paris: Maspero, 1971.

Turner, Frederick. *Beyond Geography.* New York: Viking Press, 1980.

Vachon, M., G. Rousseau, and Y. Laissus, eds. *Inédits de Lamarck.* Paris: Masson, 1972.

Valensi, Lucette. *On the Eve of Colonialism: North Africa before the French Conquest.* Translated by K. J. Perkins. 1969. Reprint, New York: Africana, 1977.

Valentin, Ferdinand. *Augustin Thierry.* Paris: Lecène Oudin, 1895.

Vallois, Henri V. "La Société d'Anthropologie de Paris 1859–1959." *Bulletin de la Société d'Anthropologie de Paris,* série 1, no. 11 (1960): 293–312.

————. "Race." In *Anthropology Today,* edited by A. L. Kroeber. Chicago: University of Chicago Press, 1953.

Vatin, J. C. "Histoire en soi et histoire pour soi: 1919–1945 et après." *Revue algérienne des relations internationales* 9, no. 4 (1974): 274.

————. *L'Algérie Politique, Histoire et Société.* Paris: Colin, 1974.

Vatin, J. C., with A. Mahiou. "Histoire et . . . histoires." *Revue algérienne* (1972–74): 803–17.

Vatin, J. C., with et al. *Connaissances du Maghreb: Sciences Sociales et Colonisation*. Paris: Ed. du CNRS, 1984.

———. *Culture et Société au Maghreb*. Paris: CNRS, 1975.

Viard, P. E. "Note sur un problème familial kabyle." *Questions Nord-Africaines* 4 (1938): 18–23.

Villot, Roland. *August Pomel: Democrate et savant 1821–1898*. Oran: L. Fouque, 1957.

Von Sivers, P. "Algerian Land Ownership and Rural Leadership 1860–1940: A Quantitative Approach." *Maghreb Review* 4 (1979): 58–62.

———. "Insurrection and Accommodation: Indigenous Leadership in Eastern Algeria 1840–1900." *International Journal of Middle East Studies* 6 (1975): 259–75.

Wall, Irwin M. *France, the United States, and the Algerian War*. Berkley: University of California Press, 2001.

Wallerstein, I., ed. *Social Change: The Colonial Situation*. New York: Wiley, 1966.

Wansbrough, J. "The Decolonization of North African History." *Journal of African History* 9, no. 4 (1968): 643–50.

Weber, Eugen. *France: Fin de Siècle*. Cambridge MA: Harvard University Press, 1986.

White, Owen. *Children of the French Empire: Miscegenation and Colonial Society in French West Africa, 1895–1960*. Oxford: Oxford University Press, 1999.

Wohl, Robert. *The Generation of 1914*. Cambridge MA: Harvard University Press, 1979.

Woloch, Isser. *Eighteenth-Century Europe: Tradition and Progress, 1715–1789*. New York: Norton, 1982.

Wysner, Gloria May. *The Kabyle People*. New York: Private Print, 1945.

Yacono, Xavier. *La colonisation des plaines du Chélif*. 2 vols. Alger: E. Imbert, 1955.

———. "L'Algérie depuis 1830: Centenaire de la Société historique algérienne, 1856–1956." *Revue Africaine: Centenaire de la Société Historique Algérien ne 1856–1956* (1956): 145–90.

———. *Les Bureaux Arabes et l'évolution des genres de vie indigènes dans l'ouest du Tell algérois*. Paris: Larose, 1953.

Zagoria, Janet. "The Rise and Fall of the Movement of Messali Hadj in Algeria, 1924–1956." PhD diss., Columbia University, 1973.

Zouache, Abdallah. "Eléments D'économie Coloniale Saint-Simonienne: Le Cas de l'Algérie." *Économies et sociétés* 43 (2009): 1321–41.

Zurcher, Magali. *La pacification et l'organisation de la Kabylie orientale de 1838 à 1870*. Paris: Belles Lettres, 1948.

Index

355

Index

naturalization, 8, 183, 186; of
   Algerian Jews, 172
Neo-French, 186, 197, 207
de Nerval, Gérard, 78, 93–4
de Neveu, Edouard, 55–8, 60, 103,
   129, 132, 137, 143, 148, 163
new white race, 196–8
nomadic style of life, 37–40, 51, 106,
   130, 133, 159, 190, 221, 222, 236,
   249
normal, meaning of, 101
novels, 218, 219; by settler authors,
   207, 208

officer corps, French, 97
olive oil, 24, 40
olive trees, 83
Organisation Kabyle, 11, 174, 188
Orientalism, 75, 78, 92, 96, 146, 147,
   206, 225
orphanages, missionary, 179
Other, concept of, 199
Oudney, Walter, 43

Parti du Peuple Algérien (PPA), 234
paternalism, 80, 91, 92, 119, 181
patriarchy, 248
peasants, French, 246, 248
Pères Blancs, 177, 179
Périer, Joanny-Napoléon, 128, 137,
   155
philology, 43, 136, 137, 147
phylloxera epidemic, 193
physiognomy, 121; of Berbers, 137
Picouleau, Lt-Colonel, 25
pieds-noirs, 177
plain, category of, 51
plain dwellers, 222, 223, 237, 249
Polybius, 21
polygamy, 64–7; attack on, 74; in
   Fiji, 67
Pomel, Nicolas Auguste, 175, 177,
   181, 183–7, 188, 192
population of colony, 183
potato, cultivation of, 83
Pouillon, François, 232
Prichard, James, 42
progress, concept of, 135
property, 245; rights, 185

Pruner-Bey, Dr, 155, 156
Ptolemy, 21
public works, in France, 8

de Quatrefages de Bréau, A., 118,
   155
Quetelet, Adolphe, 101

Rémond, M., 226
race, 88, 101, 113, 137, 152, 154, 203,
   242, 250, 251, 253; and colonial
   theory, 210–12; concept of,
   119–30, 253; hierarchy of, 160,
   221; question of, 118–45, 161
races, classification of, 152
racial ancestry, 142
racial determinism, 168
racial difference, 146
racial division of labour, 183–7
racial ideas, 196; acceptance of, 217
racial images, formation of, 251
racial theory, 163, 194
racism, 1, 194, 196, 236
Radical School of Anthropology, 159
Randau, Robert, 207, 208
Randon, General, 7, 11, 27, 28, 82,
   114, 141, 174, 188, 230
Raudot, Claude-Marie, 199
Rassemblement pour la Culture et la
   Démocratie (RCD), 235
Raynal, Abbé, 107
rebarbarisation, 198, 204–6, 207, 208,
   212
reconnaissance, 34, 53–75, 103, 118,
   134, 136, 249; as category, 35–52;
   role of physicians in, 121
refoulement, policy of, 46
religion, 136, 161; as cohesive force,
   244
Renan, Ernest, 5, 95, 135, 137, 139,
   143, 147, 151, 158, 160, 161, 162,
   163, 181, 206, 212
Renault, General, 31
republicanism, 60, 100, 226, 241,
   243, 245, 251
resistance, 79–88
Retzius, Andreas, 150
revolutions, in France, 248
Revue Africaine, 73, 141, 142, 225

Index

CPSIA information can be obtained at www.ICGtesting.com
Printed in the USA
BVOW03s0112030714

358072BV00001B/1/P